BACK TO
THE
FUTURE

THE PROTESTANTS AND
A UNITED IRELAND

J BOWYER BELL

POOLBEG

Published 1996
by Poolbeg Press Ltd
123 Baldoyle Industrial Estate
Dublin 13, Ireland

A catalogue record for this book is available from the British Library.

ISBN 1 85371 692 8

Cover design by Poolbeg Group Services Ltd
Set by Poolbeg Group Services Ltd in Stone 9.5/13.5
Printed by The Guernsey Press Ltd,
Vale, Guernsey, Channel Islands.

CONTENTS

PREFACE

Separation between past, present and future is only an
illusion, however tenacious.—Albert Einstein

For much of my life I have sought, with increasing lack of
vigour, to concentrate on matters only peripherally related
to Ireland: the Middle East, Africa, other wars, the troubles
of others. But gradually I have found myself embedded in
Irish matters, replete with Irish connections and friends,
Irish concerns, even and especially fortunately an Irish wife.
I have hardly become more Irish than the Irish but I have
been more exposed to the Irish, more involved, and indeed
more opinionated. And although I still have sought further
fields, other wars and rumours of wars, somehow I end more
often than not at my world headquarters in Buswell's Hotel
in Molesworth Street, Dublin.

There from time to time over a span of some years Philip
MacDermott and I would conjure up prospective texts—
always for others to write. I had written too much on
Ireland, much of it different but all at great length, more on
Ireland than even most of the Irish want to read. Yet there
was obviously more to be written, on the Troubles, on the
peace process or the return of war. For some long time there
were almost no works on the Protestants of Ulster, and then

when scholarly works did appear, the Protestant case and its implications still did not have a popular presentation. Sectarian horror was covered but not the perceptions of the Protestants, the Protestants now as they are, not as they should be or once were or might be. There was a Protestant case, unheard, and a Protestant reality, rarely chronicled. There was, we agreed, a book in it.

Few listened to the Protestants, fewer to their strident advocates, and few read the splendid analytical texts. Someone should write about the Protestants. And so in time the field seemed to narrow to me. Perhaps in time I might contemplate the Protestants of Ulster—not a history, of course: I am not qualified and not rigorous; I was not interested in polls and graphs. Perhaps a tract for the times: the Protestant case against the great national dream of a united Ireland. After all, I had spent my time in Ireland with the republicans, whose case might often be popular but whose means were unfashionable and whose members were not always easy to reach. Surely the Protestants could not be more difficult? Surely their case could be divorced from rant and evasion? Surely the enormous difficulties Protestant reality imposed on any lasting accommodation were worth detailing?

Accommodation of the two traditions, the two perceptions of reality—and that of the British as well—rested on the adjustment of perception to specific advantage so compelling as to warrant agreement. Those involved and responsible might well continue to believe what they chose, as long as what they chose to believe was to the advantage of all. It would require an Irish resolution to an Irish problem—one text, many interpretations—and should in truth have an Irish advocate. Still, if I am not Irish I am not entirely innocent of Ireland and the Irish, even and especially those most militant Irish in the republican movement. I am as well a Protestant, an Anglican—an Episcopalian in America; one of my family served on Anne Boleyn's jury at the request of Henry VIII. So too my daughters; often not a very Protestant family, not fundamental but still Protestant for the long run. I have lived amid American Protestants whose ancestors came from Ulster, "Scotch-Irish" in America, even if they were often neither. I have lived among all sorts of Protestants and Catholics in America and even lived in Rome at various times.

Ireland is, even for the tourist, bounded by pieties— Protestant or Catholic. For anyone beyond the country, the special mix of nationalism and religion, the nature of the country's varied tradition, the varied beliefs on the march to different tunes—all are both challenge and obstacle. But Ireland, however special, is not without parallels. Years spent amid the Zionist arguments on religion and nation, amid the Arabs focused on similar matters, are not without relevance. So too the American experience: the evangelical shop-fronts of east Harlem or the pieties of the east Texas Bible belt, the born-again Black Muslims and the rise of "family values" and the campaign against abortion that unites fundamentalist Protestants and almost all Catholics. America is always filled with examples as well as traditions.

Ireland is different and the same, Irish Protestants special but not without parallels, in America or elsewhere. After all, Dr Paisley is Dr Paisley because of an honorary degree from Bob Jones University in South Carolina. And anyone can read in the newspaper of bus bombs in Jerusalem or Tel-Aviv, where two destinies clash in a land twice promised. And there have been others who live by the Bible and the sword, seek redemption or explain politics as religion.

Still, this book comes out of neither a long-standing concern with such matters nor really the capital built up by experience but simply because so few in the Republic, much less the republican movement, understand Irish Protestants. In twenty-six counties they are invisible, in six counties defined to nationalist advantage. The real Protestants have been ignored as politically incorrect, bigots almost all, strident, unsavoury if at times ridiculous. Somehow everyone knows about Protestants in Cork or Clare without ever having met one, certainly not one from Antrim. One need be neither a Protestant nor congenial to their tradition and community to recognise that they have a case and one that, if not recognised and accommodated, ensures that a united Ireland is not a viable proposition. As long as Clare and Cork are content with stereotypes, the country will continue to be divided, for the Protestants of Antrim and Down know as little of the other tradition, Rome transported to Ireland. Everyone knows what they know and finds what they assume vindicated, sees what they expected to find. And few Catholics know Protestants except to nod to, to deploy as token, to mock or fear as bigots.

Years of grumbles in Buswell's lounge produced no other candidate to undertake the Protestant case: this one too busy, that one dead, the others committed or contaminated or otherwise engaged. And so I succumbed to temptation.

The result is not a history of the Protestants or a rigorous and authoritative analysis of their case and their cause as much as a tract on the fundamental reality of their tradition and perceptions and on the implications for Ireland. What matters to them matters to all Ireland. What they perceive is an alternative reality ignored at risk.

I have probably managed to provoke all the involved. The Protestants are not especially congenial, their case real but unappealing, their critique of nationalism and the Republic rationalisations; and their vices are apt to overshadow their undeniable virtues: a brave, proper people, indomitable, not really British or truly Irish, not this nor that but themselves, not my kind of Protestant but no matter. And their attack on the product of Irish nationalism, the Republic, a Catholic state for a Catholic people, could until recently have been duplicated by any committed militant republican. It has never been hard for critics, domestic and foreign, to find in Dublin pretensions, compromise, and self-interest—a failed entity. It has also been an entity with ample explanations and rationalisations, history rewritten as justification. Yet if the Republic is not a failed entity it is not and has never been the triumph over the odds that its advocates have proclaimed. Free Ireland is less than the dream—any Ireland would be—but often more than the cottage industry of critics, many based in England, would believe.

Still, what the Protestants have unpleasantly to say is often both in general and in particular accurate if unwelcome. The nationalists and many republicans are apt to ignore the flaws of a free Ireland in their pride in the undeniable accomplishments of its establishment and the wonders yet to come. So the Protestants' case is not heard— or rather they are heard but no-one listens, or credits them with insight or even with vision. Their British Ulster, a dream arising among unionists once the rest of the country was lost, cannot be imagined in Dublin 4, much less in Kerry. Ulster is far away, and the British are children of the Tan War. All know perfidy and bigotry but none really know Protestants or the reality of their Ulster. None realise that there is indeed a British Ulster, not a place but a perception. And none want to know, for the incandescent reality of a united Ireland shapes the perceptions of nationalist Ireland.

Few can imagine their own flaws; empathy has been noticeably absent during much of modern Irish history. The united Ireland that has been the proclaimed goal of nationalism for over two centuries possesses as rubric and as grail enormous staying power. Yet any united Ireland imagined by Tone or those out in Easter 1916, any united Ireland shaped by treaties or legal proposals or political resolutions, must be a united Ireland that has room for all traditions, all the Irish, Protestants as well. For many Irish it is often enough inevitable. British Ulster is a chimera, the Irish Protestants are Irish. For the Protestants, Irish nationalism is simply Irish Catholicism and anathema. Either a united Ireland is viable or it is not: viable now it is not, viable in the future depends on faith, not facts. The Protestants say "no" to a united Ireland and so ensure that Ireland is not united. And they have logical and compelling reasons for their position. Protestants foresee only their present separate tradition protected by the union, or assimilation. Why should they surrender to Rome, to Dublin, to unconvincing arguments?

In turn the nationalists assume that all the long cycles favour integration, the Irish united, a future perfect built on past precedent, a united Ireland and an end to turmoil and history. Certainly nationalism has been the most effective ideology of the century, and the most costly, ensuring war and chaos amid the new flags; and the Irish republic is the child of modern nationalism, if built on old aspirations and grievances.

Both nationalists, mostly Catholic, and the unionists in Ulster, almost all Protestant, perceive the future as the past replayed. Both seek to go back three moves and so change the future. Both want to rewrite history: one seeks redemption and assurance and the other vengeance and justice. And as long as the two traditions rasp against each other on often convergent orbits, the British will contend what is clearly not the case, that without tangible interests they must remain as arbitrator and mentor: right and righteous, not perfidious at all but, like all the others, history's instrument. To continue to write history backwards, to know because one knows, ensures that tomorrow never comes—not a bad strategy for British Ulster but not one that engenders much enthusiasm.

Thus, with the not unreasonable suspicion that no-one will like their perceptions misinterpreted, their grasp of history questioned, they will have to be accommodated. And this will hardly be a simple matter, for they are an unaccommodating people.

It would be foolish to imagine that this tract will change the times, make the Protestants real for many or move the responsible. There is no message of cheer for anyone. The Protestants would want an advocate and the nationalists sympathy, the scholars more documentary evidence, and the responsible a solution. So there is no need to thank all those who may have unwittingly contributed to my experience, to my travels and travails in Ireland that generated this tract for the times. Who should have credit for encouragement? Perhaps Philip MacDermott of Poolbeg, who finally agreed that since neither of us could suggest an appropriate author perhaps I should try—and he is a publisher and they are soon forgiven. Perhaps my Irish wife, who is apt to encourage any of my essays and enterprises; but families are involved without responsibility. For most of the others the result is apt to be less than expected and more than desired, not scholarly, not fair, not balanced, not really history or the practice of social science, not very promising in recommendations—part of the problem rather than the solution. Thus I should exclude those usual suspects but will not: the Murphys of Dublin, New York, Harold's Cross, and the Ó Snodaigh family of Sandymount, now offering as always aid and comfort but now as well a new generation of assistance; and as always the Brownes of Ballybunnion, the Middle East, and Dublin.

It has always been difficult to write on contentious Irish matters, even from a distance; but then only the odd public scold has appeared. In general and particular the Irish have been more kind than begrudging. And this text is really about them, about the Irish as I find them, their dreams and traditions and special perceptions. We each have our own Ireland. That is the charm of the country: some take away memories, salmon catches, hand-knitted jumpers, notes for a thesis, and delight. And some add to the debris of history left cluttering the analytical countryside. Ireland has done far more for me than I have for it. So Ireland gives and takes, and tomorrow may yet come, a tomorrow when truth is not contradictory and perceptions match reality.

PROLOGUE

THE CROSSROADS OF DUNLOY, SUMMER 1995

> Who controls the past controls the future. Who controls the present controls the past.—George Orwell

In 1995 Northern Ireland had the most glorious summer within the memory of all or the records of the meteorological service: long, dry, sunny days, real heat—a splendid time. And it was the first summer in a generation that proffered not simply fine weather and the holidays but also civic tranquillity. The province—all Ireland—was at peace. The IRA's announcement of a ceasefire at the end of August the previous year still held. Peace, at least for the morrow, had come to Ireland.

There had been no formal accommodation yet, not even formal talks about the Anglo-Irish proposal contained in the Downing Street Declaration of December 1993; but the peace process was as good, promised that tomorrow would be like yesterday. Whatever the hard men in the secret army might wish at some future time, the IRA armed struggle seemed not just on hold but over. So too was the loyalist paramilitary murder campaign. There had been no real incidents, no bombs, no atrocity by a splinter group, only

1

the clatter and scuttle of the politicians: once more talks about talks, about bad faith and preconditions.

Still, everyone remained uneasy. Blunders by someone were always possible. There always seemed to be blunders in Ireland—history as blunder. Old aspirations had not been denied, nor acceptable compromises yet proposed. One mad bomber might be able to undo the whole thing. But at least for the time being there could be a return to the normal. The wife could go to the films. The centre of town was safe. The family could drive by no-go zones, and the British army had left most streets. The knock on the door was no longer cause for terror. The flags were still up but the battle elsewhere. Northern Ireland, bit by bit, had become normal.

After a generation some assumed this normality to mean that twenty-five years of violence had changed nothing, the old ways for the old purposes were still valid. The peace process might have opened the streets of Belfast, made the roads in the country safe and the British army and RUC hardly visible, might have ended the climate of terror and anxiety; but those who walked about in peace were the same troubled people who had feared to venture out during the violence. They did not feel changed or different or transformed, only free to act without fear. Most were content to go into town, visit, walk the streets. Most still wanted what they had wanted, saw the peace process as threat or recess as much as opportunity. Many, republicans and loyalists, nationalists and unionists, had changed, but often not a lot: after all, the persistence of ambition denied and defences required had been the engines of violence during the Troubles. The peace process so far meant that none had lost and none had won. And of course no way out of the zero-sum game, the long, complex, intractable Irish dilemma, had been found, had even been offered, only the good will of individuals and of parties, factions, or governments. Sinn Féin might have opted for peace in hopes that the British would persuade the unionists to despair of the benefits of the union, who in a year were not even persuaded to take part in formal talks with the republicans. The IRA might have declared a ceasefire but had declined to decommission their arms or apparently restrain their volunteers when deploying the gun against the drug trade. There had been talk but no viable action. Still, the peace was in process, and the process low in cost and high in tangible returns.

In a sense the peace process allowed the sectarian conflicts of the past—the marches, provocations, old slurs and slogans—free and most visible play. There was apparently no reason not to continue the routines of challenge and response now increasingly visible. Without IRA bombs or British army sweeps, visible violence was less, not lethal but symbolic, still found: in churches and chapels burned, in sectarian sabotage, in vicious sermons, provocative speeches and individual provocation. During the summer of 1995 both traditions gave ample evidence that their implacable quarrel was far from over. None claimed to have struck the first blow—none in Ireland ever did; but there was always someone to paint the slogan, set the fire, throw the stone.

The peace process kept open the space to protest and intimidate as well as to indicate a way into a more accommodating future. There had always, of course, been provocation and display; but in the midst of the chaos of the armed struggle such rituals played only a minor role. Protestant marches into Catholic areas, Catholic demonstrations before British authorities, orations, riots, symbols burnt and opponents damned—the politics of ritual

3

and display, challenge and response, had become the muzak of Northern Ireland, hardly noted once the IRA dominated the stage, made the running, generated a war and an erratic loyalist paramilitary backlash. Without the violence of the Troubles the traditional displays could take centre stage again. So the great hot summer of 1995 was also a summer of arson and arrogance and provocation. And summer is the commemorative marching season in Northern Ireland, when the Orange throngs gather to celebrate those famous victories of long ago. Seemingly, in 1995, little had been forgotten and all remembered. The past was not prologue but ever present. The marchers marched as if twenty-five years meant nothing in Ulster's long history.

This was not so. Twenty-five years meant that much had changed in Ulster, including the nationalists' patience. The minority now felt that humiliation as festival no longer had to be tolerated: the examples of the gunmen years indicated that. The Croppies had no intention of lying down, even if Sinn Féin urged calm. They would not be slandered or shamed. The more determined defenders of British Ulster, fearful that twenty-five years had eroded their defences, felt that nothing less would do. The past began again. Orange halls and Catholic churches began to go up in flames—tit-for-tat minor atrocities. Everyone might welcome the peace process and nearly everyone might fear provocation, but the militant would not be restrained by decency or common sense, nor would their constituencies change their habits. This was especially true with the unionists, long fearful that any change would be loss, now fearful that the peace process was a means of eroding their defence. Even the most moderate felt that restraint, if needed, need not mean an end to the cherished traditions of the past, traditions of the majority, traditions that were legal. With republican

4

nightriders still about, a defence of British Ulster was more necessary than ever.

So the Orange marching season in 1995 could not pass off as a display of simple folk customs, a matter of marching bands and a day in the open, old, legal customs that traced old, traditional paths. Everyone knew that any Orange march was provocative—to some or to many—at best sectarian and often nasty. Even the most decent defenders of British Ulster, those in respectable pulpits or law offices or those with Catholic neighbours, knew all about the implications of marching parades. The Orangemen marched not simply to display skill on the tuba or in recollection of long-ago battles but as a means of indicating territorial imperative. This land is ours, our British Ulster, our country won from implacable enemies against difficult odds, redeemed in blood. And it was their land: they were the majority, British, aligned to London and different from the others, disloyal and truculent at times, if decent in many cases. In a few instances the unionist truculence led to violence. In many places and most nationalist hearts the marches were unnecessarily inflammatory. In a few places there was trouble.

So the efforts of the Orange Order to maintain their traditional rights to march where they chose inevitably engendered resistance by those who felt the time of intimidation was past. Some nationalists in fact went forth and provoked the unionists. The result was that in the summer of 1995, amid a peace process that inspired good will and high hopes—despite the slow pace—the province was hardly peaceful. The sudden influx of tourists had indicated the advantages of peace, and all sorts of politicians promised more and better: more jobs, more investment, more cross-border co-operation, or less. Everyone in authority scrambled to find harbingers of good will and gave glad tidings. Yet somehow much of the news out of Ireland still seemed bad, reflected no new era of good feeling. And certainly in the past every initiative had eroded in the acid rain of ancient grievances: devolved government lost, the Peace People forgotten, the Anglo-Irish Agreement failed. It was hardly a surprise that now a peace process that must make do amid rising and newly visible sectarian display ran into trouble. It seemed as if the traditional troubles, the same old sectarian troubles, low in intensity but high in emotion, had emerged from the past: nothing learned, nothing forgotten, the divisions clear, commitment implacable. No-one wanted to change, adjust the old agenda. No-one could imagine an accommodation without triumph and humiliation. And a few, perhaps not so few, evidently saw need to resort to arson, sabotage, and intimidation.

The clash of traditions, if not the focal point of the Troubles, as many in London claimed, was real. The province's sectarian troubles had always been integral to the IRA campaign, founded on nationalist grievance and seeking an end to Protestant Ulster as imposed by the Government of Ireland Act in 1920, seeking an end to partition and a united Ireland. This new Ireland would, critics said, merely be the existing Dublin republic writ large, writ at Protestant Ulster's expense. The republicans might say otherwise; they were wrong, lied, lied at least to themselves. A united Ireland would be a nationalist Ireland, and such an Ireland would be dominated not only by a Gaelic ethos but a Catholic one. Only the republicans imagined themselves non-sectarian. They had been misinformed by their own indulgences and hidden agenda: they were Catholic and so acted, defended "their people", allied themselves with other Catholics in a "pan-nationalist front". The republican movement might claim to speak for all Ireland, but the Protestants knew better: they spoke for their own, the others, the Catholic nationalists.

The British too claimed that the armed struggle was merely sectarian. The British army was a peacekeeping force imposed between two sectarian tribes, one in the majority, loyal and Protestant, the other not loyal and Catholic. In that sense the IRA was merely a Catholic force with a non-sectarian banner. Yet the major thrust of the Troubles had been not a religious war but rather a national struggle over the sovereignty of the six counties that composed Northern Ireland. When the IRA called a ceasefire against the enemy, the British forces, the war stopped. Many in power had preferred the Troubles as religious war; but once the IRA called a ceasefire and the violence ended at once and for all, the nature of that violence was more apparent. The armed struggle was non-sectarian, the enemy the British, although in reality the IRA was Catholic, its goal a Gaelic Ireland. The IRA had attacked the British forces and, under whatever flag, attacked their local loyalist allies. It had been an armed insurrection opposed by the British, by the loyalist paramilitaries, by the unionists, by the entire Protestant populace and often even by those in power to the south in the Republic, where militant republicans were subversives, if from decent families.

Many analysts were apt to point out that the IRA was nationalist, non-sectarian in aspiration, opposed by the hierarchy of the Catholic Church and focused not on religious targets but the British army and RUC. This made them pure, not religious, nationalists—except in unionists' eyes. Because nearly all nationalists were Catholics and the defenders of the regime in Northern Ireland were nearly all

Protestants—and such had been the case for generations—there was, just as London and others argued, a clash of faiths. Ireland was never really simple, and certainly it was not a simply sectarian war but rather an armed struggle with a sectarian component, large or small depending on the inclination and agenda of the analyst. The Protestants saw Irish nationalism as all but identical with Irish Catholicism and the IRA's armed struggle a focus on winning the war by expelling the British and absorbing the province into a Catholic, Gaelic entity. Within Northern Ireland the unionists felt they must then defend the law and the majority against the subversive nationalist and Catholic population. The nationalists, fearful of sectarian attack, dubious of the protection of the authorities, perforce had tolerated or in some cases supported the IRA struggle, if not out of conviction then out of necessity. In an emergency there must be some defence against a general loyalist backlash; the IRA was there where the legal authorities might not respond promptly or at all. The Dublin government was most apt to stand idly by. The nationalists, fearful of a loyalist pogrom by seeking republican protection, risked provoking just such a backlash, just what was intended to be forestalled. Such toleration, the rules of engagement and the dedication of the committed drove the IRA's long war, a war that could not be defeated and often seemed close to eroding British patience.

Too often for the unionists, at one time or another, the IRA had seemed to be winning if not the war then the hearts and minds of the politicians and the media. The IRA gunmen bombed and murdered, if not with impunity at least with regularity, murdered in Dublin, mortared Downing Street, destroyed the benign, children, those at a dog show or those at the wrong street corner, ruined whole

8

towns, slaughtered the innocent in Enniskillen or on Bloody Friday. For nearly a generation there had been Protestant anguish and fear, frustration that crime was paying and that none cared. The unionists could find no means to ensure that the union would be both acceptable and permanent. The republicans and the IRA were intractable, sure that their day would come, and the British reluctant to use compelling force. Inevitably the most loyal sought recourse in violence. During the Troubles there was then a backlash—as there had been repeatedly in Northern Ireland's past—when there was indication of a shift in the balance of domination. In the province, loyalist paramilitary violence had been reactive, defensive, legitimised in part by the anguish of the unionists but no threat to the system. That system supplied to those without other assets the right to arrogance. They often had little else, not education or prospects, no house or property, often no job, nothing tangible but misery and the dole. Their single and singular triumph was their faith as passport to esteem, the right to arrogance and for some the necessity to display the one gift of the British Ulster system. The loyalists sought to defend the system, their system.

During the previous generation of Troubles, except for one or two confrontations with the authorities, the loyalists had directed their attacks against the Catholic minority. The immediate threat to the system was the IRA, but for the loyalists the IRA was out of reach. Most Protestants assumed, not without reason, that most Catholics were nationalists. And most nationalists tolerated, if they did not encourage, the republican gunmen. When the IRA hunger-striker Bobby Sands ran in a by-election for the British Parliament in April 1981 he received 30,492 votes—surely all Catholics, all votes for subversion, for treason. Thus any Catholic would do as loyalist victim, since all were taken as a danger, as

9

nationalists and as such as surrogates for the IRA. The system had to be defended, if not against the IRA then against the surrogates—the vulnerable Catholic, symbol of the danger. And such surrogates in turn had to be defended by the IRA. Thus sectarian violence was integrated into the armed struggle—provocation, retaliation, and defence—rather than occurring plainly as a matter of religious prejudice.

With the ceasefire in 1994 the immediate republican threat was gone. The IRA was, according to the optimists, spent, the secret army no longer a real player, the gunmen's capacity eroding even if their aspirations remained unchanged. The IRA threat to the existing system or to any desirable system still was perceived as real. As long as Ireland was not one and free then the republican movement would seek to persist. To prevent republican aims, to thwart nationalists and so Rome, a defence of British Ulster was crucial. Such an Ulster could not really be any more non-sectarian than an Irish republic: the majority tradition remained a majority, at the expense of the local minority.

For Catholics, majority rule had been and would be injustice under false flags. They wanted at least fair shares and in some cases fair shares at the expense of the majority: vengeance under the colours of reform. In their heart of hearts many Protestants wanted if not all then domination. Majority control alone, a matter of constitutions and laws and fair employment practices, lacked the congenial ease of domination displayed. Such a display was felt necessary to defend majority rights in a country dominated by those not British at all but Catholic Gaels, loyal first to Rome and then to a debased national aspiration, who wanted union in a country never united, who wanted to dominate those not already dominated by Rome, who wanted, whatever was said, an end to British Ulster, the Protestant tradition, the union with England.

The stability of the ceasefire meant that the traditionalists of both sides, never having changed their assumptions or aspirations, were given opportunity to resort to display and skirmish in the name of the old cause. Such action was congenial, and greatly improved the temper of those involved in arson or agitation. The barn-burners and nightriders were engaged in display, not subversion. Their returns were as apt to be in reassurance as in intimidating the others. The Protestants seemingly wanted subconsciously to feel secure because they were secure, were inherently better, not just different, and so invulnerable to Ireland's nationalist majority. There was always the tendency to imagine that such security, such ease in mind and spirit as well as in institutions and power, had actually existed at some past time. And it was in that past that the nationalist agitators found rationalisation for arson, for they too shaped past as prologue, found justification in ancient times. They wanted vengeance for real and imagined humiliation. The Protestants, on the other had, wanted to be vindicated and their posture bolstered. Always a minority within Ireland, the Protestants in fact had always been fearful that their security, their traditions, not just their privileges, were threatened. They could count on no-one but their own, not the British really, not the Conservative Party or the London establishment. The justice of their cause, the reality of the danger, the necessity for vigilance, was elsewhere poorly understood. Thus, along with their inherent superiority, the gift of the Protestant ethic, each of the majority too received a compensating fear that the foundations of their tradition had been built on the shifting sands of British political interests. British Ulster was loyal to a kingdom long ruled by those not especially loyal to Ulster. Ulster's friends, always suspect, offered aid and comfort not as right but as political convenience, as habit, as a means to other ends, avowed or subconscious. Ulster's enemies were everywhere, not just the IRA and the Irish nationalists in the province and in the Republic but also the world media, the American establishment, much of visible world opinion. Few understood the Protestant case, fewer were convinced of its wisdom. Almost no-one, often not even its advocates, realised that British Ulster was not merely six counties given for a time devolved government, a province in Ireland, a matter for Westminster, but an all-but-mystical and largely imagined homeland for a people without proper nation, with a muddled cultural heritage, all Protestants, united on their civic virtues, general diligence, and dedication to liberty. They shared not so much a single faith, a great and ordered denomination, as a Protestant commitment, some evangelical, some passive, many militant, Methodists, Presbyterians of all sorts, tiny churches and those with grand congregations, Quakers and Anglicans and Lutherans, all united in opposition to Irish Catholic nationalism, and loyalty to the union with England as the most effective means of safeguarding their traditions, their Ulster.

Such a construction, fashioned from perceptions and faith, from hope if not charity, evolving over years, never acknowledged and seldom defined, is not easily incorporated into peace formulas, agreements, or suggestions for grand coalitions and segmented authority. Dreams are hard to adjust to the everyday. So British Ulster was and is an entity shaped in Protestant hearts, not on the map, and it has been and still is seen as under siege and obviously for a generation has been under armed attack by the forces of Irish nationalism, epitomised by but not limited to the IRA. Protestants felt that all the ramparts must be defended at all times; complacency was deadly. Even to accept the reality of change was dangerous.

In 1995, the first summer of the peace process, the first marching season beyond the Troubles, the defence of tradition became the most visible show in Ireland: the past replayed by those fearful that their day had gone.

In west Antrim the River Bann runs north above Lough Beg, past Claudy and then under the bridge at Bann View, not yet half way to the sea near Castlerock. There the road to the east of the bridge slopes up to Rasharkin. Beyond Rasharkin a net of small roads lead up and around a countryside that shelters a famous standing-stone and on down, six miles or so, to Dunloy, isolated, a crossroads on the way to nowhere, easy to miss. Dunloy, unlike Rasharkin, is mostly Catholic— 95 per cent—and all 1,600 souls scattered about the village know who is who. Mostly over the years Protestant families have for one reason or another moved on: it is more comfortable and during the Troubles more secure to be with your own.

Ireland is divided in many ways: rich and poor, urban and rural, and in the six counties of Ulster always Protestant and Catholic. A divided society is not necessarily one separated into ours and theirs: here be Protestants and over there be Catholics. This was often true—this street ours to that kerbstone, or none of them in this village. The different and alien may also live side by side, quite separately, and often did so. Peace had to be maintained, because there was no alternative to toleration. Social custom was often structured to discover the identity of the other—by name or by school—so as not to give offence, to allow a divided society to work. Such a society worked better divided against itself. Thus Protestants and Catholics were divided both by faith and often by location; and over time the location was subject to slippage. And after 1969 time had speeded up.

Increasingly with the Troubles, with violence as the norm, separation in fact as well as in faith became increasingly attractive, sometimes necessary. Whatever the motives, much of Northern Ireland, urban and rural, has witnessed the migration into safer areas. At the beginning, in 1969, some were refugees, mostly Catholics, fleeing pogroms; but from time to time after that those who have loitered, the token and the residue, have been intimidated, threatened by word or deed, often by their neighbours. Some simply found their residence increasingly vulnerable, their life circumscribed, their home a bastion and so no pleasure. Protestants moved in from the border areas closer to Belfast, and Catholics left many of the previous mixed areas, especially in Belfast, to move into secure zones. Those who stayed paid. Even with the peace process—especially with the peace process—the process continues. One Catholic family in Black's Road, just off the Lisburn Road in a Protestant enclave, Suffolk, had their home attacked fifty-seven times in the last nine years. Suffolk is isolated in west Belfast, surrounded by new Catholic houses, an island in an island, and in the middle of the two hundred Protestant families are ten Catholic families, the final minority in a province where isolation means petrol bombs and sledge hammers, rocks through the windows, no security even behind shutters.

Northern Ireland had increasingly been physically divided into sectarian areas, first in a rush but ever since as the norm. The walls have gone up—real walls: at first corrugated steel sheeting and later more elegant constructions. Good walls did not make good neighbours but check-points, areas for confrontation and the raw lines of a divided society. These walls and divisions and no-go zones were marked by the British army for briefing: here is a dangerous border, beyond this line the IRA writ runs or the Catholics are solid, over there is a Protestant stronghold. These could be traced on maps of election returns, in the markings of gable ends and flags flown.

Only the secure middle class and the mixed areas indicate a dearth of symbols, unnecessary or too provocative. Elsewhere someone rules OK. In the Ardoyne or Bogside or south Armagh are nationalist no-go zones for the British army and RUC, and the gunman is safe on the streets and the gable ends dedicated to the Republic. And in Portadown or Tiger Bay there are districts filled with loyalists, with evangelical Presbyterians and with the UVF, hard men and dour, Orangemen and their families, many with no property but all who want no Pope, no Papists here or even there.

Some of these secure zones were very old; some, like Dunloy, had been shaped by natural emigration, by opportunity, but mostly by choice, not coercion. The Catholics left behind lived beside the Orange hall and the Protestant church, closed to most custom but symbol yet. The imperatives of territorial defence still ran in Dunloy, just as they did in certain Catholic housing estates or city districts: there the Orangemen would march, not as folks out for a lark but as evidence of power, persistence, priority. Dunloy would not be abandoned except by the living, not abandoned to the Catholics. The parish was still in British Ulster. The church was there. The hall was there. Orange Dunloy lived and would be commemorated. The changes of the previous generation had been most unwelcome and worrisome for unionists and loyalists, the apolitical and the militant. Beginning disguised behind civil rights banners and culminating at the very least in tacit support of the IRA armed struggle, the minority in British Ulster had been engaged in subversion. The majority had been under siege in their own country; and here and there they had visibly lost ground, real and tangible ground, and might lose even the right to march over that ground.

For the majority, the unionists and the Protestants, those who feel British Ulster a bastion against both Rome and much that is undesirable in the contemporary world, the shift in population has been traumatic. For centuries their tradition has been dominant, defended by their own, the United Kingdom, the justice of the saved, the rewards of history. And for centuries all of Ulster, or at least six counties, has been theirs. The others, the Catholics, feckless, at times violent, beyond redemption, have lived in Ulster on tolerance, without power and without prospects. And this is as it should be. They are not just disloyal but beyond reach of the existing civil society, many decent but none within the kingdom.

For a generation the province's defences have been eroded. The old system, a meld of political supremacy at Stormont, ethnic assurance, religious conviction, the power of the purse—both the private and public purse—the ubiquitous Orange Order and the security establishment, has gone. Stormont went and with it real control. The Unionist politicians have been ineffectual, the British army and RUC so restrained that loyalist paramilitaries have been encouraged to act as defenders. London has been ineffectual. International opinion has been misguided and British Ulster misunderstood. In all ways the IRA's armed struggle—surely vulnerable to repression if the will existed—has threatened not simply the old dominance of the Protestants but also their very hold on the land. Northern Ireland should be British. And this is not so when good Protestants are afraid to live in this housing estate or at the end of that lane, or near Dunloy in County Antrim. And the more Catholic an estate, a parish, the more dangerous, the more disloyal, the more likely to be haven for republicans. In 1995 the Ulster of Protestant dreams, pure, prosperous, a beacon of order, pious, neat, productive, a grand wee country rising from faith, diligence, and hard work, was at risk. That such an Ulster never existed makes the vision no less real. Everywhere nationalists evoke an imagined past, golden ages, purity ruined by foreign occupiers or false gods. Nationalists invented an Irish-Ireland filled with comely maidens and Celtic heroes. So too did Protestants imagine a time when their faith was not at risk, their friends in power, and the majority—them, the Catholics—in disarray: a lesser people outside the pale. If times had changed there was still after 1921 a British Ulster, if under threat.

The proper order, the mythical past, the legacy of virtues and standards—all must be defended, not an inch must be ceded, especially to those intent on the destruction of the system. Consequently, an inviolate ritual, long predating the contemporary Troubles, has been regularly and ritually to reassert the authority of the dominant, those dominant by right, by law and practice, by virtue of their capacity and their faith. Thus a people militant and triumphant must display capacity and so the right of domination. To do less would be to deny their own Protestant legacy, would be to accept an unpalatable reality and would lead sooner rather than later to the evisceration of Ulster.

It is not sufficient merely to control the agencies of governance or the majority of the people: the others must acquiesce. This is as much a psychological need as a strategic

17

aim. And so, organised by the Orange Order, British Ulster marches to martial airs, to giant drums, to the tunes of the past to ensure the future and to reassure their own. They march to celebrate famous victories and stand to hear ritual speeches. They do so every year, no matter what has happened, no matter that in this townland or along the other road the faithful are long gone. Especially where Protestant writ always ran, the presence must be maintained symbolically if not tangibly and, as elsewhere, the others intimidated. The same provocative route must be used, because it is provocative—no matter decency or even the opposition of their own police, no other option will do. So the Lambeg drum beats for both traditions to hear, their own, now withdrawn and needing reassurance, and those others, assumed sullen and resentful, who still live on the land and are still within reach. Nothing is to be conceded, not an inch is to be given, and not an Orange hall abandoned or a march route adjusted.

Dunloy is a small crossroads village, its main street often a thoroughfare for sheep. There is not much other through traffic, the locals to and fro and a wave for passing motorists. It is a tiny parish where time moves slowly. There is an empty Presbyterian church, still in the hands of the faithful but no longer open, for there are few Protestant families left. And there is an Orange hall, fifty yards away in Station Road, a traditional building, stucco-surfaced with stone-edged corners, solid, built to last. Dated 1896, the time of imperial triumphalism and Orange conviction, it is the outward symbol of the old system in place. The hall, straight, Mason-square on a lonely site, now has shuttered windows, a locked steel door, and no members. Away on all sides stretches rural Antrim, fields and narrow roads, the ground dropping off to the east to the headwaters of the

River Main and the main road from Ballymena to Ballymoney.

In August 1995, as every year, the members of the local Orange lodge intended to gather at Dunloy to march and then be bussed on to the Apprentice Boys' parade in Derry, the biannual march about the walls to recall the salvation of the Maiden City on 7 December 1688 by the thirteen apprentice boys who closed Ferry Gate on the advancing Catholic troops of the Earl of Antrim. The boys thus deprived the Jacobean troops of an easy victory and began the Ulster Protestant resistance to Rome and James II that led to the defeat of James and the triumph of William of Orange. All these events had long ago been shaped into a British Ulster icon, and all are hallowed by the contemporary Apprentice Boys. The great Ulster marches— mere fete and popular outing according to some—are annual and visible rituals of Protestant triumph, marches with drums and thunder to intimidate as well as evoke past glory. History is both a patriot game and pageant, folklore and rite. In August the Apprentice Boys recall the Battle of the Boyne a month after the celebrations of the other Orange orders, and in December the stations of the siege of Derry.

There is no-one from Dunloy to march—all are Fenians, assumed by the Protestant faithful to be a subversive residue driven to the hills by the planters. Here the survivors plot vainly to reconstruct history. Always the Apprentice Boys arrive to march before moving on to Derry and then return to march again in what has become an uncongenial arena. There had been Apprentice Boys to march in Ulster since 1814, and the summer of 1995 could hardly be an exception. Why should the first year of the peace process, the first at the end of a generation of violence and subversion, be any different?

In August the old system had long gone, but not the Apprentice Boys, who drove into the crossroads on the Saturday morning, some bringing the band instruments and all enthusiasm, some with packed lunch, many in parade dress, banners and sashes and keepsakes of the past. This time there was a new reality in Dunloy, an indicator that the locals were not easily intimidated nor even content with the evolving peace process to ensure justice. Splattered white across the dark shutters of the Orange hall were slogans of the times: *IRA—Our day will come*, and *Black bastards, you will die—PIRA;* the graffiti of the times, smeared with hate by those who abhorred the system and the rituals of the triumphant. Times had changed; if nothing more, the IRA had done that. So the Orange hall was changed: daubed, roof and walls streaked with paint, the slogans crude, a monument vandalised by those who were to be intimidated.

Outraged, the Orangemen marched in the morning on schedule to the crossroads of Dunloy. The residents were equally outraged at the gall of the Apprentice Boys in tramping through a village not theirs, to give intentional insult to locals, to flaunt arrogance once more to sectarian tunes. The spokesmen for the Orangemen, those who would be more politically correct, more visibly decent, said they saw it always as tradition, a day in the country, a holiday commemorated, folklore on display and fine marching bands—and no need for the locals to take umbrage. The locals, the minority in the province and the vast majority in Dunloy, saw matters differently.

Exactly what happened that evening when the Apprentice Boys marched again on Dunloy depends on the perceptions of those involved. No disinterested witness came forward. The RUC on the road did not count as far as the locals were concerned: no-one in Dunloy considers the RUC disinterested. They are part of the problem. There were no doubts that when the marchers reached the village crossroads the second time that day there was provocation, words, a scuffle, a sword lost, police caps missing, pushing, shoving, no easy march-by, a fracas. No-one took responsibility. The slogans on the Orange hall were the work of "undesirable elements" among the young men. The Catholics had been provoked. The Protestants were merely defending their tradition. They had a legal right so to do.

The RUC, a few in the morning and a goodly number in the evening, had done their duty: names had been taken, arrests were made on Monday morning. On Monday Rev. Ian Paisley issued a statement alleging that the wife of one band member had been beaten by more than thirty republicans during the disturbances and that others, including the husband, had also been beaten; "the attack was obviously an attempt to intimidate the small number of Protestants sill living in Dunloy. Republicans were clearly telling the Protestant community that in their eyes they have no rights." There were articles, some short and one long in the *Irish Times*. Then the outside world went on with other events, the big stories. No-one followed up matters, sought roots, found the responsible: everyone involved knew what they knew.

In Irish sectarian grievance there is never a first cause. Each finds justification in history; each act is provoked by previous injury. There is a dialectic of retaliation. Everyone defends rights, not privileges, acts only if provoked, holds a monopoly on justice, on reason, on history. The divided Irish society reveals two sets of contradictory rights arising from two different histories woven from the same threads. All are agreed, if on nothing else, that the past is prologue, that the present is warped by greed, ambition, and malice, not by error or the inevitable. There is always wrong to be corrected, right to be defended, justice to be sought. History is both then and now and rarely a product of consensus. It is a history beyond the reach of professional historians, not amenable to revision or often reason.

All the Apprentice Boys wanted in August 1995 was to exercise their rights as citizens, as majority members of a democratic society, as free-born Irish Protestants. They did not mean harm, did no harm but followed marching bands along routes traditionally taken. They, as decent Christians all and citizens of the United Kingdom, had come, as they did every year, dressed in their best with their wives and friends, with the band and in a party mood. It was their custom, fair, folkloric, and just. What harm? Even what harm if the victories were Protestant and the others not invited? The locals had their own Popish and republican ceremonies. If affront were taken, that was not Protestant concern. The marchers merely sought to duplicate past precedent and were thwarted in Dunloy by those who would resort to violence to achieve what was not theirs to have: parity in esteem.

Those who had been provoked in Dunloy could find no logic in such an explanation. They knew that the very purpose of Orange marches, with banging drums and sectarian songs, was to impose ritual dominance over those of another tradition. There were no Protestants in Dunloy to celebrate long-ago victories; so the celebration was not a matter of marching bands or folk customs, not in Dunloy. Who was there to watch the parade? Who was there who wanted such a parade? The only purpose of a tramp down the narrow main street was to intimidate and awe, to display dominance—a dominance that the scuffle at the crossroads and the slogans dribbling down the Orange hall indicated had long gone.

The Catholics defended the territorial integrity of their village: no arrogant Orangemen here. There in Dunloy as the majority they felt the march was not a folk display nor a venue for political speeches but a ritual to humble those who sought only justice or peace or quiet within their own homes. Any violence was provoked. The slogans on the Orange hall were provoked. The purpose of the march was just that: to provoke and humble; and if challenged, the system, in the form of the RUC, imposed humility through a system of institutionalised injustice. The march was a ritual of British Ulster, a necessary reassurance in troubled times; and for British Ulster times had always been troubled. Nothing had changed.

In fact everything had changed, as the vandals had proved, as the title deeds indicated, and as the scuffles stressed: momentum had shifted, the ramparts were not in the same place; an inch had been taken, and more.

In Rasharkin, matters were not as clear-cut to the involved, since the village has a mixed population, divided in tradition but one in location, and the year is long. As one Catholic said about the marches, "I think people would accept them if they were peaceful; they've been doing it for years and years." They had not, however, always been doing so peacefully. A decade before, on 14 July 1986, fifty loyalists with clubs and hatchets had attacked Catholic homes in one of the worst Orange excesses of the times—nasty and vicious, according to the authorities. But that was then, and even then many of the local Protestants wanted no trouble. The Catholics were, after all, their Catholics, there all year round. The Catholics too had to live with the others and so had a selective memory—recalled only the peaceful marches; like most in the province, preferred quiet, peace if possible.

In August 1995 the march in Rasharkin had not been quite peaceful. A skirmish in front of the grocery shop had developed when the Orange members of the bands from Ballykeel and Ballymena, apparently with drink taken, had attacked the locals with beer cans and bottles on their return from Derry. The local Apprentice Boys, not eager for sectarian violence in the village, calmed the troublemakers— more so than the RUC, who the local Sinn Féin representative felt had "stood around laughing and joking with the bandsmen." The local newspaper reported, however, that the police intervened to restore order. This may have been the case: one sees what one sees. What one saw in Rasharkin was the overspill of a hot summer, trouble unwelcome, unwanted, but real enough and not limited to the marching bands of Ballykeel and Ballymena. In Rasharkin the locals had to adjust: there would be a tomorrow, and life must go on. In Dunloy, divided in spirit and distance from the others, there was less need to adjust. Decency did require disapproval of the vandalism by "undesirable elements", but the Catholics felt that the Apprentice Boys should accept that they were not wanted.

In fact at Dunloy all the old and new were there. The local Catholics assumed, perhaps not without reason, that the Orange march was not a folk custom, rather an effort to intimidate, to display territorial control over once-firm Protestant areas, to show that not an inch had been given, no matter a generation of violence, the shift of population, and the threats daubed on the Orange hall. For the Catholics, the village majority, the Protestants as Apprentice Boys were immutable, unchanging, arrogant and aggressive—had learned nothing. They were the aggressors, no longer neighbours of some sort but symbols. They, unionists, bigots all, were unable to imagine concession or compromise, and, given the opportunity as in Rasharkin, eager to deploy violence. There was no rational need to troop through Catholic areas. There was no need to stir up trouble in mixed areas.

The Apprentice Boys felt aggrieved. It was their hall that had been vandalised. It was their traditional routes that were barred by Catholic troublemakers. And in Rasharkin the incident was surely a minor matter. Outsiders after a day in Derry with drink taken had become a bit too obstreperous but had been quickly quieted by the locals and the police. Only the media hunger for sensation would be interested in a scuffle on a village street—and, of course, the newspapers were quick to report trouble. And the reports were most apt to be critical of the defenders of British Ulster.

In Rasharkin for a moment the two traditions had grated, but by Monday matters were in hand. Tempers had cooled. The village went on as always, for little had been at stake. What was at stake at Dunloy was tradition: the violence of the locals was undoubtedly encouraged by republican pretensions, certainly Paisley felt so, and the whole community, not simply "undesirable elements", was hostile. Others might stress the provocative nature of the march through Dunloy or the illogic of marching where the custom was intrusive and offensive, but such observations were by those without convictions or traditions at stake. All the Orange Order and the Apprentice Boys at Dunloy wanted was their legal right to march as they had always marched.

Even if it could not be recognised, perhaps admitted, by the marchers, such displays arose because of changes in population patterns, changes in political fortunes, changes that made 1995 different from other years, changes in Protestant prospects and Catholic capacities. No Protestant wanted to talk about the implications of these changes, but marching gave them something to do about them— something congenial, easy, fulfilling. The change in the attitudes of the distant, the authorities, the English, the international media, those beyond the immediate, the patent unpopularity of their unionist cause—all these only strengthened their resolve to repeat the march, to do something. The majority must reassert their rights. If such an act seemed arrogant, so be it. If such an act seemed intended to intimidate, then so be that too. The act was legal, historically valid, proper.

The majority who protested were either disloyal— republicans, nationalists, Catholics—or misguided, trendy critics eager to be politically correct at the expense of the Protestants of Ulster, who were a godly, decent, productive people in a grand country. They had to defend themselves, since they had so few friends who would do so. The ceasefire made no difference. The rise of Catholic power, the emergence of an IRA that if without victory was without doubt beyond repression, the increase in the Catholic population and the shift in demographic patterns, the weight of a generation of criticism and disdain—all these made no difference. Or rather they made it all the more essential that the old rituals remained inviolate in the new and difficult times. For the loyalists the problem was not that their case was poor, that the marches were an anachronism, not only unfashionable but also ineffectual, perhaps counterproductive: rather it was that no-one understood the problem. Thus all the solutions, the crafty compromises, the elaborations of the Anglo-Irish document signed in Downing Street in December 1993, the peace process itself, simply ignored Protestant reality.

There were two Irelands: one was British and one was

not; one was imbued, despite a minority of Catholics, with the Protestant ethic and the other was not; and even if one were unfashionable both were real, opposing poles in a single geographical field, separate, inherently different, without prospect of blending. This might not be trendy but was real, very real to the Protestants. Pluralism could be found in great mixed societies like America or London, but not in Tyrone or Antrim. No-one wanted mixing, not majority and not minority. For generations each had wanted more, often perhaps more at the expense of the other, but not mixing. Both traditions imagined integration as movement towards assimilation, amalgamation, extinction. Pluralism was alien to Ulster and, like mixed schools, undesirable to all, to Protestants in the state schools, to Catholics in their own schools. Each wanted to live among their own. And even when in a mixed area, they lived apart. Catholics in Ulster wanted to be among their own, were largely among their own, isolated and visible, proclaiming their national heritage and their hope of ultimate triumph. Protestants might not be just as British as the British of England but were still British and not like the other Irish, who for generations had resisted reality, resisted the legal and recognised arrangements that had established Northern Ireland. The continuing nationalist resistance had denied the majority both security and final triumph. In fact most of the Protestants no longer felt triumphant. They were alone in Ireland, and their Ireland had but six counties. These must be held or lost. Where were the Protestants of yesterday in Kilkenny or Carlow? In a small country the Protestant minority had to be vigilant in order to be separate in British Ulster and separate in order to be free.

Protestant Ireland had always, and not without reason, felt under threat, and seldom as much so as in the summer of 1995 from an aggressive "pan-nationalist front" and from an IRA despairing of the gun for the time being but still devoted to physical force. British Ulster, the Protestant tradition, the liberties of the province seemed under threat from London, where each round of reassurances seemed more hollow than the last; under threat not just from the Republic and its friends in Washington but also from much of world opinion. The Troubles had been played out for the media, and the media had found the loyalists unpalatable, unfashionable, a vestigial and passing fragment of Reformation Europe. Always to a degree misunderstood, often manipulated by their English friends, ever mindful that numbers mattered, Protestants were a minority in Ireland no matter how the country was organised, were a majority only in six counties and not all of those and not for long, according to the projections.

The Protestants of British Ulster were not typically Irish, not really British, certainly not English. They were not planters any more. They had no home but Portadown or Coleraine, had been in Ireland for centuries but were not Gaels. They were also not really dominant any more, no matter the marches or banners. They were as always under siege by the times, by the majority, by those far away; and most of all they were misunderstood, in large part not because their cause was flawed but because it was not only unfashionable but also stridently made. Who cared to hear Protestant rights trumpeted in the sectarian language of righteousness? Who cared to see Ulster reality plain, not twisted to politically correct assumptions of compromise and adjustment? And nearly all believed that it was impossible to compromise: that would merely negotiate away liberty, the heritage of their tradition. One could not adjust revealed truth or compromise with evil. Their hope—

their intention—was that the system, besieged, battered, and betrayed, must be maintained, uncompromising, unaccommodating to other tastes and changing fashions, could be kept beyond the reach of negotiation or concession.

For a small and faithful community, isolated and under threat from Rome, from the old enemies, from most modern opinion, any concession would surely be merely the first of many. It would be that first inch that would grow to a mile, the beginning of the end. Each defender, all the defenders felt that the tradition that shaped their world had to be inviolate, adamantine, beyond adjustment. Nothing could be taken away without risking everything. Over a generation, Stormont had gone, the Unionist Party had gone, the B Specials had gone, the control of housing and employment and the easy right of way for the Orange rituals had gone. There might have been "no surrender", but much had been taken.

Yet somehow British Ulster remained—not really all Ulster and not really British—and would remain as long as the faith was kept. The generation of losses had made no difference to this assumption. The tradition could still be defended, best defended and only defended by maintaining the dominance of the system and the union with England. In a divided society there was no middle ground on such matters. All that had been must be kept and protected, even if only a recollection of the past: the memories of Carson and Craig and the Unionist majorities at Stormont, the B Specials at the crossroads, and London far away, with Dublin lost in the mists. Those were the days. Just as in those days, the Apprentice Boys recalled an earlier time when the Union Jack flew from the Glens of Antrim to Dingle, when the sun never set on the empire, when the Fenians were in chains and the Governor-General in the Castle in Dublin and Belfast an industrial giant.

In 1995 the past century seemed wondrous. Golden times had always been past times for most Protestants. Those were the times as summoned up by loyalist history when the cause was triumphant, when Croppies lay down and the royal writ ran, when loyalty was appreciated and the faith triumphant, with no gunmen on the street, bombs in the cities, or a loss of nerve in London. The history of Protestant Ireland had been one long defence of justice and tradition, of right under threat from Rome and nationalism and from England by those disloyal to tradition and justice. In Ulster the faith had been salvaged by 1922, and nothing so indicated the necessity for the union as the failure of the republic in Dublin, a failed entity that still flourished on charity and emigration. Rome rule had extinguished Protestantism and established an ineffectual, corrupt, sectarian state, inherently aggressive, driven by nationalism and buttressed by Catholic perceptions. The nature of Irish nationalism was to expand to the island boundaries, a manifest destiny that could only be denied by eternal Protestant vigilance.

Thus history was a history of threat, and the summer of 1995 was no exception. And the only viable defence was to deny the future to those who would fecklessly destroy the faith and all its gifts. There could be no pluralist Ireland, no equal mix of religions, for Catholicism melded with the Celtic nature would bring ruin. The only hope was that Ulster remain British, remain safe within the union, beyond reach of the other Irish.

Such an ambition was founded on the most unpopular assumptions, denied by politicians, populists, many social scientists, and most of the trendy. Protestants knew that their religion, their cultural tradition—open, free, productive, frugal, and fair—had shaped a better society in Ireland than the ideals of the Catholics. They recognised that separatism based on religious grounds, on the assumption of a superior tradition, violated the fashions of the day, where the elite was suspect and the meek admired. Yet they knew that their Ulster to flourish must remain separate, open and decent to the minority if loyal; if not, not. The world was filled with hopeless cases, new nations filled with misery and injustice, led by incompetents, filled with grand ideals that only generated war and misery. All the splendid ideas of the chattering classes had led to disaster. The old ways—discipline, thrift, honesty, encouraged in each individual—worked. Left alone, British Ulster would work and flourish. Trendy or not, British Ulster could be viable, a beacon to endeavour and the Protestant way, to ancient English civility. The provincial majority should be heeded, not the "pan-nationalist front". Nationalism was a lesser god—and in Ireland a greedy one. History was not child of geography, the island not intended to be one, their cause valid.

Yet the visible world found the Protestants of Ulster an affront. The Ulster Protestants knew this. The television producers, American academics, foreign journalists, even it seemed at times the BBC, all claimed that the Protestants had no case, not just a badly made case but no case. The Ulster Protestants knew that they were unpopular: a few kind words by an American president, press hand-outs in Dublin, even praise from Sinn Féin could not hide their lack of real friends; and even their real friends had no interest, no selfish interest, no strategic interest, no economic interests in supporting British Ulster.

So the everyday Protestants in Ballymena and Ballykeel

kept to the old ways, unfashionable, immutable and irrelevant but comfortable. At Dunloy they would come back again on 10 September, on a Sunday, to march again into trouble, into another clash with the locals, four constables injured and an RUC revolver snatched in the melee. It was what the loyalists expected, mostly why they had come—not for general gain or to make a point but to respond to grievance perceived, provocation taken. Most had given up hope of being understood, and most knew that their case was poorly made if deeply felt. They believed, as Paisley did, that their rights were at stake, their tradition endangered by Irish nationalism and the camp followers of contemporary political fashions, that few cared about them, about the Protestant case. And in this they were right.

I

THE FLAWED CASE, THE FLAWED CAUSE

History is made by those who can say no.—André
Malraux

It is not that no-one cares about the Protestants or their
British Ulster, but rather that the Protestant case is neither
appealing nor convincing to any but their own friends.
Their case, however, is real and in many ways reasoned if
not compelling. Yet when offered, the message is often not
only ruined by the medium but also shaped to antagonise.
Speeches by splenetic divines or an angry Orange orator,
supposedly scholarly pamphlets and tracts are often filled
with sly evasions. Their public defences are too often laced
with the curses of the rude. All too often the speeches or the
tracts simply alienate.

Everyone hears Ian Paisley or the leaders of the Official
Unionists, but no-one listens. They especially do not listen
when told realities that upset their own agenda, their own
perceptions. No-one really ever did listen to the content,
and so the medium was the message. There is Paisley again,
making a scene, garnering publicity, insulting the Pope or all
the Catholics—a dangerous buffoon. There again is this
politician or that divine preaching as if Luther still lived, as

if the Pope financed the IRA, as if pogroms might be the best policy. At best the unionist arguments appeared self-serving, the unionist core values not acceptable, the unionist assumptions those long discredited, their power seemingly resting not on logic or appeal but on their numbers and on truculence.

They are a majority in Northern Ireland, albeit a majority created to be a provincial majority rather than one evolving naturally over time or long indigenous. This cunning manoeuvre in 1920 had, after fifty years, produced a long impasse. The Protestants were the majority, and so policy— British policy, Irish policy, Ulster policy—must be adjusted to that reality. They could in theory be abandoned by the responsible in London. Support there had always been conditional: the very constitutional foundation of the province, the Government of Ireland Act, 1920, had made provision that the parliament of Northern Ireland could vote itself into the Dublin parliament if Dublin agreed; a united Ireland was an option inserted by the British, not alien at all.

By 1995 an end to British Ulster seemed an item on everyone's agenda. London might renounce interests but still insisted that the majority ruled, so those who wanted the union could have the union. Still, somehow, their future had to be negotiated again. And all could hope that the union would survive once again. And it should. After all, the unionists were the majority and loyal. So they waited on events. The easiest option had been for those in authority in London over the long years to do little, and this for London's reasons, not Ulster's. Some did sympathise with the Protestants, especially during the long years of the IRA's armed struggle; others, Conservatives usually, felt that loyalty should not go unnoticed, even if the loyalists leave something to be desired in tone and image. There is an appeal to British Ulster in an age when British power has eroded, patriotism become unfashionable. And British Ulster has, in the republicans, an enemy long detested by the London establishment and especially the Conservative right. Love for the Irish, so visible elsewhere, was hard to find in London clubs and city offices and the Tory back benches; and as for militant Irish nationalists, they were mad dogs and mindless.

So British Ulster did have friends and leverage. There was too an appeal to ancient loyalties and a shared history in a world filled with new people, and so too in Britain. Few in Britain cared for the Irish, but few would actively discard Ulster friends—or so Ulster hoped. There was the Somme and all that. Much of that was long ago, and new generations in Britain cared little for the long ago, and so perhaps the capital for Ulster was spent.

Ulster's fate must rest on Ulster's present arguments. The fact remains that now the unionist case, if sound on historical grounds, replete with constitutional and legal merit and representing a majority of those in the province, has done little to disguise the sorry record of that majority or the uncertain foundations of history, law, and justice. The shadow of majority oppression composed of the excesses of the Stormont system, the bigotry—once fashionable, not, as now, publicly despised—the excesses of a Protestant state for a Protestant people, lies across the political landscape. For nationalists there is another case and another majority, and both are more congenial to general opinion. Even the excesses of the IRA have not cancelled out the legacy of Stormont. And many accept that the IRA is not representative of nationalist opinion while at the same time assuming each Protestant a bigot if not a paramilitary. Few seek evidence that in the Republic, the other Ireland, there was prejudice, injustice, that the nationalists had constructed a Catholic state for a Catholic people; and those who do so find that this does not legitimise the unionist record. For those who seek bigotry there is still ample evidence: why else do the Orange bands thump their way through nationalist towns past sullen and insulted Catholics?

On record as well as in theory, the Protestant case, regardless of the medium of presentation, has rarely attracted more than the converted. Anti-Irish sentiment in Britain is general and indiscriminate: any Paddy will do, Protestant or Catholic, unionist or not, all are Irish. Those who favour the unionists are apt merely to agree to mutual enemies in the IRA gunmen or the troublesome little people in Dublin. There are not many natural unionists in Britain. Within the Conservative and Unionist Party there are, of course, still unionists, but often very still. They are apt to be sympathetic to the majority and to those loyal to the Crown more than to the agenda and attitudes of the Irish unionists. They do not like the idea of compromise on Irish matters, giving in to the pretensions of the Paddies. And their concern with Ireland is usually momentary and fades after the most recent atrocity. Only a few, like Enoch Powell or Ian Gow, have been dedicated. Powell came to the province and represented South Down until 1987; Gow resigned as a junior minister in protest against Conservative Irish policy. Even Margaret Thatcher, a natural unionist with little sympathy for any Irish ambition, went ahead and negotiated the Anglo-Irish Agreement, a betrayal that enormously disturbed and distressed the unionists and led to Gow's resignation. The agreement was a painful symbolic betrayal that Thatcher hardly intended and barely noticed.

The Protestant case must therefore be defended with vigour to attract any attention and must often be made as a political case when the compelling drive arises from religious concerns. Religion as politics is not popular in the West, and the rise of Islamic fundamentalism and the Balkan conflicts have merely intensified this distaste. The more advanced liberation movements seek secular rationales: so the Palestinians attacked Zionists, not Jews. Not until later, with the prospect of peace and the rise of Islamic fundamentalism, were there religious crusaders, the Islamic Jihad and Hamas. The Palestinian fedayeen had been terrorists and quite modern, even trendy; but the Hamas was inevitably seen as primitive, atavistic, incomprehensible. Religious fanaticism, even religious conviction, does not play well in the Western media; Cyprus and Sri Lanka and Afghanistan are aberrations in New York or Stockholm. So a Protestant case in Ireland, and one made shrilly, has ensured that much attention will be unsympathetic.

The Irish nationalist case is far more congenial, its advocates especially in the last ten years in America far more elegant and effective, eschewing advocacy of the armed struggle for influence in Washington, leaving the old republican support network to cake sales and prisoners' relief. Irish nationalism has moved with the times—and no more effective convert than Sinn Féin putting aside the Armalite for the peace process and so winning friends and influencing the public, moving on the offensive.

The Protestant case is hampered as well because it is defensive. The majority in British Ulster want no change in an arena where everyone else assumes that change is crucial to stability. Such change seems highly likely to come at the expense of the majority. What they want is to be left alone to shape the province as they imagine it once was, with no serious threats to governance or society. To aspire to a golden past may be acceptable for new nations but not for a provincial majority with a flawed record. The glory days for Ulster never really existed. For centuries Ireland was a battlefield on issues irrelevant today, even when the banners seem the same. The United Irishmen were not united as the Irish we know now; Fenian is today a racial slur, not a political description. Ulster has always been changing, in size and in context, and for over a century, until 7 June 1921, merely a historical Irish remnant within the United Kingdom, not an embattled fortress. No-one knew the size of the Orange card, the edges of Ulster, the limits of loyalty. No-one now, of course, cares about the details but analysts and scholars who seek truth, not advantage. For them a golden age is hard to define, difficult to locate. For most Protestants the golden age seems to mean the fifty peaceful years of Stormont—not prosperous, not without disturbance, but the baseline for most in Ulster, the good and the bad; and mostly it is the bad that the others, the minority, remember.

Any unionist must carry about the record of the Stormont regime; to do so with enthusiasm alienates nearly all, and to do so with apology makes any present argument difficult. Stormont is a relic of what most consider the bad old days when the Unionists institutionalised injustice or at best ruled without gentility. What the majority, those old enough, can recall is relative security, assurance that as British, as Protestant, the majority was inherently superior to the other Irish. For the majority there was only limited and necessary discrimination: the system had to be protected; this was natural and necessary and authorised by London if from time to time attacked by the anti-partitionist governments in Dublin. Even with the end of Stormont, direct rule—not power-sharing, not some interim assembly that would lead to a weakening of the union—works, works for the majority. Devolution, not without support, may be dangerous, weaken the union. Independence is a fantasy, inevitably reveals a short half-life when proposed by radicals or loyalists not so loyal or a hollow threat summoned up in a moment of crisis. All the cross-border contacts by churchmen or paramilitaries have been futile, exercises in illusion. The covert efforts to find common ground, like the great marches of the Peace People, have found only that change is unwelcome, not perceived to majority advantage. And even those who want change do not want to change themselves, are content with their own perceptions. So no change is the ideal option for the whole province and for most of the Protestants.

At the very least the responsible in London and Dublin feel that adjustment of present reality is necessary; and many feel that such adjustment should be open-ended, so that at some time Irish unity will occur naturally and without pain. This is exactly what the Protestants fear, and so they cling to the past, to the union, to their deepest convictions, however unpopular. And since little support can be so attracted, little is sought: the case may be made but rejection is assumed. And this has resulted in a long and often irritating dirge about the times and the lack of support when support is owed. Even those sympathetic to British Ulster find the combination of a shrill presentation, patently self-serving analysis and institutionalised self-pity to be less than appealing.

Then there is a further Protestant problem. The majority—repeatedly scorned in the intellectual forum as primitive, ignored in world forums as marginal—must accept as well, and do accept, that they and theirs are not an especially appealing people. Their virtues are often transmuted into vices: plain speaking sounds crude and cruel, honest is taken as blunt, suspicion of authority is defined as truculence. A love of the simple seemingly means scorn for the rites and rituals of all others. No-one notes the carefully organised sermons of orthodox Presbyterians, the elegant formulations of canons in the Church of Ireland, the reasoned appeals of the reasonable and educated. The general Protestant desire for freedom and democracy, for English civility, for an open society, is seemingly denied by their record in power. Elegance and wit and simplicity of presentation are in any case rare in the turbulence of Northern politics, where the tirade is a weapon of choice. And the Protestants of Ulster have seldom denied themselves the hard word.

Always their visible advocates have been the least effective on the general stage, appear as bigots in a time of tolerance, intransigent when flexibility is vital, loud and arrogant when they advocate simplicity and candour. They speak to their own constituency at the lowest level and apparently to advantage: no-one seemingly feels it is possible to be elected to office in Ulster appealing to generosity or good will, or even addresses issues beyond the union. Even then every moderate presentation is driven from recollection by the iteration of the awful. And seemingly year after year, every campaign, at each grand Orange march, some primitive calls down the wrath of God on the Pope's minions or urges bonfires for the IRA. And this is what is broadcast, quoted, remembered.

So a "no" by those who trust the people and their judgement, suspect power and the state, seek freedom and decency, to most sounds merely as just another hard word, another "no"—a refusal to admit error, countenance compromise, or enter the new age. The Protestants, no matter how various in reality, how refined and proper, how telling their case and sound their argument, are apt to be represented by the strident. And so their cause, valid or not, has hardly warranted consideration: the medium has been the message for most, and those who seek further find hypocrisy and a less than convincing historical record. And what they find is that the majority in British Ulster can be weighed in the balance of contemporary fashion and found faulty, their cause flawed, their society failed, their history shameful, and always their advocates rude and abrasive.

The Ulster Protestants certainly are not fashionable and so inevitably are misunderstood. They have no easy gifts, no happy face, no heritage to exploit or stereotype to market: no cheerful nation they, not especially creative if hard-working, not especially amusing, not wry or charming. Their poets and artists are neglected, their virtues missed, their simple, sound lives appear only narrow. In Ulster the Protestants know they are not congenial, not an easy people. Harsh in speech, uncompromising in disputation, narrow, too often self-righteous and always burdened by their record, and forever puritanical, they are not "user-friendly". They are easy to bait, and travel poorly. They know all this and often despair. Their creative exceptions, the poets and artists, the humour of the province, the temperate virtues of the people, get lost. Hard work must be its own reward. Piety may mean productivity, but the modern age seems to admire consumption, style over substance, admires aspects and attitudes alien to Ulster.

And so the province, eager for work and discipline, somehow no longer prospers. It seems that logic, decency, the truth have no takers, because the messenger has worn an unfashionable outfit and chosen to speak straight. When no-one listens there is a tendency to speak louder. No-one likes shouting, even the truth shouted. The defenders of British Ulster know this and so are apt to make their case for local consumption, where no defence is needed, only reassurance given. No-one could and no-one in British Ulster does ignore the scathing assaults on unionist proposals and positions, assaults on Protestant concerns and cares, on their arguments, their logic, their historical position, their rights, assaults on their Ulster. And that Ulster—British Ulster—is shaped by minds and hearts, not by lines on the map, is a province of the faithful, not simply six counties of Ireland. Ulster so perceived has a long history, a golden history of freedom and defence, sacrifice and loyalty to the Crown, to liberty, to virtue. The greater the anxiety of the defenders, the more intense their defence, the less effective the defence. Their defenders become apologists, academic, political or pastoral, and address the saved, who need hardly listen. Once again speaking to those who do not listen or rather listen only for key words to cheer, old slogans to admire or past glory to recall, the defenders are not engaged in a dialogue. They are engaged in fact in a dialogue of the deaf, and are often deafening. Paisley speaks to his own for their purposes and his: reassures and warns and encourages through rant and Biblical quotation and a provocative posture. It is what they expect and it is what they get.

Such a dialogue with one's own is hardly unique to Ulster or to Ireland: the great anti-partition campaigns of de Valera and MacBride were similar exercises in evasion, preaching to nationalist prejudices, since reality was beyond challenge, certainly beyond any sacrifice Dublin might contemplate. And so too in Ulster, where truculence as policy is persuasive and bigotry in public not without reward.

The more modest and more elegant Ulster defenders

simply deploy their wares with greater restraint, but only before the converted: the Unionists speak to unionists, and the gunman of the UVF seldom speaks at all. None expect much understanding, and few receive it. All expect perfidy and calumny, and often receive it. Only the very few seek a dialogue, and those often are disappointed.

Even the unionist-Protestant appeal to British allies inevitably seems a mix of suspicion and complaint, whining about fears seen as fantasies in Manchester or Glasgow. Rome rule does not generate concern in Bradford, nor Papal influence play well in Finchley. More in Britain worry about Islamic fundamentalists than the intentions of the Roman hierarchy. Few travelling amid all races and colours on the Clapham omnibus with tickets issued by Sikhs worry about the Pope or care much about the Irish: all in Ireland are Irish on the Clapham omnibus. And so too the case for a British Ulster rarely fails to alienate those at Westminster or Whitehall. The Ulster Orangemen are those who, decked in campaign medals and waving Union Jacks, stone the British army and the RUC, their army, their police. In Ulster, loyalist paramilitaries shoot the innocent in the name of the Crown, have shot the soldiers of the Crown out of loyalty to a tradition few in Britain recognise as British at all.

And there is nothing easy to be done. The Unionist politicians can never be sufficiently assured. They trust no-one. They are ready with no concession to make life easier in Whitehall. They will never give an inch in a British society constructed on compromise and concession. And when a devolved arrangement was managed despite all, as at Sunningdale, the loyalists preferred to bring the whole delicate structure down rather than endure compromise. They would have flooded Belfast with sewage, ruined the province rather than share. One and all seem intractable;

and the one converted to some moderation, a Terence O'Neill or a Brian Faulkner, even at last a William Craig, is immediately discarded and the gates closed.

All unionist politicians may not rant: some may mumble; but they seemingly mumble the same old tunes. They may speak with the posh accents but, whatever their war record or the design of their tie, they are hardly one with the establishment, itself increasingly less posh. Even Margaret Thatcher, a unionist by conviction, an advocate of British Ulster, a friend of hard security and the hard word, felt obliged to negotiate behind Ulster's back and without Ulster's consent to produce the Anglo-Irish Agreement. It was an agreement to ease the turbulence without allowing Ulster a veto—or for that matter allowing Ulster a word. Everyone, even the prime minister, knew that the word would be "no". That this was a reasoned and logical, perhaps accurate, political judgement did not make the prospect of one more refusal any more welcome in London.

In Ulster, often the best that could be imagined was that tomorrow would be like yesterday. Change was not just risky but dangerous. Harold McCusker spoke for British Ulster on the agreement:

The agreement deals with my most cherished ideals and aspirations. On three occasions in the week prior to the signing of the agreement, on the Tuesday, Wednesday, and Thursday, I stood in the house, having been told in essence by foreign journals what the agreement contained, and it was denied to me that an agreement existed, or had even been reached.

I went to Hillsborough on the Friday morning ... I stood outside Hillsborough, not waving a Union flag—I doubt whether I will ever wave one again—not singing hymns, saying prayers or protesting but like a dog, and asked the government to put in my hand the document that sold my birthright. They told me that they would give it to me as soon as possible. Having never consulted me, never sought my opinion or asked my advice, they told the rest of the world what was in store for me.

I stood in the cold outside the gates of Hillsborough Castle and waited for them to come out and give me the agreement second-hand. It is even more despicable that they could not even send one of the servants to give it to me ... I felt desolate, because as I stood in the cold outside Hillsborough Castle everything that I held dear turned to ashes in my mouth.

That the British government had been callous and callow in Irish matters, that McCusker had reason for resentment, still did not transform his response when heard in London into more than another whine. He stood before Hillsborough as protester, not as petitioner, stood on ground that could not be defended, and so had given London an open field to impose the limited agreement with Dublin.

The agreement did not warrant such anguish, and the implication that unless loyalty was repaid then British Ulster would wave no Union Jack was guaranteed to annoy as much as the drama of the faithful spurned at the gate. McCusker was making his case to his own: they felt betrayed, they were outraged and fearful and anguished. They needed reassurance. This they were given in a form assuring them that all others, Thatcher and company, the British in general, sold on the wonders that would soon arise from the document, would be alienated if attention were paid at all. First to thine own people be true, and in truth the majority in Ulster always waited to be abandoned. They knew they cost more than they returned, no matter how often they tolled their sacrifices and their contributions. For

45

those in England the province was a drain, dreary and costly—worse: a bore and Irish. The Ulster Protestants knew that somehow residence in Ireland eroded their worth: the English found Ireland distant, amusing, irrelevant, and distasteful, and Ulster was in Ireland and not even amusing.

The complaints, the insistence on the purity of the Ulster case and the inviolability of political stance, the very cherished ideals and assumptions, were held nowhere else, certainly not in London, not even by Margaret Thatcher. Ulster had few friends and those rarely an asset. In fact the few converts to Ulster loyalty, like Ian Gow or Enoch Powell, came as surprises, unexpected by Northern politicians, who had become used to their isolation, an isolation made more painful because of their patriot virtues, their loyalty, their dedication to the Crown, their advocacy of all that was best in England. Yet few took them at their word. Most new "friends" for Ulster had been American fundamentalist divines, far-right chancers, racist fellow-travellers or neo-fascists.

The rest of the English establishment and most opinion, not only in Britain but everywhere, had little sympathy with Ulster, with McCusker's assumptions and ideals. Opposition to the Anglo-Irish Agreement and to the prospect of peace was assumed invalid or indecent. What did the unionists want—a return to the bad old days? Over a generation no assembly, constitution, devolved parliament or adjustment had met with favour. The Protestant case seemingly was always negative, defensive, grounded in prejudice and sold by bigots. Few in fact bothered to listen seriously to their case against the agreement. The depth and intensity of opposition seemed to bear little relation to the text: the monster rallies, the great signs and the sermons, the new organisations and the constant protests, mobs deployed, disobedience authorised, petitions despatched—a vast campaign to what end? The most telling indication of the nature of the overreaction was that the paramilitaries did not feel the agreement warranted murder. What had been lost? What was long lost was what had generated the anguish: the confidence that Ulster was British for good. This fear ran through the Ulster body politic like a fever. The Protestant case was a defence that failed to defend. Their case was seemingly so unappealing that rather than attack the flaws, many simply did not bother. Why go through the failures of Stormont once again? Why debate the constant negative?

The Taoiseach, Albert Reynolds, in the midst of the Anglo-Irish negotiation boldly tacked the loyalist agenda to the Downing Street Declaration, but few read it. Who cared but the English establishment, who found Protestant paramilitaries only slightly more appealing than Catholic gunmen. Who wanted to listen to defenders without votes? Who wanted in fact to listen to unionist politicians with votes? No-one really listened to anyone, content that a forum had been given. Some observers, some academics might listen, but rarely did they hear more than the self-pity and anger, rarely did they credit logic or reason or compelling argument to the loyalists. Everyone knew not only what they were like but also what they were saying. So no-one does listen, not really. When they did during the peace process they heard a variation of McCusker: the old litany of betrayal adjusted to the most recent change.

So, year after year, the advocates of British Ulster are reduced to addressing their own and their few friends, ignoring as hopeless the others in Ireland, many in Britain and most of the distant. Everywhere there is at best a lack of understanding and often an articulated distaste for

Protestant Ulster. Dublin waits, as always, to transform the majority in Ulster into a fading minority in Ireland. In Northern Ireland the minority will in any case, according to demographic projections, be a majority in a couple of generations. The polls in Britain indicate that a British withdrawal from Ireland is desirable. Nothing is certain in Britain. The establishment in London may fall into the alien hands of Labour; and even with the Conservatives in power there was the agreement, the Downing Street Declaration, and unionists reduced to an unwanted fringe except when votes were needed. From Fortress Ulster a generation of Troubles had brought no comfort in Ireland or in Britain.

Further afield there have always been hard words for British Ulster by the prominent and powerful, critical coverage by television commentators, unsympathetic investigation by scholars and analysts. What moves and motivates Ulster Protestants is discounted. Every effort to explain, to make a case for British Ulster, seems futile. No-one even believes Ulster means "no" when Ulster says "no". No-one accepts that there will be "no surrender". And no-one bothers to give fair hearing to the assumptions that have led to such strategies of denial. It is as if a whole people were howling into the wind.

The winds this century have almost always blown against Ulster interests. The British—and for that matter the Irish Protestants—never wanted a partitioned Ireland. No-one did. The British wanted a country as closely held as possible, and the nationalists as much freedom as imaginable. No-one wanted Northern Ireland, and none but those in the majority there have ever felt moved to defend it. At best London accepts it as what the majority now wants, but most of that majority assume that the British too believe in the inevitability of a united Ireland, some day, some way. They have now said they have no interests in Ireland, no strategic interests, no economic interests, no interest at all, not even selfish interests. They have also said that Ulster can be British as long as Ulster so desires: so the province rests on a local majority vote, not on justice, not on the unity of the United Kingdom, not on law, not on right, not as a matter of justice.

From the first, Ulster was different, a province run under special rules. Ulster is an attachment—a costly attachment—without the right to remain British. Westminster does not let any other majority opt out of the United Kingdom. There is no feeling that the British people, their government, their political establishment are really committed to British Ulster. Even a loyalist majority may not be sufficient if London decides to jettison the province, to "persuade" the majority to find a future outside the kingdom. This may not appear so when Conservative leaders defend their dedication to majority interests, but many in British Ulster feel that it could easily be so. At least then the Ulster case can be a comfort, a tolling of old loyalties forgotten, reviewing old threats others cannot see, a display of present grievance, and this wrapped in righteous indignation that all should come to this—Dublin's anti-partition campaign, the speeches of Irish-American campaigners, nationalism disguised as civil liberties agitation, the armed struggle of the IRA gunmen, the pan-nationalist front, a peace process that may promise subjugation if London blinks. For the majority there has been half a century of provocation that no-one but they notice. There was need to defend the majority, erode potential rebellion, deny advantage to the subversives; there are no subversives in Leeds or Chelsea, the gunmen and bombers in London are the overspill of Ireland. A bomb in Rotten Row or in the City ought to have sharpened minds, but none in British Ulster is sure. In Ulster anyone can see that there are reasons for an armed police force, for emergency legislation, for fear of the minority. There is evidence: the roll of the dead, the ruins scattered by the road, the slogans smeared on walls, the reality of the secret army, still there, still armed, waiting. Yet most assume that the majority is despotic, that the nationalist majority in Ireland is not aggressive—assumes this despite the IRA campaign, despite nationalist aspirations. Hardly a Dublin politician can be found who opposes reunification—some day, not soon, but some day. One Ireland is so natural, so appealing, so logical that no nationalism can understand unionist resistance or Protestant fears. Somehow it is always the loyalists at fault: at fault for being loyal, for being British. And no-one gives considered attention to any unionist argument and so leaves the field to Kick-the-Pope bands and Orange oratory, to the screeds and pamphlets and sermons at the Free Presbyterian Church, to the sullen, often bitter explanations in the golf clubs and odd corners of Westminster. The Protestant case makes for unpleasant hearing, since it is not shaped to be heard by the disinterested, not intended to convince but rather to vent anguish and frustration: it is a Protestant case for a Protestant people.

Who now fears Rome or a Polish Pope? Even the Italians voted for divorce. Even the Poles failed to support the Pope's candidate in 1995. The Roman church has enough problems elsewhere to worry unduly about a small province on the margins of Europe. Even the unionists' strongest point—that they are the majority—can be discounted: everyone knows this is an artificial majority created to allow the Protestants to dominate the loyal core of the province. Everyone knows the use made there of majority suffrage, of majority economic and social power—no matter the provocation or the example of the other majority in Catholic Ireland. Everyone is familiar with the sins of the unionists. Everyone seems to know the imperfections of a partitioned country and the inevitability of One Ireland, only opposed because of irrational religious fears. The Protestants of British Ulster thus seem archaic, still seized on matters long decided. No-one else seems to accept the prospect that Rome rules now in the Republic and would rule the whole of Ireland if the gunmen had their way. And none see the Republic as black-spot but rather as an emerging success story with a charming woman president, low inflation, and prospects for high growth. The Irish are a delightful people, gifted poets, with grand universities, a grand countryside. Ireland is a great place to visit; even the American President wanted to play golf at Ballybunnion after the political talks. The Americans come and the Swedes, the Germans and the Italians, and the English. None ever seem unduly concerned about the failures of the establishment. And with the peace process the day of the gunman seems over, and none happier than the responsible in Dublin.

And if those gunmen have few friends abroad and few announced in Dublin, their cause seems somehow to attract support. The Protestant paramilitaries are seen as butchers. Despite all the atrocities, those far from the reek of cordite and the endless funerals still find the IRA somehow romantic, the hunger-strikers and lads in trench coats, or so some of the beleaguered unionists are apt to imagine. There is horror at the massacre in Enniskillen, and then everyone forgets and Sinn Féin becomes the media flavour of the week. It is not just unionist imagination that gunmen-politicians of the "pan-nationalist front" can be found in the office of the Taoiseach, in the White House in Washington, on the evening television news. Gerry Adams, late of the IRA, currently president of Sinn Féin, was 1995 telly star of the year, and his colleague Martin McGuinness of the Derry IRA was on the lecture tour advocating a united Ireland at university venues. Irish nationalism seems trendy—not too fractious, as in the Balkans, not too fundamental, no ayatollahs, if still the odd IRA bomber, instead rather congenial to the innocent who assume geography is destiny and so Ireland as one island should be one nation, united.

It is this consensus against British Ulster that frightens and angers the majority. Everyone knows that religion no longer matters, that confessional issues are atavistic, deployed by Islamic fundamentalists or Balkan killers, not in western Europe, certainly not in the United Kingdom. Because the Protestant case is Protestant it is dated, just as the unionist case seems negative. Thus the Irish Protestant realises that his case is tainted but can do nothing: the fear is real, his analysis convincing, the history of the country actual. Catholicism is an issue. The Protestants see plain the reality of Roman power, now hidden in a "pan-nationalist front". The only hope seems to be, as it has always been, the union. The Protestants can see what Catholic nationalism has wrought in twenty-six counties, really wrought, not what Bord Fáilte sells or the Irish-Americans buy.

Such a vision may not be fashionable but to the majority is real. To be convincing, to have an impact, to warrant consideration even if not sympathy, a case needs to have credibility, not necessarily accuracy. And the Protestants' concerns are not taken as valid by others, the media or the American administration, the British public or the elite European newspapers. President Clinton may come, may make splendid speeches, may urge peace, but every unionist knows at whose expense such a "peace" will be constructed.

Even a lecture by Ian Paisley is not going to enlighten Clinton or the Americans or anyone else. At best the concerned, like Clinton, will listen but they will not hear. The Protestants, accurate or no, are not credible. No matter how moderate at the moment, Paisley and so many others have long spent the capital of toleration. And none are so aware of this as those who have nothing to offer but the truth as perceived, have no defenders left but their own. They feel a proud people misunderstood, often forgotten, loyal to their heritage and so ignored.

Thus the spokesmen for the majority in Northern Ireland, self-appointed or officially recognised, grow frustrated and so more ineffectual. They shout louder to attract attention, and such attention is attracted to the raucous medium, not the message. The rage and violence of the tirades, reiteration of the irrelevant and irrational, have become the Ulster style. The cadence of the quarrel is repeated and repeated and so easily dismissed. In nationalist Ireland the reverse seems to be the case: the nationalist argument is made over and over again and somehow accepted each time as valid, no matter the inconsistencies, contradictions, and distortions. With nothing to lose and much to gain, Dublin can use the soft word to hide a flawed case made to a congenial audience. The Irish in Dublin say they want only peace and accommodation and decency, and certainly not to be lumbered with six counties filled with unionists. Few in Ballymena believe this. Dublin and the Northern nationalists of John Hume are one with republicans on the inevitability of a united Ireland; so they say not this generation, but this is merely to stay an execution for convenience' sake. What they say is heard.

What the unionist has to say does not convince, often falls outside the conventional Western dialogue. The

Protestant fears have no meaning in a tolerant pluralistic society where such matters were long ago settled or ignored. Enoch Powell may have worried about massive immigration into England but was thought quaint, querulous. Those who fear alien religions or races—Muslims in France, Mexicans in the United States—are apt to be labelled bigots. The Germans do not like too many Turks nor the Italians the African influx; but at least the "Orange bigots" are open in their tastes. And the Ulster Protestants are apt to neglect the fact that the Germans, given their history, hardly advocate racial purity or the Americans, given their history, the dangers of diversity. The defenders of British Ulster— claiming to be a majority—articulate their fears too readily, too enthusiastically, too late in the century for most, even those who might be sympathetic to the plight of an isolated and beleaguered people. Thus, when sympathetic attention has been paid to Ulster Protestants, those so attracted are as bad as enemies: English crank conservatives, fundamentalist Protestants from afar, and ideological predators—all those who are in fact bigots. As a result the unionist case has been further discredited. By your friends shall ye be known.

Known by their friends and their vitriolic spokesmen as well as their record as read by liberals, the Ulster Protestant is in fact not known at all. If known, however, the culture and the case for a British Ulster are seldom welcome, filed under bigotry and forgotten. The message is unwelcome. Past conduct is deployed to deny any present explanation. The Protestants are assumed to be incorrigible, still lusting after domination, out of time and so out of fashion, beyond reason, still frightened of Rome. Many assume or find it convenient to assume that what the unionists really wish is to dominate Northern Ireland under the false flag of majority rule, a rule to protect them from an imagined threat, a rule to maintain not simply a Protestant state for a Protestant people but also all the privileges and entitlements of the triumphant. See the Sons of Ulster marching to Dunloy. And of course some do want this and do so announce from dais or pulpit, do march against the present to preserve the lost past, thus confirming what had been expected. In the end, even to keep what remains of British Ulster still safe for a Protestant people, if under siege, the unionists must rely on Britain. And so the union is crucial for the defence of British Ulster, and British Ulster is distinguished as much by its enemies as its principles.

Those principles are not only British but also Protestant; and in another time and place this would not matter, but this is now. Now the Protestants believe, still believe, that the province is under threat from a society shaped by Catholicism. This is axiomatic in British Ulster. Most important is that the majority in Northern Ireland truly believe what they believe, hold not alone a case but also a perception of reality that is immune to right reason or compelling force. Rome, triumphant as an Irish nation, would submerge—without force or inquisition—Protestant liberties and so the freedom of Northern Ireland. The Protestants would be assimilated into any united Ireland— and this is the goal of all Irish nationalists, all Irish Catholics: Albert Reynolds says not within his lifetime, but how old is he? How long does British Ulster have, according to the actuarial tables? The time for defence is now. Some of these Ulster Protestants may yearn for the golden days of domination, some may be bigots; but the Protestant case does not rest on personalities or congenial postures.

In fact the Protestant case against Irish nationalism is in many ways sound, their defence of a British Ulster not at all unreasonable, and their concerns legitimate. Whether this is

55

accepted or not, their case must still be addressed, if not answered, or there will never be an accommodation that takes the gun out of Irish politics. Perception creates reality out of the available, out of personal experience, and out of the climate of the times. They are what they now are, and if tomorrow the siege of Derry were proved to be myth, none would greatly change, for the minds of those on the road to Dunloy are contemporary creations. What the Protestants believe is as important as what others assume exists; they certainly will not change their perceptions because of logic manoeuvred to achieve an accommodation congenial to London or Dublin or the fashions of the time. Perceptions do change, but not easily, and rarely to others' advantage. If two and two make five, a proposition not without appeal, then this is held to be the answer and should be so considered—not accepted, considered. It is the Protestants' perceptions, if not their imagined grievances, that must be addressed. Rome rule may be an anachronism in London and Washington and may be denied root and branch in Dublin (despite evidence to the contrary) but is a clear and present danger for most Northern Protestants.

This is what matters in contemporary Ireland. And what matters as well is that the fear is not without justification. Protestant anguish is rooted not simply in a reading of reality but in one reality. The Republic is a Catholic state for a Catholic people, whatever the laws may say. And that state is not the success its citizens may assume. There is not only a Protestant case but there is also one with substance. Beyond the case, the reality or the imagination, the perceptions of the majority, there are the Protestants themselves, little understood by Catholics, difficult and intransigent, their community and their concerns the actual obstacle to any united Ireland that envisages the dissolution of sects into a common nationality. And those possessed of the revealed truth, as are the Protestants, a truth stripped down, clear and hard, are not apt to adjust to the misperceptions of others. There seems no reason why they should not continue to withhold their consent to an arranged funeral of their faith and their accomplishments, their history and their hopes. Why should they indeed? And an Irish-Ireland with a single government will not be free, much less Gaelic, as long as the Protestants refuse to consent.

There are, then, real reasons, not imagined and unrelated to present political fashions, for Protestant refusal to consider not only one Ireland but also interim arrangements. The nationalists are largely innocent of the nature of the Protestants of Northern Ireland, other than stereotypes and exaggerations, and of the depth and rationale for the denial of the wonders of a united Ireland. The advocates of British Ulster are in reality so far removed from the image projected by nationalist assumption as to prevent any meaningful dialogue. To go forward towards the nationalist dream, towards a united Ireland, without lasting divisions, present events—especially present Protestant perceptions—must be considered as a Markov chain: the future determined by present conditions, not the preceding path—not history as prologue but the present posture as foundation. And now the Protestants must be taken at their own estimation, their case weighed as valid option, perceived by all in Ireland as a burden unneeded. The present is an opportunity unappreciated, because reality is less congenial than imagination.

There cannot be Irish unity if the diversity in Ireland is so great that the people are partitioned not by a physical border but by a psychological divide even more impenetrable because hardly recognised by those who urge unity. And this is so. If the long dream of nationalists, articulated by Tone and pursued by various means and with mixed results, is to culminate in a united Ireland, then the terms of that union must be shaped to the reality of the Protestant people, their perceptions and aspirations. And so the Protestants have a case above and beyond recourse to logic or law or history. They are themselves and not subject to easy change or to facile definitions. For generations their case has been ignored as unworthy and illogical, their separate existence assumed to be accidental, their ideals and dreams mistaken as merely self-serving, and so their future all but determined. They would blend or emigrate; they would in time accept the role written by a Fenian hand. But they have not and will not, will insist on union with England as protection unless offered greater advantage. This since 1921—before 1921—has been the case: in unity with England there is strength to defend Protestant traditions, in unity with Ireland extinction through assimilation.

In many ways little has changed. Dublin has looked into its own heart and found what Ireland means, what lies ahead for all, for the Protestants especially, and found the answers congenial, as they always have, and cheap. On the national issue the Irish-Irish have always been loath to sacrifice, suspicious of risk and at best tolerant of the few more driven by patriot motive. That was not a game for the Irish but one to avoid. So toleration was rare and limited: too much patriotism led to complications, took a penny off the milk, made the decent and responsible too radical for general taste. Given the change, the electorate voted for peace; given an opportunity to rise, most stayed at home seeking peace and quiet. The Irish did not fight in the past but retired to round towers to wait for better days.

Partition for the Irish-Irish is institutionalised evil but one that others had best remove: the United Nations, the Americans, or the British, negotiations or time; the IRA and the gun are too risky, too precipitous, to be avoided. So Dublin has, as Ulster Protestants see matters, cunningly arranged to appear benign when they are mean but greedy, to encourage others to do what they will not undertake, whether the American President, the British government, or even the IRA, and wait on the tides to cast British Ulster adrift. This may give the Irish establishment too much credit for cunning but is not an unreasonable reading of history, however unpleasantly received in the Republic, where the myths of the patriot game are still taken as history. In this nothing has changed—or will change in Albert Reynolds's lifetime. Nothing has changed in that London still wants the easy life, the immediate fix, if not at the present cost. It is true that the enormous secondary benefits of moral superiority that their Irish tutelage gives them would go if Ireland went. Still, in that event England would probably be content to be rid of the Ulster Protestants if the departure were to be wrapped properly in triumph and praise. Then again while England may have no selfish interests in Ireland, the establishment, those in the clubs and the City, those in power, all have an enormous psychological investment in Ireland: for eight hundred years the Irish have refused to be English, to admire the civility of the other society, and so stand as affront. No arrangement that can be shaped as Irish triumph rather than English magnanimity will sell.

In the past the English have accepted expediency in imperial withdrawal as disinterested magnanimity. Why not in Ulster? Those far-away critics want only that their assumptions and prejudices be confirmed: peace if for a Protestant price, prosperity pledged but not underwritten, an Ireland that need no longer trouble anyone, and so the fashions of the times vindicated. This is all possible if the game is not zero-sum, if any nationalist gain is not unionist loss, if there can be free Protestants in a free Ireland. And the unionists, the Protestants loyal to Britain, say "no." And they must be proved wrong, not merely truculent.

No-one much wants to hear the Protestant case and no-one in Catholic Ireland wants to know about real Protestants. In fact few in the Republic know Protestants at all: all imagine they do but there are no longer enough Protestants to go around. In any case, Protestants in the Republic are imagined to be just like us, Irish and decent; their grandparents were another matter, and the Protestant a hundred yards the other side of the border is very different. The Northern Protestant is a bigot, Paisley both horror and show, not like the locals. The locals are no problem. What is wanted in Dublin is a solution, not problems, not Northern Protestant reasons for intransigence, or evidence concerning the Catholic ethos in the Republic.

Accommodation seems so much more likely if manipulated by principles excluding the Protestants, their perceptions, their case, their very reality. Surely a deal can be made with their interest in mind, a deal that can be imposed without violence? They can be persuaded. They can even be threatened with poverty, the Catholic birth rate, worse conditions, English perfidy—and threatened because few believe their fears justified or their case valid. Unity, later rather than sooner, is for the good of all. The British could persuade them, or logic might work or time. And always, unionist perceptions are assumed to be fantasies and their Protestant reality simply imagined. Ireland and Ulster are not as they claim. The others—the real Irish, the Gaels, the Irish-Irish—know better, know best: the arrogance of innocence. The Irish in the Republic have always known what they know and have always managed to adjust patriot history, private priorities, a Catholic ethos with imagined toleration, always found fault elsewhere and never given up hope that their fantasies would take form; the pot of gold at the end of the rainbow earned by others would be theirs by right of claimed inheritance: no title deed needed, no great effort. No wonder any Irish initiative, every Dublin accommodation suggested, engenders Protestant suspicion: no movement is better than slippage.

In the real Northern Ireland there are all sorts of Protestants, a considerable spectrum of rich and poor, evangelical and conventional, urban and rural, elegant and mean; but almost without exception they share the conviction that British Ulster is best served by the maintenance of the union. And always what is on offer, from London, from Dublin, from false friends, from the well-meaning, would erode the union, ease the ties, not strengthen them, would underwrite slippage. And this remains intolerable and so inspires opposition. Unlike Irish nationalists—the few militant republicans aside—who aspire to a unity that would require no sacrifice, the Irish Protestants are determined to maintain their separate and threatened tradition at all costs: no surrender. They, like the republicans, have possession of a revealed truth and the responsibility for a temporal chalice, not the Republic but British Ulster. They cannot cede a dream on the instalment plan. This is their conviction. That such a "negative" attitude engenders no sympathy beyond the majority in six counties makes the posture no less real and perhaps more adamant. Yesterday was felt to be better than tomorrow's prospects. Change has inevitably been at Protestant expense: no Stormont, no B Specials, the Orange halls empty and

61

vandalised, and laws favouring the minority. Violence has paid, but not loyalty. And even with the shift in the tides the present is preferable to any of tomorrow's options.

Such a persistent negative attitude is more than irritating: it leaves no room for conventional politics or compromise, not even hope for the attrition of reason or time. Ulster always seems to say "no," even before asked, even to advantageous suggestions. In fact at the end of the day the unionist posture has really left no need to present a pleasant face and a telling case to those not committed to British Ulster: there is no point, no-one listens. Why explain? Say "no." Only a few disinterested scholars, and most of those only lately, have investigated their world. The media and the social scientists clump around the nationalists, the IRA, the civil rights activists. Most outsiders avoid the Protestant heartlands, seldom circulate among the everyday people who are not in paramilitary organisations and do not attend the Free Presbyterian Church. Only when the bomb goes off and they are victims does anyone notice, and then it is soon back to the vigil at the Falls Road for the latest from the IRA or a drink at the hotel bar for the gossip. Hardly anyone needs a quote from the Unionists, and there is always Paisley. No-one cares about the everyday Protestant. And those Protestants, the everyday, they do care about the good opinion of others but can find no way to present themselves, their Ulster, to effect. What they want no-one else wants to hear. Even during the peace process, when everyone was said to listen, to heed, to reach out, the Protestants felt no empathy, no understanding. They understood that all the adjustment would be on their part: they would be persuaded, not do the persuading.

So the Ulster Protestants, isolated and atavistic, misunderstood, aggrieved, unpopular in part by choice and in part by necessity, have seldom sought to influence anyone beyond the corridors of Westminster, and there not always successfully. They know they are unfashionable, have repellent spokesmen and are not a congenial people— virtuous, productive, pious, true and loyal, righteous, but not congenial. Their efforts at explanation have been failures. Even the well-meaning and decent attempts to explain have often been unbalanced, received as special pleading, and have not sold. The injustices of Stormont are not easy to justify, and as everywhere in Ireland—and elsewhere, of course—introspection is rare and evasion of responsibility pervasive. Stormont might not have been as awful as now accepted, but the apologists have convinced no-one, and if they did the impact would be minor. The B Specials and multiple votes and sectarian housing allocations—the whole Orange system—are not easy to explain in any case, not now, when the past is packaged as nationalist assets and not easy to unwrap. Stormont is a weight. No apologists can quite lift it, explain away the practices of the past to present advantage; in fact few try, and those who try are read by few, are hardly even a comfort to their own. And all religious concerns are liability: no-one wants to hear about the Anti-Christ. What everyone but the unionists wants is accommodation—accommodation by the majority. Even their friends in London assume that adjustment and concession is possible. It is assumed that there must be give in Protestant positions, flexibility in real Protestant interests.

Seldom has a community been not only so frustrated by the times but also so little understood by all—even by themselves. Almost no Catholics understand the nature of Protestant reality, and those in England or further abroad who are familiar with the fundamentalist Protestant mind—

the dominant strain in Northern Ireland—have been exposed to an attenuated and isolated variant. The Presbyterians of Scotland are not as Presbyterian as those of Ulster, nor the evangelical missions of Alabama as evangelical as those of Antrim, nor the Masons of Toronto as pure and pious as those of Fermanagh. And the pure and pious in British Ulster are such that at times the province seems barely incorporated into the United Kingdom. In Britain church membership has dribbled away over the years. There pluralism is essential in a society enlivened and strained by immigrants of all colours and creeds, where secularism is rampant and flux constant. Ulster may be Protestant and the Protestants may claim to be British, but this is so only in the sense that they are not like the other Irish, the Catholics, north or south. They are, in fact, rather like the Catholics in that they are also church-going, socially conservative, pious and puritanical—characteristics in short supply in Britain—but they are these in Protestant shape, different in manner from those imposed by Rome. The result is that the Ulster Protestant is *sui generis*, a breed apart, bred and nurtured in a special climate.

So the Protestants are special—and they feel special, but not always to advantage. Being special has been to be isolated, misunderstood, abandoned, often disdained, at the mercy of greater events and currents. They have become an island people eager to be part of the mainland but without a visa. They are a people shaped by a special vision of the past and present and so difficult to incorporate in an easy future. Their perceptions are never given weight. Few in fact understand the compelling power of such perceptions for the involved, accepting instead their own Irish vision as real, their own nationalist agenda as natural, their own political predilections as universals. It is this consensus against British

Ulster that frightens and angers the majority. Everyone knows that religion should no longer matter, that confessional issues are atavistic and should not be encouraged. It is all right for security purposes for London to claim a responsible role in Ireland because of religious strife, but not for those religious differences to be given precedence in any accommodation. Religion is to be contained, domesticated, or at least kept in churches or at prayer meetings—kept out of politics. Everyone knows; but those in Ulster see daily the reality of Roman power, now hidden in a pan-nationalist front but all too obvious on the gable ends or in the poems of an IRA hunger-striker like Bobby Sands or the social policies of Dublin, and most of all the empty Protestant churches in the Republic. Catholicism as well as republicanism lives along the Falls, in the lanes of south Armagh—and in Dublin. Such a vision may not be fashionable but to the majority is real.

So the spokesmen for the majority in Northern Ireland shout louder to attract attention, and such attention is attracted to the medium: few bother with the message. The great thundering salvos from an Orange pulpit may comfort the faithful but only alienate those who hear the din and not the words. The means of transmission abrades: the rage and violence of the tirades, reiteration of the irrelevant and irrational. The cadence of the quarrel is repeated and repeated and so dismissed. When attention has been paid mostly by cranks, the case has been further discredited. Even the decent and undeniably respectable converts like Ian Gow were few, and others, like Enoch Powell, have come as outcasts and failed prophets. Who dares to speak for British Ulster? Who can? In America and on the Continent there is always a futile scramble by television producers or academic chairmen to find a respectable unionist spokesman to match against the certified nationalist experts and specialists. "Could you tell us, sir, what these people want?" And no-one listens to the specialists either. And this is not true for the nationalists. The old republican Noraid warhorses who sang "Kevin Barry" and supported the lads have long been replaced by sleek and elegant ideologues, well tailored, well versed, well connected, reasoned voices of the New Ireland. Even the British publicity establishment is at times bested— no longer has a downhill run against terrorists and mad dogs. And for British Ulster there is often no voice at all or the savage echoes of those who march to the Lambeg drum.

What matters is that the majority in Northern Ireland truly believe what they believe. With or without spokesmen, fashionable or crude, unlovable, that they believe is what matters, not how they speak or how they are seen. They hold not a case but a perception of reality that is immune to right reason or compelling force. In fact the Protestant case against Irish nationalism is in many ways sound, their defence of a British Ulster not at all unreasonable, and their concerns legitimate. Compelling force does not change minds—and who should know better than Irish republicans? What the Protestants believe is as important as what others assume exists: they certainly will not change their perceptions. They are what they are; and there are too many to ignore, to wish away. They have to be fitted into any accommodation. They must be convinced of advantage to shift their perceptions: one more barrage of nationalist logic or international condemnation will hardly do.

The republicans believe the loyalists' views are merely transitory, matters not of conviction but convenience, and once the British are gone all will be well. British Ulster will be an illusion and the Protestants will be Irish. The other Irish nationalists may be less sanguine but are equally sure that adjustments can be made to ease the unnatural or self-serving fears of Northern Protestants; laws can be written, positions offered, kindness on every hand. So too those further off: compromise is the essence of democratic dialogue, and so the unionist will in time bend. And so everyone, if not knowing what is best for Ireland knows what is better than the Troubles: any arrangement. And so the concerned generally choose not to address the uncompromising convictions of the province's majority but rather to make up congenial Protestants and moderate unionists, malleable and imaginary players in the Irish game.

The Ulster Protestants are shut behind the gates, unable to compromise their faith, their British Ulster, and so unwilling to surrender and unable to explain. They may henceforth refuse to play in Ireland's end-game, make no move, wait on events; but they cannot in the end be ignored, easily manipulated, or made tidy for present fashions. Shaped by the perceptions of the faithful, hard-edged, four-square and intractable, British Ulster must be taken whole, will not go gently into any accommodation unless for advantage.

2

BEYOND DUNLOY: THE PERCEPTIONS OF THE DAY

Practical politics consists in ignoring the facts.—
Henry Adams

Everything is remembered. Nothing is forgotten.—
V. I. Lenin

The world, Dunloy and Rasharkin, Ulster and Ireland and
Britain, varies according to witnesses, varies as do individual
perceptions. At any moment most of these witnesses arrive
with prepared minds, minds shaped not so much by history
as by experience and previous assumptions, not burdened
with tradition but predisposed to the accepted verities. What
they see is what they see. Anyone standing by the road may
have varying interpretations; but the real is real, the fields of
Dunloy are real, the Orange hall tangible, and real too the
ambitions, intentions and prejudices of the crowd. This is
mostly apparent to all—anyone except those from far away.
Anyone can see hate as easily as a pub, fear in any face.

At Dunloy and Rasharkin, Protestants and Catholics,
nationalists, unionists, republicans, and loyalists, those who
watched and those who marched, all the Irish involved on
the Sunday in August, those in for the day and those by the

68

roadside—all were involved in the long, complex and disputatious history of Ireland. Their actions, not their perceptions, would be recorded, if not with a flourish still in time for the evening news and the papers the following day. And their interpretations, Catholic interpretation or Protestant, were not really at great odds. Mostly those at the incidents saw in like manner if not through the same spectacles: their history was shared, even their most special perceptions were often mirror images of the others. After all, real slogans had been daubed, the march was over disputed land, there had been scuffles; and mostly the involved not only knew what they thought but also assumed they knew what the other thought. Each and all imagined the other as they did themselves, and not always with invidious distinction.

And the various distinctions and differences were largely evoked from their own experience, not imposed by the past or even learned from texts. They saw what they expected to see and had learned to expect. They knew themselves and the others, the arena was small, the exposure lengthy. Their present had an inhibiting if not determining prologue. They had, if they chose, historical roles but mostly made do with the moment, wrote their own script. One moment angry as the beer can glittered through the air and the next transformed into a footnote in a yet unwritten text. People make no history, but rather authors insert people into history as prose, or others recall events as legends, a slowly changing oral account. Each one present at Dunloy, active or passive, became part of at least two histories, texts remembered if not written. All had been shaped by what happened, was happening, and would be by what was written; but most of all they were all shaped by experience and example and were thus part of the quarrel as perceived.

They had all been shaped by osmosis, the slow seepage of their culture, assumptions absorbed without question but from living sources. History was important but not a determinant: the slogans on the Orange hall had not been written by the moving hand of history but by "undesirable elements", elements not unmindful of history but inspired by the real world: the armed struggle, the times and the Troubles, the reality of Dunloy, and the examples to be found elsewhere in the summer of 1995.

All, the involved, the observers, the media and the distant, felt that history was being replayed; the pieces moved as much by fate as by momentary anger—not wrong but not really right. Meaning, not content, is each year adjusted: the Siege of Derry is now a nexus of assumptions that those real people at the siege would hardly credit, not recognise or understand. The very words have different meaning: the Irish then are not the Irish now, the victory for another cause in another time but for three centuries adjusted for special purpose. History is open for use, the past can be plundered or ignored or adjusted to need—and on the cheap, with the cost hardly apparent to the investor. History is often what is needed. So history is not destiny and at its most compelling may indeed be prologue but not the text.

What the many seek, no less than the elegant or complex, is simplicity, a ready answer, order among the buzzing confusion. The formula accepted may have internal consistency, answer both great questions and small, but inevitably reality must be adjusted, no less for the elegant as for the simple. Those who do not write on the faith must still accept the vision. Inevitably such a vision when applied at the crossroads at Dunloy is less than coherent. No matter, patriot history confirmed bias, self-serving prejudice;

invidious distinctions fill the mind if not with order then with explanation. All can, if need be, be blamed on history. And few are about to point out the contradictions between the world imagined and the world as lived, between the Taig and the man next door.

Two human faces offer the viewer an infinite variety of differences. No two people are alike; but two hundred faces are a crowd. Mostly there are "them" and us and the one down the lane. And that one, the different one, the other who is known is and was perceived as quite different from the great mass of the different. Those others in mass were all different, different in tradition and agenda, different in religion and capacity and inclination—and if not threat then provocation. Almost without exception the threat and provocation, the intractable differences, the integrity of the confrontation were taken as history's legacy.

This heritage is passed along wittingly and subliminally—not a sudden gift—and most certainly orders the confusion of the present, explains, identified, made the complex simple. Everyone does this, all the Irish, and so create many Irelands, most easily classified. Their Irelands are congruent. Each notes the totems of the other but is not moved, knows their own role and vitality, sees the others clear but differently. Those others move to other voices, other tunes. This congruence does not make them all more Irish than not, except in alien eyes, does not produce a common civic culture, although one does exist, but rather ensures the structure of their quarrel, the dynamics of an Irish dialectic more complex than a bipolar chart. In any case, each and all within the province, in Ireland and in Britain shapes the real to perception's expectations. It is the clash of these perceptions buttressed by evidence, the historical records, that so complicate the task of those who would unite all

71

under the common name of Irish and so a united Ireland or seek a secure British Ulster, essentially a Protestant Ulster for an Irish Protestant people. What matters is what matters, and this is determined by a meaning accepted when offered and so imposed and then internalised, integrated. Then a new order is established, so easily that it seems old, always there, the nature of reality. Everyone looks at a special Ireland, sees what is expected, accepts what matters. It is not just that the Apprentice Boys march to a different drummer, they march in a different Ireland, see what the nationalists do not. And so too the Catholics at the crossroads, so too each nationalist standing sullen on the parade route, standing in a quite different Ireland.

Despite idiosyncrasies of person and place, many in Ireland find the same Ireland, their Ireland, to be everyone's Ireland. And so too the Irish, the Protestants and the Catholics, the rich and the poor, the urban and the rural, the old, the young—all different but all in some way Irish. Some feel exhilarated by this and others only lightly touched—mostly British, deeply Protestant, Irish by geographical accident, not heritage or breeding. They do not inherit that Ireland but construct it, built it not over a day but a lifetime, although most is in place swiftly, the child perceptual parent and subsequent change difficult. Such an heir may not be burdened or compromised by the Ireland perceived, but most are: the accepted truth, the wisdom of the district is easy, conventional, convenient, interest-bearing and apparently cost-free, congenial to emotions and conforming to evolving expectations. The past thus becomes prologue.

For coherence everyone must order experience and is so taught, at home, at school, by experience, observation, and osmosis. Few everyday people imagine that their perception is not reality, their habits and customs not general, so natural is the process of adaptation. They become Irish, more or less Irish, without effort and find about them others more or less like themselves, Irish of a sort, who fit neatly into categories. As Presbyterians they act as expected, as Presbyterians, just as most parents act like parents. They perceive a role without planning but with purpose; most hardly need to seek out a mission once the role is established, and the role comes with perceived reality in place. Some Irish Protestants may be born again, but the shift in perception is one of intensity: still Protestant, still British, still not quite Irish if in Ireland, still among one's own but now empowered by revelation. In any case, if one feels British then one is—no matter what republican ideology claims or the people in Britain think. Who knows better than the Irish what is Irish reality? All need only look into their heart. What is imagined is not without reality and certainly always with consequence. Eamon de Valera said he took no oath, and so he did not. If Ian Paisley says the Pope is the Anti-Christ, who would deny he so believes? If the Apprentice Boys see nationalists as Catholics avid to assimilate Protestants, then is that not what they see?

But all of what is seen is not set in amber, unchanging and unchangeable. Reality, even perceived reality, is not static. Over time there has been picking and choosing—marriage in and marriage out, the fortunes of war and private choice. Mostly genealogy is assumed to buttress present reality. History only matters when needed. One arrives a member of the tribe: one is what one is, one or the other; and one is not the other, the other Irish. And few understand the other outside the narrow and necessary contacts, and few seek so to do. "For what fellowship can there be between light and darkness?" Intimacy is rare and alien. Not many want a mind cluttered by options and painful distinctions. Each persuasion remains in the private, closed world, at ease with their own, in their pub or their kitchen, with their true friends, at their school or church, certainly at play and often at work unknown to the others. Intimacy is rare and alien. Familiarity breeds distinction: none so alien as the man on the other side of the wall, the family next door who chain the swings, the neighbour who wears a fáinne or the neighbour dressed as an Apprentice Boy in marching trim. The isolated heart is not so much grown cold as content with existing reality, the stereotypes of the day, invidious distinction. Prejudice is simply to know already without need of reflection, a comfortable and general posture, a vital necessity in most matters: for what is experience but to permit the organisation of reality without each time beginning at the beginning? Old perceptions are not necessarily invalid.

Perception is all, makes one of diversity or unites the various as a single people, gives order to chaos. Perception may transform a people into a nation, impose right rules of conduct, make nearly anything possible and often anything permitted. Perceptions give agendas, discipline to society, make the Italians loyal to the family and the Germans loyal to the state, the Americans optimistic and the Japanese suspicious of the individual. Some can see a heroic people in a sullen mob or report the destruction of the enemy, because this is as it should be. The fisherman of Conamara can be pure or primitive, exemplar or failure, most Irish of all or least successful. If by taking thought one can still not add a cubit to one's height, one can turn a whole people into monsters or rationalise greed as divinely inspired, make a peasant king or a king a tyrant. For some truth is a function, not a fact, and shifts with need. What ought to be becomes what is. All that is necessary to shape the world is imagination, the need for order, and the inevitable slow adjustment of perception to the tangible. There is always adjustment.

Stereotypes need not be either inaccurate or demeaning. Many perceptions are not simply convenient: the Jews have a foundation for insecurity, the Germans a fear of their nature. Peasants—mean, narrow, fearful, prey to great tides and inexplicable events—often seek tyranny as a means to order and admire cunning, secrecy, and self-interest, and do so in Andalucía or Moldova. Peasant perception allows persistence in a hostile world, makes the best of assets others find unpleasant, and most of all evolves not simply from past rubrics but present reality: time moves slowly for the peasant, and so too perceptions. Yet even the most useful stereotypes need not be for ever, not even those of the peasant, however compelling the collective memory. Age may fine-tune perception. Tomorrow need not be a repeat of yesterday though usually is. It is easier to stay the same, and so many change but little.

The clash of perceptions about what is and should be Irish are not now and never have been an academic matter: a generation of Troubles has cost over three thousand lives, ruined a generation, corrupted the law and decency, crippled the economy of British Ulster, traumatised the people of the province, diluted civility in Britain, and narrowed freedom in the Republic. It would appear that perception has a price and that those perceptions emerge as the legacy of intractable quarrel.

Great empires have been overturned. The whole map of Europe has been changed; the position of countries has been violently altered. The mode of thoughts of people, the whole outlook on affairs, the grouping of parties, all have encountered violent and tremendous changes; but as the deluge subsides and the waters fall we see the dreary steeples of Fermanagh and Tyrone emerging once again. The integrity of their quarrel is one of the few institutions that have been unaltered in the cataclysm that has swept the world.

The Irish, the Protestants and Catholics, those who sought a free Ireland and those who defended the union, could afford their quarrel; the country had been no battleground, nothing in the crash of empires had suggested that the traditional perceptions of Tyrone and Fermanagh were not still valid. They were valid in 1918 as they had been a generation before and would be for much of the rest of the century, shifting a bit under pressure, adjusted to novelty, viable and persistent: they were not, however, inherited whole, did not ensure that Ireland divided was integral to history. Ireland at the end of the century was still quarrelsome, but the arena and the agenda were not quite the same, even when the language did not notice the shifts. Contemporary Irish events needed subtitles so the interested could read the dialogue that no longer related to the action.

For generations the Irish have quoted one's past to prove present perfidy. From 1914 on, each decade has seen militant republicans give up physical force for political action, insisting that not they but the times had changed. Each decade has seen the militant republicans cite chapter and verse to prove that the times are not different, only the faith of those who would abandon the dream; MacNeill ("I am definitely opposed to any proposal that may come forward involving insurrection") and de Valera, Peadar O'Donnell and Seán MacBride, Cathal Goulding and now Gerry Adams, are simply the most recent in the long line of apostates according to Republican Sinn Féin. Those in

Ireland who cry peace also have their old warcries quoted in response. Who would believe those who now cry peace who once made war with relish? Historical quotation is a fine art and effective weapon. History is in Ireland what one makes it. The country may be filled with real gravestones but the inscriptions are constantly being etched for more contemporary purpose.

History is taken not whole but with care and regularly. With rare exceptions, all the involved were apt to assume that the their quarrel had evolved pure over generations, centuries. The complexities of the past had long been reduced to patriot history and rationales: the Boyne and the Flight of the Earls. Free will was for church, not for Ireland. Change might come in a Papal encyclical but not in the resentments of the moment. Catholic or Protestant assumed, for such assumption was convenient, that not only was past prologue but future too. History was alive and well in Dunloy and Rasharkin and Antrim. And many in Ireland feel that history is to blame, not the events, certainly not themselves, who simply respond naturally, simply.

For there are many who do not distinguish between past events and a written text nor imagine the compelling power of the present. True enough, those in Dunloy and Rasharkin have been shaped, if not unwillingly or unwittingly by their past, by their mutual past varying, interpreted but inevitably potent. But now in Antrim is now, the assumptions and perceptions of the involved learned, not inherited, often learned without lessons, without conscious effort, but not inherited as chiselled text. Yet still history as imperative has more appeal than present rationalisation and responsibility. Who wants to admit the charms of bigotry or the lure of easy hatred? Who wants to take the responsibility for the first stone thrown? All believe that whatever else, the

Troubles are part of history. In a zero-sum arena, this one's loss is that one's gain, amid those who seldom find communality. This is as true for those who arrive new to the scene, French journalists and English social scientists, as it is for the Irishman in the Irish street: all believe in the weight of tradition. Every book begins with potted history, the assumption that tradition not only has substance but is a burden, that the past is in every Irish knapsack, untouched, to be gnawed raw. Everyone begins at the beginning, none with more surety than the specialists and the ignorant, one seeking reason and the other rationalisation for heart's desire.

The scuffles in the two Antrim villages, the post-Trouble troubles, the stereotypes and flawed causes, the hidden agendas and small kindnesses, seemingly emerge as directives from the past. There is no analysis to be found, no matter how quantitative, without indication of historical precedent and imperatives: a rush through Celts and the Boyne, Home Rule, Easter 1916, and Bloody Sunday; and only then the models and charts, the rest of the story, the real text. In Ireland everyone seems to arrive as a blank slate for the times to inscribe. The present creates itself from historical evidence; the first Provisional IRA chief of staff, Seán Mac Stiofáin, born English and Protestant, created himself Irish—not the first alien to be more Irish than the Irish. And the French television producers, American newspaper correspondents, Italian economists or English neo-Marxists, all accept the strictures of Irish history. History rules OK.

Irish history explains all and excuses much. The United States, for example, has no history in the Irish sense: two generations could remember the civil war, but that is gone. Each generation learns holidays and a few scraps, for what makes an American is not the heritage of the past but the agenda for the future. Each new generation of schoolchildren learns, haltingly, about the founding fathers, who were building a nation when their ancestors were the refuse of Europe or hidden in the bush of Central America, peasants in China or even in Kerry. History for such Americans is neither prop nor rationale nor burden but an exam in school: history in America is over, and tomorrow is a better day. Not so in Ireland. In Ireland many remember as yesterday the Boyne or 1916, not just as peasant memory, not as the heritage of an oral tradition but as a living presence—but only so because the living have chosen to make it so, to make history into reason and justification, pretext and ruse for an action agenda. In Ireland there is little understanding that there is a difference between history as lived, the event, and history as created, as text. The past is actually past and largely irretrievable, lost but to memory and professional scavengers with limited resources and narrow intentions. So what happened is what the specialists say happened, what historians and poets, soothsayers and village explainers say happened—limited to some degree by the evidence. There are those who remember not only Bloody Sunday or Bloody Friday but the Boyne and the Famine—not the real battle or the actual starving but the residue retained for present purpose. History as text is a matter of perception. Evidence can always be found or ignored.

There were generations who wrote without great concern for the issue of sex roles or class. History was once the province of Great Man or events determined by the unfolding of God's intention. Kings counted not the meek. An Arab chronicler once wrote that this year nothing happened but that the *hajj* to Mecca was interrupted;

otherwise a year without relevance. There was no need to note that the disruption was caused by Napoleon's occupation of Egypt, the arrival of the West in the heart of Islam and, of course, not an inconsequential year for France and for the West. For the Arab scribe, all that fell outside history, outside relevance.

Most of those in Dunloy and Rasharkin in any case have not read history, have not read even the patriot history of stark certainty. Most simply know their past, the memorised dates amuddle with stereotypes, caricatures, and hearsay. They do know that history is important, validates the present, and history like God is omnipresent—if, unlike God, not omnipotent. And beyond history each knows the others, what Protestants are like or the secret life of Catholics, what the Orangemen want and the virtues of the old faith, who to trust and who not to trust, who is a danger and who mere voyeur. The Irish, Catholic or Protestant, know their own and the others and so can explain the present, deploy the past, have a context for their quarrel and their life. Their history is neither the real events nor their rigorous reconstruction but assumptions arising from experience. And that experience is made now, this decade or last, composed of lessons taught on the street and at home, taught by intent or learned from the ethos. This is history as lived, what gives shape to the chaos, what gave meaning to the scuffles at Dunloy and Rasharkin. What matters is what those involved think matters.

The cool and elegant texts of professionals, scholarly, balanced, and authoritative, are what scholars and professionals perceived. In time and in part such history may win the day over failed generalisation and fireside tales, and then again may not, mostly has not in Ireland in any case. The patriot history of republican commemorations or the conclusions of Orange oratory is what the committed perceived. What those involved in the events of Dunloy and Rasharkin perceived was a present given meaning and coherence by what they imagined had happened and what they perceived about them, by analytical assumptions learned neither at school nor as a result of a close reading of the past but from everyday experience. And from such experience learned over and over, generational attitudes arise and are repeated: those suspicious of external authority, recalcitrant at the prospect of discipline imposed, hardly realise that such attitudes might arise from historical experience—need not so realise, since the response is still valid. The Irish, it is said, expect life to break their hearts, and not without reason. The Irish thus arrange their lives to minimise heartbreak.

Everywhere, whatever history teaches must bring with it advantage and ease as well as prescription to be welcome. In Ireland, then, bad times expected are not as bad times unexpected. A Protestant need not read history to know that at Dunloy there is a threat from the truculent crowd: a glance at the Orange hall will show not the past but present provocation. This threat fits an expectation that Protestant tradition is always under threat—not an unreasonable assumption given the events of the past and the country's Catholic majority. Others elsewhere fear not the morrow nor imagine a constant threat; Americans are optimistic, assume every problem has a solution and every people eager to emulate rather than threaten them. One cannot easily teach pessimism or optimism—easier to blame history for such attitudes

Irish history seems important because the Irish assume that it is and so convince the disinterested. What happened at the Boyne or at Bloody Sunday in Derry or during the

Famine, all history, is evidence and explanation, pennies on a scale already weighted with certainty. What those in the crowd at Dunloy or Rasharkin see is what they expect to see: a tangle of generalisations and individual perception shaped by experience, by assumptions, and by recourse to the ragtags of easily available historical generalisation. The Irish, like everyone else, make themselves up each day from contemporary sources, not from the strictures of the past. They are product of that past and their parents and the times and constantly in flux. Underlying attitudes— pessimism and optimism, suspicion of power or pride in reason—arise from long cycles, but even these are open to adjustment. Yesterday matters, but not all the yesterdays equally.

What did or did not happen at the Boyne, who are the real Irish and who are not, the impact of long cycles on present events, does not really matter much, at times does not matter at all. The truth does matter, and will in time have takers; but in written history truth is perception that does not deny the evidence of the past, perhaps revelation, perhaps chronology, but rarely pure, if potent. And written history is apt to matter only to those who read, the bookish, the reclusive, and in time to the record, the great chain of classics and accepted verities. The Siege of Derry or the Battle of the Boyne were real enough, winners and losers famous, but the implications at Dunloy have long been attenuated by time. The olden Apprentice Boys would not recognise themselves on the road to Dunloy. King William has been reduced to a banner and gable end as symbol of present concerns, not as dictator over present action. Habit, fear, prejudice and arrogance could as easily be found at Dunloy as the children of time. These individual perceptions are rarely amenable to scholarly discourse, to the impact of revisionist history, or even at times to right reason or common decency. They are not inviolate but often quite recalcitrant to change. It does no good to contend that all men are equal when the evidence is to the contrary, or to predicate a revolution on the principles of a class struggle in central Africa when there are no classes in central Africa. To insist that British Ulster is an illusion will not convince those who see it clear. One cannot by an act of will stand back from one's perceptions. Even to recognise the reality of another is painful. To insist that all in Ireland are Irish will not convince those who know they are not Irish but British. Words may take on reality but many rest in shallow graves, from Bolivia to Bosnia, who mistook the word for reality.

It is often easier to see the mix of experience and action at a distance. The Italians govern poorly, fear the morrow, are pessimists at heart and cheerful for the moment. Effective civic culture can be defined and traced in the peninsula, some provinces more and some less comfortable with governance. Good government has been rare and distributed unevenly for centuries, as has prosperity, but the local variations have a central theme everywhere. All Italians suspect those in authority, for good historical reason but mostly because everyone suspects those in authority, and such suspicion is warranted and generates advantage. The Italian works best in small groups, works better with those who live within sight of his door, friends and neighbours and best of all blood kin: the family is the safe, sure and basic element. In Italy small is effective: the partisan bands, the Ferrari racing team, the Mafia, commando units, and the Brigate Rosse—families all. Great armies and grand government inspire no great loyalty, are imagined as prey and predator. This is the nature of Italians, and it is still their nature even after the economic miracle and fifty years of tranquillity. And this is for good reason, since experience has validated assumption. Old lessons are retaught and can readily be adjusted for the Common Market or the information revolution or the scandals that put a political generation under indictment. Italians are like that.

The Irish are different, if often not very different. Small in Ireland is also cherished, and the family and the farm. Civil authority is assumed imposed. The centre—Dublin—is the site of entitlement and intrusion, alien even to those who live on the North Circular Road. Much authority is assumed imposed, somehow alien. Easy acceptance of any central directive may be taken as surrender, concession to the powerful. In Ireland, politics beyond the parish—and parish politics are vicious, since so little power is involved—is potentially lethal. No good will is readily granted: the nation is still amazed that TB was eradicated by central government, a triumph not paralleled in the bovine world, where disease has been shaped to ensure entitlements, not cure. Beyond the parish lurks exploitation, and so evasion and duplicity become operational virtues.

The Irish countryman is apt to find punctuality the imposition of an alien culture and so arrive late at the pub if expected by colleagues. No thought need be given to such matters. The rules of the centre, as in Italy, are suspect. The powers that be are to be evaded and exploited, even in small matters. Government away off in Dublin is to monitor entitlements, not to intrude in real life.

This lesson is applicable at present, as it was when land tenure was not sure and worship restricted, when an Englishman ruled from Dublin, when the countryman was not in the ascendancy and rebellion no option. The old peasant lessons have been readjusted. The Italian fills in the forms, instructs his lawyer, plans his holiday, assuming without thought that those in charge are irresponsible and inefficient and often malign, so one must take care, without the need to quote Machiavelli. The Irishman still arrives in time to sell the cow and then have the pint, and what more is needed? No-one likes to pay tax, neither Italian clerk nor Irish countryman; but evasion for one is a pragmatic matter for family advantage, for the other a small, rebellious triumph achieved with cunning. Like the Italian, the Irish countryman doubts the legitimacy of the centre, even as a patriot, doubts even in matters of the hour, but is apt to be evasive rather than reasoned.

Everyone is like that or else alien, and everyone in Clare or Ringsend or Dunloy has learned to be like that, has not been forced into history's mould but has had experience and expectation vindicated. To operate in Rome one must be Roman, and so too in Cork. A German's thirst for order and punctuality, fences where none were before, gates locked, cropped trees and straight lines, in Munster are merely irritant, ineffectual, counter-productive to German aspirations. Ireland works to a different rhythm—if, the German might think, at all.

People learn as they go along, not from William of Orange and not alone from school or parents but from the tacit and assumed. No-one teaches the Italian to doubt the future or the Irishman the proper time for tea. Neither explains the inexplicable by recourse to the intrusions of the condottieri or the lack of land tenure. Historians may and sociologists do, but the everyday get by with the ways of those about them to shape their world. Such perceptions can change but seldom do: change is painful, free will not free. Some in contemporary Ireland find advantage in change, like the computer specialists of Dublin 4 and those who see European institutions as opportunity. To be punctual and orderly has rewards, not alone at the bottom of the balance sheet but in pride. Some in Italy are optimistic about the future in general. It was not, however, the progressives and entrepreneurs that most believed in a fair future but the terrorist generation that sought vengeance because Italian reality did not reflect the precepts of the sociology class or the formal public agenda of politics. Decency had been promised and corruption delivered, no surprise to any but the students who took to the streets with guns in their surprise and anger. Promised change, they had been short-changed, not by history or the long cycles but by a corrupt system that rewarded habit and custom.

Change for everyone is seldom agreeable, more likely to be imposed by necessity than created for good cause. Some attitudes are hard-wired, part of the person beyond corruption or common sense. How to discard duty or honour or lust or pessimism? Honour and lust and pessimism as precepts may evolve, but over time and not to instruction. Beauty is in the eye of the beholder, and so too hate and loyalty. Perceptions must, however, be learned. Generations of Irish Catholics have expected the worst and so have often been surprised, but never disappointed. Events are often surprising, inevitably not quite as foreseen, and so perceptions must perforce be adjusted over time: most adjust as little as possible, and some never change but die with their convictions that the world is flat or thrift is impractical.

Coherence requires ordered perceptions, no matter how arbitrary or misleading such order seems to others: thunder as God claps, disease arising from dank ground, those with blue eyes inherently superior to all others. In Ireland it is what matters to the Irish that matters, what they perceive as real and relevant, what they have learned not from the texts and not out of the past but as a living tradition that shapes perception. These perceptions, if anything, caused the incident at Dunloy. And if no ready explanation can be teased out of Dunloy or Rasharkin, certainly those perceptions and assumptions can be described without recourse to the Boyne and the Famine.

Dunloy in 1995 is very much of its time and place, the actors self-taught, their temper and disposition the product of recent influences, some passed along the generations but moulded to present needs. Each saw what was real, what was imagined, what was expected, and each responded without need for reflection. The accumulated result, despite internal contradictions or the lack of evidence, generated the reality of the moment; the day at Dunloy or the scuffle at Rasharkin was not a captive of the past but the perception of the moment. Irish history did not shape that Sunday but rather the Irish did, and they in turn were not so much children of history as themselves. What mattered at Dunloy—and so matters in Ireland—is what those involved believe real. The evidence of history, the actual text of tradition, the tangible and foreseen, do not provide vision, only collaborating evidence. What the various Irish saw variously at Dunloy was quite real. And if they see what others do not, the others may be at fault or not, but the vision is no less real. For the believer the statue turns, the earth moves, the earth is flat. If the Catholics at Dunloy see arrogance in a bowler hat, oppression in a marching band, then this is so for the Catholic, and perhaps for the Protestant. If the Protestant sees subversion in a smeared slogan and the gunmen smirking by the side of the road, then this is so for the Protestant, and perhaps so for the Catholic.

No history book, no factual text is likely to adjust their

mutual and not necessarily contradictory vision. They see what they see. And what they see is for all purposes what those who would accommodate their quarrel must accept. History as text may be rewritten, made fair, indicate that the past was far more complex, the Protestants less than monolithic or the Catholics not always victim; but history as lived in Dunloy will little note nor long remember such discursive asides to reality as lived. In this sense history does not matter in Ireland, is not first cause nor even proper evidence. What is crucial is what is imagined, what is assumed. Most people think in stereotypes, are prey to emotive reasoning. Few need books or laws or social science to explain the present, the present at Dunloy or the present in Ireland. And their explanations, so often repeated, so long in formation, so intense, so natural, are rarely questioned, almost always taken as real if examined at all. One's own assumptions are true and those of the others false, possibly faked but surely misguided. We are Irish or we are not. Unity is inevitable or not. They are bigots and we are the reasonable ones.

Thus those who marched in the tiny arena in Antrim arrived on the road with their perceptions set and their aspirations in part hidden and in part visible; justice and vengeance, security and triumph, reassurance and a day in the country were all on display or hidden away from the observers, from the others, from one's own and at times from oneself. And whatever else, the Protestants of British Ulster are real, no matter how misunderstood, implacable, indomitable, and often unpalatable. What Protestant Ulster, what the many and various Protestants of Ulster, what the defenders of British Ulster and their allies see is what they see.

In fact such a world view is so at odds with both fashion

and the assumptions of nationalism that at times it seems that none but their own can accept that there might be a Protestant case. Protestants are simply apt to be seen whole and awful, misguided at best and malicious more often. Away from Ulster those concerned, those moderate in manner, the reasoned, the decent, the foreign analysts, many at Westminster or Washington, have always chosen to believe that the Protestant case is monolithic and inherently flawed, self-serving, a violation of history and often the acceptable assumptions of Western society. If the case were real, accommodation would be if not impossible then improbable. Problems must have solutions, zero-sum games add up to a congenial total. So the Protestants are misguided and must be redirected.

It is as if the Protestant majority, the few moderates excepted, have taken a wrong road. Those who would march at Dunloy or pelt the crowd at Rasharkin are—alas—bigots, beyond the law and reason, without justification. They not only should change but will change, discard the husk of error, see the future in a bright light: make a deal, turn Irish, accept compromise. And besides, the militants are few, loud but not representative; for years and years the nationalists have reassured themselves that the Protestants are truly moderate, actually Irish, open to compromise. The Protestant case is simply a non-starter in a post-modern world—irrational, aberrant. Their coarse spokesmen and arrogant orators are as one with reasoned explanation and carefully wrought academic proposals in the popular mind. They advocate separatism when decency favours amalgamation. They appear even in academic gown or barrister's wig with banners emblazoned *No surrender* when negotiation requires flexibility. They alienate their would-be friends, even their English patrons.

The Protestants are unfashionable. But the Protestant perception is not only real but also not without merit. Truth is often unfashionable. And even if historically dubious, legally attenuated, morally suspect, the Protestants have a case believed, a case made, a case accepted by the majority and so a factor in Irish affairs. And it is a case that cannot be wished away for English convenience or with the assumptions of Irish nationalists presented still once again as revealed truth.

In fact those who would deny the Protestant case—their opposition to an Irish-Ireland, their fear of the Roman church, their absolute commitment to the union, their denial that geography is fate—often present an equally flawed case arising from adjusted history, unstated assumptions, other stereotypes, and equally flawed logic. The nationalist aspiration, however reputable, fashionable, viable in the ideological market, is unconvincing to the defenders of British Ulster. Observers and analysts are comfortable with nationalist aspirations, with Dublin disclaimers and assumptions, and so miss the reality that such a case is no more valid or realistic or historical than the British assumption of their own disinterested involvement in Irish matters. There is of course a British case as well and one equally special, self-serving, dubious in detail but at least easier to sell. This is so especially since the British have far more interesting goods on other markets, interests to consider other than Ireland, and so can, if reluctantly, be flexible. So London has increasingly assured all that only moral responsibility is a British interest, hardly noticing the enormous psychological benefits such an imposed burden returns. And so London offers to those in Ulster good will, if only from time to time when Ireland becomes visible. The British announced a late responsibility without selfish interest, feel a special Irish destiny: London has the last word, because the Irish have never earned such a right, a right that comes only with English civility.

Thus Belfast has been repeatedly appalled that its loyalty has not been repaid in kind: no Stormont any longer, only deals with the IRA in Chelsea, then Sunningdale and the Anglo-Irish Agreement, the Downing Street Declaration, and more deals with the IRA; and always lies, evasions, and lack of consultation. Instead lectures to spongers, lectures to bigots, lectures none want to hear, for none in British Ulster feel appreciated. The nationalists too are regularly appalled that English perfidy does not erode over time nor their assumption that when their attention is attracted they will this time for certain tidy up the other island: Britain rules OK. So the Dublin establishment was stunned to discover that in November 1984 Margaret Thatcher did not see the Forum options as anything more than three Celtic flavours of poison—"Out, out, out"—and so not viable options at all. Dublin has for so long listened solely to its own nationalist devices and desires that it was impossible for the responsible to imagine British reactions. This was a common perception with the Unionists, who also could not imagine that London would not take them at their own estimate.

The British, on the other hand, showed a remarkable consistency in Irish matters: they presumed from time to time, when they could be bothered, that intervention would at last introduce reason into the Celtic equation, make the Irish into English at last; and if not, London could wait until London did actually rule OK. Dublin and London both were slow to realise that they played by the same rules: what was good for London was good for Dublin. This, since it was more important to Dublin, was easier for the Irish establishment to accept and for the Unionists to oppose.

Other assumptions abounded in Irish matters, not because they were repeatedly contradicted, as in the case of the British government, but because they were often beyond testing. Dublin assumed that the nationalist options could be sold to the northern Protestants, since they were so appealingly wrapped, so logical, so much a part of an assured future. Dublin's dismay at Thatcher's response to the Forum options was a rare example of assumption entered in a free market. Usually assumptions need never be tested for truth. The Anglo-Irish Agreement and the Downing Street Declaration simply ignored the core unionist constituency, and could in turn be ignored within British Ulster once it was clear that the text was aspiration, not agenda. Over and over again, those involved in the Irish crisis, as in the case of the New Ireland Forum or the "Not an inch" action school, have assumed that repetition is the equivalent of proof: two plus two may not be five, but the proposition in time takes on a certain substance, offers certain returns, beyond easy questioning.

Everyone says they listen to the others but no-one really does. Everyone knows those of the other tradition but they do not. Everyone insists they are engaged in a dialogue. They wait, listening, and then simply ignore the noise as irrelevant: the usual republican propaganda, the usual Dublin whinging, the usual Orange bigotry. They listen only so as to have time to talk, to repeat the verities.

Why bother to listen to what everyone knows will be said? In Ireland empathy with the others is rare, as is introspection. Ritual repeated over the years transforms amenable formula into assumed reality and then revealed truth: unity is inevitable, England is perfidious, Protestants are bigots, and Roman Catholics are bent on the conversion of the saved.

Believing your own words is not a novel posture for nations or individuals. Believing in your own righteousness is not a characteristic limited to Ireland; but then the Irish case is not as special as many assume. The Irish problem is both special and general; but the involved have been seized within the same dialogue for so long that the impasse seems unique, and so history is more important than the present. Certainly accommodation has proved beyond the reach of the entrenched minds, beyond the desires and capacities of those along the Antrim roads and in positions of power. In Antrim in the summer of 1995 a nationalist case, a unionist case was made by recourse to the familiar ceremonies and defended by special pleading disguised as truth. All those involved in the Troubles, Catholics and Protestants, British and Irish, nationalists and unionists, and those who drop by for the spectaculars, have so long repeated their own assumptions as truth that all assume them true and so real: geography is destiny and Rome is aggressive, the Irish feckless and the British disinterested. The New Ireland Forum thus imagined that nationalist truth as perceived within nationalist Ireland was true for all. This did not prove to be the case. The British still imagine themselves neutrals in Irish matters. This is hardly the case, as the postures and positions assumed since the peace process evolved into more than text. The Protestants know in their heart of hearts the cost that Rome rule would impose: inferiority and oppression imposed by the lesser breed. And actually no-one has disproved this case, because no-one has bothered to listen, much less answer such a preposterous proposition.

In fact as long as no-one contradicts the heart's desire of those engaged in the crisis, all these contradictory or convergent cases remain alive and well and operative. These cases have varied appeals and have been presented to differing effect. The British have spent past ideological capital and deployed considerable talent to effect on the international market. And the British can afford to be flexible, for they have only secondary benefits to lose. It is difficult for the Irish, loyalist and especially nationalist, to imagine how little Ireland matters in Britain, where crucial by-elections, backbench squabbles, new stock issues and rumours about the royal family are always more intriguing. Ireland is an irritant and source of atrocity, an arena with little prospect of glory or gain. So the British can be and often appear to be if not quite disinterested at least uninterested. No-one, least of all the British electorate, likes to contemplate the hidden cost of a dirty war or the reality of English arrogance and anti-Irish sentiment. Instead English responsibility and civility is proffered on the international market, and accepted.

So too have the Irish-Irish sold well, once they made it clear that Dublin was divorced from the gun. This was always the case, except for moments of midsummer madness on the further fringes of the orthodox spectrum, but took a generation to make clear. The Irish rebel is a universal stereotype: Brendan Behan wrought more for the republicans than the Republic could have imagined. Everyone, especially the English, has tended to forget that those most opposed to the gun are those who first cherished it: no-one like a republican to let a subversive starve on hunger-strike or intern those who quote their old rhetoric back to them. The Irish, increasingly moderate in demeanour and in their demands and always in real life, have made the decent Dublin perspective generally acceptable. They converted the Irish-American establishment—those with money and office and respectability—to Dublin's views. Irish rebels belonged on the stage, not as gunmen reeking of cordite and massacre but in the hearts of the Kennedy clan or Senator Daniel Patrick Moynihan. So new, sleek Irish spokesmen appeared in America, at odds with the old ones, publicans and plumbers, minds stopped with Kevin Barry—new sleek spokesmen who were as one with Dublin 4 and the decent Dublin case.

The nationalists can afford to be moderate in tone, for the IRA has made the hard running, just as the English can adopt a high moral tone since they are the legitimate factor in the Troubles, the target of the gunman's attack. So the Irish have a decent case and one easily believed, and so too the English and one easily sold. Not so the Protestants. The British case is deceptive, no less to those who assume that they are disinterested; the Irish case is dubious, relies on natural rights others will not cede, on hope over experience. No matter that both seem reasoned while that of the Protestants seems only strident and atavistic.

The Protestants have been poorly served by their own, and so their perceptions have been denied or ignored by almost everyone: the other Irish, the English, the distant, most scholars, nearly all journalists—the explainers—and even the everyday consumers of events in Chicago or Osaka or Madrid. Protestants have no real friends, no reasoned advocates, and at times no hope of better days. They feel trapped. They can afford neither to be flexible nor disinterested, even fair, for all is at stake. They cannot afford to be moderate in tone, since no-one listens unless they shout, and often not then. Unlike the British, they do have interests at stake—not a life-style but life; they do not give moral example, good advice or patient tolerance but their all to British Ulster. Unlike the Catholics, the Protestants do not have a fashionable national cause. They are not even sure if they are Irish at all, or what positively they want: not a nation, not even devolved government at the moment, not what they have, not what is on offer, not really what they once had. They know what they do not want, but this is not the sort of case that attracts effective friends abroad, even those in America with Irish Protestant roots. No-one caters to the Protestants beyond from time to time some muted concern about Unionist votes at Westminster—and this is politics at the most local level, not evidence of a Great Protestant Case.

Dublin knows little of any Protestant case against a united Ireland and so moves towards the future quite innocent of an Ulster reality that, undesirable or no, unfashionable or no, will not be moved by wishful thinking nor understood by repeating old saws. The English in London know them somewhat better but may actually like them less; Unionist anxiety raises the cost of British moral intervention. And kind and genial chaps like Terence O'Neill are long gone, so the best that was on offer was a mumbling James Molyneux, who, if decent, was also one of his own: deputy grand master of the Orange Order and sovereign Commonwealth grand master of the Royal Black Institution—not really the clubs of the Tories. So even the Unionists lacked entry into the English establishment.

The Americans neither know nor have tried to know the nature of British Ulster. President Clinton came in triumph to the province to give benediction and receive a welcome, for who does not favour peace or want to detail opportunities, not obstacles? And so Clinton came and listened, listened even for twenty minutes of Paisley, and, like the other Americans, heard not, not even the echo of their own Protestant fundamentalists. Washington was always more apt to listen to the articulate, first the British embassy and then the new, elegant Irish-American spokesmen. Americans assume that there are opportunities, Dublin that there are prospects, and London that moral responsibility pays—everyone assumes as true what pays.

The varied assumptions, the perceptions of the committed, do have a grounding in reality. Some Protestant stereotypes are accurate. Some politically correct behaviour is correct. Sometimes right ensures power as much as might. Generally, however, proximity and exposure have not led to insight about Protestants or about the other parties and certainly not led to introspection. So the involved have taken comfort from repeating the familiar formulas, so that for Dublin, British Ulster is an oxymoron, and for the unionists it is a compelling reality always under threat. The Protestants have not only been unable to sell this reality except to their own but have also, in word and deed, antagonised all with their efforts to do so. What they have done is kept the faith, given nothing that could be held, made impossible as far as feasible political co-option and compromise. And so, so far, they have avoided the most dreaded end of all: amalgamation into what is perceived, not without reason, as an alien and lesser culture: Gaelic Ireland. In a sense they have come into their own, found that "No surrender" is a viable option, since it means doing nothing —every politician's dearest option. Doing nothing has, after two years, meant that nothing has been done, the Protestant case made at least for the moment.

What is necessary if that moment is not for ever is to see Ireland as the Protestants do—all sorts of Protestants. Nearly everyone outside British Ulster, a mystic entity that is home only to the loyal, assumes, and has assumed from the start, that the Protestant case is flawed beyond redemption and that their Ireland is caricature. In reality the Protestant case does indeed rest on self-interest, faulty texts and comfortable prejudice but also on the assumptions of the Reformation and the experience of a generation of Troubles. Their world view is alien but not awful. If not compelling to all, their case, their reading of history, their experience is real, quite presentable, if rarely quietly presented. Their Ulster imagined is not imaginary. Their Ulster must be addressed, not ignored or denied or translated into the Ulster imagined by Dublin or barely considered by London. British Ulster is a reality within the Irish equation, an unknown but not an imaginary number dreamed up by bigots.

The nationalists, seen from Orange halls and evangelical churches and from the lanes off the Shankill Road or from Portadown, do not resemble the people imagined in Dublin and Cork or for that matter those found in south Armagh or off the Falls Road. And the Irish perceived by Protestants are not simply caricatures in Orange sermons or pub slurs but can be found in charts and graphs and novels as well, in the results of survey research and historical texts. Such Irish Catholics can be found as example too in the hill farms of Armagh and the terraces of the Bone. The decent and educated bishops, bankers or gentry, the Protestants in the Alliance Party or who are at ease in London or even Dublin "know" nationalists; and such analysis is not bigotry or bogus. Many decent people find Irish Catholics cunning and sly, priest-ridden and manipulated, parish-bound and unappealing. And certainly some Irish Catholics match the profile. Some would not even consider the stereotype critical. Dublin 4 would. Dublin 4 is the new Ireland—and that Ireland too is not without fault.

The Protestant perception of Catholic Ireland and Irish Catholics is solid, if not always sound or convincing. It is certainly one Ireland. For Protestants much that is Irish is rotten, or at least unappealing. That the Republic can be found at fault should hardly surprise Irish Catholics, Irish nationalists, so long target of their own poets and radicals and playwrights and sociologists, so long damned as bigoted, provincial, parochial, puritanical and narrow by each other, by those who would introduce discipline or beauty or end the murder machine or establish the republic. In truth, the Republic is much as Protestants suspect rather than as its citizens assume. In this they are one with generations of Irish Catholic critics. So Protestant perceptions are not an unreasonable foundation for a Protestant case. The Protestants assume that their tradition is not only under threat but also superior to that of the nationalist, their British Ulster even amid the Troubles a splendid country, Protestant Fermanagh better than Catholic Mayo, productive Belfast desirable, not the soft, dirty city of clerks and corruption that is Dublin. Even their fears have foundation, and so their ideals have merit. No observer may agree to their ethnic superiority or even to the inherent dangers of Catholicism, but the Republic is hardly a success story, or the failures of Irish society and character simply Protestant fantasies. The easiest means of denial has been to pass over Protestant reality: ignore the blemish in the sparkling Irish eye—the flawed state, the lack of development, the insular society of political strokes and business connections, the one scandal after another—and focus on the revealed truth, the desired reconciliation. So Dublin takes the gloss of the surface prospects, the reflection of the dark glass, makes no effort to see through but remains content with that image mirrored back.

If there is ever to be accommodation it will not arise from such formulas repeated, innocence assumed as insight, ignorance as policy guide. An effective reconciliation must involve more than surrender. The prejudice of the moment, no matter how hallowed, how often repeated, how logical, is still not analysis and never an effective foundation of settlement. The Protestants in real life are not especially appealing in a pluralistic, secular era, nor their integration into Ireland more likely. Their reality displayed is thus no easy road into the future but, if anything, an indication of just how improbable most present formulas remain. Good will does not move entrenched assumptions. Pieties are for platforms. Everyone wants peace, but not at any price. And so to read the Protestant price, as asked, is sobering for those who prefer to parse only their own papers and platforms.

This does not mean that an accommodation is beyond capacity, but rather that present Dublin and London strategies are limited in application. The "pan-nationalist front" is simply a wide-spectrum deployment of the old aspirations in sync with real British interests. British Ulster is still outside the equation. British Ulster is not even existent for many of the involved: only misguided or truculent unionists, too Irish to be British and too British to be Irish, and so best thought about tomorrow; listen but do not hear, note but do not mark.

The truth may not set Ireland free, but a wilful refusal to accept Protestant perception, the reality of the Protestant case, to understand the nature of the majority community ensures futility. Good will will be wasted, and time, time that may not come again, the patience of friends and even the opportunities of the moment. Perhaps full understanding is neither required nor desirable: too much reality can be depressing. If all agree that the problem is that there is no solution, then there never will be a solution, even movement. Some, if not full, understanding of

Protestant Ulster is required. How can there be an Irish nation, a united people, if the majority in Ireland remain wilfully ignorant of the minority? How can the common name of Irishman be made to cover men who want no part of an Ireland as imagined by nationalists or republicans? Yet how can Ulster stay British if the British have no interest in such an entity? How can the Ulster Protestants continue to be loyal to a union that Britain wants to dissolve?

No vision can be imposed on Northern Ireland or on all the Irish. There is no compelling power to coerce unionists into an Irish nation assumed alien, nor to coerce the London establishment into staying if the British want to go. The IRA has tried bombing the British out for a generation, without great effect, and finally accepts, not that physical force will not work but rather that it will not work yet in the quantities available, but that once gone the Irish Protestants can be coerced into being Irish. Republicans assume they can be persuaded to that effect, but this ignores the reality of British Ulster and the persistence of the Protestant perceptions. The Protestant vision as presented must then be ignored, has been ignored, but cannot be eradicated by an act of will simply because it is uncongenial to Dublin or London or Washington; even the gunmen know this much or have learned this much.

And as long as those who stand by the road in Antrim or march to the old tunes persist with present perceptions, there can be no accommodation. Yet the Apprentice Boys play the same tunes though they march in different times: they know it; the church is empty, the Orange hall is empty, the peace process moves on and they down the road. The band plays on and on but the marchers must go home again and wait on events. Mutual exhaustion may offer respite, time for change wrought by others, moulded by prosperity or novelty; but then a return to turmoil may also be on offer as time passes. The new can be recast in old patterns. Perceptions matter, not history's imperatives nor promises nor the intervention of the powerful and wise. Perceptions shift. People may take what they say they want, may simply take what they can get if they cannot get what they really want. If the Protestants only really knew that what they really wanted could be real, then at least their agenda could be public instead of uncertain. And what they really want may change too: a people may live hoping for vengeance for a very long time, but not for ever.

Everything is subject to change, even when there is no change. Any change must, however, encompass Protestant Irish reality: even an unexpected, unimaginable British withdrawal would leave Protestant reality intact—perhaps betrayed at last, even intensified. The Ireland of Ulster Protestants is a nexus of the tangible and the imagined and has been beyond reach of the Catholic majority, beyond their focus and their interests, beyond imagination and so beyond manipulation. And Protestant reality must in some form be incorporated into tomorrow.

In sum, in a small, closed country, peopled for three centuries by neighbours who are ignorant and innocent of any but their own, local perceptions have seldom been challenged, tested, applied to the actual. What the Irish know they know, and so far they want no options that may grate. Few really want to sacrifice for posterity, much less the morrow. Few ever are drawn to sacrifice: poets, patriots, the mystic are rare in any society, even the Irish, where all have had their day. Modern sacrifice is mostly involuntary: great wars, the attack on the Somme or the involuntary losses of strategic bombing, final solutions or ethnic cleansing—no volunteers there. Given a choice, most opt for the quiet life, peace even without justice. The nationalists know the future from Tone and Pearse, from reading patriot history. Many in Ireland simply hope that the future will arrive without price, without great effort, because justice of sorts has for generations been promised. And so too do Protestants await justice, but with more anguish. Republican history, nationalist history is not wrong, only different from that of the others, the unknown Protestants with their flawed assumptions and aspirations. The Protestants in turn know their Ireland and their Catholic neighbours as well as need be for the moment, know just where they have taken and would take the country; what else is necessary? Everyone seemingly knows everyone, everything, past and present, just not the future, only the future that ought to be given the prologue and the revealed truth.

What the Protestants know, what the Protestants are and imagine, are not secrets. What they want, not always what they will take, is what they say they want. What they see about them is not so different from what others see: Catholics and gunmen and decent people, stereotypes and the lad next door. The Protestant world is still quite different, different as imagined: the songs are different and the imperatives of the day. The Belfast terraces may look alike but for the gable ends; but the Protestant people move to a different drummer, not so much to a Lambeg beat as to the cadence of their faith. They look across the glen or the peace wall and see what they expect to see. They look about Ulster and see what is there for them. Their assumptions about a united Ireland, the Republic, the wages of Irish nationalism, the role of the Catholic Church have not only salience but logic. Yet if the dream is different it is also congruent: everyone wants freedom and order, a decent living, a wee garden and pride of place, their own Ireland

and not sorrows but soft rains and country lanes, happy pubs and good exam results.

Everyone wants to be happy, wants of course everything. The Protestant case seemingly perpetuates Ulster as a zero-sum game, each unionist gain a nationalist loss, each Protestant loss a Catholic advantage: but this too may be assumption and not reality. First, however, those Protestant assumptions that form the foundation for the Protestant case must be described—in a sense no great obstacle if one can believe the discourse of pubs and the content of sermons, much less the findings of social scientists and the text of newspaper leaders. Then Protestant Ireland, British Ulster, must be seen, not as imagined, not even as the disinterested and distance would describe but as shaped by those involved. And nearly everyone is involved, certainly everyone in Ireland. So each looks about, if not through that glass darkly then certainly with set ideas and hidden agendas, and sees not a wilderness of mirrors but at best yesterday's reflection, a ghost on the glass, and at worst one's own image. Even the hardest of facts has been adjusted to assumption, geniality turned into sloth, productivity into arrogance, avowal into deception. At least the perceptions of the involved will usually evoke acceptance by those who so declare: this is, indeed, the way we say we see matters, and this is probably how others see us.

Reality is what one makes it. Mostly the easiest and most comfortable reality is a day like yesterday: the ghost shimmering in the glass. The long cycles can be reinterpreted: pessimism can be shifted into prudent management, rank optimism can be tempered. The long cycles of history are not inviolate in application: "history" can be adjusted, precepts can be adjusted. This is especially true if there is advantage, compelling pressure, to impose change—and there is always change: time runs on and on, the band marches to an end and goes home. Tomorrow is never like yesterday, and often quite different indeed. And yet tomorrow will always indicate the reality of those long cycles. In Ireland the perceptions have not needed to change for advantage—and have taken but not needed history as explanation and excuse. In Ireland isolation is impossible—where can one live beyond neighbours?—separating the traditions without carnage exhausted political and social creativity. In Ireland the intolerable has for the fundamentalists been made tolerable but exhausting: the forces of darkness are forever just down the road. Dreams are left, and duplicity, but not the energy to assimilate once separation has been imposed, contrived, constructed from clashing destinies.

History is not destiny, any more than geography or skin colour, unless so willed. People dispose and define and interpret—and dividing Ireland has been far more difficult than imagined, far more difficult to maintain. There thus may be advantages, not in assimilation, the muddle of traditions, but in less investment in separations. Then, again, separate traditions pay separate returns. And change always requires investment. Perceptions are sturdy but in most relevant cases not eternal: there is no pessimism more easily discarded than that of an Irish emigrant on the promised shores of America accepting the values of the society, flaunting the tangible returns of labour bought.

Reality is what one sees, how the tangible is shaped. Thus one observer sees a hilly half-acre in Tyrone not worth planting and another sees ancestral heritage snatched from fate and history, while still another glances across a ploughed field like all other ploughed fields—someone else's concern. The plot may, if a battle be fought, assume enormous worth for an afternoon, may if no-one wants crop or cattle in far markets be left fallow, offered to a builder, may be abandoned or incorporated or sold as act of treason. The land is always there, but not the meaning. Land is tangible, matters in context, and context is shaped by perceptions. So too the great Irish institutions: British Ulster, the Republic, vengeance and vindication. What is really real, really important is constructed by people, not nature. One can stand by the grave for an IRA funeral amid the ring of soldiers and police, under a low grey sky in a steady rain on a summer day and be within the republic—the real republic, not the one in Dublin but dream made real, a tangible entity held in the hearts of the mourners, the colleagues of the Volunteer. That Irish republic cannot be measured by the acre, is not visible to the British army sergeant or the RUC constable with ten generations of Antrim ancestors, or even the priest beside the coffin. That republic is in the hearts of republicans, a living thing, no less real than British Ulster. The Boyne is an idea, not a place, not a dream like the republic but no mean creation, for it matters to every Protestant, even the elegant and ecumenical. What matters is what matters. And in Ireland it is not even certain who is who, much less what is what—what is real, what imagined, what amenable to change, and what is even Irish.

3

PROTESTANT PERCEPTION: WHO IS WHO?

An angular people, brusque and Protestant,
For whom the word is still a fighting word.
—William Robert Rodgers

Once the march is over, the Guinness gone, the sandwiches eaten, and the lads all driven home, each Protestant is left with his own, with himself. Each, beyond individual virtues and foibles, accepts a place among his own—and his own can be ranked, described. They are the Protestant people, to themselves alike, all different but all the same: unionist and pious and loyal to their tradition.

These shared attributes do not create an Irish Protestant nation but only people who are Protestant in Ireland or Irish Protestants. Despite pop history, polemics, and fancy, they are not a racial group, not united on doctrine, not members of a tribe, and so are not easily placed in the spectrum of faction. All claim to be British, but none reside in Britain. All are citizens of the United Kingdom—but so too are their Catholic neighbours. Even the nationalists from the Republic can take the boat train to Liverpool and disappear into the mass, swiftly on the dole, eligible to vote, usually very soon indistinguishable from those who have been in residence since the Normans or before. Thus any in Ireland can fit easily into Britain, forgo their roots, become prime minister with a name like Callaghan.

Being a Protestant from Tyrone or Down does not seem to make one any more British, just as representing south Down made Enoch Powell no more Irish than Margaret Thatcher—both unionists of a sort. Thus being Protestant unites most in Northern Ireland only in not being Catholic and fearful of amalgamation. They are all one on the constitutional issue: the need for union, but always for religious reasons, even if those are assumed to shape the nature of society, Protestant piety producing English civility—but then such piety does not seem necessary in Britain, where religion has declining appeal, generates no conviction but empty churches and disputes over the priorities and prerogatives of the royal family, defenders of a faith few profess. Being Protestant in Leeds or Newcastle is a tick on a form, a private matter, not the subject of an identity crisis.

The problem of identity arises in Ulster because being Protestant is insufficient to organise the province as more than a devolved and local establishment of six-county dominance. There is no British Ulster nation in the geography books, only in all-but-unrecognised Protestant hearts, and then no nation. They are not people distinguished by colour, language, or even origin. Each stranger must be weighed for creed, questioned, examined, assessed for indicators and symbols; the great difference is hard to distinguish: the Catholics are not black, nor do Protestants speak in strange tongues. There may be two traditions but there are not two visibly different peoples, no two nations.

Being Protestant does not put the faithful into a single

complex transnational galaxy, as does faith in Allah, nor for that matter into an ethnic pool, as does being Greek—or even Irish. Ulster Protestants have allies, fellow-fundamentalists, overseas Orange colleagues, but a mere scattering across the far corners of the old empire: friends, not family—colleagues only. What moves those Protestants in Ireland is not doctrine but the special threat of Irish Catholicism, unwelcome in Alabama or Ontario but not the central organising principle of society. And very few over a century have imagined such a society as anything but adjunct to or integrated with Britain; even the Maronite Christians of Lebanon could envisage a Christian Lebanon with flag and postage stamps and a man at the United Nations. For British Ulster, being Protestant and in Ireland is ample grounds for entry, the only grounds. And once there within the walls, the great and urgent requirement is to stay, keep the gate closed, the local subversives cowed, maintain the siege, not venture out under banners of conquest. Persistence is triumph enough, and the others trapped inside ample hostages to superiority assumed.

Yet just being Protestant does not augur well in a world structured by the nation, where faction is apt to be ethnic and religion mere reinforcement: not even all Arabs are Muslims nor all Italians Catholic. Present fashion and contemporary ideology favours the submerged nation, the Latvians or Armenians, recognises even the aboriginals of southern Sudan and the tribes in Rwanda, accepts rebellion in unheard-of Asian republics as explicable. Even the Islamic fundamentalists seek not simply Allah as solution but an Iranian Islamic republic, an Algerian Islamic republic, an Egyptian Islamic republic. Just being united by creed, a Christian creed, and otherwise quite like one's neighbours, seldom seems to make it worth resorting to violence, worth the troubles that have been generated in Northern Ireland. All the visitors, the wise and the blasé, the learned and the innocent, find motivation difficult, the violence over trivia so inexplicable. Why should a variant of Christianity matter so much after all this time, when elsewhere all such matters no longer matter? The French can manage Muslims, and so too the British cope with various races and creeds. The Americans are a muddle, more Jews in New York than in Tel-Aviv and more Catholics than in Ulster, and all sorts to be found in America as Americans, once from Fiji or Silesia, Kerry or Sénégal, but now citizens. No-one cares about their faith or former fatherland.

Even in the chaos and horror after the collapse of Yugoslavia the successor armies sought not only vengeance but also a state, a place for their emergent nations—all but the one religious faction left adrift as Muslims in Bosnia. The others found national homes: a greater Serbia, fellows in Albania, a return to Montenegro as refugee, Croatia emergent, Slovenia recognised—all, that is, but those united only in faith: the Muslims. They were ethnically similar to Serbs and Croats, not Turks or alien at all. They often shared the same history, more so than the Albanians, shared the same language and culture. They were simply South Slavs assimilated long ago to Turkish religious priorities. And so with nothing but Allah they were the odd people out: the sure losers, not strong enough to shape an Islamic state, not so few as to be subject to a final solution—the option of choice for many of their recently declared enemies. Their tribulations indicate for Northern Ireland the fate that mere devotion to denomination may have. The others in the Balkans or Africa or Europe marshal more than creed as magnetic core, just as do the Catholic Irish.

Why are Irish Protestants in six counties of a small

country so special, so seized on matters long settled elsewhere, so recalcitrant on questions of doctrine? Why are they so quick to assume, so certain that a variant form of worship determines all else—government and individual character, productivity, social structure, and the limits of sin? What is, indeed, an Irish Protestant? As Wellington reputedly pointed out, being born in a stable does not make one a horse, did not make him Irish, nor Francis Bacon. The others, the everyday people seemingly can be more or less Irish, more if they speak Irish and live on rocky islands, less if they have English names and grace the Malone Road. What all share is that they are not English—but those in Northern Ireland who are not English and not Catholic, not nationalists and not different in birth or breeding from those who are the Irish-Irish, find in themselves a difference in faith worth an absolute commitment. They may not be sure of who they are exactly but are all too determined what they will not become.

What they are can have various answers, variously shaped and displayed, resting on differing evidence. The curious can examine novels and poems or memoirs, best of all talk to as many as possible over a long time or, as do the social scientists, survey a sample, reduce the sonnets and diaries to numbers, charts, and graphs. All means are valid, some more than others, but none is complete, none really very scientific. Those queried formally are apt to reply as moderates rather than bigots, evade hatred, seek to please, move towards the middle: fewer unionists always say they will vote Democratic Unionist than do so when in the polling booth, for militancy has a bad name elsewhere, if not in Ulster, and the Irish Protestant cares about the decent opinion of the distant, does not want to seem a bigot, even if biased. Many do not know their opinion until asked, just as many cannot imagine future action until the future is now. Pub talk is pub talk and rarely even when guided rises to analysis. And novels are novels, not sociological tracts. Sociological texts, even those written by ethnographers intimate with the subject, do not arise from a lifetime spent among the Protestants, among one's own or one's neighbours, a lifetime of pubs and chapel and casual interchange.

No means is ideal, but in most cases the results indicate that Ulster Protestants have difficulty in defining their basic identity: Irish of a sort, more than simply unionists, all Protestants but Ulster Protestants, British of course, but more and less British. Entry into British Ulster demands religious qualifications, enthusiasm and commitment but first sectarian identification. Once within the system, identity is a problem, but not those excluded. The Orange Order was erected on anti-Catholicism, and so too the Unionist Party. "It is difficult to see how a Catholic with the vast differences in our religious outlook, could be either acceptable within the Unionist Party as a member, or for that matter, bring himself unconditionally to support its ideals." The others, those Catholics denied entry into British Ulster, were a danger in 1934 according to Basil Brooke: 99 per cent were disloyal (up from his previous estimate in 1933 of 97 per cent) and disruptive. How could they be otherwise?

In Ireland being Protestant means not being Catholic, being at risk, seeking alliance and incorporation within the provenance of the Crown. Being merely a member of the majority tradition in a world cluttered with ethnic claims, national determination, and tribes flourishing flags, the Irish Protestant often feels compelled to be more than Protestant, to fit a more applicable definition. What matters of course is being Protestant; but then what? The Catholics are all

Catholic and Irish nationalists, stress fairly or not their Celtic ethnicity as well as their shared history. They have a language, even if they do not speak it, a national history, even if they exaggerate it. They have a flag and a constitution and a dream of unity. They are Celts in spirit, if only in the most limited ethnic sense; for they, like Protestants, are a muddle of indigenous and invaded, Scots and English, Norse and Welsh and the residue of Picts, Vikings and Danes, and others. The Republic's international football team is a melange of blacks and browns, Cockney accents and Irish surnames, but Irish. The Provisional IRA had an Englishman as its first chief of staff, and a present leadership with names like Adams and Bell and Morrison is hardly indication of Celtic ethos.

The Celtic tradition in fact was largely a nineteenth-century invention, a hazy patriot's history of battles lost, martyrs, round towers, jigs and fireside tales bartered as Homeric rivals, and the long struggle to be a nation once again—when, of course, Ireland had never been a nation, never united except by invaders. Irish nationalism, like Irish creativity, was indeed often elaborated by Irish Protestants. They are the ones who helped save the language, revive the ancient glories, and sought national independence. The first republican to die was William Orr, a Protestant; the founding father was Theobald Wolfe Tone, a Protestant; the first President of Ireland was Douglas Hyde, a Protestant. The great woman hero of the 1916 Rising was Constance Markievicz, born in London as Constance Georgina Gore-Booth, hardly Celtic. Irish nationalism may have fallen into Catholic hands but there is an Irish national tradition for all Ireland that Ulster Protestants do not want to share and cannot emulate. They are merely Protestants. Observers find this insufficient, and Irish nationalists find it no reason not to be Irish.

In the Republic no-one frets about who was Norman or Dane and who has an English surname. No-one is any longer much concerned with the invention of a Celtic tradition or even who digs with the other foot. St Patrick may not have been Irish then but he is now. None of this matters in theory and largely in fact, for now in the Republic all are Irish. True, almost all are Catholics, but still all are nationalists, Protestants and Catholics and Jews; there are more Jews in the Dáil than Protestants, and an Indian as well. What makes them Irish is that they feel Irish: who in the Abbey knew that Micheál Mac Liammóir was not Irish, or who among the IRA gunmen cared that Mac Stiofáin spoke Irish with an English accent? They are certainly not English—or not any more: that is the most Irish characteristic of all. And it is the one most galling for those within British Ulster, for they too are taken as Irish by the English.

The Ulster Protestants are apt to miss the fact that to be Irish is not really a matter of birth or breeding, Celtic surname, or manner of communion, but rather a refusal to be English. And one cannot simply be British by displaying the Union Jack, painting the kerbs, marching to Derry and back, draping a sign over Belfast City Hall. One must appear British to the British, and the Ulster Protestants are not so much British as a historical responsibility, a community loyal to the Crown—citizens now living in Ireland, and so taken as Irish.

The others in Ireland, the nationalists, also have an identity problem, one that has been solved by will: I will be Irish despite my birth, my heritage, my religion. And so said the Protestants and Jews and Catholics, those with English names and birth places and those without, those who spoke Irish and those who would not. From Belfast or Ballymena this is not apparent: the Irish seem Irish, mostly Catholic, entirely Celtic, an alien people, another nation. The defenders of British Ulster, not really a nation, accept the reality and the power of the Irish-Irish: a people chosen who chose to be as they are, are as they are now largely without reflection or question. It is a great strength that the unionists—a mere political faction—do not have, that Irish Protestants—merely a religion, if a potent one—do not have. The Protestants of Ulster, residents of an imagined British Ulster, united in not being Catholics, fearful that they will be melded into the national majority, are still not sure of their identity but only their distastes. Being Protestant is crucial but somehow not quite enough. What more is there that makes them them? They know not so much themselves as their perceived enemy and their unifying religious commitment. Yet if they do not know exactly who they are, they know all too well what they do not want to be.

British Ulster is an invention, like Celtic Ireland but equally real, except that it is not a nation, not really a province, not this and not that but most of all not Catholic. And in British Ulster a Protestant finds difficulty in imagining his own national stereotype. Everyone knows the personal virtues that the faith brings but not exactly the nature of the believer: Irish and not Irish, defender of Ulster as ideal, British but not resident in Britain, not this and not that but always Protestant and at risk. None can really imagine a Catholic as Unionist, although there are many Catholic unionists—not least the great convert Conor Cruise O'Brien—but many of those responsible, certified and successful who see no harm and considerable advantage in citizenship in the United Kingdom: still Irish, still not candidates for the Orange Order or the DUP. They are residents of Northern Ireland, not British Ulster, which is exclusive, not inclusive.

In fact the peculiarities of the divided province, the long history of trouble, the available sources, the historical record and the convenience of the site have attracted enormous interest from those who specialise in such complex societies. Over the last generation Ireland of the Troubles has been increasingly troubled by the swarm of scholars attracted by the province as a Petri dish: conflict in a divided society, an armed struggle, all sorts of constitutional experiments, political initiatives, and points of analysis. Northern Ireland has generated thousands of books—many significant, some related to the perceptions of the people involved as well as to the laws and budgets, body counts, or election results. The first analytical sweep was made just before the onset of the Troubles in 1968 by an American professor, Richard Rose of Strathclyde—before Ireland was more than marginal, a green and misty land of poets and old men walking greyhounds. Rose appeared at an ideal moment: the province was normal, or as normal as it was apt to be, the IRA border campaign over, the prospect of détente between Dublin and Belfast a reality, peace and quiet and hope for progress on the political menu. And so Rose could undertake his surveys just at the right moment to give a baseline for all subsequent data: this, soon after mid-century, was what people thought about themselves and the others, what they thought without worry of the gun or fear of the morrow.

What emerged was that the unionists, the Protestants, were not too sure who they were or what they were but did not seem to feel that this was something that mattered greatly. Then the Protestant might declare himself as British, or from Ulster, or Irish.

British: 39 per cent
Ulster: 32 per cent
Irish: 20 per cent
Sometimes British, sometimes Irish: 6 per cent
Anglo-Irish: 2 per cent
Don't know: 1 per cent

This was a relatively clear indication that Ulster Protestants were not only not very sure of what they were but also might have indicated that they did not consider the label significant. Only one out of a hundred did not know; the others were divided. None were divided on what really mattered: the maintenance of the union. That union ensured freedom and a flourishing tradition, or so all assumed. These were the last days of assurance, arrogance, and confidence that the system as evolved was largely permanent.

As time and the Troubles passed, the "Ulster" identity lost favour. Once there were those Protestants who felt less British than others: Britain had not always been a comfort, nor the established church nor the system to each and every Protestant. The Presbyterians once long ago had founded dissent with the United Irishmen, and those who went to wee country churches had little in common with the landed gentry, or they with the Methodists or the evangelical shop-fronts of Belfast or Derry. The Protestants were hardly one in many matters, but this did not matter greatly, since each was sound on the constitutional issue, the primacy of the Unionist Party, the role of the Orange Order, even most of the time of the social and economic system. As Basil Brooke noted, "Ulster has only room for one party ... Recent economic issues should not divide Protestants." And such issues never did: the dream of the Protestant working class finding common cause with their Catholic comrades played the same role within radical and republican tradition as did the expectation of the conversion of the Jews in Christianity.

Within the Protestant community, within British Ulster, there were differences in intensity, in social or economic agendas, especially in bad times, in attitudes and sometimes in values; but they were differences, suspicions, not faction. Some wanted more wages, some the swings unlocked on Sunday, some a university for Derry, and others more social welfare provision; but none wanted anything that might risk real division, endanger the union. And the Troubles that began in 1968 did not erode these old suspicions and potential quarrels but rather made them obsolete; Britain was vital to Ulster's future. Everyone must be British, more loyal than the royalists, more loyal than the English, and so not more English but more British. After a generation an Irish Protestant, like the sign for so long across Belfast City Hall, is British. All the Protestants are British, even if not resident in Britain nor so considered by those in Britain. A Protestant may be from Ulster or Northern Ireland but is British first—except in Britain.

So those who would be from Ulster in subsequent polls shifted down to 20 per cent in 1978, down to 14 per cent in 1986; and so in 1989 another survey indicated:

British: 68 per cent
Northern Irish: 16 per cent
Ulster: 10 per cent
Irish: 3 per cent

The Protestants vote Unionist, for this is the British party; if there are two unionist parties they compete as to which is more British. The Protestants are loyal to the Crown and to Britain, to imperial history and the symbols of the kingdom, and so to Ulster and Northern Ireland as British. The attempts of radicals, mostly associated with paramilitary groups, to shape an Ulster identity, to contemplate an independent Ulster, have fascinated everyone except the vast majority of Protestants. They do not want to be independent, they want to be British and so to maintain the union. They seek not differences with the British but amalgamation.

The state schools in Northern Ireland teach imperial history, the ceremonies recall sacrifices for the Crown, the avowed standards and norms are those of Kent or East Anglia. Why not? If Ulster is not actually British the province is certainly part of the United Kingdom, as much so as Scotland or Wales—more so if it were not for the quirks of geography. Belfast might, almost, be an English provincial city—a bit seedy, too many police, a few visible political oddities, strange graffiti and painted kerbstones, but the city certainly seems like any city in the English midlands, seems so to the Protestant inhabitants. It seems so to those who see what they want to see and see Ulster as British and themselves as British of a sort. This the polls indicate: the longer the Troubles, the more apt the Protestants to find legitimacy in being British.

Anyway, such divisions of class and interest and faction seldom persist, are subsumed in the need for unity on the constitutional issue—a boon to those whose interests might be threatened by other issues and agendas. The Orange Order may have fallen on difficult days but then there were those to march at Dunloy this year, as there were last year. And parity of esteem may be offered—demanded—and the Catholic minority often favoured, but the Protestant majority is British first, and that should do.

The Catholics, on the other hand, tend to consider themselves Irish: 60 per cent did so in a 1989 poll, and 25 per cent of the rest selected "Northern Irish"; only 8 per cent thought themselves British. Which is as it should be, since the Protestants did not think of them as British either, even those who favoured the union, who voted for the Alliance Party or found Ulster prosperity and prospects congenial. They are as invisible as the Protestants living over the border in the Republic, where they have been abandoned by the unionist conscience, sacrificed long ago to ensure the survival of the rest. Comfortable Catholics unattracted to nationalist aspiration were still "other"—Irish—to Protestants.

One facet of being British is abhorring Irish national ambitions, which are imagined to be identical to those of all Northern Catholics: they vote for Catholic parties, support leaders who do not find republicans abhorrent, may even sympathise with Sinn Féin, a front for treason and murder. A few individual Catholics may be acceptable, but most Protestants are hardly aware that many Catholics would not welcome a united Ireland, may be Irish but are not nationalists and abhor republicans. Many are content with a British Ulster, find profit and security and feel no Celtic longing for a nation once again.

To Protestants, however, British Ulster is Protestant Ulster, filled with the British—themselves. Whatever patriot history proclaims, British Ulster is a late invention, shaped to keep out of Rome rule what could be salvaged: a Protestant majority in part of Ireland. Before Home Rule agitation Ulster might have been different, more Protestant, beyond the Black Pig's Dyke, but was no more "British" than Kerry. The British traditions scavenged from Masonic rituals and sectarian habits, the necessity for a defence of freedom, the loyalty to their Protestant tradition found focus in the evocation of Ulster: a place but not a place, not nine counties in any case. Even the six core counties were not pure, not British Ulster; would that the others, born and bred in Antrim and so Irish but Catholic too, were gone. Their presence made a pure Ulster impossible. The best that could be managed was to ignore the Catholics of Northern Ireland; and to a remarkable degree until 1969 this was done. They were outside the defending institutions, the Orange Order and the Unionists Party, outside the workings of Stormont or the hiring practices of the great companies, outside, on the dole, living on their own with their own, rarely seen at sports, never in the local. After 1969 it was not possible, but still desirable, to simply ignore what must be tolerated: the 40 per cent of the population that is Catholic. It is convenient, necessary, to ignore what cannot be altered. Those within British Ulster had already left outside the other Irish Protestants, and so these were forgotten, no longer a care or a concern, beyond defence. It is not these lost people, living amid the Irish, but the Catholics still left in the six counties that concern the unionists.

For some not inconsequential unionists the local Catholics were simply "those traitors who live in our midst." Tens of thousands regularly voted for murder, for Sinn Féin. Whatever else, they, the Catholics, were not British, even when they abhorred murder and gunmen and the IRA, damned atrocity and praised the law. They were still alien. And the Protestants are now all "British", with the risks and advantages that this offers.

The Irish were Irish because they were born and bred Irish, have always been Irish—and mostly Catholic, despite Tone and the other Protestant renegades. Back in 1968 this is what the Irish thought too: 93 per cent of the Catholics assumed that they were Irish—and why not, they were, born and bred—while only 41 per cent of those who declared themselves British felt they were born and bred British; 80 per cent of those who identified with Ulster felt born and bred. Being British was a choice, while identifying with Ulster was a matter of nature. Northern Ireland Protestants largely felt it was a matter of living within British rule or a pride in being British that made the difference. The real British were Protestants—except in Britain, where such things did not matter. There the British were all shades and creeds; there the British were apt to consider all those from Ireland Irish. All the more reason to be British in Ulster, for Ulster to be British, to know at the very least what you are not—not Catholic, not Irish-Catholic. It did not matter that one was born in Ulster, in Armagh or Antrim, did not matter that one had Celtic ancestors from Scotland or an Irish name, did not matter at all, because all Protestants were British. The Shankill Butcher who killed Catholics for pleasure was Lenny Murphy. Some of the Protestant paramilitaries had not only Celtic names but Irish Catholic grannies but were still British. You are what you are.

What the Ulster Protestant imagined, reduced to numbers, indicates that the perceptions of the two traditions in Northern Ireland were different, often unrelated to objective evidence but still real. Thus the Ulster Protestant was politically British and, being British, being Protestant, was by necessity productive and so prosperous and thus produced contentment. This remained true for the involved, despite any evidence to the contrary, including personal exposure to attitudes in Britain or a name like Murphy—no bar to position in a Protestant paramilitary organisation as long as the other credentials were sound.

Many Protestants felt they were middle-class, but all felt

better off than Catholics. They could overlook their own miserable housing or unemployment or the lack of decent social services, because, after all, they were by definition better than the others. The British of Ulster were better off because they were British, better if just as poor. The Protestant families living in a one-up and one-down without inside bath or toilet, with dank walls, an unhealthy diet and only the comfort of the dole still knew themselves better off than the others. Thus in one poll only 33 per cent of the Protestants felt they were working-class, in contrast with 47 per cent of the Catholics. They assumed that being British meant being middle-class, despite the actual job they did—if they had a job at all—the size of their cheque, the education of their children, or the criteria of the sociologists and the state. This was true in 1921 and in 1968 and is true yet.

The key is not so much being British as being better. Most nations are pleased with their identity—until emigration or traumatic defeat. Most long-standing groups— nations, tribes, factions—assume themselves decent, some publicly assume themselves superior to all others at birth. They are the people. Their language, their culture, their life are best of all. A few so inclined divided the world into the people and all other living things. For a few the world is divided into us, the chosen—Maasai, Dakota, Israelis, Boers—and the others beyond the pale. There are the Chinese, a billion, a special universe, and then all the others, some rich, some poor, some powerful, many arrogant, but none Chinese. Mostly, however, societies are content with themselves; if not, every effort is made to adjust society to hide doubts, as with the Germans after 1945 or from time to time with Latin American countries, always promising, never triumphant.

The result is that the saved, the people, are better off:

Islam is the solution if not to poverty then certainly to salvation, which is what really matters. There are always those who live behind open gates or without fear of assimilation. An American is defined by a green passport, rewarded by the system, by the city on the hill built by pioneers and open to the huddled masses of the world. Work hard and you too can become an American—any colour, any creed; some have an easier time but all sooner or later are American. Not at all like the Tuareg of the Sahara, who glory in their desert even if without sure drop to drink or crop to grow or friend to trust and who fear not assimilation or immigration but the weather. They want only to be left alone—and who else would be a Tuareg, blue-faced and hard, and who else would want their sand? So they can be themselves and rely on the desert as defence, just as the Americans are defended by optimism and great wealth.

And for Protestants, they were within their own special pale, better because they were British. Yet being "British" in Ireland could not be the whole story, as it was with the Irish being Irish in Ireland. The Irish Protestants in Ulster were special in special ways. The ideal that shapes a Berber in the desert, an American marine or a Kenyan Kikuyu is not always apparent in each individual, but each knows the ideal, the proper stereotype: the virtuous Frenchman or the typical Greek. These are the shiny reverse side of stereotypes: the aspiration and the admirable, the individual determined by the content of his character, brave or cunning, prudent or rash, bold or not—what the many admire, what the leadership, the pastor and the patriots praise and seek: the ideal. The Ulster Protestants had their own ideal, their own ideas about themselves and even how others imagined them.

When polled for a survey, the Protestants chose their own salient characteristics in an order that over the years did shift in intensity but has for a generation been basic. Firstly they are British, and then loyal to the Crown— ordinary people, determined, decent; a fine industrious people. This is what they assume they are: not Irish nor arrogant, not bigoted but decent citizens. Some ticked Orangeman or conservative—power-holders; but first they were the loyal British and then ordinary, determined, and respectable. And each is a decent Christian, a Protestant Christian, a conviction that empowers and endows each with certain characteristics and responsibilities, makes each better and different from the others, those Romans across the peace line or up the road at Dunloy. The others may indeed be civil in discourse, well-meaning, but are Catholic, Irish nationalists, if not armed still dangerous to the British, to Britain, and so an intolerable intrusion into Northern Ireland that must nevertheless be tolerated.

Most Protestants aspire to what might be called the virtues of the Protestant ethos: piety demands productivity and hard work, not necessarily just for personal advantage but for the soul's sake. Work is God's work. And the virtues of discipline and obedience, characteristics found in the Ten Commandments and the requirements of the Boys' Brigade, are assumed to abound in British Ulster. Any Sunday sermon is apt to draw the line from the acceptance of Jesus Christ to the righteous, godly and sober life, industrious and productive. It is a life determined not by ritual or form but by individual responsibility. The Romans lack this responsibility, rely not on revelation and redemption but on ritual. Not so the Protestants: everyone, the meek and the rich, men and women, the clever and the limited, if Christian have responsibilities, must contribute to the civility of order and the productivity of society. They are the plain people of British Ulster moved by the Holy Spirit, not the strictures of doctrine, not excused by confession but sure to be judged by the Lord.

They all, Methodist or Presbyterian, orthodox or non-conforming, independent or elder in Paisley's Free Presbyterian Church, each lay preacher of the Elim Pentecostal Church and every one of the gentry at Morning Prayer, are wholesome, proper, righteous, God-fearing. They are often born again into Christ, but always devout and active Protestants, church-going, God-fearing. Some are washed in the blood of the lamb; others sit in bespoke suits and Sunday hats with minds idling, as have their ancestors by habit for generation, at Sunday service at the Church of Ireland. And there the service is low, simple: no movable feast, no permanent altar or censers, no trumpet voluntary or elaborate vestments; the Anglican elegance thins out in Antrim. Everywhere in British Ulster there is a feeling, not articulated in survey and polls, that a life in Christ, a Protestant life, ensures a civil society, a productive society, a society that challenges the old assumptions of Rome and Europe. The Ulster Protestant does not believe that doctrine, duty done, display and decoration, the rules obeyed, will supply much credit on judgement day. They know this is so; for theirs is a God with thunder, a zealous, jealous, demanding God who checks each pint, checks the hours invested in productive labour, numbers evil thoughts and sins of omission. And at judgement day not reprimand but Hell fire waits, flames that burn, pitch that sears, real, excruciating, tangible pain for the sinful damned to a Hell reeking of brimstone. Each Protestant not only must pursue the good but also does so as reasoned choice, given the options. Life is real and life is earnest in Antrim and Tyrone.

These northern Protestants know that their virtues are often ignored as others seek instead for faults, seek means of exploiting what has become in a materialistic century unfashionable.

Beyond the check-lists, at the end of the century, the Protestant does not so much feel better than the Catholic as more equipped to produce in the contemporary world. Those who have not done well in this contemporary world are apt to feel betrayed—doubly betrayed, because they see across the peace line their Fenian competitors with a secret army, a "pan-nationalist front", a leader on the telly and they deserted by the gentry, and even Paisley ineffectual. Still none would be Catholic, and all assume times will be better, for them as Protestants, for they are better, are they not?

Thus simultaneously the Protestant feels more akin to the times, a British citizen part of the main, not a Celt on the island margin of Europe, and marginalised, because the affirmation of his faith, the plain speaking of a plain people beleaguered, is not fashionable or very productive in worldly returns. Yet it is their religion that makes them a success—and mostly they see British Ulster as a success, warped by nationalist intrusions. If peace does come, the pan-nationalist front fails, then British Ulster will be prosperous, despite the economic and social evidence of the century. They are convinced that their piety translates into productivity, has done so and will do so again. This faith does not shun questions or rely on rituals and dictum but arises from commitment.

They are, then, ordinary people, questing and querying, dedicated to life, liberty, and prosperity, to the individual's freedom, to the righteous life, to their traditions and so to the union with others like them in Britain.

What is distressing to all is that not only the Catholics do not understand them but also those in Britain and those represented by the media. And this matters: their image counts, and their actions—actions on which they are and should be judged—should be better understood. For a decent, godly and productive people threatened by dark forces, they feel they are seen by too many—those who should know better as well as those innocent of Ulster—as imperfect, primitive, narrow, bigoted, and biased. And they are not, do not so feel. They must speak out against the forces of darkness, a duty, a responsibility. They cannot be still even if the fashions are against them. And the fashions of the time are licentious, dissolute, and secular. In a sense they stand alone against sin in a sinful time; and it is not a popular posture.

In fact their image even across the cultural divide is not as grim as they assume; the bigoted Orangeman of political oratory is less repelling than imagined. Not everyone in Leeds or even New York accepts the times as decent. Not everyone in Ireland imagines each Protestant to be a bigot or all Protestants unsavoury. And the Irish Catholics within the province, given in the same survey a similar list of characteristics, all sorts of choices from the media to the provincial vocabulary of Lundy and Croppy, listed power-holders as number 1. This was what the Protestants expected: after all, they were mostly in power—but as a result of their tradition, not just their numbers or London's aid. What the Protestants did not imagine was that Catholics would see them as bigoted, which they did, selecting this characteristic ahead of "loyalist" and "Orangeman". It was difficult for the Protestants to think of their analysis or their conduct as bigoted: they merely spoke the truth as it was. It is in any case hard to imagine oneself bigoted, especially if possessed of religious truth.

Even if opinion surveys are apt to generate moderation in response, the Protestants expected the worst. They did not in the survey get it. The Catholics knew the Protestants as people as well as stereotype. "Ordinary people" made the Catholic list as well as "determined" and "brainwashed"— the last, perhaps, an excuse for those obviously Irish who persist in claiming to be British. So the actual Catholic stereotype was not as harsh as Protestants imagined.

And so too for their own stereotype of Catholics—more moderate than the bottles tossed, the Kick-the-Pope marching bands, the rationales of the loyalist paramilitary or the slurs of the pubs. So too did the Catholics imagine that Protestants would fill their lists with slurs: Taigs, IRA men, murderers, republicans, Papishes, Sinn Féiners, priest-ridden, breed like rabbits, bigoted and lazy. They too assumed the worst: ourselves as we assumed the others see us. The Protestants did not, perhaps because some of these labels are taken as true, taken for granted but not to be selected even in the secrecy of an opinion poll. In fact the Protestants' stereotype, if hardly complimentary, shapes a reasoned characterisation for Ireland's Catholics, who are after all also ordinary people, if Irish, nationalists, many republicans, and all dominated by their church. A few are bad, terrorists and gunmen, but not every Catholic. Most Protestants know that. The few who rush out to shoot Fenians are shooting symbols—or using the troubled times to shoot anyone. Nearly all Protestants stay at home, abhor violence, assume that their largely unseen Catholic neighbours do the same. Clearly the Protestant is apt to see the Catholic as an amalgam of the vices of the Roman church, if ordinary at bottom, while the Catholic assumes the Protestant sees each of them as gunmen. And this is quite different from their own view of themselves: Irish, long-suffering, ordinary people, insecure, decent and deprived and unfortunate but a fine people, nationalistic and reasonable.

Any survey over the past generation produces much the same result, with one or two shifting trends: the decline in the Protestant's Ulster identity is one of the more pronounced changes. The earlier surveys' results indicate that most responded with remarkable uniformity: there was a consensus on such matters. The stereotypes tended to avoid extremist words. And the surveys indicated real differences not readily apparent in the slurs of the street or the assumptions of the commentators. Each community was not just the same but different. Nearly half the Protestants (49 per cent) felt the law should be obeyed even if a particular law is wrong, but only 28 per cent of the Catholics agreed. Easy to see which tradition would sympathise with civil disobedience, and why. While 74 per cent of the Catholics opposed the death penalty for terrorism, only 19 per cent of the Protestants did. Since in Northern Ireland treason and the gun are more readily associated with the IRA, despite the long toll of loyalist killing, it is hardly surprising that the majority would want to pursue and punish those who would resort to the gun. So whether or not the Catholic response was nationalistic, protecting their right to protest as well as the IRA gunmen, a matter of provincial politics or one shaped by the broader tenets of the Roman church in such matters, the fact is that a Protestant could on the results assume the majority more law-abiding and more eager to punish terrorists than the others. The polls indicated just what the Protestants assumed: the others were more tolerant of national vice, were more subversive, dangerous. That most Catholics did not favour breaking laws or ignoring terrorism, that many

Catholics might answer the poll for reasons other than theological or national, could be ignored and the evidence employed to authenticate a stereotype.

The Catholics might be decent but they were nationalists, and the most nationalist of all were republicans—gunmen and bombers. Paisley knew who broke the law at Dunloy and why, without need for investigation. He knew his own and them. And so too did Catholics in Tyrone or Cork. They need not ask for whom the Lambeg drum rolled: it rolled for them, all of them.

Still, many of the stereotypes actually held in Northern Ireland are not quite what might be imagined. If anything the Protestants have had a clearer image of the others, although neither imagined the others as evil. In sum, the Protestants had a more positive image of themselves: they were not insecure, and why should they be? And Ulster Protestants see the others as ordinary but seduced by nationalist aims. Thus any Catholic will do for most loyalist gunmen: all are nationalists, equally symbolic. Those others, the Catholics, imagined the worst, assumed that Protestants saw all of them as gunmen when they were in fact merely ordinary folks in a society dominated by Protestant power-holders, an image largely held by the Protestants as well but shaped to traditional virtues. The only difference in loyalist militancy was that the gunman did not care if the target were decent or not, active or not, republican or not, as long as the message got through when a dead Catholic was found beside the road. The point of the atrocity was to be as visible as possible—old men shot in a country pub during the World Cup or punters in a bookie's shop, the drunk wandering home or the lad at the wrong corner. The more decent the victim the more monstrous the act, and so the more impact. Surveys do not, however, focus on loyalist gunmen or their motives but on the general stereotypes of the people living in a divided society.

Away from survey and social scientists, beyond the need for decency and moderation and among the more militant of either persuasion, certain attitudes may be stored for lack of local use and more congenial, more traditional assumptions displayed, often in traditional ways: a shower of beer cans or graffiti dribbling down a wall, a slur over tea or a nasty joke. There is joy in disdain, comfort in bigotry and venom, and pleasure in the failures of others. The nasty images are easily displayed, easily packed for later use but arising from basic assumptions not always ticked off on survey forms or pondered by television panels where good taste reigns.

It is these assumptions that are reinforced by the rituals of domination and the rites of arrogance and rebellion. A republican Easter commemoration is about the Easter Rising but also about the ultimate fate of the Protestant tradition. And this tradition of triumph, often without a patina of toleration and decency, is displayed at many Orange rituals. In a group the decency of individuals can easily be forgotten—or become paramount as risk is taken to ensure that a tomorrow is possible, that harm and humiliation do not destroy the civility of a society that must tolerate the different. So there were those at the kerb in Rasharkin to calm the militant and protect the Catholic, just as there were those at Dunloy who deplored the graffiti and the turmoil on the streets. In Dunloy no Protestant really needed to be protected, since the Orange marchers were hardly in any more danger than the locals, and the RUC were on hand in any case. Those locals, Catholics, might at a pub or race meeting be decent, might be so at work or over the purchase of a cow, but for generations those in Ulster have been able to think in general terms, act in general terms, because the stereotypes were not only accurate but also arose from a certain innocence about reality. The Protestants might come out of the survey as less militant, might reveal toleration and community loyalty as well as the stereotype virtues, but the big picture had for a generation only grown to a sharper image: the big picture had no time for particulars, individuals, those who as exception made defence more difficult.

More or less the surveys over time tended to confirm common wisdom: that none of the assumed stereotypes was as harsh as might be imagined. The worst was often mistakenly assumed: they think us brutal or feckless. In fact each incident indicates that there were decent, moderate people at work; just as the explainers tended to explain the harsh word to advantage, so did the moderates make no highly visible statement. The deed that always attracts is spectacular and violent, and "violent" is not apt to be ticked on survey lists. So the Protestants as individuals are more moderate both in attitudes and actions than has been assumed but also in mass have proved as bigoted and aggressive as charged.

The seedy bigotry of the golf club fertilises violence, allows explanation for atrocity, adds to the weight of the necessary rationalisation for murder. Many Protestants who abhor violence, would not touch a gun or condone a bomb, still feel no qualms among their own about turning stereotype into slur, and some unexpectedly indicate a militancy not found in surveys or sermons or even patriot oratory. A generation of violence erected on imagined history of provocation and defence has in good part as foundation the dark side of stereotypes—Protestant stereotypes and Catholic stereotypes. Perception matters, indicates symbols and targets and the fate of the drunk making his way home along the wrong road.

In real life, in the chatter of pubs or the privacy of homes, the stereotypes live quiet lives. Sensible Protestant people, no matter how bigoted or biased, know that Catholics are not all gunmen or murderers or even republicans but merely Irish Catholics, decent enough but lumbered with the imposed vices of their religion. Thus the historical stereotypes of the feckless, foolish Catholics, encouraged by priests to have large families, encouraged to accept ready answers, encouraged by their imagined grievances to see a nationalist solution, is very real. They might not have voted for the gun when they voted for Bobby Sands on the Sinn Féin ticket, not voted for murder, as some claimed, voted merely for one of their own and for an Ireland none expected to achieve—but still they did vote the republican ticket. Each went alone into a booth and voted for a gunman: 30,492 votes. So each Catholic, however moderate and decent, is a subversive. Kevin who lives across the lane or Bernadette at the shop may be decent, have always been decent if never in the door, but are Catholics, and so intolerable. These ones are our Catholics, moderate and no danger, but the others are different; and so most ecumenical campaigns, the camps and mixed schools simply add to "our" Catholics or Protestants, leaving the others as irredeemable as always, perhaps more so. And yet, as always, they must be tolerated. What must be done is to shape contact to decency and evade intimacy.

The decent neighbour met in the lane or at the pub can best be approached by narrowing the range of contacts so as not to give offence, so as not to know, so as not to cause trouble. Politics and religion are to be avoided, and most subjects beyond the weather, the match, the news from afar.

One can feel the magnetic forces driving away the other, eager to flip over to the safe subjects, subjects that do not matter or can be used to vend off intimacy and so insight. The result is an amazing ignorance, almost an innocence, about the others. That the survey stereotypes fit reasoned and observable patterns, indicate the reality of the people as much as prototypes, is all the more remarkable. With the decline in mixed areas and the rural isolation imposed by the IRA's armed struggle, the divide is even greater than the historical self-imposed adjustments in a long-divided society. Despite not knowing many Catholics and never knowing them well, the Protestants' imagined Catholic is not unrealistic: what is unrealistic is the Catholic's assumption about that image.

There is nothing like the easy insult to merge with the many—or so many assume. Some insults are so local as to be untranslatable for the visitor. What is a Taig? Some have in display become a recognised aspect of the Northern Ireland conflict: Orange bigot or Green nationalist as labels now travel, even if Taig and Lundy do not. They continue to play well locally, however, when neighbours are apt to seek to harm without too great provocation.

So it is not that the survey indicates more moderation than imagined but the fact that such moderation comes moderated by the persistence of prejudice. And some of these judgements are shallow, lightly held as convention, and some are not, buttress murder. When Lenny Murphy, the Shankill Butcher, was killed by the IRA, eighty-seven death notices were placed in the *Belfast Telegraph*—some kith and kin, some perhaps showing solidarity against the intrusion of the IRA, tipped off by other loyalists, but some outward and visible evidence of the nature of militant Protestant assumptions and stereotypes. All those loyal to

British Ulster bear some responsibility, if not for Lenny Murphy then for other murders done in Ulster's name and so theirs.

Such judgement in advance—knowing what one knows—arises from self-interest, observation, reality adjusted to expectation, and lessons learned. Few of those lessons arise from real experience or actuality but are assumed valid. Those who live side by side physically are seldom exposed to the full reality of the other, twenty years a neighbour and never in the kitchen, sons interchangeable on the street but nowhere else. The various persuasions may meet in the pub or swim together, play golf together, sit opposite a chessboard but not meet on any other common ground. The further up the class ladder the more politic the meeting, but distance remains; money does not matter, any more than skill at boxing. Only now and again will Protestants even support from afar the Republic's football team; and everyone knows whether a world champion, a boxer or a runner or a Nobel Prize winner, is one of them or one of us.

Many assume that observation can reveal the difference. And much can be observed. Catholic families are larger than Protestant families. Whatever the reasons, there are many Catholics on the dole. Catholics fail to trim their hedges. They listen to every word the parish priest has to say on any subject. They play games on the Lord's day, vote for Sinn Féin, the advocates of IRA murder. They may be as neighbours decent but could be deadly Taigs. The RUC have come to take away the most unexpected terrorists: the girl next door, the lad who would take his taxi anywhere. And anyway, being decent does not mean being just the same: different is different. They are all members of a lesser but still dangerous tradition.

There are Catholics who fit the moderate Protestants' stereotype and those who fit the harsher judgement of the bigoted, who do not want their minds cluttered with individual exceptions: better the monsters known than the nice woman met on the bus. Many of the stereotypes are old yarns and traditional lies. Many of the stereotypes, good and bad, are confirmed by disinterested data as generalisations. It is easy to assume that the greater proportion of Catholics on the dole is due to sloth rather than lack of opportunity. If they lived like Protestants they would have jobs like Protestants—or so said Terence O'Neill, and he a prime moderate: he called the UVF the "evil thing in our midst."

It is frightfully hard to explain to Protestants that if you give Catholics a good job and a good house they will live like Protestants. They will refuse to have eighteen children. But if a Catholic is unemployed and lives in a hovel he will rear eighteen children on social welfare. If you treat Catholics with due consideration and kindness they will live like Protestants, in spite of the authoritarian nature of their church.

In the meantime it was assumed that those imagined Catholics living with eighteen children continued to do so, unredeemed by conversion to British standards. And in any case, anyone can see ample examples along the Falls Road, in the lanes of Tyrone or Down, in the statements issued in Dublin, on the television news, in the papers. All these authenticate what has been learned at home, on the corner, or in the bar. The Pope tells the Irish how to vote on abortion: every newspaper tells us so, and therefore the claims that Rome rule is not relevant mean little. And Catholics do have rituals and confession, and more children; these are facts, not just Protestant facts.

The Protestants' view of Catholics is largely shaped early

on and merely confirmed by the media, by events, by a reality already understood. The Apprentice Boys at Dunloy knew the nature of those Catholics at the crossroads; it was at Rasharkin that the locals knew them by name, not as stereotypes but as neighbours who would be there on the morrow. Paisley, from further off, knew republicans before he saw them, without seeing them. It is not necessary to know a Catholic or to have a Catholic neighbour to fear and so hate Catholicism and so Catholics. It is not even necessary to hate a Catholic: what a loyalist gunman hates is the Catholic religion and so the faithful.

What all those that Antrim summer found by the side of the road were Catholics on land once Protestant, Catholics emboldened by IRA violence, by the events of the Troubles and by the prospects of the peace. They were Catholics, nationalists, irresponsible, feckless, priest-ridden, bitter, superstitious, and provocative—Taigs. They were symbols of change for the worse, dreadful because of their religion and their ambitions. No-one knew their names, aspirations, family, or kitchen chat, only their religion. And that was enough. Once the streets had cleared, the marchers marched off to their homes, they, the Irish, the Catholic Irish, again became decent enough, if still limited by belief and habit and prone to nationalist rhetoric. And those who had marched far off to Ballymena or Belfast disappeared into their own tradition none the wiser, not exposed to people but to the forces of the Pope.

Stereotypes work on various levels, are often no more than necessary to make orderly a confused world and so rest on right reason as well as self-interest. The Catholic the Protestant describes is not unreal, not without substance, can even be found with survey and polls, the median Catholic. The average Catholic, the typical nationalist, republican or gunman are not imagined but conjured up from a real society of real people, of ordinary Irish people. The key assumptions are never tested for whole areas of human life, and the perception of others is not touched at the shop or the pub or across the hedge. To do so might cause trouble, give insult, appear nasty or impolite. Thus contact with Catholics does little to reveal Catholicism; and there is no great sense of loss, for each tradition assumes that the other is known, fits the stereotype en masse.

The Protestant perception of the Catholic Irish, Irish nationalists, all of them as one, makes little distinction on matters of the border. North or south they are one, shaped by their church and by their grievances, confined and shaped by Rome, docile in theological matters and so uncompetitive in the world of production and ideas, the world of getting and spending. In the south they have failed at state-making and in the north failed as a minority. Their church has failed to educate talent, failed to ensure the persistence of social discipline, has not been able to offer the returns of free thought. A Catholic society for Protestants is a failed society, with all the resources of the church focused on keeping the flock within the faith and so denying them free will and hence the chance to succeed. Only in pluralist Protestant societies can Catholics succeed as individuals— and Northern Ireland is a divided society under siege. This means that the Catholics do not participate nor live as Terence O'Neill suggested they might and as they do in Liverpool and Camden Town.

So Catholics in Northern Ireland rarely succeed, fail in a Protestant state for a Protestant people, live on the dole in hovels with their eighteen children, and have failed in a Catholic state for a Catholic people, live on the dole in republican hovels with eighteen children. Their Catholic

Ireland has been a failure. And elsewhere many of the same limits and characteristics could be found: Italy or Spain, where the church played a dominating and so debilitating role in society, in shaping civic culture. Elsewhere the old Catholics may not rule OK. If the Catholics have to compete in Manchester or Chicago or Munich, and succeed, then the hold of the church must by definition have lessened and a more effective Catholic citizen have emerged, no longer dominated by an authoritarian church.

Once the power of Rome is eroded change is possible—but not in Northern Ireland, not normally. It is Catholic society that is dangerous, not the individual. President Kennedy succeeded in America because he was an American, an American Catholic amid a Protestant majority, a majority safe from Rome's threat that could tolerate a Kennedy, encourage a Kennedy. In Chicago and New York the descendants of Ulster Protestants have in all arenas had a splendid record, presidents and bankers, generals and scientists. Not in Ireland, not for Protestants, who knew little of the real Italy or Spain, or, for that matter, Chicago. The problem was that Rome in control imposed values that Protestants found irreconcilable with their own aspirations and the reality of modern life.

In Ireland the Irish-Irish were for almost all Protestants firstly religious creatures; and this is what the Irish Protestant of Ulster opposed: their religion. And from that religion all manner of undesirable social ills flowed; and so Irish Catholics were apt to carry their burden with them. In Ireland, in Ulster these ills were readily apparent if not always discovered in fellow-workers or the chap next door. Seán might not be feckless or violent, not fail to appear on time or keep his garden tidy, but there were indicators: the number of children, the choice of sports, the games on

Sunday, the little signs that made him different—surely he voted for nationalists, surely he accepts Roman doctrine, so certainly he was different and fits the greater pattern, decent or not.

All this was to the good, except that the Irish Protestant still had something of an identity crisis. Knowing one is different does not mean knowing exactly who one is, only who one is not. The ideal, the idea in fact of being British was largely an invention, a term borrowed to cover Ulster conditions. And British Ulster was a late Protestant and unionist concept. Once the idea of Home Rule arose, the opponents, mostly Protestants—and most Protestants were concentrated in the north-east of the country—favoured the union. Ulster gradually emerged as an arena of interest—Protestant Ulster, where, if the worst came to the worst, a redoubt of the dissenters could be shaped outside Rome rule. British Ulster did not emerge out of historical Ulster, out of an evolving shared past, out of incipient nationalism, racial pride or even religious separatism but out of immediate political need: to keep as much from Rome rule as possible. And this was done by those loyal to the Crown, those dedicated to the union; and those who would be ruled by Rome were left with a remnant filled with Catholic nationalists that had to be defended but could not easily be defined. Who indeed were Irish Protestants but Protestants living in six counties who wanted to stay within the United Kingdom? In the beginning they were no more and often less.

By the time the Apprentice Boys marched on Dunloy a British Ulster had emerged, vague in boundary, magnetic in appeal, not established in the hearts of all Protestants but a concept that gave some legitimacy to fear and suspicion, some grace to sectarian suspicion. And no matter, for all those loyal to British Ulster and incidentally the Crown and London and the rest of the United Kingdom knew that they were not Irish-Irish, not Catholic, not like the others, whatever else. And the others, really known not at all, were well known nevertheless: Gaelic, Catholic, children of a lesser god, legions of darkness. And so those loyal to British Ulster must maintain their defence, keep closed the gates, for their perceptions have shaped the reality they imagine, determined who is who.

4

PROTESTANT PERCEPTION: ROMAN CATHOLICS

... The Roman Catholic Church would seem to be the effective government of [the] country.—*The Irish Times*, 12 April 1951

The Catholics have been interfering in Ulster affairs since 1641.—Ian Paisley, 30 August 1969

For everyone in British Ulster, Catholics are important, because of their potential to do harm. As to what they are actually like, most Protestants know them only too well; how could they help but know them, since they are all about?

To a rather remarkable degree, the Protestants of Northern Ireland determine the nature of the Irish Catholic by their assumptions about themselves, their society, and the uncertain nature of British Ulster. They assume that these perceptions, this reality, arises from historical evidence, hard data, the rigours supplied by experience and exposure: they know what they know, because they really, really know it. This is an illusion. They know what they know because they have been told so by their own, acquired their perceptions by osmosis hardly tempered by experience, and certainly not as a result of some sort of historical imperative. History in Northern Ireland is what one makes of it; and for the Northern Ireland Protestants the Catholics are largely what they make them out to be. Recourse to assumption decked out in history, logic, statistics and experience is in large part necessary, since the Protestants know so little of the Catholics. They assume, however, that they know what matters. And this may indeed be so, since their world and their actions are determined by their perceptions, the big generalisations rarely contradicted by exceptions, personal experience, or unpleasant reality. First, know thyself and then all else falls into place; who is who is easily answered and who they are obvious.

People are often more comfortable with generalisations than with the inherent, intractable nature of the individual, somehow all too often an exception on examination; stereotypes are easier and not without rigour and utility. For the innocent, Brendan Behan is the typical Irish rebel. The real Brendan Behan—creative, amusing, emotional, very Irish and a decent sign-painter—was no prototype of a rebel. The real rebel is apt to be narrow, focused, a puritan with a secular faith, dubious of humour, alien to the arts, rigid, a very serious sort, and yet in most ways indistinguishable from those in the queue at the supermarket or on the way to Mass—not a stage character at all. And each Irish rebel is different if the same—fits a pattern and does not: some women, most men, some old, most young, all dedicated and all but one or two Catholics.

It is, however, a pattern people seek and discover. What is wanted is the typical terrorist, the average Catholic. Thus even the individual, the token, the one truly known, met in a peace camp or simply at the pub, will not disrupt the general. This one or that becomes the alien known, becomes our alien, not token of the others but exception to the rule, a rule only made more firm by the evidence of the exception—one of the difficulties that those who would resolve the Irish conflict by fostering cross-traditional contact are apt to neglect.

It is easier to note the Catholic as a type: slothful, manipulated, irresponsible in detail if devout on Sunday. It is easy to imagine them all, easier than having a drink with the lad and finding he likes the same rock music and plays football, a West Ham fan, and thinks the required rebel songs silly and the parish priest a dunce. Then one must make the lad the exception; but if no lad is known then there need be no exceptions. The UVF thus has found that for victim any Catholic will do, since they know them all even when they know none. For the Protestant, not quite sure of his own identity, there is the double problem of knowing thyself as well as knowing the other. At least the Catholics know who they are: Irish Catholic nationalists. At least for the Protestants their own stereotype is easy: the sound, the prudent, the productive, God's own people, redeemed—and British, of course. And the others, the Fenians, are not: not British, not proper Christians, imprudent, wastrels, profligate, not redeemed, beyond redemption. Better to imagine the slothful, drunken Catholic, surrounded by squalling children, living on the dole, slipping off to Mass on the way to the pub, there to sing his rebel songs, to contribute to Sinn Féin, and there to waste God's day. In fact it is far better than meeting the harried, desperate husband, unemployed, willing and desperate, determined that his lot will get out of Unity Flats and into a decent school, and not at all concerned with the authority of Rome or the agenda of Sinn Féin. Better to imagine the Irish rebel, cold, merciless, cruel, a nationalist monster, than to meet the frightened boy at the end of the lane given a gun but little guidance, given hope of glory but no clear mission, while at home the parents, desperate, frightened, wait for the inevitable, hope for a cell, not another funeral.

No, for the Protestants, and for that matter for the British army and the RUC, the responsible, the British in Britain, the redeemed and loyal, the Irish as monsters and mothers of monsters, terrorists all, makes sense, seems real. The IRA has done monstrous things, and the nationalists, all Catholics, seek the same ends and so need not quibble about means. Generally they are disloyal and dissolute; and the evidence is all about.

General types are what arise from Protestant perceptions—and, indeed, from the evidence, for there is data to reinforce assumption and anecdote. The individual may not be an exception, may have compensating virtues, but in general the Protestant imagines Catholics, in many cases must do so, for he or she knows none. And Catholics in general do fit patterns, social patterns, economic models, categories and class, that differ from those of their Protestant neighbours. They are different even if they look the same and speak with the same accent about the same weather, even if each is special. So it is the category that counts, and perception shapes both, despite and because of the data.

There can be no doubt that the Catholic is devout, attends church with a regularity found nowhere else in Europe, surpassing even Ulster Protestant figures on church-going, which are the highest in the Protestant world. The Catholic goes to Mass, is seen going, is noted if absent. The IRA gunman can always find a priest. The radical is apt to read Marx but marry in the parish church—and there are few in Ireland who read Marx if more now who marry in the registry office. In fact while there is a decline in church-going, in those who appear for communion and confession each week, the vast majority, urban or rural, North or South, rich or poor, can regularly be found in church.

Protestants are apt to have very little idea of what transpires in that Roman church—the nature of the sacraments, the details of ritual, the language of the Mass, or the content of the sermon. It is assumed that Catholics go to a Roman church that guarantees absolution and salvation, requires obedience and rituals, are surrounded by icons and images and the odour of incense. There in church they have their faith validated by attendance and their salvation assured, their sins forgiven, their ties to Rome renewed. There the Catholic rituals take precedence over revelation or the word of God. In fact strange, exotic rituals are often suspected—those within the church and those abroad, those hidden and those discussed, all mysterious. Certainly for most Protestants all is a mystery: the Rosary, the pilgrimages, Lourdes, the wafer and the confessional—exotic means of maintaining obedience.

Thus Catholic piety is seen as intensifying the attitudes and assumptions of Catholics. Such worship is not a virtue, as it is within the Protestant faith, but a reaffirmation of institutionalised error, error yet unreformed, reaffirmation of doctrine counter to reason. The individual Catholic may be decent, but the religion is not and the institution not, and Rome as contemporary religious and secular power malign. Of course many Protestants are far more discriminating, see Rome as different and undesirable but not institutionalised sin, the Pope no real player and the Vatican no real threat. Some, on the other hand, see with blinding intensity Rome as the force of darkness and the Pope as the Anti-Christ.

In Northern Ireland the church-going Catholic goes to a

church not simply different from all others, as would be the case in New York or London or perhaps even Edinburgh, but into an alien institution. The Catholic Church, while a church, while urging virtues and decent conduct, is basically opposed to the revealed truth, opposed to free will and reason, opposed to democracy, and imposes an ethos that denies freedom and so productivity. The individual is seen absorbed into the Counter-Reformation, shaped by Roman doctrine and so less able to participate in the civility of society of the province. Individuals somehow may cope with such indoctrination but the mass does not, the Mass imposes on the mass, the Pope on the people, Rome on Ireland. This is what engenders fear and suspicion.

This assumption may be mild in the moderate and elegant but it is rawly expressed by the crude Christians and the dedicated bigots. Rome rules, and this is not OK. Not only is it not OK, it is also evident to Protestants that Roman rules impose lesser social and personal standards than Protestant pieties—again these are attitudes and assumptions, not easily revealed in survey research but readily noted in front rooms, over tea, in the pub or on a train among one's own.

The Roman church is assumed to shape behaviour by threat or by habit in a way quite unlike other churches. Roman Catholics are not redeemed, not saved by Christ but rather signed up at birth to a regime of rituals that guarantee salvation in return for obedience. Their habits are overseen in detail by their priests, who impose discipline but do not evoke the Holy Spirit. That Protestant divines insist on the most scrupulous behaviour, impose standards on all manner of things, from the use of the swings on Sunday to the seating in chapel, is no matter. What counts is that the parish priest is assumed infallible, that Rome dictates conduct so that no questions need be asked, no singular effort made to be saved, nothing at all but obedience is required, dissent therefore unimaginable. And if the Protestant church has a fundamental aspect in Ulster it has seen rebellious disputation, producing a wide spectrum of choice, a selection of doctrine and seemingly observance. The visitor may find most Protestant churches alike, simple, plain, few with elegance and none with decoration. Not so the congregations, who find each different—more Presbyterian variants than there are Presbyterians in Munster. Not so with the Roman church: the one in Dingle is one with that in Derry, all the rituals alike and imposed from afar, all housing belief that is not to be tested. For the Catholic it is obedience for ever, despite the futile contemporary efforts at reform: democracy in administration, women as clerics, divorce as a right. Catholic alliances for reform or adjustment or keeping past habits have short half-lives, make no changes in what Rome wants, what Rome imposes. None of these dissenters has produced schisms or change: the Roman faith is still inviolate, resolute, intractable, still Roman, authoritarian.

Thus if one in doctrine and that doctrine imposed on all facets of life—except the odd drink with a Protestant friend or the kind word across the hedge—the church is everywhere to be found, ordering, authorising, imposing the faith on every act. No exceptions are permitted by Rome unless imposed by a greater power. So with the death of the first President of Ireland the assembled Catholic government of Eamon de Valera sat in their limousines outside the church, prohibited from attending their colleague's Protestant funeral service—no exceptions, no divorce, no compromise, no state education or secular hospital, no need for right reason or free choice. Rome claiming all is thus seen as responsible for all: the size of families, the lack of social discipline, the soft edges of a society where even major sins are easily forgiven at confession. This is the church where the gunmen marry, where they come on Sunday and are not turned away, where they are buried under an IRA volley with the parish priest, reluctant or no, at the side of the grave. Gunman, banker, farmer, thief, once within the church always within the church, guaranteed entry into Heaven as long as form is followed. Rome handles all that matters.

The Protestant does not imagine this perception of Rome to be a mirror image: that evangelical pastors and Church of Ireland prelates are often engaged in micro-managing society, imposing doctrine on detail, locking the swings and denying the validity of ecumenical conferences. Not so all Protestants; but all Protestants are apt to see Rome, not unfairly, as monolithic and intransigent, a cabal of elderly cardinals dominated by a Polish pope, a Roman pope. So an omnipotent, omnipresent religion must by definition be responsible for imposing a Catholic reality on a Catholic people—a reality best seen at a distance, away from the individual exception. Even the individual, however, is apt to fit the perceived pattern: attends Mass with a large family, misses appointments, lacks seriousness of purpose, plays games on Sunday, wears a cross, and marches not to a Lambeg drum but to an alien anthem. One sees what one expects and often expects what one will indeed see.

The patterns found are not patterns imagined. Ulster Protestants may be a minority taste but one with many takers, and not all in Ulster. Assuming that the social values of the church are imposed is obvious—and so too other matters of faith and morals that come as infallible. The Roman church is conservative, long suspicious of the secular, free will, individual rights, the play of ideas or the creation of alternative artistic visions, the thinking citizen or a state education; for many, a Catholic university is an oxymoron. The church has opposed not only abortion and divorce—as have most Ulster Protestants—but at one time or another much of modern analytical thought, the scientific method, the national state—all those endeavours of the spirit or the mind not controlled by Rome. The more limited in British Ulster prefer the conspiracy, assume cabals and strange rituals and plots. The Protestant knows that the Orange Order is a social society, a marching band and a band of brothers, not a conspiracy, that their churches are open to all, that there are no Protestant conspiracies or Orange plots, as the Catholic may imagine; but they know as well that Catholics are engaged in a great conspiracy, wittingly or no. From the Jesuits to Opus Dei there have been such societies, visible and invisible, all dedicated to increasing the power of the Roman church. All are part of the great conspiracy. Thus Catholicism, Irish nationalism, the IRA and the Irish language, the Republic in Dublin, the Ancient Order of Hibernians and the GAA are merely facets of one world. In contrast, one could hardly call Protestant Ulster one doctrinal world: the Free Presbyterians are no allies of orthodox Presbyterians nor the Pentecostals allied to the Church of Ireland. Doctrinal diversity is the very nature of the Protestant community. That all look much the same in their conclusions, predilections, values and voting habits does not matter. The Protestants know that they are not one; each exercises a free will denied to the Catholic, and all shape different institutions.

Both traditions actually share much or at least appear to do so in the alien eye. Both want to shape society to the good, want traditional values, family values, their values imposed not simply in the process of governance but in everyday life: censorship is not a Catholic invention, nor alcohol damned only in Protestant sermons. It is a fact and hardly denied that British Ulster is church-bound, publicly pious and, when the opportunity existed, has often politically imposed religious doctrine: no games on Sunday, special pub rules, pleasure regulated if duty not required. Few advocate divorce and none abortion. In fact pleasure is suspect and damnation of one sort or another assumed. Life is real and earnest and the highest standards preached if not always displayed. Both traditions are socially and economically conservative. Both suspect an excess of the secular, the trends of the times, the lure of easy money or sensual pleasure—even as both sample the available. Both give great weight to ecclesiastical concerns, live visibly godly lives, go to church and take heed of the sermon.

Northern Ireland is a godly province, if often riven with schism and by the issues of the Reformation. Paisley is hardly alone in seeing Rome through sixteenth-century spectacles, a vast, multicultural conspiracy intent on reasserting authoritarian doctrine on the West. And there is always evidence. In 1995—not 1595—Pope John Paul asked his Irish flock to vote against divorce as a civil right, asked his own Polish flock to support a faithful candidate, denied those who would reform the church, would allow women as priests or allow priests women, opposed the liberal ideals and programmes of Latin America, gave every evidence that the Roman hierarchy was an active and self-interested player on the international scene. In fact the Pope had spent years crisscrossing the world, organising the far places, had even come to Ireland, if not to Ulster, everywhere expanding Roman influence and Roman control. Pious, talented, and shrewd, he was not one for the easy word, for compromise or concession to the Protestant ethic. His doctrine and his career simply enhanced Ulster Protestant assumptions and fears: the Roman church as conspiracy and crusade, the doctrine monolithic and authoritarian, the communicants obedient. Catholicism is a danger to freedom and their own faith.

In west Belfast or south Armagh the Roman church was represented by the parish priest, by teaching brothers, by religious orders, by the constant intrusion of the faith on the people's daily rounds. The Protestants saw little of this in their world—even if others did—but imagined a seamless web of conviction and commitment by the other tradition. Thus everything from the Belfast Brigade of the IRA to the curriculum in the classroom was permeated by Catholicism. Their schools, hospitals, pubs, their games and factions, their homes were separate and unknown—all part of another world, a covert world. The wise, sophisticated and elegant did not see this as conspiracy or as conscious, but most assumed that there was indeed a Catholic ethos, one different from and less desirable than the Protestant ethos. The two communities were alike—everyone admitted that: both were puritanical, pious, parochial in vision, and seized on matters that did not concern greater communities. Both suspected the secular, had values not found in the market, although Protestants assumed that their piety might easily be judged by the bottom line; productivity arose from diligence required by the faith. They assumed the Catholics felt that faith followed and ritual obeyed were sufficient, rather than life daily judged by a jealous God, a zealous God. The Protestant way was superior because Protestants could count not only their spiritual blessing but also the tangible returns. These were real matters, whether the benefits of smaller families or the salaries paid for hard work, not imagined, not assumed, not simply perceptions but there to touch. The Protestant ethic paid. One need but look about Northern Ireland and contrast Catholic society with Protestant. Catholics had larger families, less schooling, limited careers. Catholics were more apt to be unemployed, to emigrate, to remain on the dole. Catholics were more apt to have poorer housing, more persistent health problems, more limited professional prospects, fewer certificates, and to hold more menial jobs. Catholics were seldom found among the economically successful, on the university staff, in positions of power and authority. The figures, decade after decade, remained constant: the Catholics were, by any criteria, not simply a minority but a failed entity.

The Protestant conclusion was not that the existing power structure, maintained in all sorts of ways, ensured such results but rather that the other tradition was a prime cause. Large families demanded by the Roman church's diktat meant that less could be done for more. Parochial schools meant that time spent on doctrinal matters was taken from science or literature, and so Catholic pupils were not as well prepared or were prepared by teachers who often lacked the qualifications demanded in state schools. The indulgences of the Roman church meant a failure to conform to the standards of modern society: punctuality, discipline, dedication, accuracy in detail and a work ethic that ensured productivity. The attitudes fostered by that church meant an irresolute, careless people demonstrably inferior if not in chat and decency then in character and capacity.

Catholics did not deserve esteem, much less offer parity. They did not trim their hedges, paint their windows, appear on time, cultivate the corner of the field. They could be seen as poor and poorly served, beyond remedy or reform.

Naturally British Ulster did not and should not indulge them, avowed constitutional enemies—offer jobs and education and houses to those who would destroy the system. Why give the killer a razor? Why bother to strengthen subversion? The Catholics would taint all they touched in any case, fail to show up for work, ruin the houses, have eighteen children and overload the schools. They were denied entry because they did not believe in British Ulster and so support Northern Ireland, the connection, the union. Instead, trapped by their faith, they longed for unity. And unity would submerge the Protestant virtues, destroy British Ulster, to the advantage of no-one, not even the local Catholics.

This analytical vision, abetted by visible evidence and the statistical data, assumed that the Catholics were lesser because they were Catholic and had always been so; that a high birth rate ensured indigence, that parochial schools stinted conventional subject matter, that good jobs were available for the talented. British Ulster might in other circumstances have offered all a level playing-field. In Northern Ireland those not Catholic were forced to defend their tradition, even by means not especially palatable in Britain. That was simply the nature of history. And history, for the Protestants, had shown the nature of Catholicism, and so of each Catholic.

Everywhere the Catholics were lesser, could be seen as lesser, had always been lesser. It was then no step at all to assume that not only was the culture lesser but also that all those within such a culture were inherently lesser. The content of one's character was shaped by faith, and culture could be judged by rigorous, quantified criteria. Inferiority flowed not simply from the faith but also from a flawed Irish nationalist ethos, imposed and shaped by a great transnational Roman church. The Irish were Catholics of a peculiarly pernicious variety. Such concepts, articulated or not, meant that inherently Protestants were different in kind, not simply opportunity. And so they should be superior in most aspects of society that mattered; and so they were, except in a few facets of Irish life that hardly mattered: jigs, jokes, random athletic skill, and the odd poem—the triumphs of the minor and the marginal, the sporadic appearance of isolated generosity, not the basis for civility, governance, a stable society or steady productivity. In matters that mattered the Catholics did not matter—only appeared when violence, ruin and chaos offered careers to the violent Celt. The gunman's trade was appealing to those lesser people who could not create, only destroy.

Much more telling was that most Northern Catholics had access to the same data, the same anecdotes, the same reality, and came to much the same conclusions. They were potentially grand, but history and malign fate had betrayed such prospects, rather than religion or their national heritage. Once as Celts, as Irish, they had been splendid, but fate had snatched away power, leaving them on the margins of events, perpetually impoverished, reduced to the corners of their own land. There had been a golden age, long gone, and since then in Northern Ireland oppression, only occasionally eased but never gone. Neither Irish nationalism, which shaped a Free State in the south, nor British decency had by 1968 transformed the reality of British Ulster. Catholics were inferior in all ways that mattered, because they were Catholic.

And some of the minority in Ulster accepted that such inferiority arose from Catholicism and from their Irish heritage. It was not that Catholics were discriminated against—this was obvious—but that Catholics were deserving of discrimination. The most effective form of oppression is to persuade the victim of the justice of the power structure. Many Catholics accepted inequality as inevitable and their due. Many more did not, dreamed of olden days, aspired to personal improvement, kept the faith in the aspirations of the republic, made do with what was available. They were nationalists dreaming of a day long gone and tolerant of subversion as a national virtue. And a few of these felt that their hope lay in using a gun, sooner or later, if not now then later. These were the republicans, fervent, recalcitrant, persistent, the paladins of a Pope they claimed not to respect, outriders of a Dublin government that denied them, the terrorists and nightriders known to every Protestant in British Ulster: driven to violence because even they must recognise the virtues of Britain, the power of the Protestant ethic, the failures of institutionalised Irish nationalism.

Yet despite this analysis, despite all the evidence, despite a century of example, all the Protestants knew was that in the heel of the hunt their salvation rested in London. If London betrayed them, then the power and glory of the Protestant establishment would serve for nothing in the face of Catholic numbers: no defence would do; and so the long-predicted doomsday would not occur. British Ulster would end not with a bang but a White Paper. In the meantime a rigorous defence was the best means of maintaining the union—a union that offered little to the suspect and seditious. Judgement day, however, seemed distant to those scruffy lads in cheap clothes and thin shoes standing on Derry street corners without work, without prospects. No matter if Protestant defender or Catholic rebel, the lad on the corner, the girl with a dead-end job, their parents without work or hope knew who was who, who mattered and what mattered.

Northern Ireland was not only a society shaped by class, as was that of England, each in place, each acknowledging their role, their status, swiftly checked by accent and demeanour, no matter the quality of the jacket or the state of one's soul. There were gentry and workers, shopkeepers and lace-curtain Irish, the upper middle class and the lower middle class, bankers and clerks, and each assigned by accent and assumption and habit. This in various permutations had been the way for generations, and would be so, despite all sorts of vast social change, in the future. Class mattered, but in Northern Ireland there was caste as well: two traditions, two populations that in theory and often in practice never mingled but when necessary shared a province. The majority had power and possessions and presumptions. And the great salient determining difference was religion.

Those in the minority recognised all this, recognised that in most ways they were inferior and still in 1968 accepted that such inferiority might well be justified, by their culture or their church, by their character or their history. They felt inferior because by objective standards they were inferior. They were not a risen people in 1968 or 1969 but an aroused one. Before that, after that, they were a people who each day rose and hoped merely to survive, today like yesterday. In 1969 vengeance and triumph were both a dream, if somehow the country were united, but until then were at rest on the top of the shelf. Once order collapsed in 1969, in considerable part because of Protestant inflexibility, uncertainty disguised as arrogance, at least the minority could watch vengefully as the IRA sought power with the gun, and found power, if not control, a role as well as a mission. One did not have to be superior to shoot a constable—although it helped—and so the lesser breed could bleed the stronger. And increasingly the stronger looked both vulnerable and intrinsically no better than the minority—not inherently superior at all.

The Protestants, no matter how poor, how grim their house, tattered their clothes, narrow their spirit or vicious their vices, no matter how bad their teeth or sour their spirit, felt superior, and so were, until the Troubles. They were so in their own eyes, and this was ample. They did not care that the Irish in the Republic might find them arrogant without cause, despotic by nature and by permission of the perfidious English—who in turn might find those very Protestants pretentious, difficult, and in the end Irish. The Protestants could look about Northern Ireland and see that Catholicism was flawed, its adherents failed, and for that matter look to the south and see a republic that was little different: a Catholic state—the Falls Road writ grand—an equal failure filled with people who were poorly clothed, poorly fed, poorly housed, exchanging cows and pints, burdened by large families and short working days, unpunctual, drifting, without discipline and, most telling, unable to create a viable economy that would keep the Irish in Ireland. The Protestants seldom bothered to look south: there was no need to summon further examples of Catholic incapacity with so many and such telling examples to hand. These examples, like the stereotypes of both traditions, gained in authenticity by simple repetition. There was never a reality check on failures or accomplishments, on the dynamics of provincial society. Everyone always knew what they knew without need to differentiate the map from the terrain. The Protestants felt superior and so were. The Catholics were inferior in most ways and in most ways accepted their lot and so too the judgement of the majority—or did so until the present Troubles shifted perceptions.

In 1968 the great change began, ushered in largely by a small group of young people who, arriving at university by virtue of a new Education Act, found themselves neither inferior nor superior but victims of injustice. They believed therefore that by taking thought, by acting, by protesting, the reality of the moment could be changed. Although Catholics, they did not feel especially Catholic and sought example not within Catholic radicalism but in the American civil rights movement, in the trends and tenor of the times; television, films, magazines, the avowed positions of politicians in London and Dublin had a relevance. They chose all but unwittingly in their adopted means a variation of the great Ulster rituals of domination and resistance: the march. And they chose a strategy that, given the psyche of the Protestant establishment, would all but guarantee success.

Civil disobedience in Ulster meant that violence would be ensured: a strategy of non-violence nearly always means that others will be violent and so to the advantage of the provocateur. One plans on deploying the violence of the other, and so the strategy must take place within an arena that does not permit absolute coercion; to march against Hitler in Nazi Germany, to speak against Stalin in the Soviet Union, to defy the dictatorial life-presidents may generate martyrs for some cause, but the cause is often crushed as well. One can be provocative only where provocation may be tolerated. In Northern Ireland in 1968–69, Stormont and the system could for various reasons, good and bad, recognised and not, respond only so far with state violence. The playing-field was far from level but the game could begin.

The Protestants' superiority rested on uneasy foundations; all the evidence of history and the visible world assured them that from domination domination would flow. Tomorrow would be like yesterday, as long as any challenge to present reality was intimidated or denied. The system was pure, absolute, and seamless, and so any loose thread might unravel the whole. The social net was elegant and splendid, glistened like a great spider's web, but was fragile—effective for consuming the occasional gadfly, the IRA gunman or the communist radical, but still a structure with only so many contact points. Any assault on the inherent stability of the system was therefore dangerous: British Ulster, unlike England or France or Australia, was fragile, in large part because of geography. British Ulster was safe in the hands of the majority, but they in turn lived on an alien island and were often treated as such by their own in Britain, called "Paddy" off the boat train, had their Ulster banknotes refused, found their accent mocked—became Irish and most of all perceived as different.

And so the reverse side of arrogance was fear. Their fear was of being denied, their loyalty without value and their British Ulster seen as burden, not ornament. British Ulster was different in that it was always under siege, always at risk, always in need of local defence as well as London support. And habit and history indicated that the most effective response to provocation was swift and compelling oppression—oppression that would reinforce the inherent superiority of the system, a superiority that the rituals of the majority, the tangible power of the devolved government and the mesh of economic and social control ensured. Such coercion need not be lethal—republicans could be interned, marchers end in cells with banged heads, and agitators intimidated—but need be firm. The Northern Ireland establishment in 1968–69 did not see that such a traditional response could no longer be kept from general view, isolated in the province, where everyone knew the rules. Coercion could no longer be invisible coercion, even if on a small scale and lacking in intensity. Television made all sizes equal and all coercion brutal, intense, relevant. There were real dangers in Northern Ireland, real tensions and banked fires that no-one in London knew, for they did not know the Irish, the republicans or British Ulster, and, until television, had not needed to know.

Television had changed the arena: the game would be broadcast and the standards of the responsible West would prevail. Repression must be politically correct, decently done and in good cause. Yet the system in British Ulster was in matters of coercion raw and arrogant, untutored in politics, behind the times and soon obsolete—fifty years lost with as many feet of television film taken of the RUC clubbing Gerry Fitt, member of Parliament. Northern Ireland lacked the talent and the consensus to be accommodating and the skills to be coercive in a media-friendly environment. Nothing was more guaranteed to mobilise minority opinion in Northern Ireland, reawaken nationalist responsibilities in the Republic or gain the sympathy of the foreign and the interest of London than recourse to "non-violent" provocation that ensured excessive retaliation. The bear could be baited by the weak without fear of being eaten whole, scratches and maulings guaranteed and welcomed. And so it proved, once the bear was baited, bloody heads on the television news, a police riot, Northern Ireland an issue and a round of drinks for all the agitators: non-violence worked. Provocation had engendered the most violent result and ultimately, if unwittingly, the armed struggle of the IRA and so the Troubles.

There was little the Northern Ireland system could have done differently: like the scorpion, its nature could not change, even if advantage could be perceived. Provocation by a ragged band of trendy Catholic students with hand-lettered signs and borrowed ideas set off alarm signals and a disproportionate response. Civil disobedience worked. In the next two years the minority was awakened to the reality that they were not inherently inferior but victims of conscious injustice. They were not in the classical sense a risen people, certainly not mobilised or, as the civil rights advocates assumed, empowered, but rather a people angry, endangered and tolerant of a defence in their name, a campaign in their name, an armed struggle that ensured that they would remain threatened and so need a defence. This was not apparent to many in 1969, just as a few had never accepted the inherent inferiority of the Northern Catholic. This imperial ploy to make the colonised guilty of their own slavery had always been obvious to some. What had not been so obvious to any was that the minority had the assets and capacities to do more than suffer, accept history's penalties, accept even the validity of Protestant assumptions. The advocates of non-violence had found a use for indignation and dedication. They sought and found a way to lever movement into history, even if they did not foresee that they would begin the great avalanche into the Troubles. By 1969 they had changed the nature of the Catholics of Northern Ireland and so the perceptions of all, especially the Protestants; but they had not changed the essentials, not changed events as imagined: all the pieces were still largely the same, if not as static.

The Catholic people were not mobilised, not really a risen people, even if they formed at times large crowds, but rather were given and seized the opportunity to adjust their perception and so Northern Ireland reality. By 1970 the Catholic population did not feel inferior but denied. They would thus risk provocation by others, risk the little that had been kept for the prospect of gain, gain not from the menu of reforms—votes or jobs or houses—but gain in pride and so prospects: equality of opportunity. This was an especially delightful prospect because in this case equality ensured vengeance, since it would be a triumph over Protestant perceptions and assumptions. Asking for what was fair would humiliate the others without penalty. The majority was thus almost from the first defensive and outraged: the meek were inheriting the earth, their earth, their bit of Ireland, their Ulster, not so much by force—that and the IRA would come later—but simply by changing their mind about reality, a reality so long imposed by Protestant perception as assumed real in Bangor and Tiger Bay and Ballymena.

The next twenty-five years would see a British effort supported by decent opinion, the Dublin government, Irish nationalists and the Northern Catholics to transform the tangible evidence of Catholic inferiority. Everyone wanted to be part of the solution, not the problem. Jobs were to be given and houses, votes and the keys to Derry, places in universities, roads in the hills; the tangibles, the hard facts of domination were to be changed. And the ethos of the day left no room for Protestant argument. These were reforms that had to be tolerated or supported. And many Protestants were not opposed, since they had no choice and had not changed their minds: no manner of concession would change the debilitating results of Catholicism on the communicant. Many continued to believe that the Catholics were going to be inherently inferior, no matter what.

The Catholics no longer so believed. They would no longer stand idly by and watch the Orange march in sullen silence. Even the marchers knew that the hostility on the kerbside at Dunloy or Rasharkin was a provocation that arose from shifting perceptions—and not merely Catholic perceptions. The Protestants over a generation had not so much accepted Catholic equality achieved through reform, external interference and the return of the IRA gun but rather accepted that their own worth had somehow been diminished. They, if superior, should have felt superior, coped with provocation and violence effectively, acted instead of being ordered about by others, been in control instead of on the defensive. There was great uncertainty and considerable frustration; the verities of generations had changed. No-one knew exactly how. No-one knew exactly who to blame.

As the Troubles continued, the better people seemed to be badly done by: scorned as spongers, denied access to a hearing in London, left poorly defended. The old system decayed and collapsed into faction and schism: Stormont gone, the gentry discredited, the Unionist Party in bits, old lands lost, new laws imposed, new overlords sent from London, the Catholics given this or that, houses and jobs and concessions, and the British army in the streets but not out shooting gunmen. The golden days were gone. No-one knew what was what, even who was who any more. No-one knew an easy remedy. No-one was at all sure that tomorrow would be like yesterday. And no-one could afford to admit that anything had changed, in case everything changed.

"Not an inch," when first offered, had meant that all six counties would stay as the base for British Ulster, and even this was no longer so certain. One might fly banners emblazoned *No surrender*, but others had the power to surrender whenever they chose, for whatever reasons they chose. Thus everything had changed—and in many ways nothing had changed. After twenty-five years bigots could still burn churches, Catholic bigots and Protestant bigots. Ideas about the other were different but still arose from assumed stereotypes and the consensus of the tribe. Perceptions had changed, but not always a lot and not always in ways useful to any peace process.

Twenty-five years after the civil rights marches began to twist along northern roads into an idealised future that vanished into the bombs and murders of the Troubles, the Protestant perception of reality had shifted: some things old, some things new, and a shift down the spectrum of certainty. There was less change that might be imagined, because the best strategy was often to do nothing, to seek to repeat yesterday, to go over and over the litany of faith, the elements of the belief, so as to drown out risk and change. This constant and comforting reinforcement of old assumptions when all about could be seen to shift and shimmer meant that in many ways the Protestants had double vision, saw as they had in the past and as they wanted to in the future but driven to integrate too many new realities into the old pattern. The Catholics were not what they had been nor the Irish nor British Ulster, and yet much was just the same. The answers to "Who is who?" were not as easily given, so most resorted to repeating those answers found in the back of the book, the authorised version, yesterday's solutions. No-one exactly believed the old answers or could easily answer who was indeed who.

What is significant about the shift in Protestant perceptions over a generation is that there was a shift; for if there is ever to be an accommodation, much less a resolution, of the Irish zero-sum game then the perceptions of all must change. Reality can be shaped to assumption and so to advantage: the Catholics were made to feel inferior because in tangible ways they were inferior. The cause of that inferiority was defined by the majority to advantage and gradually accepted by the Northern Ireland minority, to their cost. Advantage is in the eye of the beholder: invidious distinction, physical beauty, pride of place arise from an imaginative act. Black can indeed be beautiful, if so believed. Catholicism can indeed be a badge of incapacity, if so believed.

A generation of Troubles has not induced a sea change in many Protestant assumptions, despite the erosion of evidence to that effect. The Protestant may now cling more closely to the British identity and associate nationalism more closely with IRA violence, but many, if not all, of the basic perceptions remain. The fundamentalist Protestant world view still shapes British Ulster—still a most Protestant province. The Catholics, the nationalists, still fit the old basic stereotypes. There is a Catholic ethos. This ethos is not as effective in generating a civil, productive Western society as is the Protestant ethos, no matter that Northern Ireland has not been an economic success either—that is not wilfully ignored, simply not relevant. Those within British Ulster are making a case against the reality of the Republic, against Irish nationalism, not a case for the alternative found in Northern Ireland.

What analysts for British Ulster analyse is Catholic impact. The more Catholics, the more intense the ethos, the less effective the society in Western terms: Rome is not the core of the West but a drain on Western energies, a sump-pit for creativity, free will, and the benefits of the enlightenment. All this is just the same—and yet, and yet, the IRA, the epitome of Catholic ambition in Protestant mythology, has worked, and has no effective Protestant competition. Catholics at least know how to kill, how to manipulate British and world political opinion, maximise their assets; and, given the playing-field of Ireland and Britain, the Protestants have had no satisfactory answer. Thus the Protestants, once fault is found with others, with the British government, with Dublin and Washington and the media and the times, once blame is allotted elsewhere and even within the unionist response, then adjustment must still be made on the nature of the Irish, the Irish individual, the Irish stereotype—them. The Irish beside the road in Dunloy are perceived as different from those who stayed inside a generation ago, the windows shut to the Orange tunes, minds closed to Orange triumph. Now the Irish not only stand by the side of the road, defiant, but stand rebellious. What is imagined is the New Model Irish.

This stereotype is no more to be found in real life than in the results of social science surveys: that the Catholic Irish individual is decent if a nationalist, limited by the church but, all told, not unlike everyone else. And most believe that being nationalist implies a toleration if not support for Sinn Féin and the IRA. The Protestant believes this symbiotic relationship far more intimate than the average Catholic believes that the loyalist paramilitaries are unionist outriders: they are as apt to be seen as British pawns, not Protestant equivalents of the IRA. It is an analysis that the loyalists find both demeaning—do they not carry out operations, have titles, defend their own?—and irrelevant, in that the UVF and the UDA are defending British Ulster, in tandem with the legal security forces, not pawns but players, with sure missions and roles. They defend their own against the nationalist attacks, and those attacks are rationalised as valid by the minority in the province and the establishment in Dublin. And the Catholics are both dangerous and effective in their deployment of violence and ineffectual and improvident in their exploitation of peace. And most still believe that the limits imposed by the Catholic Church prevent the minority from fully exercising their capacities—terror aside. Such judgements, private and general, are apt to be founded in allusions, asides at work, in the midst of kitchen conversations, and in raw terms in the speeches of the fundamentalist politicians and the screeds of Orange divines.

There has been a remarkable consistency in the perceptions of the Protestants. The great change has been in adjusting to the shifting evidence to arrive at much the same conclusions. In 1967 few Protestants, not the Unionists nor the Orange Order, not the man in the street nor the power-broker, gave much thought to the Republic. There was no need to consider the twenty-six counties. No-one went there. No-one was very interested in what went on there: the Protestant community was eroding and had always been less provocative and less Protestant than those in Ulster. The ascendancy had been elegant, the middle class comfortable, clerks, retired colonels, none so raw as to march to the drums except those close to the border, and the poor seemingly more apt to seek comfort in the unions than in unionism. They, the lost Protestants, were lost to memory and to any future agenda. Those in Ireland were far away, lost and gone for ever.

Once the IRA armed struggle became self-perpetuating and horrendously visible in 1971, the Republic as model for a future Ireland had to be considered—not as prospect but as horrid example. Thus the Irish of Ulster remained for a time as they had always been and the Protestants focused on the Irish of the Republic as indicators of what a future united Ireland would offer. The basic, generic Irish-Irish model remained, the great shift being the acceptance that in matters of subversion Catholicism, if it did not encourage efficiency, was no obstacle: the IRA gunmen, often incompetent, with inadequate trade craft or common sense, without decency or proper planning, still managed, still persisted. The power of the Crown was somehow frustrated by an Ardoyne corner-boy or a South Armagh ploughman. Still, the gunmen and bombers as well as the solicitors and teachers were all the same, one with the incompetent and corrupt in Dublin.

The Irish Catholics in the twenty-six counties supplied the same kind of evidence that once the social and economic statistics of Northern Ireland had done: tangible failure. Each new political decade shows promises made and not kept: the Republic was going to create a viable economy, was going to be self-sufficient without ground rents or dependence on Britain, the new Lemass-Whitaker initiative was going to establish export industries, and then came the men in mohair suits followed by the slick new breed with portable phones to ring back from Brussels. All failed to end unemployment, maintain any transitory gains, create a viable economy. All that was done was give ample evidence that a Catholic Ireland for a Catholic people was a certain loser; matters might improve, but not much; novel initiatives lacked the needed resolve and discipline: a mobile phone does not make a Catholic into an entrepreneur. The chartered accountant with a TCD degree and time spent at Harvard is only one more Catholic with a gadget and a slogan, one more inherently ineffectual, inefficient Paddy, even if togged in a Louis Copeland suit. For those who doubted, the numbers of the unemployed still, despite all, despite the initiatives and the state bodies and the computers, were prodigious—statistical evidence of Catholic incapacity.

The Protestants could dissect the Republic with clean

hands; the Irish had only themselves to blame, could measure themselves on the standards not only of the West but also their own that the founders and followers had so often proclaimed. Who must emigrate, not even offered frugal comfort? Where were the scholars and the artists but in exile? Why was there a fear of violent crime and the revelations of priestly abuse? Where were the Protestants of yesteryear? And the Irish nation, all Catholics, was everywhere found lacking: the Republic in Dublin as failed entity. And with the onset of the peace process even the Fenian republic to be found in every Irish heart, including that of Gerry Adams and Martin McGuinness and the other not-so-old gunmen, had failed at last, had at last failed to inspire one more generation of futile funerals.

What was left was the ruin in Dublin, the creature of an establishment doomed from the beginning by their nature, by their lack of enterprise and civility and freedom. How could it be otherwise, for they had shaped a Catholic state for a Catholic people. And in British Ulster they all knew the limits of the Catholics, their neighbours, the lad down the lane, the killer in the dock, the idler by the road, the father of eighteen children. They knew these Catholics even if in fact they knew them not very well or not at all.

These Catholics so well known in no way resembled the image that the Catholics had of themselves. Of course, neither did their mixed image of the Protestant resemble the real Protestant. First, for the Irish Catholics there were two quite different categories of Protestants: ours in the Republic and those in control of Northern Ireland. The former, in Dublin banks or Monaghan farms, were just like us—except Protestant. And were not many of the founders Protestant, and Yeats and Shaw and the others? And the ones to the north are different, a strange, imagined mix of the horrid and the hilarious, hard, cold men but make the most outrageous speeches about the Pope or Maynooth or a Republic they have never visited. Paisley is merely the most visible and often the most ridiculous—"I have reason to believe that the fowl-pest outbreaks are the work of the IRA." So for the Irish-Irish the Northern Protestants are different, tolerate sectarian murder and yet are Irish, make silly speeches and threaten the lives of Catholics, a people quite contradictory and mysterious and, of course, rarely met. They do not come south, but then those in the Republic seldom go north. There they would find that as visitors they are already well known to the Protestants, because they are Irish Catholics: residence in Tipperary or Tyrone makes no difference, Irish Catholics are Irish Catholics. The Protestant knows them well and their faults and failings. And so they knew what such as they might summon up as state and nation, as model for an all-Ireland future. And so they deplored the project, abhorred the prospect, and focused on the demonstrable reality of the Republic, a failed entity.

5

PROTESTANT PERCEPTION: THE REPUBLIC

In the South they boasted of a Catholic State. They
still boast of Southern Ireland being a Catholic
State.—James Craig

Irish economic performance has been the least
impressive in Western Europe, perhaps in all Europe,
in the twentieth century.—J. J. Lee

The Protestants of British Ulster, knowing the nature of
Catholicism and the habits of Catholics, see both as
determinants of the Irish state, a Catholic state for a
Catholic people and so inevitably flawed if still dangerous.
What Protestants seek in the Republic is validation of their
assumptions about the inevitable nature of Rome authority
melded with Irish nationalism: a failed entity. When policy
and the times so require, the Unionist political
establishment also wants the Republic as threat—a role for
years on offer to the IRA until in 1971 the threat became
manifest rather than imagined.

The Dublin establishment is more often viewed not so
much as a conglomerate of special interests engaged in
distributing entitlements but rather as a greedy and

ambitious Catholic cabal eager to absorb "their" six counties. So Dublin seems committed, if quietly at times, to the persistent national aspiration—a dream that requires no investment, no commitment, no sacrifice, but remains a consideration, since the aspiration attracts international support and denies Northern Ireland stability. Dublin exacerbates all-Ireland instability both by latent or actual encouragement to the republican gunmen and by pressing on London and the naïve international community a pan-Irish national goal: Irish unity at the expense of the Protestants.

The Protestants feel that their loyal and unswerving commitment to the union, the sacrifices in war and peace, the long and painful struggle against gunmen and subversives and their rights as a provincial majority have garnered insufficient returns. They do not feel reassured about the future: British Ulster is still at risk. Dublin is still waiting for someone, whether the British Labour Party, the American President or the United Nations, to shake the Ulster tree so that the six-county apple will drop. And London's defence of the orchard does not seem as vigilant as might be expected. Major or Thatcher, Churchill or Lloyd George, all promised vigilance, but still the province seems always to be at risk; all-Ireland lost by partition, devolved government lost, and the B Specials and the power of the Unionist Party gone. If Ulster is right, as London so often claims, why is it always necessary to fight? And why so often has ground been taken away from the loyal instead of defended?

British Ulster has always been vulnerable, everywhere vulnerable and so everywhere in need of defence. No-one seems to understand that any compromise will erode existing defences and so lead to further compromise and finally absorption into an all-Ireland system that by any criteria will be a disaster. British Ulster accepts both the enormous dangers inherent in compromise on the constitutional question and the dreadful prospects if defence fails, fails at all, falters even an inch.

What unionists have increasingly felt to be ideologically needed, especially after the rise of the IRA's armed struggle, is to display just how dreadful any such all-Ireland entity would be. Unionist fears must be and can be justified. The main issue is no longer the identity of Home Rule and Rome rule but rather the evidence that Rome rule in twenty-six counties has been a disaster. If the prototype of any united Ireland is the Republic—and this has really always been the nationalist assumption—then certain debacle awaits. The majority in Northern Ireland, against their will, may be driven into harm's way. So as far as the Republic is concerned, the Protestants aspire to displaying the reality of the ruin for all to contemplate. The Republic is a failed entity. The national dream, because of the malign influence of Catholic, Gaelic society, has led to disaster. Irish nationalism can by nature only lead to tragedy, a futile, authoritarian society without grace or enterprise, a tragedy for the Catholics already and tragedy proposed for the Ulster Protestants. This is not some fervid Orange speech, not hyperbole, but reality: look at the record, read the statistics, see the evidence beyond the travel posters and Government claims.

Free Ireland has largely failed to fulfil the dreams of the founders and often the needs of the people. Free Ireland is an unhappy state filled with unhappy people, despite the charm and the superficial glamour, the new buildings, new fortunes and new men. These new men are no different from the old, pessimistic peasants keeping what they can, how they can, suspicious, obedient, amusing and at times dangerous. Irish pessimism arises from a historical tradition that indicates that one's heart will be broken and that hope is a foolish investment. All suspect that any triumph is passing—and are so encouraged by the Roman church—and endangers all others, all the other peasants. One does not so much begrudge success in Ireland as fear that evil will be attracted by it. Do well and be damned, write a book and you cause trouble, be different and notice will be taken. The high flower must be cut to camouflage the rest of the weeds from the reaper. And green Ireland is a land of weeds, for it is assumed that sooner or later the reaper will come for the high flower. Even the weeds are bound to suffer: the ambitious will be denied, the price of a pint will go up, and the crop will fail.

It is not so much a nation of begrudgers as a nation without hope of a better day. Only the comfort of the church and the memory of the past are steadfast. So there is no proper investment, no real creativity, no freedom, and a full church at Mass time. It is only the Protestants under the threat of a zealous god who believe that material progress is not only possible but also a reward for piety. It is only the Protestants who demand liberty for each to find God, to live freely, to seek liberty and prosperity and so pursue happiness. The Protestant ethos is different. And this is the basic beginning of all criticism: the nature of the Irish Catholics ensures failure.

Unfortunately this judgement, as declaimed by the fundamentalist of Northern Ireland, has almost always proved unappealing to the distant and disinterested. It seems a good case ruined—and especially a good case difficult to make at a time when traditional values are discounted, when religion is seen as a Sabbath recreation, not a life commitment, for many in the West. In British Ulster other rules run, other than in England and especially other than in the Republic. The Protestant lives close to God, not to a church, leads a life constantly monitored, where salvation and revelation are vital. Redemption empowers and transforms each new soul won, changes the very atmosphere of the province. One must be saved to live a righteous, godly and sober life; and often one must seek to save the lost. For Protestant Ireland most of the Catholics, the national majority, are long lost and seemingly beyond salvage. Few knock on Catholic doors to spread the gospel or seek converts. The Irish Catholics are a failed people muttering about old wrongs, members of a lesser tradition, a dangerous tradition. The Irish Catholic in all thirty-two counties is both irresponsible and manipulated, is always improvident and often dangerous. In Ireland their tradition is so pervasive and persistent that few Protestants, few even of the most evangelical, imagine winning the country for their faith. Rather the others, the Romans, can be left to their own devices—except those in the six counties, who must be watched as subversives, lost but not without purpose.

This Protestant analysis adjusts, distributes and shapes all data, so that reality is what best fits the existing image. Catholics are as Catholics imagined and so the Republic as expected. And this is hardly novel or necessarily fatal. There is much evidence of the flaws in the Irish national dream and the accomplishments of emerging independence. There is considerable criticism by those who have suffered or failed to benefit: artists and poets, émigrés and republicans, radicals and social critics. For the unionists there is overwhelming evidence, no matter the circumstances or the apologies, that Irish nationalism has failed to produce as promised.

All data is adjusted to this aim—and much data needs no adjustment. Before 1972 the existence of the clause in the Constitution establishing the "special position" of the Catholic Church was cited regularly by Protestants as evidence of the reality of Rome rule. In 1972 the removal of the offending clause did not change Protestant analysis. The removal was cited as irrelevant, a matter of propaganda, an exercise to trick the unwary. And there can be no denying that the clause did exist, did indicate in a tangible and visible way that the Irish state was a Catholic state for a Catholic people. Removing the words, as far as Protestants are concerned, was cosmetic, not a shift in the essential nature of the Republic.

The Protestants know that Rome rules. The Irish people, polled in 1995, might accept a constitutional right to divorce, by a tiny majority; but the vote was grudging and the Pope had actually intervened to urge his flock to vote against the amendment—which they did in great numbers. The Republic seems really as Rome-driven in 1995 as in 1972, as the Free State was fifty years before. De Valera never made any secret of his priorities on even the smallest matter, much less the nature of the country: "If I had a vote on a local body, and if there were two qualified people who had to deal with a Catholic community, and if one was a Catholic and the other was a Protestant, I would unhesitatingly vote for the Catholic."

The litany of Catholic interference is there for all: the brutal censorship to curry favour with the clergy, the unyielding hierarchy, more authoritarian than the Pope, imposing standards on all, insisting that every child of a mixed marriage be raised a Catholic. This was in violation of many local customs and, Protestants felt, of common decency. So too was the ban on Catholics attending Trinity

College, Dublin. There were rows over contraception, censorship, and social reforms, and always the church view prevailed.

And in Northern Ireland they kept to themselves, their own schools and hospitals and rites. In the Free State every word written, each play staged, all films were held to Catholic standards. The finest artists were driven abroad, if not by poverty then by the Pope. It was a priest-ridden state. No dancing at the crossroads, no visiting Protestant churches, no future in Holy Ireland for the Methodists or Presbyterians. The Church of Ireland had been marginalised in the Republic, the congregations eroding, St Patrick's and Christ Church empty, the country parishes closed, the bishops wheeled out as tokens at state ceremonies.

The republic of the IRA man Seán MacBride was no different, no less sectarian, no more republican. When the Government introduced social legislation in 1951 in the form of the Mother and Child Scheme of Noel Browne, the Minister for Health, the church interposed its authority: "The Hierarchy cannot approve of any scheme which, in its general tendency, must foster undue control by the State in a sphere so delicate and so intimately concerned with morals ..." The minister was brought to heel by MacBride, whose attempt to explain away the Government's decision not to introduce the legislation Browne described as a "model of the two-faced hypocrisy and humbug so characteristic of you."

In power, republicans were as subservient to Rome as they had been rebellious in opposition. The passing years seemingly had made little difference but in the subtlety of Catholic intervention. Still, in many matters, from abortion to divorce, the church publicly entered the discussion. In the Republic the province of what was solely Caesar's was narrow indeed. Anyone need only visit the Republic, if few unionists did, to find formal piety, public obedience, symbols of Rome, attitudes and sermons everywhere, the parish priest ubiquitous in many matters and the Roman church unrepentant. Nothing really changed: television came, and the Angelus that came on the screen every evening was so natural that none noticed, or noticed St Brigid's Cross as the RTE symbol. Catholicism and the Irish were as one. The only faction to draw repeated Roman scorn—the republicans, the gunmen with their secular faith—were buried by the clergy in holy ground, commemorated with the Rosary, still Catholics like all the others.

The slick, modern Governments of FitzGerald and Haughey, focused on rapid development and general progress, just like the Governments of their successors, Reynolds and Bruton, were still priest-ridden. All, nice words or no, wanted to absorb Northern Ireland. All were Catholic. There were no votes in the Republic for the secular, few anti-clericals and fewer radical critics of the church. Over the years all that changed was that the hand of Maynooth and Rome was more hidden. The Roman church might have discovered more obstacles to domination, the wares of secularism and the doubts of a new generation, but then Rome had always found ways of coping, to command, to control, even under less promising circumstances. The Dublin Government was more of the same, whether led by Reynolds or Bruton or the old men in dark suits with rosaries in the pockets.

At times each nationalist leader made bobs towards Protestant opinion in Northern Ireland—for the Protestants of the Republic were assumed one with the country. These gestures evoked little enthusiasm, even within the Irish electorate, even when sold as crucial in modernising the country and absorbing British Ulster. Neither Ulster Protestants, Orange bigots nor northern Catholics, harsh and demanding, generated much enthusiasm in the Republic. More often than not the electorate showed no interest in modernising, demonstrating for access to contraceptives, accepting abortion or divorce or the ethics of the Sunday press, nor any desire for adjusting to acquire the six counties that all assumed would come sooner or later as right. Why change? So the changes were grudging and cosmetic and in no way disguised the power of Rome. This the Protestants accepted as axiomatic, and no vote on divorce, no speech by the Taoiseach, no plea for parity of esteem could sway the convinced. The Roman churches in Dublin 4 and Dingle were still filled on a Sunday and the Protestant pews empty.

What was thus perceived mattered to Protestants, still mattered to Protestants. It mattered no less and perhaps more once there were efforts in Dublin to disguise Roman reality with false toleration and the illusion that church and state were not one. Of course they need not be one institution, for everyone was Catholic and so too all nationalists. What the Protestants detested and feared was Catholicism, not the ordinary Irish, not the Government's policy on exports or tax refunds. Catholicism was ubiquitous, it determined values and agendas and so the intrinsic nature of the Republic. Abortion on demand would not change the ethos, nor would the clergy permit their flock to make such a demand, regardless of the law, and so the laws were irrelevant to reality.

True, the Irish-Irish were a rude and barbarous nation, but the real cause of failure was the insidious influence of Rome. Thus for nearly all Protestants Rome still has much to do with the governance, with the whole society. In the Republic, Rome not only rules OK but will also continue to do so. How could matters be otherwise? What distinguished the Republic from Northern Ireland was that in British Ulster the Protestant ethic ran and British civility. It is the nature of the Irish-Irish, of Rome, of the objective conditions found to the south in the Republic to shape the nation to Catholic needs. The people must be submissive. The teachings and authority of the church must be unchallenged. Ideally Rome wants the ideal enacted in law, but this is not really necessary: the faithful know their role and their fate if they stray. And few stray, and fewer complain. The most egregious scandals come and go, even appear on the evening news, but doctrine goes on for ever. There is for the Protestant ample visible evidence to this effect, whether in the large families or in authoritarian social legislation. The Catholic ethos moulds society. There is also the failure of the Government, of the nation to reward talent and discipline, their failure to encourage enterprise and proper investment, their failure to do more than ensure that the church has a predominant role to play and so to maintain a hold on the communicants. Such an agenda may offer salvation but at the cost of subservience and a failed society.

In sum, those twenty-six counties, however organised, however named, are both threatening and failure, and most of all an example of the debilities that Rome rule has brought in part of Ireland and would ensure in all Ireland in the event of reunification. Partition has meant twenty-six counties abandoned to a misery that the oppressed citizens accept as just and inevitable. Partition was opposed before 1921 for these very reasons: Ireland ruined by Rome rule. And when all could not be protected, then the Protestants withdrew behind the walls, faithful to their own, and ignored the muddle the Catholics made of the rest. Partition, now defended by unionists, means that six counties have been saved from the inevitable consequences of Rome rule.

The Ulster Protestants may not know the Republic intimately, at first hand, but they know what they know. And they do know the local Catholics in British Ulster very well indeed—or so they assume. And these Irish Catholics are the same: same religion, same ambitions, same flaws and failures. The Irish Catholics of the province are thus perceived as no different from the residents of the Republic, different only in their more limited capacity to contaminate society. Long-visible evidence of inferiority, too many poor, too many on the dole, too many with large families and drink problems, none very productive, few evincing enterprise, most content in misery until stirred first by outside agitators and radicals and then by the atavistic appeal of the IRA gunmen—these local Catholics want what they do not have, do not deserve, cannot create. How can they, for all of them are shaped by the ethos of Rome. At times similar faults can be ferreted out of Continental examples: Italian government instability or the instability of Spain, the flaws of Québec or the record of Rome in Latin America; but mostly the Protestants look no further for example than Dunloy or the Ardoyne. To the south in the Republic, the visible faults, failures and even foibles of the northern Catholic have intensified, dominate all, because there is no Protestant leavening and leadership. Without Protestant example, without the benefits of British civility, the Republic is lost.

It has been easy for unionists to imagine such a republic: in fact it is crucial to do so, since few know it at first hand.

There was no need to do so as long as British Ulster was challenged only in theory, not in practice by real gunmen, by British doubts, and by world opinion. Before the Troubles, Dublin was merely one more imagined and imaginary villain in the Orange stock, to be sold over the counter when requested. Details were not needed, evidence not required—any item would do for an Orange oration, a Unionist speech, or a good sermon. After the Unionist system came under the gun there were more buyers and a greater need, but no sudden accumulation of new data. The old Orange system collapsed. Unionism divided. Stormont was gone and the B Specials. The rituals of domination and assurance could not be heard over the bombs and guns of the IRA. This armed struggle that the British rules of conflict allowed to persist did not change the accepted truth about the other Ireland. So the reality of the Republic did not intrude on the image, even as evidence was sought to embellish that image. Just as the country lanes and city streets had become a real battleground, so did the sale of the Protestant case become part of the struggle. The Protestants feel that they had a good case, as majority in Northern Ireland and as critic of the Republic.

In fact the Republic's reality is often just as the Protestants imagine: much in the Republic is flawed, many core values have been discarded, general aspirations have failed, and hypocrisy and self-interest are rampant. The Protestants are not the only ones who contend that the Irish state is an amalgam of special interests, the establishment excessively privileged, self-indulgent and arrogant and the populace too often incompetent in matters of investment and development, not enterprising at all in such a bleak milieu, and so the ambitious are avid to emigrate. For Protestants the Republic is a failed entity: read the *Irish*

Times, the attacks of the critics, the conclusions of economists, the preservationists, the artists, the students and Greens, read the Irish-language activists and the liberals, the columns of *An Phoblacht*, the opinions of Continental politicians, and read the statistics of development. Irish Protestants are not alone—only the romantic, the innocent and those responsible for the ruin find rationales.

The Republic in northern Protestant eyes, distant, alien, mysterious in many ways and unpalatable in all that matter, has changed little over time. The Protestant image at the end of the century is nearly the same as it was in the twenties. The consequences of Rome rule that dominated Protestant thinking for a century have merely been proved in twenty-six counties. The only difference over the years has been the shape of the threat. For fifty years the Stormont system had deflected the threat—never truly a serious matter except for a time when a neutral Ireland might have levered support into unity but did not, until 1919. Then objective conditions, a momentary failure of nerve, a Labour government in London and the impact of alien ideologies made Irish nationalism a more lethal and so tangible danger. In 1967 the IRA could be summoned up as spectre; in a few years there was no need to send a summons, for the cities were filled with ruined buildings, with no-go zones and the smell of cordite. And this violence was the overspill of nationalist ambition.

The argument that this horror arose from the failures of the old system, weighted voting, sectarian practices, and misery unfairly distributed, arose from the very system that had succeeded in keeping nationalism at bay, is rationalised away by many: the others were as sectarian in all thirty-two counties, and such means were necessary as well as traditional. What still should matter is that Protestant opinion and unionist opinion is majority opinion in Northern Ireland. The majority should rule or at least be given fair hearing. More to the point, and excluding the matter of fairness, the Protestant case has always focused on the variegated ills inherent in their enemy and their own virtues—and what political or national or religious case has not? And why should the lads on the road to Dunloy be different, held to higher standard, asked to be balanced and decent when the paint is still wet on the vandalised Orange hall? It is in Dublin, miles away to the south, that the real problem arises, that the real problem always arose.

This Republic is still a foreign land but filled with those not at all foreign, for their sort can be seen in the local nationalist community. Both sets are equally contaminated by Catholic culture, if not inherently by birth and breeding then certainly by exposure. All men might be born free but if born in Leitrim or Carlow will not long remain so without the comfort and guidance of a faith other than that of Rome. The great difference in the Republic is that the huge majority of Catholics has shaped society to Roman and nationalist assumptions, aspirations and agenda and so revealed what reunification would bring to British Ulster.

A united Ireland as imagined by nationalists would be the present Republic writ large: even the militant republicans, often in the past as critical of the Dublin establishment as the Northern unionists, given a whiff of power made swift common cause with the pan-nationalist front of John Hume and Fianna Fáil. And all the other rainbow parties, every faction, the old Stickies and the Labour people—all signed on to the new pan-nationalist thrust. In Dublin all assume that reunification would generate a novel and wondrous society, free to all, free for all. This is just what the IRA and the nationalists have always proclaimed, that it would be non-sectarian and fair to all. This is the same IRA that shot Protestant farmers off their tractors to buy the border land. Such a republic would not be secular, not open to all but as Catholic as the present edifice built up in Dublin over the years.

The Irish political establishment always assumes as right the whole country—one need not look at constitutional provisions but into the hearts of the Irish-Irish. They have, one and all, decade after decade made clear the future, perhaps not achieved with violence, perhaps not achieved soon but always inevitable: an Ireland united. Ireland would then be a nation once again, or rather a nation for the first time ever in control of the whole country; but it would be a nation with the Protestants taken in on toleration, assumed pliable, converts to the ways of the Gael—merely Irish, not British at all. As new citizens they would soon adapt, soon find esteem and success and comfort, soon discard their old loyalties: and these loyalties were not seen as liberties and rights but as residue of empire. They could be easily discarded.

As for the others, the nationalists, the Catholics, no sacrifice need be made. They could offer a few places in Government, a little legislation rewritten, good words, and then the Irish would settle down to wait for Protestant differences to go. And in this matter the unionists felt the nationalists were right: once their liberty was gone, once the Catholic ethos became dominant, their old attributes would go—productivity, enterprise, propriety, and freedom. Their virtues would evaporate in the Roman miasma that floats over the Republic and drives the ambitious to emigrate. Then the Protestants could stay and atrophy, amalgamate, or, like so many others, emigrate.

Any united Ireland would by necessity be united on Catholic terms and for Catholic benefit, no matter the promises or legalities. There are not enough Protestants to transform the ethos, not a critical mass, not enough to convert the obedient or inspire the lethargic, to break the habits and customs of the tribe. So unity does not mean diversity but an end to the British ethos in Ireland, British civility and liberty, an end to the Protestants of Ireland. One need only seek the Protestant community in the Republic or seek British enterprise in Irish development statistics to discover the future.

Unity is inevitable, a mantra repeated over and over, year after year, until even the simple accepted the proposition as valid, and yet it was a proposition never defended by logic, only by repetition. Being on the same island did not make Haïti and the Dominican Republic one. Yearning for a great homeland had created chaos and war in the Balkans for centuries. Hawaii was American and much further from the mainland than Antrim is from England. Those in Dublin felt their cause so just that sacrifice would be unnecessary: others would bring an end to existing injustice. There was no logic except that engendered by ambition and faulty reminiscence, old myths, lies, patriot history. For generations in anti-partition campaigns the nationalists had appealed to reason, to British decency, to world opinion, to Washington and the United Nations, subliminally to the gunmen of the IRA—and often not so subliminally. The power of the dream never seemed quite so compelling as to engender the necessary sacrifices to seize the "national territory" or sufficiently applicable to make flourish what had been ceded. Unity would come, must come, but at someone else's expense. Prosperity and a grand Irish renaissance would come, but later, after unity. It was an Irish response: an evasion of responsibility, a failure to speak plainly—cunning, crafty, Catholic, and typical.

Whether eager to risk for the cause or no, there could be no hiding Irish ambition and Irish intentions. The six counties by right, because of doctored history and bad law, because of geography, were to be amalgamated into the Republic, no matter what the Protestants wanted and probably with the connivance, albeit reluctant and disguised as duty, of the British establishment and the enthusiastic support of the distant—the Americans, the Europeans, and the guileless and naïve. In Irish Catholic imagination British Ulster was artificial, doomed, merely a lost green field soon to be reclaimed without concession or compromise. And the result would be ruin for Ulster, ruin on a greater scale, 32-county ruin if not chaos and escalated violence. Some predicted anarchy and chaos; some, in London anyway, merely foresaw sullen acceptance and then perhaps prosperity at last but certainly an end to the "Irish problem". Most found the prospect of coercing the unionists daunting, given the risk of sectarian slaughter and the enormous actual cost involved. No wonder even the faint of heart in Whitehall and Downing Street hesitated to turn over the loyalists, the unionists, the faithful to the pan-nationalists. Ulster would have no option but to fight, and Ulster would be right.

And suppose Ulster did not fight? What then? That Ulster would acquiesce, that unionists would become nationalists, that the loyalists would become Irish was further evidence of wishful thinking that was so typical of the lethal dreamers in Dublin or the Falls Road, or even Westminster. What then? Who would pay? Who would underwrite Irish sloth, Protestant loss, the suppression of Ulster gunmen?

Such obstacles were to be left to the future. The form of the united nation, the one Ireland, was for later. The means was for later. What was wanted was to begin a process that made later inevitable. Then the six counties would drop into the waiting Dublin basket without cost, without violence, without plans and preparations: a strategy dear to Irish hearts. Nothing need be sacrificed, little changed. None of the nationalists can even imagine uniting the twenty-six with the six, bringing the centre of power north to Armagh or Belfast, jettisoning the clerks and clerics of Dublin and beginning anew. Uniting Ireland does not mean unity at all, not an end to Catholic dominance in all matters, not an end to the establishment in Dublin, not an end to Irish sloth and debt and the easy life. Unity means more of the same, no change but that imposed on the Protestants, no cost but that picked up elsewhere. It would be a country soon ruined, a Protestant people soon discarded. This is on the record: where are the Protestants of Kerry, the Protestant republicans, the Protestant poets and prelates, bankers and small farmers, the people once prized in theory and driven away in practice? And where would be the Protestants who submitted to Dublin desires—in a decade on the boat, exiles from their own land, Ballymena now Dunloy, none to march to the different drummer. And if not, if still in Ireland, they would be serving their time, watching their children marry elsewhere, the farm sold to Murphy, the business without markets and the chapel closed, Armagh Cathedral a tourist site and none to remember the past on Poppy Day.

Unionists always knew that nationalism always implied a unity that could only come at Protestant expense. De Valera felt that his 1937 Constitution could simply be extended over the six counties. This was the whole point: the country dominated by those who had already ruined what they had. The nationalists mostly did not even pretend otherwise. De Valera's Constitution made special provision for the

Catholic Church but none for those of other faiths likely to be included in the reunification. De Valera offered only frugal comfort, not hard work, enterprise and productivity. In the twenty-six counties happiness was the pursuit of the lost six counties and the assurance of ultimate salvation offered by Rome. The nationalists accepted that concessions would have to be made: civil service positions offered, guarantees written down, pride and esteem guaranteed. Time, of course, would remedy all such costs. Time would make Ireland one. It was all too evident to unionists, loyalists and the disinterested that time had eliminated diversity and prosperity in the twenty-six counties. With unity through a peace process, through a failure of nerve in London, through outside intervention or a failed Ulster defence, the inevitable outcome would be the Republic writ large. The existing establishment would be in place—same parties, same priorities, largely the same people—if the 1994 peace process worked as Dublin and the pan-nationalist front imagined, and always the same agenda. The Angelus might no longer be heard in the evening on radio and television in every home—a concession to northern sensibilities—but unheard airs are sweeter still. All Ireland would dance to the old tunes: fifty years to eradicate southern Protestants and another fifty for those in the north. All were Irish, were they not? All in time would be as Irish as the real Irish. In other words, this or the next and future establishment would remain established and so the Republic remain an instrument in Catholic Irish hands. These hands might not be quicker than the eye but were still sly. So nothing had changed, and if unity were to come, everything in Northern Ireland would change. The country was one, and so a fully failed entity.

For fifty years Unionist opinion hardly felt constrained to

damn Irish nationalism, a spent force. Then came the Troubles and the necessity to point out why such a force had failed, how nationalism had led to debacle. The Republic is seen as disaster institutionalised, a calamity on the instalment plan glossed over with wishful thinking and travel posters: sheep and old men and green fields and the wee white cottage, a never-never Ireland that sells group tours to a Catholic state for a Catholic people. And it is for all, Catholics or the few others, a failure by almost all standards. These Irish-Irish people live on remittances, casual corruption and the uneven distribution of entitlements. Agriculture has produced no capital and capitalism has produced no jobs. Only the Government and taxes have grown. The arts have suffered, and education is flawed. Science cannot even cope with native cunning and bovine TB. Nationalism has ruined the larger part of the country and would do so to the province, not out of spite but because of the inherent nature of Catholicism.

Few in the Republic, all dazed by their own advantage and imagination, can envisage how grim Ireland may seem to others, those without access to the entitlements of the state, those without the comforts of contacts or the freedom to criticise and comment. Those in the Dáil or Government offices, the chattering classes of Dublin 4, the comfortable and even those who have stayed to live on the taxes of others, feel Ireland grand: a nation of saints and scholars, a nation easy and comfortable, safe and beautiful, fast modernising, an attraction to visitors, a source of general admiration. Everyone loves the Irish. And so Bord Fáilte publishes grand posters of scenic Ireland, Georgian doors, green fields, and happy people: everyone loves the Irish, even when they have the wind in their face and walk a rutted road.

Loved or no, the statistics of prosperity, the failures of policy and the futility of most national endeavours, from the welfare system to all sorts of economic and social gauges, indicate that all is not well. Behind the doors are ruined building sites, the green fields are badly tended, the people often not so lovely close up. Everyone prefers the posters and has ready explanations for the difficulties so special to Ireland, so beyond remedy. On this the establishment has almost always been one in offering reasoned explanation why Ireland should not be harshly judged, should be a special case and has always had to cope with unique problems in difficult times. Ireland was special. It was a small island on the margins of events, without resources or a comforting climate; the people were poor, the British government execrable, and history unkind. And despite all this there had been great progress: bogs drained, factories built, new roads and new schools, Irish had not been lost as a language, nor was the country without influence in international councils. The Irish pound was the equal of the pound sterling in 1996 and inflation was down, credit sound, even emigration dropping, if not unemployment. So there were still problems—but then aren't there always. And hadn't the Irish coped?

Essentially they had not. In the first place there were fewer Irish to cope, fewer than might be expected or might be desired. Elsewhere in Europe populations had grown, and done so without hampering development. In contrast the Irish population declined. In 1841 eight million lived in Ireland, most in misery; a century later the population was little more than half that and static, not miserable but hardly flourishing. The population after the Famine continued to decline as living standards rose, if slowly, if not to western European standards. Only a single burst of economic optimism in the sixties produced an upward blip in the slow decline. Even at that, far fewer people than elsewhere, fewer marriages, later marriages, emigration and religious vocations seemed to indicate that the slow rise in living standards had been achieved by cutting the population; not enough could now go round more easily. Elsewhere there was more to go round, more in Denmark or Finland, and more to receive it.

Between 1910 and 1970 Ireland recorded the slowest growth of per capita income of any European country except Britain. And even the bottom of the polls, Britain and Northern Ireland, did not lag as badly as Ireland in national income. Only massive deficit spending produced promising national income figures after 1970 and kept some at home who would have left—or could have left if American immigration law had not changed and the British market not proved fallow. Once a creditor nation, Ireland spent to stay even with others and borrowed to aspire to a European standard that could not be generated within the country. Even then the people could not be kept at home—another of de Valera's aspirations denied. Ireland lacked enterprise, effective development policies, general prosperity, and the capacity to march in common with the Common Market.

The politicians claimed that population growth generated unemployment and so economic failure: the Government could not keep up with even the existing population and had to run to stay in place. This was a reality only found in Ireland. Even at maximum, with an annual population growth of 1.4 per cent, a rate not far from that of the United States at 1.1 or Japan at 1.2—where in both cases growth continued—the Irish could not create jobs. The Government could not ensure growth and could not raise standards to Continental levels without borrowing. Even in the years of great and unprecedented growth, 1960–1974, the Irish fell short of European standards. Ireland had to borrow. And credit was good. And when prosperity came to some in the nineties there was still no answer, no end to unemployment, no real end to the loss of talent, no end in sight to the difficulties—never admitted as failures, only the price of history or a passing phase subject to transformation with a new initiative, next year's statistics, the fruition of adjustment.

The borrowing was not invested for productivity but to keep society content. And then the debt had to be repaid. Ireland had a seriously flawed economy—a different kind of failure from the low population, slow growth and high emigration years of the pre-war era but still a failure. Taxes were high. Foreign investment was unsatisfactory. Manufacture tended to be last into Ireland and first out when world conditions so suggested. Industry was not viable. New directions led to blind alleys once the Asians competed or the market changed. The allocation of funds to create employment was ineffectual. Jobs were created but at great cost. And then jobs were lost at great cost, and the dole queues snaked out to the street. Ireland's unemployment rate was unique in Europe, an indicator of a failed society as far as the Protestants were concerned. In fact they were hardly alone in finding Ireland at fault.

Ireland's economic performance must count as one of the most striking records in modern European economic history. The apologists for the Irish state always had explanations: the inherent limitations that made the Irish example special, explicable, excusable, unique. Ireland had not failed but triumphed over high and peculiar odds, should not be held to general standards. The Irish were more spiritual than materialist in any case—so said de Valera, so said they all, even the economists. And there was nature's narrow providence—no gold, no diamonds. There were history's costs and geography's penalties. Neither alone nor in combination will Celtic spirituality, a paucity of natural resources, a gloomy climate, a marginal geographical position, a tiny economy in a great sea shifted by other tides and a history of oppression produce an explanation that will stand contrast with the successes of others in Europe, not even as well blessed. Ireland is special, as are all countries, but not especially handicapped. In fact it might well be considered especially blessed.

History in Ireland is long ago. No great wars fought over the fields, no pogroms or devastating battle losses, cities bombed to rubble; no ethnic cleansing, no final solutions, no great plagues or famines, no wandering Panzer divisions or mad tribes intent on murder—nothing this century on a grand scale but the losses in the great wars in faraway places. And those at the Somme or D-Day were all volunteers for war, not the innocent bombed or slaughtered or starved out of policy or whim. Ireland has suffered none of the catastrophes that have afflicted almost all of Europe. Ireland on the margins has been safe, tranquil, neutral, and lightly touched with the winds of war. And there on the margins the world economy may not always favour the small; but then over the last century at times other small economies have flourished, often benefited by great tides. More hours of sun would hardly ensure prosperity for a land blessed by moderate climate, good land and a congenial topography: no sharp mountain chains or vast acreage near the Arctic circle, no land saved by dikes or baked by Mediterranean sun, and certainly no jungles or swamps; and even the bogs yield fuel. And after all, the tourists do come, many not for their roots but for the soft, gentle rains and the green fields, the ruins and the Guinness. And, true, there were no great mineral hoards, if some oil and gas, no coal or iron or uranium; but then other flourishing economies made do with even less—imported materials, exploited their talents, exported with a vengeance, and flourished. And where were such assets in Finland or even Italy? Denmark too had to rely on fields and cattle, Denmark too had a great and not always generous neighbour, and Denmark suffered real occupation and real wars. And Denmark flourished.

And most certainly the spiritual Gaels gave every indication that they too wanted to flourish, and so litigated, arranged the most profitable marriage or real estate purchase, exploited the Government or their neighbour, sold the one cow with cunning care. Those who emigrated and triumphed in the alien market returned in full pride with photographs of the house and car and accounts of success in Melbourne or Toronto or Chicago, no shame in the tangibles, no apology for spirituality lost. Who would excavate denial at a horse fair or the finer things on a building site? Not most of the Irish, concentrating as do most on getting and spending. There was surely evidence of work done if frayed edges, good enough to pass. There was surely evidence of work wanted, any work at home, but few could make work for themselves. Everyone truly wanted at the very least frugal comfort, and only a few found that— and a few drove past them in the Mercedes.

There was, however, no general success in Ireland, not enough getting and so no effective spending, no saving, no investment but instead high unemployment, high taxes, high emigration, and high hopes abandoned each decade. Always disappointment, and never anyone responsible for failure. The parties were interchangeable in irresponsibility, no strategy effective except in the elegant and sophisticated explanations of the appropriate bureaucrats, once with charts and graphs and later with projections and economic strategies and more lately with computer projections, but always with assurance. Emigration was sold as a natural and inevitable and perhaps not undesirable Irish solution to an Irish problem. Irish spirituality was a loser's prize in the free market.

Irish history has repeatedly been misread as ample excuse for the lack of returns on greed, the rise in the debt, the decay of even the existing social standards. The Irish truly believe their island has been ravished by war and ruined by violence: look at the Troubles and over three thousand dead—less than the Northern Ireland traffic toll, less than a day's killing in a real war, horrid but hardly the figures to confound a Polish Jew, a Kurd, or an Italian. History this century has been kind to the Irish, mild and soft as the climate. The Irish have been largely left to their own devices and after 1921 to their own free state, not fully free but free to pursue liberty and prosperity and, as every Ulster Protestant is quick to note, to fail in so doing. And so who is to blame if performance is flawed, not rewarded? Whither Irish enterprise, Irish performance, productivity, disciplined commitment to achievement? The Protestants had no doubt who was to blame: Rome rule merely stopped short of penury for all at the prize of obedience. And that obedience can be challenged only through poetry and exile.

In response, about all the Irish could note, sourly, was that the failures were not limited to the twenty-six counties but were replicated in Northern Ireland. There the Protestant ethic, the fundamentalist commitment to performance, the assurance of material returns arising from divine satisfaction seemingly were of no greater avail. The province too had apologists who pointed out the special costs of the Troubles, the greater impact of partition on the smaller state, and the cost of a sullen and subversive minority. This, however, was of far less concern to the unionists, the loyalists, who looked not into their own account books but those of the Celtic, Catholic heart of the Republic. No need to bother about the mote in one's eye. In Dublin the local apologists could not hide the unemployment figures, the emigration figures, the debts, the declining number of Irish-speakers and the rising glitz of glass office buildings run up by the mohair men. None after a time could make much of a case for growth that arose not from productivity but from using borrowed money, promised Government money to tear down Georgian and run up gimcrack. The result could only be sold as "development" for a few years. Foreigners were brought in with money and skills to accelerate development and instead took the money, exploited the opportunity, and all too often left disappointment and debt behind. Even the effective local and international development, the good projects and the clever schemes, did not change matters greatly. Then outside those proud new glass high-rises built on the ruins of ascendancy Georgian were the vast, monotonous housing estates, each citizen with a garden and central heating or a tiny flat, or more likely hundreds and hundreds of shoddy houses, houses in rows, houses stacked as high-rise, cramped rooms overlooking a field of mud for the poor, detention camps for those on the dole kept at the end of the bus queues. The few Marxists might carp, the students always found fault, the Greens and the artists—all the begrudgers of the everyday complained as expected, but so increasingly did the sensible and sound. The countryside was ruined by unrestricted buildings, one bright white cottage after the next. The towns were decaying, the roads crowded with cars few could afford, the schools class-ridden and the administrators found in trendy restaurants.

J Bowyer Bell

All this might be forgiven and was hardly unique to Ireland, but the numbers were special: too many unemployed, too few viable economic centres, too much debt, too little real shift in the pieties and prejudices of the provincial, and too many emigrating. Scandals might now be in the newspapers instead of whispered across the hedge, but the same dreary social problems generated those scandals: ignorance, avarice, bigotry, suspicion of novelty or elegance, puritan ethics in public and private prurience—and always preference given to one's own, competence rarely rewarded. Ireland did not work well and did not work to general advantage; things might be better, some things for some people were better, and Ireland was not the only country with problems and scandals, but something was still wrong and visibly so. The agendas of the founding fathers—Pearse or Tone, certainly de Valera or even Lemass—had not been achieved, often not even addressed. Amid the emigration figures, the closure of hospitals, the failure of foreign factories and the intractably unemployed, the pleasures of the elite with credit cards grated. There were not only the flash cars bought on the never-never cramming the new roads but also new houses and new fortunes. How did former politicians end up with mansions? How did the price of everything go up and wages not keep pace? How could the middle class afford school bills and the poor hardly aspire to schools at all? Where did the money come from to keep open the trendy restaurants, the Dublin night clubs? What had happened to dear, dirty Dublin and the comfort of the country? What sort of place had Ireland become? The old days might be bad but even the new rock stars felt the country had been sold for returns soon wasted, for private profit.

And what was left for the Irish: a rising crime rate, the

pollution of the countryside, the bleak life in the housing estates, the endless emigration of those who wanted to stay, the erosion of family values, and little of substance in the new imported customs. The time of the comely maidens dancing at the crossroads had long gone, leaving empty dance halls, an abandoned countryside, violence in the cities, and the grandest triumph, Irish rock music, for export. Ireland was ruined on borrowed funds that brought neither growth nor tangible benefits for most. The country, hardly a nation once again, had become a dumping-ground for all the used fashions, tacky trends and transient fancies of a secular Western world. To walk up Grafton Street in Dublin is to see the same people one might find in Hannover or Chicago, dressed the same, humming the same tunes, but in Ireland waiting not for their ship to land but for it to sail. It was not, despite the glitter, the flash clothes, the statistics of promised growth, a happy country, if not as ruined as the Ulster Protestants were apt to claim. Much was the same that was a comfort, much was for the winning, much could happen. In a sense, however, the churches might still be full, but not Irish hearts. Those who did well spoke well of what had been accomplished and ignored the rest. Those who did not like the new Ireland could leave— and many did; or they could whinge about their betters— and some did.

All this, the malaise of the Republic and the accompanying anguish of social critics, the alarm of the creative, the new fears of pollution and urban blight, and even the hard word of orthodox republicans, was grist to Protestant analysis, analysis that need not begin at home. The Protestants look south to failure and so found it. Ireland may indeed have generated saints and scholars, but in this century the Irish, most neither saint nor scholar, leave for more promising opportunities. There seems no need for any new saints when the Roman church—despite everything, despite revelations and scandal and arrogance—can survey the full churches with satisfaction. As for scholars, they are apt to find chairs in far places, as do those without certificates and further schooling. For Protestants the one constant has always been the cost of Catholicism. Ireland may indeed be pious and easy, a safe society for a sedated people, but the parish priest still rules. And the rulers are corrupt: the only opportunities are divided among patrons, the bishops live as they choose, the vote is a matter of exchange, and the Dáil merely monitors entitlements. Those who have get. Cunning speculators have grown rich by Government contracts, invested for quick gain and built for turnover and for the Mercedes and long lunches. And the church has accepted the present exploitation: no Celtic liberation theology, only full churches and the odd scandal. Anyway, the poor are out of sight, concentrated in housing estates or urged to emigrate: no room for those who know no-one. Each a defender of the faith, none defended by the faith.

All this the Protestants take as a given, not gospel, not on the evidence of their own eyes but from the public record. Ask the republicans. Ask the Irish. Walk the streets of Dublin. Read the *Irish Times*. Whither Ireland? And any time the statistics give hope, the Irish pound does well, a new building goes up or the dole is not cut, there are those who say now the unionists will see the virtues of reunification: they care not for the Crown but the half-crown. This has been an abiding illusion, since economic prosperity for Ireland has been as elusive as unity and the fault always elsewhere: as soon as prosperous the Protestants will sign up. Sure aren't they Irish?

The Protestants, not even sure that they are Irish, certainly not Irish in tongue or heart, not content with subservience to church and a state operated for an establishment recently bounded by parish visions, see in the Republic a dreadful future. No number of half-crowns could ever change that. And economic prosperity will always be beyond those without liberty, without freedom and a work ethic, beyond the reach of any Catholic nationalist regime. How appropriate that the vision as nightmare could be found early on in the 1924 *Catholic Bulletin:* "The Irish nation is the Gaelic nation; its language and literature is the Gaelic language, its history is the history of the Gael. All other elements have no place in Irish national life, literature and tradition, save as far as they are assimilated into the very substance of Gaelic Speech, life and thought." In the language of the IRA and Falls Road this was "Brits out." Ireland in the future was to be Irish-Irish: a 32-county Free State that would not be free but would be Catholic in nature instead of catholic in aspiration: not only not Protestant but also not pluralist. And from 1921 this is what the nationalist majority wanted and assumed would occur; partition would put no permanent barrier to the march of the Celtic nation and so the Catholic Church. As for prosperity, that would be in Heaven, with frugal comfort ample for a supposedly spiritual people.

This Republic imagined by the unionists, the loyalists, the Ulster Protestants, quite one on this as on most matters but not all means, is a bleak, clear, demonstrable failure. It is a failure in secular matters. It is existentially corrupt in spirit. It is the sum of the Catholic Irish flaws. It is the inevitable contemporary failure when Rome, much less Rome as shaped by the Irish, is permitted to have control. And this failure neither glitters nor shines but is hidden by the misty nostalgia of the dreamy Celts and their descendants, by the nostalgia for a glorious and imaginary past and a promising and imaginary future. Seventy years of testing is ample: all the nationalist explanations and excuses have long been used up. This is the Ireland that the nationalists have produced. This is the future now. It can be weighed and is found wanting, not only by Ulster Protestants and radical nationalists but also by any fair observer. If Northern Ireland were to be amalgamated with such an entity, all the virtues of British Ulster would be lost—and so too the future of Irish Protestants. They would simply sink into the same bog.

First, then, Irish society—the establishment, the Government, those of one sort or another in charge in Dublin and out in the countryside—has through policy and private intervention failed to produce a viable society. Ireland is and has long been a remittance state, unable to maintain its population, supply the basics of middle-class Western society or engender sufficient economic growth to indicate a prosperous future. Second, the existing society, maintained by two centuries of emigration and warped marital practices, by misery for the poor and draconian taxes for the productive, is closed, narrow, warped by priestly injunctions and provincial values. Irish society drives the best into exile, censors the clever and independent, razes the old, and builds only for profit. The sleek new Euro-bureaucrats with their laptops are one with the men in mohair suits, those who skim the limited cream produced by the Irish milch cow. The Irish establishment is irresolute, greedy, closed to advice or variety, often genial in public but mean in private, a cunning but irresponsible elite ruling over a people feckless and amusing and prone to violence if the cost is right. Third, the Ireland of scholars and saints, poets and musicians, a country with the wind at one's back and a jig at the pub is myth packaged by the tourist board and sold to visitors in an advertising campaign. There are no tours to the bleak housing estates that ring Dublin, no visits to the mean hill-farms, no list of this week's emigration total or last week's convictions for armed robbery and drug sales. The real, ruined Ireland of the nasty rich and the sullen poor is papered over with posters of the ruins of Cashel.

Ireland is a splendid place for the rich, for golf, for tourist tours, for those who want to evade taxes elsewhere or drop by to tug on their roots. It is a grand place to watch the horses and feel the rain; but for many in the twenty-six counties, outside the circle of greed, it is a limited, dank, unpleasant life. The Republic is an island republic ruinously ruled by Roman vices, by habit, by still another generation of Catholic peasants newly brought to university degrees. And as for religion, that is the singular foundation of all the flaws of the Irish state and Irish society. For Ulster Protestants the overwhelming cause is not the Gael but the Catholic imperative.

The Catholic religion ensures a closed society, requires obedience, and offers rituals, not inspiration. It inevitably produces a flawed society unless diluted with other influences. A Roman Catholic society is content with the promise of salvation and the pleasures of the moment. In America or even in Germany such a prospect is avoided because of the presence of sufficient Protestants. In Ireland there are not sufficient Protestants, were not in the twenty-six counties and would not be in thirty-two. A united Ireland would be dominated by the Irish Catholic ethos, and this is what the Protestants of Ulster abhor: a society compelled by habit and history to obey at the cost of free will, access to God, and a decent, productive life.

Such a vision of any present or future Irish society can seemingly be buttressed by the real: statistics of emigration or the failure of industrial investment. The Roman church is just as dreadful as imagined by the Free Presbyterians: the newspapers in the Republic are filled with revelations about the Catholic clergy, arrested drunk, arrested for molesting children, stealing from the parish, lying in public. And always there is the continued intervention of Rome in Caesar's business. The system protects the child molester because he is a priest. The system closes this publication because of sexual prudery or fails to distribute that one because the orthodox are affronted. The authorities see that there is no promotion for the intemperate critic of the church—the one church. Don't ask the Apprentice Boys on the Dunloy road but ask Noel Browne what Rome can still do. Ask those who advocate not divorce but abortion, ask anyone in the parish who dares the priest, loves beyond the altar, or violates the norm.

There is little room in such an Ireland for another church. The Protestant cathedrals are empty, museums for the tourists, the country churches sealed, those in the suburbs sold for office space, the congregations wasting. There are at best one or two token Protestants in the Dáil, and a scramble to find a token representative on this committee or that. There are not enough Protestants to go round. Vast public concern about Protestant feelings simply hides Catholic interests: they seek divorce not for the Protestants but for their own convenience and as argument that the Republic is mature, secular, changed, when it is not, remains indolent, confessional, the same. Everywhere the Ulster Protestants look, especially in the pages of the *Irish Times* or the *Irish Independent*, there is evidence, compelling evidence.

The sleek and well-educated civil servants in Dublin departments, the countryman who represents his own in the Dáil, the decent tradesmen, the clerk and the solicitor, the big farmer, all the contented, content that they are still in Ireland, content with their share of the wealth, cannot countenance such a statement. Their Ireland is vital, alive, various, changing, soon prosperous, already promising. They may in the past have lived in a Catholic country for a Catholic people—and not surprisingly, for 95 per cent of the citizens were Catholic. Those days are passing, or past. They do indeed go to Mass on Sunday. Does not Paisley go to church on Sunday? Ireland is pious, north and south. There is room in the Republic for all, will be room for all in a united Ireland. And in the West national differences are fading—the Balkans an aberration, the Caucasus far away, the Basques forgotten. Ireland is thus in and of the new Europe, attracting investment, shaping a new infrastructure. Ireland will be part of a single market, a single culture, both popular and elegant, a new world built on the old. Ireland and so Europe is eager to settle the Northern problem and move on to peace and prosperity and for Ireland even an end to forced emigration. There is nothing greatly wrong with the Republic—nothing that time and skill and good will not manage.

And not only is Ireland OK but it also offers—whatever the ultimate form of the Irish nation—security and opportunity for the Protestant. Piety is no sin. Church-going in Limerick or Sligo is voluntary and no different from that of the pious church-goers who worship as Free Presbyterians or at an evangelical hall. Christian morality is an asset to the state, to society. The Pope does not rule Ireland: his wishes were not reflected in the vote on divorce. And family values are little different north and south. The hierarchy is open to criticism: the newspapers were delighted to spread the failings and foibles of the clergy. Scandal is scandal, north or south. And most within the church are decent, dedicated, pure in heart and mind and no longer aspirant to parish domination. They do not want to convert Protestants but to welcome them, offer parity in esteem and freedom of worship. Being Catholic in any case was not the obstacle to development elsewhere: the Italian miracle, the Irish-Americans rising to power and prominence, the triumphs of history, Florence or Vienna or Paris.

And so the nationalists, while accepting some criticism—the economic statistics cannot easily be denied—deny the whole charge. Ireland is not so awful nor the fate of Protestants in a united Ireland so grim. Nationalists can, but rarely do, point out the general failings of the Protestant state for a Protestant people on terms beyond the oppression of the minority Catholics. To disinterested observers British Ulster appears equally narrow, equally an economic disaster, equally cosy and corrupt and far more sectarian and divisive than the twenty-six counties. Yet the nationalists, other than focusing on the injustices done to nationalists and the sectarian nature of British Ulster, are not apt to detail the flaws of the province. For the nationalists there is no real need to detail the specific flaws of the failed entity, for the great failure is that Northern Ireland exists—what matter details? Too many details of past flaws too often repeated may make future conciliation and accommodation more difficult. So better to get along by going along—and there is much to go along with: a common suspicion of the British, a common distaste for republicans, a common island, and even the comfort of all Irish quarrels.

The only remaining real quarrel is for Dublin the manner of accommodation; the peace process, all assume, means movement, however slow, towards a common destiny. It is not the nature of British Ulster that is to be criticised but its existence: unnatural, maintained artificially, to no-one's benefit. Its very existence is unfair, sectarian, unnatural, and so must go in time. The radical nationalists assume the sooner the better, but the wise would as soon see the process vastly extended, not in Albert Reynolds's lifetime nor even his children's, later, much later, when costs can be paid by others, if there are more costs to be paid. No-one likes to think of the Troubles as a down-payment on unity, more an abnormality.

So, unlike unionist critics of the Republic, nationalist critics of Northern Ireland focus only on the national issue, relying on logic, history, and sentiment, seldom deploying economic development figures or housing statistics. These have been ignored in arguing the case for unity, the case against partition, and so ignored when deployed by the unionists against the Republic—not really the issue for nationalists—except to strengthen the assumption that, since they seem to matter to others, the Northern unionist is most concerned by the fiscal terms of accommodation, the half-crown not the Crown. And such a concern can be met by material goods, unlike the great dream of a united Ireland, which generates, or at least once generated, spiritual energy and aspiration not easily deflected by petrol prices or the gross national product.

Thus the Protestant case against a united Ireland is a material one that most in the Republic have over the years chosen to discard—the self-interested message of bigots and braggarts underwritten by London taxes and London interests. Why bother at all? Why counter development statistics, social welfare benefits or dole numbers when these are not the issue but rather the justice of the national cause?

Anyway, the unionists have so blotted their copybook, have ruled so badly when given the opportunity that no case need be made. Certainly Dublin has never imagined presenting a closely reasoned account of the returns of a Catholic society for all—for all those Protestants now gone, for all those Catholics who must accept instruction. What Dublin stresses is the national case, which needs no statistics and is politically correct for the times—the problem with any religious argument. The Protestant case is seen as self-serving and irrelevant, because there are no takers. Certainly there are no takers in the Republic and few who bother to respond. Most abroad find the Northern Ireland case unconvincing, because few bother with the attacks on the Republic but on the record of Stormont and the evidence of sectarianism.

The limitations and shortcomings of the Irish state in any case have ready explanations: no-one in Ireland is ever responsible but rather history and geography, powerful external forces and bad luck. Everything, every time, seemed to rest on the national excuse: we did not begin with a fair start. The nationalists evaded responsibility—a response long inculcated by Catholic habits, where responsibility was assumed by Rome and obedience left as ample return. Dublin's explanation, at times made explicit but always to be found over the pint, in political discussion and as basis for all else, consisted of a litany of grievance. Any conversation concerning Irish history tended to fall into dissertations on just grievances: the past as ruin, exploitation, concessions wheedled or extorted by recourse to physical force. Patriot oratory was taken as real; economic theory was shaped to independence from London in all things. Everything that was English should be burned but their coal. Everything should be Irish: buy Irish and in time the Irish will prosper—and if not there will be ample for frugal comfort. To go with that comfort would be a pure and decent society without the temptations and sins of the modern industrial state.

Yet the end of all Irish economic strategies, all social planning, all the wisdom of the Roman church or the free market, all the plans and development boards, all the building and renewing and ravaging, was that the country was not viable. Employment had really only increased within the huge state bureaucracy, and the cost of jobs was high, as were the numbers of unemployed and the numbers who emigrated.

In sum, Ireland, if a nation, had generated an establishment that existed on entitlements, the misery of the poor, the departure of the ambitious, and the gratitude of their betters. Any Protestant could and did see this at once, recognised the sloth and feckless Catholic behaviour transported to government or administration. Any Protestant critic could and would cite the repeated waves of emigration, the unemployment totals, the greed of the new men, and the ruin of the countryside. No member of the Irish establishment would or did pay any heed. The Northern unionists had no right to criticise—after all, indigenous criticism from radicals, ecologists, historians, the Greens and the indignant students as well as much of the press and great numbers of citizens had not saved Viking Dublin nor moderated the urban horror. This simply proved the Protestant contention that in a Catholic society criticism is an affront, the governing bureaucracy is shaped by the authoritarian aspects of church and therefore society. The Irish deserve their bunkers.

The Protestant criticism appeared to be self-serving, warped, deploying any evidence that could be effective, whether accurate in detail or even congenial with logic. In economic matters, for example, the Irish record was poor, but over the last generation there had been real progress, and progress judged against successful European standards, not those of the Third World. In 1995, according to the European Commission, the rate of Irish inflation was low, less than Britain if more than Finland and Denmark. The total Government debt as a percentage of the GDP was high, higher than Finland or Denmark or Britain but far less than Italy or Belgium, and the budget deficit was low, lower than Britain and Finland if a bit higher than Denmark. Ireland was about average in Europe and much better than Greece and Italy—and a bit better than Britain. Investment had not always succeeded, not always produced lasting employment, but no record was perfect. And the balance of the economy had changed, had become more than minor market and exported livestock. Ireland was on the move, congenial to high-tech manufacture, filled with a skilled labour force, constructing an advanced infrastructure—on the high road, despite the persistence of certain problems.

Of course the great change was the increasing separation of the Irish economy from the British and the decline of the largely unprofitable agricultural sector—still an emotional and ideological commitment but hardly a factor for the Irish future. Ireland might still have high unemployment and many might emigrate, but the country was hardly the disaster area the unionists were apt to depict. Each scandal had resulted in higher standards. Each egregious development blunder had engendered reform. No-one, no institution, was above criticism, not even and especially the Catholic Church, seeming by 1996 the favourite target of the media. And who were the unionists to criticise, given the historical record and the economic failures of Northern Ireland?

Few Protestants were apt to focus on the emigration from Northern Ireland, or the unemployment rate, or the remittances that arrived each year from London and Brussels, or to dwell on the ruins imposed by urban planning as ruthless and ill-conceived as that of Dublin. In fact if there were defending to be done, the unionist tendency was to explain away the Stormont regime, where criticism was justified in some part.

Yet the nationalists' case was not open and shut. There were unionist explanations and other statistics. Discrimination was not the province of one community; the inequalities were shared. The times in any case had changed. Still, it was the past failures of the political system that were defended rather than the general record of that system. Whatever its virtues and vices, to the disinterested the accomplishments of British Ulster with the Unionists in power or out while the British government ruled directly from London through the Northern Ireland Office were limited. Ulster consumed, did not produce. The Troubles simply meant that more went for security than before—how much no-one could really tease out of the statistics, for nearly any expense had a security component, from urban planning to traffic control. A reasonable figure was that 45 per cent of employment was security-related, while all the other industries and agencies dried up, closed down, failed or puttered along as always. Before the Troubles, British Ulster had not paid and its advocates could see no real economic advantage in Irish unity, so the remaining assumption was that after the Troubles the province would still not pay. British Ulster as ideal had nothing to do with the failure of DeLorean, the cost of the RUC, the price of Malone Road reality, or the number of high-tech jobs to come.

The Protestants tended to dwell on perceptions and intangibles, the feel of freedom, the validity of the Protestant ethic, the failure of Catholic enterprise—and, if need be, the record of the Republic. Anyway, and as always, statistics were a two-way street, open to what the traffic might bear. One analyst might see high Catholic unemployment in Northern Ireland as a result of discrimination while another might see it as obvious outcome of sloth and reliance on charity. And the honest, simple Protestant did not dwell on reasons but on knowing that he or she was different, better, saved in many ways. And besides, it was easier to find fault with the others than defend one's own. What the Protestants sought they found, and did not imagine. And what they imagined often became reality. Just as the Irish nationalists sought explanation for the failures of the state in the legacy of the past or irreversible present conditions, sought to evade responsibility, so too did Protestants deploy history and the Catholic ethos to explain the perceived disaster of the Republic. And, like many others, they evaded any responsibility for similar failures in Ulster. Ulster had been the victim of history, world forces had subverted shipbuilding and linen, the DeLorean fiasco or the failure of Lear aircraft had been imposed, not indigenous error. The Troubles, arising from Irish ambition, had ruined the province. London was not sufficiently committed to Northern needs. Despite all this, much had been done, most of those needs had been met, and even the old charges of discrimination had produced reform legislation, new rules, new commissions, and new opportunities; there was new housing and new roads and new investment.

What is crucial is not whether the case is valid but that it is believed: this is Protestant reality. The adjusted analysis was in fact almost a mirror image of the case of the Dublin apologists. Unionist minds were also closed to emigration, unemployment, deficit spending, and economic failure; the Protestant ethic did not produce general prosperity in British Ulster any more than Rome rule had in the Republic. The two sides passed like ships at night in a dark fog of perceptions, guns firing at different targets. The unionists did not defend their record of accomplishment where they were vulnerable but only the political positions necessary to counter subversion, while the nationalists too fudged their own record to attack the sectarian politics of the Unionists. Everyone used 1969 as a base-line as if nothing much had changed—no reforms, no three thousand dead, no IRA or UVF or vast investment in the province. The unionists attacked and the nationalists attacked and no-one minded the shop or defended how the books had been kept. The nationalists attacked the political record of Northern Ireland, imagining that the Republic needed no defence. The unionists saw failure, but only in the Republic, only by Catholics. For unionists the focus was Irish incompetence. The nationalists' attack was on historical injustice in Northern Ireland. So an attack on discriminatory hiring practices at Queen's University was subversive for many unionists, and the disappearance of the Protestant population in the Republic was ignored by most nationalists. The mutual emigration loss was assumed to be a nationalist problem, the mutual failure of enterprise not a problem at all, and the damages of a sectarian society a matter for the unionists.

As was the wont of all, few talked to the other's point, few listened to the other; and when an exception was made, none seemed to hear what was being said. For years assumptions went unchallenged, because on such matters there was a dialogue of the deaf. No-one wanted to hear what no-one wanted to hear. Much of the "dialogue" was crafted to appear real but was not, and nowhere was this more true than where the disputants were closest, in Northern Ireland, where the wall between British Ulster and nationalist residents was all but impenetrable.

The Ulster Protestants, and so too the Irish Catholics of all thirty-two counties, were really only interested in reinforcing previously held convictions. Still, the unionist attacks on Dublin accomplishment were valid and could only be answered in part. This was seldom done: the Irish special case satisfied Dublin. They ignored the past failures of the state and claimed the future by right and so infuriated the unionists. The figures on the failures of the Republic and the disappearance of the Protestants were revelatory only when read and considered, and few in the Republic did. Few in London bothered: they knew little of Ireland, and this was often too much. They too, like everyone concerned, knew what they knew: Britain was part of the solution, not the problem, was neutral, fair, just, and decent. Old grievances were too old to count, and new initiatives were without ulterior motive or even secondary benefits.

The Government in Dublin found it convenient to take the British establishment at its own valuation; the returns were more promising than pointing out the enormous psychological investment London had in Ireland or the various more recent grievances arising from both the dirty war and British arrogance. Better accept the British disinterest as real, hoping that from time to time the British would accept Irish interests as mutual—an enormously difficult feat for an establishment disdainful of the Irish and whatever the Irish might advocate. Far better for Dublin to push the national issue with moderation, point out unionist flaws. Far easier to ignore the Protestant case as irrelevant and politically incorrect. And few observers elsewhere examined the unionist case: the media knew who must be to blame.

So almost all unionist criticism of Irish society was judged unfair, outdated, the skewing of reality, the efforts of bigots and rascals to misdirect attention. Even the British seldom bothered to support the unionists, seldom bothered with Ireland in fact. And so the Irish-Irish case congenially presented by reasonable men seemed more logical than the shrill attacks of unionists, provincial gentry or Orangemen in funny costumes, ministers better suited to revival meetings, and evangelical ministers holding office. Who could listen seriously to such as these? Free Ireland had not done badly. Irish family values and pace made the country pleasant to visit, pleasant to stay in. Dublin was small, sophisticated, charming, and soft in the gloaming, filled with articulate people and still some Georgian vistas. Censorship was mild and rarely applied. Artists were awarded bursaries, given tax relief: a Northern poet who had come to Dublin had won a Nobel Prize; what more could one want? Social structure enforced by law was the society the people wanted. Many from afar admired it, admired the new Ireland with a woman president, computer factories, and rising standards. The Irish now could impose their wishes on divorce or even abortion: the Constitution was open to adjustment to respond to secular demand. The old ways were gone or going. Even the IRA was closed for lack of popular demand and there was no real prospect of a gunman's return; the militants, sullen and covert, returned to the shelf. The church was on the defensive and the national debt down. The people flocked to the arts, filled the theatres, read new books, attended the museums. Brian Friel was on Broadway and Irish actors in the films. Irish popular music topped the charts. More people knew of U2 or the Hot House Flowers, a new group on the world tour every year or so, than remembered Bobby Sands. The unionists exaggerated: Irish society was and had been—north and south—conservative, narrow, pious, often self-righteous, suspicious of the exotic, and provincial, and so too the laws. The quick and the bright had often come to confusion in any of the thirty-two counties, especially in those more rural counties where time moved slowly. This might change— Dublin as an art centre or Belfast home to poets—but neither Protestants in Ballymena nor Catholics in Dingle were apt to advocate abortion on demand or the distribution of X-rated videos or champion the trendy art ideas of London or New York. Few in Ireland would skip church or welcome marriage in the registry office. Some did both without shame. Times had changed, even if most were pious in deed and often thought, voted against change, suspected the unfamiliar in concept or prose, or opted for yesterday as guide.

Ireland, however, even rural Ireland, had not been frozen in place. There had been changes, and, as the Protestants pointed out to all, if few heeded them, one of the most visible changes was the disappearance of the Protestants in the Republic after 1921. In matters of piety in the Republic, it was the services not attended and then not held that attracted the comment. The Protestants had been isolated, marginalised, and ultimately made unwelcome. The Irish-Irish had been subservient to Rome. The non-sectarian republicans became in power sectarian, Catholic defenders. And much was imposed without public declaration. Every Protestant knew this—and many Catholics would admit it. In Catholic Ireland, Rome rules OK. Over forty years after the Mother and Child Scheme, Rome still felt doctrine should rule, even in the divorce amendment, with the Polish Pope comfortable with intervention. Imagine the uproar if the Pope had told the American or French electorate how to vote! Holy Ireland still existed, nationalism a patina over Catholicism and Catholicism still unrepentant, ambitious, authoritarian; the issues of the Reformation were alive and well in Ireland. And the Protestants, uncertain of their role, content in British Ulster but not in Ireland, noted that in Irish-Ireland, in the Republic, their own kind had gone, empty churches, the great houses burned and the small ones abandoned, no place for the Protestant to flourish. The Protestant critics had to hand very telling incidents. There were the teachers fired for non-academic reasons, a librarian without a job, novels banned for the sake of general morals and ample quotations from reactionary bishops. For those who cared to look, in novels and in real life, in attitudes and assumptions, who cared to listen to the Angelus each night on state radio and television, the Republic was a sectarian state; that it had become so without pogroms or a final solution, without violence, was evidence of the insidious nature of the majority—expulsion by ethos.

The Ulster Protestants spent a great deal of time looking at what others felt were exceptions and oddities, because the great threat was perceived, not evidenced in blood or even much legislation. The special position of the Roman church was best noted by the disappearance of the Protestant community, not in a teacher fired, and noted by the privileges and immunities of the priests. The militant Protestant found ample evidence of the hand of the parish priest. There was a double standard in personal conduct and a Roman intrusion into all matter of Government business.

The Irish Protestant need only look, and there was the evidence. The Irish Catholic did not look. The Roman interventions were so accepted, such a natural aspect of society, that the Catholic nationalists never noticed any contradiction between religious duty and state responsibility. Few in Dublin cared to remember Dev waiting in his limousine or the other evidence of Roman rule. Few cared to note the absence of Protestants on the Irish scene. So benign had been their gradual disappearance that most in the Republic hardly noticed their going. And certainly those they knew were no different from the other Irish; except on close questioning, few actually knew any Protestants, for there were not enough left to know. Irish freedom had not seemingly been extended to Protestants. Even after generations of freedom in the matter of divorce, two referendums were required, and the final favourable vote was a tiny minority. Freedom was not intrinsic to conservative Irish Catholic society, as it was assumed to be in conservative British Ulster.

Irish-Ireland had always been a Catholic state for a Catholic people: so said the Constitution, so voted the politicians, so assumed the people. And what else could it be but Rome rule? Regardless of the specific agenda of the hierarchy, the Irish people were Catholics and so acted like Catholics—or Catholics as imagined by Presbyterian elders and evangelical ministers and the Church of Ireland gentry in big houses. And nothing had been offered to change their perception of the Republic: it was still a Catholic country and all that this meant, a lesser society with limited tangible accomplishment and no welcome for dissent, no place for Protestants. Catholic Ireland peopled by those inherently inferior could only display its limitations inherent in an authoritarian sect, could but fail to prosper, inevitably would shape a society narrow, parochial, obedient to dogma, uncreative, yet imprudent and prone to violence. The Irish had always been wild and very uncivil.

This was and is the Republic seen by the Protestants of the North. This Catholic Ireland is by no means imagined, a rude stereotype sold in Sunday sermons and during the oratory of the marching season. The Republic is in many ways just the failure that the critics in Ballykeel and Portadown perceive. The grim numbers of the debt and development statistics and emigration are there. The dole queues are real; so too are the isolated new housing estates without facilities, holding-pens for those without the wit to emigrate. Poverty in the countryside is more difficult to find but just as vicious, and the old people at risk from criminals, just as in the cities. And at the centre, very near the tourist trade, are the drug dealers and the same old poor driven to the same old crimes. It is a nation that has not saved its language, kept its people at home or cherished its artistic heritage but instead has imposed the standards and visions of the publican at the crossroads. The state has written into law the strictures of Rome, and the establishment, replete, well-fed, shameless, has put on the Celtic mask to welcome the tourists at festivals and summer schools. It is a land that had no place for the Protestants, a lost people. It is a land that has no place and can be no attraction for Irish Protestants of Ulster. And their perception of Dublin is not imagined, just ignored by those chattering in the new French restaurants over expense-account lunches or hanging about the rear of filthy pubs waiting for a dealer. The Irish have staged their presence so long they are hardly aware of reality, certainly not reality as an aspect of the national issue.

In any case, for Ulster Protestants no Dublin excuses or

historical explanations can change present reality: Rome rule has meant failure, failure on a national level, failure in daily life, failure to be constructive, creative, and productive. The Republic is a failed entity, a province with a seat in the United Nations and delusions of grandeur run on next year's overdraft. Ireland of the Gaels is fallow, not fertile, closed, not open. And so say they all in Ballymena, along the road to Dunloy. Irish-Ireland has a final solution to Irish Protestant history but not one that can easily be imposed on British Ulster. There is nothing the Ulster Protestant can imagine the Republic might have on offer worth taking: no common heritage, no love of tongue or tradition, no unity of purpose, no common enemy or agenda. No scholar can summon up a mutual heritage or any politician a common programme. British Ulster imagines itself different and so it is different, a matter of perception. Unity would end diversity. Unity would compound existing failures—and the Protestants see Dublin failures everywhere.

Even if the Republic were as successful as Japan, an economic miracle, if in some strange alchemy Rome turned into dynamic instead of plague, tangibles will not open the door to the kingdom of God and will not save the Ulster soul. Money matters, but not much, not in contrast to the civility of British life, the imperial heritage, the long roots of Protestant freedom. The nationalists have often chosen to assume that driven by the Protestant ethic the Northern unionist would accept a united Ireland for his purse's sake: money would tell—the cherished half-crown delusion. Change the statistics, shape prosperity, and the unionists would queue up to be within a single successful country. Just as republicans saw the Ulster Protestant as Irish badly dressed by the British, so too did many nationalists see that same Protestant as merely an economic man driven by fiscal imperatives. What the Republic needed was to succeed, Ireland to be made attractive to the others: the pound would rise and the economy flourish, the Constitution could be changed, parity of esteem offered, positions and prospects dealt out, prosperity promised, all possible once partition had gone. In fact the returns of peace have repeatedly been shaped by nationalists in economic terms to attract the economic man, just as parity in esteem has been offered to reassure the other tradition. All this is wishful thinking and demeaning, assumes that the Protestants are false to their faith, open to offer. And the republicans have rarely bothered to tender an offer, since they are assured that Irish Protestants are unionists only as a tactic, are basically one with the majority, will discard the Union Jack, the Lambeg drum and the Ulster dream once the British have ceded sovereignty and there is no option but violence.

And violence for what? British Ulster is an artificial concept. Ulster as a state is not viable, has no history or heritage. The unionists and the Protestants, the advocates of British Ulster, will sooner or later accept the undeniable benefits of Irish unity. Loyalties will change and so become Irish loyalists, as Irish as the Irish—for the real Irish are assumed to be nationalists, certainly not residents of an imaginary British Ulster. More or less, in a greater or lesser degree, all the Irish-Irish are apt to agree. Those in the six counties are first of all Irish, born and bred in Ireland and so Irish like all the other Irish. The Protestants are assumed to be less dedicated to their faith, their land and their history than the dominant tradition, more open to tangibles, and so in many ways a lesser people maintained for British interests. British Ulster is not really British and only a bit of Ulster but contains Protestants who are really Irish. What is needed is to equal or remove advantages supplied by the

British, and the Protestants will then be as one with the Irish-Irish.

Only very considerable innocence of the dynamics of British Ulster encourages such analysis. Dublin no more wants to hear Ballymena than Ballymena wants to hear Dublin. And those Catholics along the road at Dunloy are nearly as far from the marchers as those in Dublin, just more vulnerable. Proximity in Ireland is apt to encourage ignorance rather than the reverse: toleration cannot abide too much reality. In any case there is no realistic prospect of all-Ireland prosperity other than the returns already in hand from two years of the peace process. Certainly some costs and some profits are down: security costs are down, MI5 with no sure Irish mission, compensation payments down, less work at the hospital trauma centres; but then glaziers have lower sales and the black economies of both traditions have uncertain futures. Even with the most imaginative projections beyond the tourists few see vast changes if the border goes.

And so why even imagine unity? A united Ireland offers no enhanced market, no new pool of capacity, no suddenly released economic—or for that matter psychic—energy. Historical problems merged are still problems. Those unionists who rightly stress the limited economic appeal of a united Ireland are apt to stress the existing failure of the Irish economy and ignore the failures of both British Ulster and Britain. Ireland is a black zone, with economic and social statistics unmatched in western Europe except by Britain. Alone or together no-one has done very well. The unionists are not really interested in economics other than as an indicator of the lack of Irish-Irish capacity and enterprise. They are not interested in the price of amalgamation—if so they could any day go off to Britain and abandon Ulster. They are certainly not interested in their own economic record. All the chatter about cross-border institutions cannot hide the reality that a free, united Ireland dominated by a Roman majority would be simply more of the same, six more counties to add to the unemployment, the failure of industry, the rigidity of society—and for the six counties, all this without the undeniable benefits and entitlements available from Britain.

Worse, with the promise of penury comes the certainty of an end not to Protestant domination, as the reformers plead, but to Protestant existence. No matter the excuses, the reasons given, the free choices made for marriage or gain, the disappearance of whole categories and classes as the times changed, the fact is clear that the Protestant community in Irish-Ireland has all but gone. Why would this not be the case in a united Ireland? Again there would be a Protestant minority, rich or poor, but one that would inevitably face similar choices in an uncongenial ethos. They too would move away from the countryside and then from Ireland, see marriage, education and opportunity elsewhere, drift away to be noted in statistics, plaques on the walls of churches abandoned. Their heritage would be forgotten, their accomplishments dust, their halls smeared with graffiti—Dunloy done large. And then all thirty-two counties would be Irish-Irish, as the nationalists want, and would be Catholic, as Rome expects, and British Ulster would be lost, as both foresee. Even if there were iron-clad, copper-fastened guarantees to the Protestant minority, even a return of twenty-six counties to the Commonwealth, if not the United Kingdom—an accommodation with a certain small appeal—these would hardly transform the country, still inhabited by a majority of Catholics and these sooner or later somehow to dominate by osmosis, by the gradual propagation of their agenda, by the absorption or isolation of the minority. This is the Catholic nature, given the opportunity. Look at the record, say the Protestant divines and Orange orators. Look at Dunloy as well as the empty pews in St Patrick's and the token Protestants in the Dáil. And this inevitable process is what matters, not the bottom line, not any shared tradition, not similarities or mutual advantage, not the declared benefits of unity but the reality that is to come: the imposition of Catholicism on all. The minority in a united Ireland will inevitably convert, amalgamate, or, as in the past, emigrate. There can be no accommodation with the Republic.

Somehow British Ulster has managed, if not easily, to adjust not only to the minority about them but also to the majority in Ireland. "Not another inch" is possible without too great risks. Such adjustment can be made without giving an inch of what is vital, a land won from history and defended for three centuries despite the odds. British Ulster, cursed by geography, poorly understood, seldom appreciated, has persisted, especially this century. No longer ask what British Ulster can give but what British Ulster must maintain to be free.

So the Republic has become a nightmare to the Protestants of British Ulster, all Irish communality long lost: who cares who revived the Irish language, led the Irish Volunteers, won Nobel Prizes for Ireland? Those Protestants are dead and gone, replaced by a pan-nationalist front, a front for a failed Catholic entity. To the citizens of the Republic, to most of the nationalists, especially those in the diaspora, the Protestant image of Ireland is awful, a self-serving caricature of a fearful and vindictive people. To the more disinterested the actual success of a free Irish state leaves much to be desired, especially in contrast to the congenial image projected by apologists, the assumptions of the Irish establishment, and the impressions of the tourists. Much that the Protestants depict is quite true, more true at one time than another, not all true at the same time. Ireland as a small democratic country not greatly rewarded by nature or perhaps by history has emerged as a warm and genial society, largely safe and often creative, admired abroad, core of a great outreach that touches far places to their advantage. This is the Ireland imagined and admired in the Dáil, at the pub, in lecture halls. It is the Ireland that works. Much that is in Ireland does not work at all or very well, and this is apt to be denied. Mostly those who are critical are judged malicious or naïve, knaves if they criticise or fools if they accept the Ireland of the tourist poster. All in Ireland realise that while there is great hope yet, the promise of the founders of 1916 has not been made good. Those responsible feel that this time or the next matters will be made right, the debt paid, emigration over, the unemployment problem ameliorated. The Irish problems are amenable to Irish solutions, are tangible matters, not, as the Protestant insists, matters of the ethos. And the last real problem, that of partition, once ameliorated, will release the nation to full prosperity, if not tomorrow then in the certain future.

The Protestants continue to see a stagnant 26-county entity driven by obsolete and decaying financial institutions, lacking in social services and social graces, mean, bleak, divided by class and caste, badly ruled, and inevitably doomed by the very nature of Catholicism in command. Change is illusion. The next time will be like the last time, illusion sold by the bureaucrats of the day. All Irish wonders are shaped in the future tense: the record will not really bear the weight of the nationalist dream. And this in reverse is the view from Dublin as well: Ulster as nightmare, a bleak province that, because partitioned off from the rest of Ireland, is inevitably doomed by the very nature of that division. Both see the other as failed, and neither is without evidence. Ireland has not done especially well in many matters; and certainly a generation of Troubles has merely emphasised this.

If anyone in Ireland chose to notice, most distressing for both unionists and nationalists would be the reality of the United Kingdom, with or without British Ulster. There can be seen a very similar pattern of failed development, limited social benefits, a damaging class structure, ineffectual political leadership, a miserable poor, truculent and potentially violent in their estates, and ethnic quarrels. There has long been an often irresponsible elite, a history of bad choices, and as exports unruly football fans, unwanted manufactured goods, machines that do not work and cars that do not sell—and arms bought by the shoddy. If the United Kingdom is not a failed entity, however composed, it is a failure in contrast to Continental success. This for the Protestants means that the British way into the future holds little rational promise—a proven failure despite the local Protestant ethic, despite the assumed civility of British society, more efficacious governance, and a more desirable historical tradition. The faith offers no returns. The Lord's work does not prosper, and the bottom line remains unpromising. This would be, if examined, an unpalatable conclusion. For the nationalists who are apt to define being Irish as not being English, refusing to stand in queues, to arrive on time or to play cricket, their republic statistically, on paper and in real life fits the British model closely. In fact Ireland is easily encompassed into the local pattern, one more of the British islands, no different in the charts than the Isle of Man: English-speaking, Christian, old and quarrelsome, divided by class and dreary by nature, some progress but no miracles. In fact from London Irish-Ireland is no different from Britain, not special at all, quaint, on occasion prone to violence, inefficient if poetic, a mix of resort and slum, a show staged by peasants.

Of course this refusal to see Ireland as special infuriates the Irish-Irish, just as the refusal to see Ulster as British infuriates the Irish Protestants, united on this one matter that both find unpalatable: British perceptions. Ulster wants to be successful and integrated, and the Republic wants to be different and successful, and neither is the case. In economic growth the only difference is that Ireland, north and south, is statistically a tiny bit better off than Britain. Irish nationalism and pride or no, Protestant tradition or no, Ireland and Britain are one in their failure to compete in the West economically over the century. They are one in the collateral problems of social welfare and criminal justice, educational opportunities or class distinctions, and elite responsibility. There has been vast improvement, great growth, times are better all round, but only in contrast to the base-line. In competition with France or Germany, Britain and Ireland have been all but marginalised: in contrast with the Japanese or Americans, whether in patterns of economic development, prospects for education, advancement or comfort they more closely resemble a Third World entity. Comfort can only be taken that British and Irish culture is safe, that the quality of life is a reward, that the times are changing, that the irresponsibility of the powerful, the habits of the parish and the greed of the establishment are going or may be going, that the failure of justice or the persistence of snobbery is a passing phase. Still, Ulster would be even then no different from Ireland nor Ireland from Britain.

All this is quite immaterial to the Protestant case. They are content that their ideals are superior, that a traditional love of simplicity, freedom and Protestant fraternity establishes a better and more productive society—if not quite yet then as soon as the Troubles are over and nationalists no longer a debilitating threat. It is not, however, even the failures of the Irish that appal the Protestants but the success of the Irish in absorbing or expelling the others, the Irish Protestants. Where have all the Protestants gone if Ireland is a non-sectarian, tolerant and genial society? Why have they gone? They have gone because they would not amalgamate and could not prosper. And this is the major complaint and the one hardest to deter: the Republic is Catholic in people and therefore society and hence in the nature of institutions and assumptions. The republicans may feel this irrelevant, the nationalists feel it no bar to a pluralist society, but for the Protestants it is the unalterable reality that really needs no further evidence, no charts or graphs, no data. The Protestants seek invidious distinctions, not countervailing evidence. They know what they know.

This is the root cause of difference and the explanation of all other failures. Their own failures may not be so explained, nor those of the British in Britain, but this is not the issue. The key difference for the Protestants is that their province has protected the Protestants, and the province is in turn protected by the union. British Ulster is safe for Protestants. Long practice has kept the mixture from mingling, kept the different different. Divided traditions mean that the majority is still viable and the minority only present. The partition of society into them and us, the empowered and the isolated, those within the British tradition and those without, means that domination keeps the province from being swallowed by the Dublin establishment, the professed goal of Irish nationalism. This is the great difference—not the unemployment figures north and south, nor emigration nor the imagined benefits of liberty and dissent, nor new motorways nor the tidy towns nor the lack of a British economic miracle. Any deal would open British Ulster to dilution and so death by instalments.

In Northern Ireland the crucial strategy is to rely on loyalty to the strictures of the faith, by a defence of history's heritage, by holding firm to past example, by resisting any change under whatever guise: Ulster says no. For decades Northern Ireland did better economically, offered better benefits and access to Britiain's dole but did not feel engaged in competition with the other Ireland. That Ireland was simply ignored, defined as failure if dangerous and forgotten, unknown and unwanted, seldom visited and labelled awful. There was until 1968 no need to say "no" too often, only to keep the Orange troops in line, the Unionist machine ticking over, the system happy. After 1968 a more active defence was required and the "no" more necessary than ever, since London kept saying "yes." Then the unionists' focus shifted to the specific failures of the Republic heretofore ignored; the nationalist future must be shown, to Ulster Protestants, to the British, to all, as inevitably bleak. So the Protestants persist in a defence of every inch against the driving currents of Catholic nationalism that would by erosion or an armed struggle, by confusing London or by evoking world opinion, impose ruin on the entire country, as had been done in the 26-county Republic. There Irish nationalism is a proven failure.

So in the end the Protestant perception of the Republic, the inevitable child of the Roman church, is what matters. Unity with the rest of Ireland would simply mean an end to Protestant Ireland, to the British Ulster tradition, a fate worse than the swift slaughter of great battles and no less sure, a fate that might come with a whimper or with thunder but a prospect that is best countered by present defences: the gates closed, minds shut, the Republic known, feared, damned.

6

PROTESTANT PERCEPTION: A UNITED IRELAND

Unity has got to be thought of as a spiritual
development, which will be brought about by
peaceful, persuasive means.—Seán Lemass, 1971

The Irish Protestants of British Ulster know or assume that
they know the Irish Catholics, those nearby and those away
off in the Republic. And they know what a failure that
Republic has been, alien ground for Protestants and fallow
for all others. Thus they know what any future united
Ireland would portend: more of the same, the past as
prologue, a future that would doom not simply British Ulster
but all Ireland to an ineffectual, authoritarian regime of
squalor and surface charm. They are not apt to be persuaded
that a united Ireland will come through persuasive means—
and are all too aware that when such means have failed then
physical force has been the nationalists' other option.

For generations, new levies of republicans have arisen,
dedicated to a united Ireland, an Irish republic, that
shimmers with incandescent promise, a proposition
established in all Irish hearts, a concept worth any sacrifice:
death, corruption, prison, or shame. And during all those
years this aspiration, this united Ireland has been equally

real if differently imagined to the Irish Protestants of British Ulster. The potential reality of such a republic is not all that both share, for they live on the same island in the same way, speak to differing purpose with a recognisable accent, are alike in the alien eye but not in the perception of reality.

For the unionists, those loyal within the United Kingdom, the perception of reality is shaped, not as most nationalists imagine but, as they themselves insist, insist over and over without attracting listeners or converts, by the nature of the Roman Catholic Church. This is everything, gives integrity to the quarrel. The Roman church is so pervasive, so prevalent and persistent, so prone to absorb and so control the fringes that all those within its purview will succumb. In Ireland unless defended by numbers or a border, the vulnerable will inevitably be more Catholic than Irish. This has always been so in Ireland, the essential nature of the Irish shaped by Catholic doctrine.

Beyond the insidious doctrines and prevalence of the Roman church, the society of the Gael is a secondary but real disaster, less threat than failure, a failure due to the very nature of the Irish-Irish. And that central Irish nature, a compound of invader ethics, island habits and an imaginary golden age, was at best marginal to the great trends of the West and at worst a wild and barbarous core that saw indolence as grace and violence as recreation. The Gael was the last froth of the Asian invasions that had devastated the West, lightly touched by the Norse and outside the power of the English, really outside the Pale even within living memory. No matter the historians or the advocates of a single tradition, no matter the facts or the reality of Ulster settlement, those in British Ulster feel that, if Irish, they are not one with the heritage of the Irish-Irish, above and beyond the matter of Rome, a Rome that has had such a disastrous impact on the inherent Gael nature. Such a heritage, a mix of the barbarous and the elegant authoritarianism of Rome, engendered the Irish-Irish, beyond enlightenment, beyond the pale. In a sense Irish history is the 800-year failure to make the Irish into the English. More often than not those who come to Ireland are more altered than not, become not more Irish than the Irish but different. British Ulster is different and so evidence that in six counties Irish Protestants are not like the Irish, but not still English or Scots, and so not even British according to those in Britain. Vulnerable, uncertain of their legitimacy, fundamental in their faith and fearful of their allies, the Irish Protestants have shaped a British Ulster. On a small island with the Crown's writ restricted at best to six counties, the only hope has been isolation from the Irish-Roman miasma, an ethos so compelling that those shaped are hardly aware of the price of their inherited faith. The unionist is not so innocent and so, recognising vulnerability, tenaciously defensive.

Thus, knowing the Irish Catholic and knowing from the examples abroad and in Ireland where their domination can lead, the defence of British Ulster has been special. And it has been especially difficult because the dominant Protestant ethos intensified by historical experience and the special Irish conditions has been fundamentalism not moderated by time, the corruption of power or the ease of accomplishment. Fundamentalist Irish Protestantism, if not the Church of Ireland, has always felt at risk from the more orthodox, the established, and those less moulded by their faith and more prone to accommodation. And Ireland has always abounded with these, the vast majority lost to Rome, those adhering to the conventional congregations, those whose dedication is not total or pure or absolute. Thus the fundamentalist has been trapped amid sinners, among the half-hearted, the dissolute, or the misguided. There have been too many to defeat, too many to convert, too many to manage effectively—and this too was the case when the arena narrowed to six counties. Those pure in faith are in a minority in Britain and in Ireland, even at times it seems within the Ulster Protestant community. They are not really united with their own—the other Protestants—in Ireland and certainly have found it difficult even to imagine being united with all the Irish.

Their status is especially dangerous because the revealed truth is always at risk and can best be protected when there is no option, no competitors, no other orthodoxies. The danger of the Roman church, the danger of those more established congregations was a historical legacy. The faithful born again in Christ wanted to live their entire life in Christ. This they often found difficult amid those not yet redeemed or not fully Christian. These others were assumed to be pawns or proponents of the forces of darkness, not simply stray lambs as yet not saved for Christ. With or without power, they could not easily be ignored and so were often subject to proselytising at best and often scorn and disdain. All those not saved were not simply lost but often dangerous and so not to be tolerated.

This had always been so, as the Puritan clergyman Joseph Cotton, who lived between 1584 and 1653, during the great era of Reformation and reaction, said: "Toleration made the world anti-Christian." In the past those Christians, Protestant fundamentalists, puritans and pilgrims, those born again in the Blood of the Lamb, who tried to establish appropriate forms of worship and life had often found safety only in flight. They established their Dutch Reformed Church in South Africa or utopian communities in America.

They left Britain or Ireland as emigrants from conformity and established their Pentecostal sects in Tennessee or Kentucky and, often unhappy in Tennessee or Kentucky, moved on where the word and the spirit directed them.

New orthodoxies arose, some restricted to a shop-front and some, like the Church of Jesus Christ of Latter-Day Saints—the Mormons—quite grand, a major religious establishment dominating the state of Utah and found knocking on front doors in São Paulo and Bombay. These fundamentalists not only found toleration of those not yet redeemed difficult but also often found the state intrusive, unsympathetic to the word of God as received relating to social and familial matters, to taxes or war or the keeping of the Sabbath. Some had also found Ulster too difficult and had also fled to America. There some prospered. Some maintained the habits of Ireland, often a propensity for violence and a disputatious concern with the revealed truth. Some kept the faith despite secular temptations. And some or most entered the mainstream of American life. There, including especially those from Ulster, they appeared regularly on the roll of presidents or as simple voter, the successful man next door or the Baptist elected to Congress. They established a great Bible belt in the American South— and a less defined zone in the American psyche—but could be found throughout the world.

Where the first émigrés had sought freedom to worship they had found in Ulster unexpected problems, natives who persisted in their old ways, often a government in London that submitted to the orthodoxies of the day. Those who stayed in Ireland, especially in Ulster, were often moved by conviction either to coercion or conspiracy that after centuries and at great cost made parts of the country secure—for the moment. The majority was not saved, even the ruling class was often lost, but the confluence of interests meant that a Christian life was still possible, as long as those interests kept Rome at bay and Britain on call. Then Ireland so united could be home for the Christian.

What was always needed was a defence against Rome, Celtic habits, and Irish nationalism. Despite the Protestants converted to nationalism, most, including all fundamentalists, felt that Irish nationalism was shaped by Irish Catholicism: the great crowds were mostly Catholic, the leaders and followers mostly Catholics, and the advantages to come were Catholic. No wonder the appeal of a united Ireland did not attract: Ireland would be united under false flags and united in opposition to Protestant interests and Protestant existence. The defence against such an eventuality, largely in the hands of the British establishment, collapsed in 1921 before the weight of numbers and the tides of fashion. The costs of British Ireland were for London too great.

So British Ulster rose to defend the faith and the faithful, the loyal, those dedicated to the union as safeguard of their tradition and freedoms. And to defend their own against the national majority they had structured an effective system despite the presence of the subversive minority within the gates. The system not only imposed Protestant control and ethics but made the subversive minority in the six counties impotent, all but invisible, and the vast Catholic majority in the rest of the country irrelevant. The dream of a united Ireland safe for Protestants had gone, a dream lost; but the alternative, largely the unintentional and unwitting device of Ulster Protestants, proved satisfactory to the residue provincial majority. The system at no great cost ran for fifty years without unduly troubling London, if to the considerable disadvantage of the nationalist minority caught in British Ulster. Ireland was out of British politics, Northern Ireland out of reach of Dublin, and a united Ireland a matter for history books and patriot oratory. The northern nationalists, a minority in Ulster, were merely the tide-wrack of history, alien to Ulster, tolerated by necessity, always dangerous if not as magnet and model then as subversive to the freedom of all. They could not be simply ignored, because they represented subversion within the gate: Catholicism and Irish nationalism had unrequited national ambitions. This was all they had.

A united Ireland was so unlikely that few could imagine its form. A united Ireland might be within every Irish heart but it emitted only a blinding and compelling light, not details. For fifty years no-one in British Ulster need ponder real proposals and prospects, only watch fitfully the guttering but persistent hopes of the few who kept their hopes alive, advocated if not physical force then external intervention. After all, the Irish, all those in Ireland, deserved to be a nation once again. For the Irish Protestants of Ulster this was nonsense: there was no Irish nation and so need be no state, no united Ireland; how could light and dark be one?

The Irish Catholics assume that being Irish is different from being Catholic, while the Protestants can see in the Republic that to be Catholic determines the very nature of Irish state and society, transforms the people perniciously, inevitably, even shapes the Jew and the Methodist. This is the danger of the republic: the threat to the faith. And the nationalist dream in action, in the Republic, was for unionists obviously, visibly a failure—a failure ensured by Catholic habits, subservience to authority, lack of responsibility, rituals instead of righteousness. Irish nationalism was, like the Irish national state, shaped by

Rome and by generations of Irish illusion and sloth. This was the model for any nationalist united Ireland and so impossible to accept, much less support. There need be no study of constitutional arrangements, federal models, or adjusted advantages—if they had been offered, and before 1969 they seldom were. The very concept of a united Ireland for all, Protestant or Catholic, unionist or nationalist, remained just that: a concept, a notion whose time had not come.

After 1969, when the republicans found a means of deploying physical force, some effort was made to shape a description of the new Ireland sought. A federal Ireland was the republican goal until its proponents, Ruairí Ó Brádaigh and Dáithí Ó Conaill, were replaced by others. Academics and analysts, locals and foreigners, published proposals and models; all, like the republican aspirations, suffered from a lack of realism. In a zero-sum game the unionists would simply countenance no form that any might suggest for losing, for the end of British Ulster. It was especially trying that all the forms proposed for uniting a divided society largely addressed political issues when for unionists and loyalists it was religion that mattered, that divided by nature and made unity a contradiction in terms.

In this analysis the Protestants could find no real ally that feared Catholicism in a secular age, no real ally that damned the Republic for failing to achieve normal Western standards. Worse, all the logical and compelling arguments of the advocates of British Ulster were twisted, turned against them. The Reformation is dead. Catholicism is a mere competitor in religious matters and increasingly less effective in the West. To focus on religion as a factor is not politically correct. Even their allies in London really had a British imperial agenda, a distaste for the Irish, and other priorities when they supported the union. For them Ireland was never a pressing matter and the Irish republican a mere irritant, not the threat imagined by the unionists.

In fact elsewhere the Irish did not annoy or threaten but attract. The Republic may have had faults, but small, marginal; without great resources it had nevertheless prospered, had influence far beyond the population and had made friends everywhere. The Republic was decent, Irish nationalism was no bad thing, and the aspirations of the unionists in contradiction of the tides of the times. Thus a united Ireland seemed possible to everyone but to those who were to be united, the Protestants of Northern Ireland, and their friends in London, who saw their prospective departure not as Dublin's gain but as British loss. Those who sought to explain just why unity was an illusion found no audience. The nationalist analysis, on the other hand, was seemingly immune to statistics, to the sight of the dole queue or the emigrants in line for an Aer Lingus plane to Boston or New York. Such an analysis seemed to ignore the IRA campaign, supported by Catholics, shaped by Catholic imagery and ritual and directed to Catholic advantage. No-one heeded British Ulster but instead drew up constitutions and arrangements and accommodations: all would be surrender, some swift, some incremental, but all fatal to the Protestant tradition.

For Ulster Protestants the rise of militant nationalism after 1969 simply intensified an anguish that led again and again to a refusal to act for fear of error. Every suggestion, proposal and compromise was turned down, promptly, fully, without discussion. Doing nothing was the first choice: not going to work during the strike against Sunningdale and power-sharing and the Council of Ireland, not voting for compromise candidates, not accepting the Anglo-Irish

Agreement, and perforce not showing adequate enthusiasm for the ceasefire and peace process. If history had lessons to teach, the Protestants, still unionists, still loyal to the old connection, felt that change since 1916 had done their cause harm: British Ireland divided, Stormont challenged and destroyed, the IRA armed struggle, the Anglo-Irish efforts to find a means of reducing costs and chaos at Protestant expense, and finally a peace process that was constructed on a British statement that London had no interest in Ireland beyond that of the people of Northern Ireland—and even that process did not proceed as swiftly as the republicans wanted.

The charms of a united Ireland were constantly offered in varying combinations and mixtures but always as inevitable, sooner or later, easily done or imposed. The majority of the people of Northern Ireland were informed that demographics would in time make them a minority, informed by one and all that their fears were groundless when they were not, lectured and hectored, their contributions to the Crown discounted—spongers. And somehow they could not explain what a "united Ireland" would mean, would inevitably mean to them, and could not explain that the people of Ireland could never be united and so no single Irish nation could emerge from all the blueprints, schemes, and drafts.

The most galling fact was that no-one listened—or everyone listened and no-one heard. All the scholars, lawyers and theorists offered plans and models and structures. None would do, or could do. Each, for the fearful Ulster Protestants, was more woolly than the last: formulas of amalgamation. What mattered to the Protestants was what they believed: what they saw they saw, and they saw a united Ireland as a slow death for a grand people and a fine wee country. No federal constitution could change that. This had always been so.

While there has always been an Ireland, there had not for a millennium been one Ireland, and even then not one nation. The Ireland of the Celts, who imposed their language, customs and most especially their elite on the locals, is everyone's beginning. Celtic Ireland was more a matter of myth than reality, a place to find the requisite historical seeds of the long Irish problem. And nearly everyone who analyses Ireland is apt to seek an early beginning. Yet, as the Ulster Protestants are quick to point out, a united Irish nation has never existed. Ireland has most simply been part of the British Isles, ruled with more or less efficiency, more or less intact, from London. Ireland in whole or in part has been united with Britain, not a separate nation, not since the Celts and Danes and the myths. True, the Irish and even at times Irish Protestants have resisted this arrangement but even then rarely produced a united resistance to the English. The Protestants opposed the Tan War, and many nationalists were more than eager to settle for far less than a republic. The Protestants who supported rebellion and the United Irishmen did so only briefly and for reasons at variance with those of their Catholic allies— were thus not historical allies of a united Ireland but momentarily willing to revolt in order to be left alone, not to be partner in an ideal Ireland.

This ideal Ireland, a united Ireland that is the subject of song and story, the stuff of history and the aspiration of nationalists is essentially an invention of the Enlightenment, a far more complex invention than patriot history is apt to imagine, mixed with provincial and historical grievance and cultural differences. The Irish nation arising from Tone's aspirations, both from the ideas of the

Age of Reason and the ancient heritage of parochial rebellion encouraged by new ideas and momentary English weakness, collected symbols and history. The imagined Ireland was goal and grail and subject to various indigenous take-over bids. Whatever else, the nature of Ireland as imagined, as nation, arose in the nineteenth century. Before that, to be Irish, to be from Ireland, was different and had other connotations. In the seventeenth century or the eighteenth, essays on the Irish meant different things, addressed different categories, and cannot be read as if written by Sinn Féin. Much that has gone on in Ireland has been filtered through modern expectations and assumptions, turned into patriot history and so a rationale for violence. Much that is and would be united Ireland is not simply speculation but imaginary.

The modern Irish nation, like other modern nations, imagined a special people, communal bonds, a common civility, often one language or one faith, and aspired after a single governance. Much of the nineteenth century was devoted to the tribulations of this concept, the denial of freedom to some and the costs of reunification and centralisation to others, and only a very few modern nations managed to emerge intact. Other dreams and other causes often intervened; other nationalities, other ambitions, the new classes and the old faiths intervened.

For many the Irish nation remained a concept of the Enlightenment, secular, general, the harbour for all Irish aspirations, but for others became identical with the vast majority of the Irish, long penalised by British suzerainty: the Catholics. These, claiming primacy of place, had long found expression mainly in persistence in ritual and sullen obedience. Now there was an Irish nation as well, open to all but most welcome to those who were by habit Catholic, an institution avid to transform their flock into obedient and effective modern citizens and so no enemy of an Irish and inevitably Catholic nation. It is largely the national dream, more secular than not, more geographical than ethnic, more attuned to European events than the actual complexities of loyalty and faith in Ireland, that has won the day—won in twenty-six counties, won the Catholics but not the Irish Protestants of Ulster.

They have remained true to their opposition to nationalism, despite their own complexities and divisions and varied agendas. They see still and always a united Ireland as a Catholic Ireland, the more dangerous when not so recognised by its adherents. British Ulster re-reads Irish history, just as do nationalists, seeking a past as prologue to present intention.

The nationalist and republican case is that to be Irish is not to be Catholic or anything else. One can be Irish and also be a Jew or a Unitarian; Englishmen play on the Irish World Cup team; Shaw, a Protestant and Irish, lived in London and wrote in English; Beckett, a Protestant and Irish, lived in Paris and wrote in French; Yeats, a Protestant and Irish, lived in Dublin and wrote in the spirit of the Gaels, and died abroad. For the nationalists, especially for the republicans, religion is irrelevant: England is the never-failing source of Ireland's political evils. To be Irish is not to be English. One may speak Irish and know every jig, or live in a great house in Down, send the son to Eton and give on Poppy Day and still be Irish. The national dream is that as a single political entity, one nation will both remove the malign influence of England and release the creative enterprise necessary for Ireland to flourish.

And no Ulster Protestants accept any of this for a moment, at any time, then or now or later. A united Ireland cannot exist, because there is no Irish nation: some Protestants may convert to nationalism, some may speak Irish, but Irish nationalism is inherently Catholic—Catholic in numbers, Catholic in ethos, Catholic by heritage and inclination. And Protestants cannot be united in ethos and heritage and remain Protestant, cannot by the numbers resist and will not by inclination accept assimilation. Quite simply, the northern Protestants feel that not only is the nationalist case rot but demonstrable rot. On this all the divisions and differences, the clashing ambitions and agendas of the many Protestant variants in Northern Ireland agree. In fact on the crucial questions related to the Northern Ireland problem, most differ only in the matter of timing, the necessity for a show of public decency, and the relative importance of reaching out to those of the other tradition. Even the most ecumenical, those most likely to see Catholics as much like them, are as one with the loyalist gunman on the nature of any united Ireland proposed by Dublin.

Irish nationalism and Irish Catholicism cannot be divorced and if not identical are in any combination alien to Protestant values. The IRA gunman who shoots a neighbour, a part-time RUC reservist, off his tractor kills a Protestant, intimidates a whole category, opens the prospect of land to be sold and a family to flee. An Ireland united by the gun would hardly be an easy place for Protestants. An Ireland united by coercion, by British pressure, by a unionist loss of nerve or by intervention of the contingent and unforeseen would be little different.

At the sharpest of edges, the defenders of British Ulster see that they are Protestant and the others, the gunmen and their spokesmen, the big names in Sinn Féin and their friends in the Dublin Government, are all Catholics. Other

Catholics may condemn such violence, may not, as do some Irish politicians, profess a yearning for a united Ireland—some day—but are one of a kind: Roman Catholics. A few have been converted to the virtues of unionism, a few, like Conor Cruise O'Brien, no friend of Catholicism and dedicated enemy to republicans; but these are hardly representative of Irish opinion any more than the odd Protestant within the IRA represents unionist opinion. Thus even those who cherish their Catholic neighbour and seek toleration and accommodation do not do so at the expense of the special traditions of British Ulster or in a first step towards a united Ireland. All the various formulations of a united Ireland cannot disguise a Catholic majority. That is why there is no non-sectarian means of appealing to a Protestant by a Catholic. There can be no new Tone, no explanation that the IRA is an equal-opportunity killer that would now be convincing. To foresee no unity within a lifetime has no appeal to those who have grandchildren. To be told that parity of esteem awaits in a republic that has adjusted, if at no great enthusiasm, its old sectarian ways is unconvincing.

It is not simply a case of seeing what one wants but seeing what is clearly there: a Catholic national revolutionary movement that relies on violence to intimidate the provincial majority. It may be apparent that the Irish-Irish epitomised in the IRA core of the republican movement are not ethnically pure, but all are Catholic. They may be dedicated ideological socialists rather than close readers of Papal social edicts but they are Catholic. Most of the republicans and nationalists go to church. They marry in church, confess in church, die within the church. They are Catholics at the beginning and at the end. The republicans are Catholic even when they complain about the Pope's plea for peace, the interference of the clergy in hunger-strikes, or the parish priest who wants no part of an IRA military funeral. The gable-end murals use Catholic imagery. The hunger-strikes acted out the roles of Catholic martyrs. And so too is Irish nationalism shaped by Catholicism, and so the Irish nation would have no comfortable place for Ulster Protestants. This has meant that no Protestant has spent great effort in defining the nature of such a nationalist aspiration.

The evidence for Protestants—and even for some social scientists—is absolutely convincing. It is impossible to separate Catholicism and Irish nationalism: how could it be with only token Protestants available in the Republic or in the republican movement? The ideas and ideals and assumptions of the church permeate the movement, the Republic, and the Irish nation. And this has meant that few Catholics have spent great effort in defining the meaning of a united Ireland. The nationalist united Ireland, federal or unitary, broad or narrow, is a matter of governing institutions, while that of the Protestants is one of the people—a contradiction that cannot be covered by any form of governance.

As it is, in fact, only a rigorous defensive and the separation of the two traditions make it possible to tolerate the minority in the far smaller arena of Northern Ireland. Fundamentalist Protestants generally and in Northern Ireland particularly find alien proximity dangerous. Even without Christian competition the fundamentalist persuasion reveals a history of dissent and dispute, heretical notions, and organisational disagreement. The result is an example of Protestant freedom of belief. In the Roman church dissent against form and organisation and practice cannot shake doctrine and dogma and cannot often lead to reform. In the world of the fundamental Protestant, seemingly anything can lead to dissent that has resulted in a long chain-reaction of splits and schism and new starts. Many of these Protestant splits and schisms can be tolerated, if deplored. At times this is not possible: those with the revealed truth must emigrate or impose their vision on the others. One cannot easily tolerate the presence of the false. Then toleration is a grave risk to the saved. Such toleration, because of historical reality and the sheer weight of numbers, is necessary in Ulster but a risk. "Toleration made the world anti-Christian."

For the majority of Protestants, certainly for the articulate and devout, governance should ensure the prospect of a godly life, therefore a righteous and productive life, a life lived in Christ and in fear of judgement. The more elegant and less fundamental at least feel that society should not make the free exercise of religion difficult or painful, nor should the state intrude in such matters. The free and full exercise of religion is in many societies not possible because of government intervention but in others because the dominant culture will not tolerate the different, the pagan or the heretic. This is the case in Ireland. To claim that the Irish nation once united will not be divided because of religion or will not put the minority at risk is dishonest. The Irish are apt to accept authority, deny dissent and impose the general will with more alacrity than other Western societies—or so some surveys and all Ulster Protestant observation indicates. To pretend otherwise is more than dishonest, it opposes the very history of the Irish state in this century. Where have the Irish Protestants gone in the twenty-six counties, and why? Not because of pogroms or legislation or the anger of the majority of the people but because the nation exudes a Catholic miasma alien to

Protestants. For a Protestant to live in the Republic is to exist perpetually as an outsider, conscious of the reality of sin that touches not those cleansed from sin each Sunday before Mass, alien to the values and agenda of all, the solicitor, the clerk, the driver, or the little old woman crossing herself. They are Catholic and Irish, and the Methodist or Presbyterian is made to feel less so, less Irish, no matter the generations of ancestors or the proclaimed ideals of the state. All Ireland seems to be shaped by a great and secret conspiracy so ubiquitous that none can remember the details, only how to act in ways often mysterious to reason or to analysis. The Protestants may be part of this ethos, no different from the rest, but are still separate from the rest in many matters—which are said not to matter but in fact do. The country is a vast net of family connections, parish contacts, agreed standards listed on no agenda, a conspiracy that cannot welcome a Methodist even while making the Methodist welcome. And the Methodists or Presbyterians of British Ulster want no welcome, only to be left in peace.

For the Ulster Protestants the united Ireland proposed by scholars and analysts, by politicians, by the pragmatic and popular, comes in various configurations, a matter of divided powers, shared responsibilities, electoral systems and civil rights. The details and models of governance would still not be united. Such an Ireland would be consolidated under some acceptable form of government, ruled democratically by consensus with all the complications of a divided society and a troubled history factored into the final formula. And such a transitional and imposed unity would gradually be transformed by the Catholic ethos into a truly united Ireland with no role for the Protestant and in time no place.

This is the united Ireland imagined by the Protestants of Northern Ireland. Such an entity may have novel form as suggested by scholars, momentary advantage as promised by many, may be a creature easily described in texts and contractual agreements, may be a republic or not, the Republic or not, but can never be united. The Protestants perceive an emerging Ireland unrelated to the authority to issue passports, the responsibility for designing postage stamps or repairing the road. The Protestants of British Ulster are opposing not bits of paper or political programmes but the nature of any Catholic society. The united Ireland perceived from inside British Ulster is united only in the imposition of authority by a government of the majority: it is a nation defined only by an island, not by a people, not by consensus, not by heritage or tradition, only by necessity and the coercion of others. They imagine the future as the institutionalisation of a nightmare, not the realisation of a dream where only the details need be worked out. British Ulster cannot be a part of a united Ireland, because such a concept is in violation of the basic premise of existence: the Protestants in Northern Ireland can only exist apart from the main, exist as they are largely pure, undiluted, intolerant of others and sound in their own province, though not a real province, not part of historic Ulster, hardly part of Ireland, rather a province of the spirit that cannot exist amid an alien tradition. Therefore a united Ireland would arise almost at once from the ruins of British Ulster, the province destroyed and so the people lost, not united under the common name of Irish but dissipated, exiles and emigrants or assimilated.

All those provisions and provisos, protocols and assurances that may be woven seamlessly to form a united Ireland are snares. All the models and plans and constitutions are delusions. Ulster may not always be right but Ulster can only rightly remain if safe from amalgamation. What the others say unites the Irish instead makes those in British Ulster into the others. There is no overarching form, no splendid republic for one and all, but only one people, the majority, absorbing the rest. Then the Irish Protestants, no mean people, will be found not united in a new and energetic polity but merely as names on grave markers, names on maps and in history books. They will become a people lost, emigrated, exiled or transformed, done meanly by other people.

This is the united Ireland imagined by those marching down the road to Dunloy. This united Ireland is easy to describe, easy to fear, dreadful to contemplate, and beyond the reach of constitutions or compromises, beyond the pragmatic, and beyond matters of delegation of authority or separation of powers. This united Ireland is not that of Tone or Emmet, not that of 1916, not the republic for which so many sacrificed and died, not the free state that awoke hope in Yeats and Hyde and the others, and not the entity proposed by social scientists, politicians, and optimists. This united Ireland would be institutionalised ruin, transforming Irish Protestantism into an incident. This united Ireland would soon transform the country into a seedy Catholic parish maintained by charity and tourists. This is the united Ireland perceived in British Ulster.

7

A MIGHTY FORTRESS: PROTESTANTS AS PROTESTANTS

A mighty fortress is our God,
A bulwark never failing;
Our helper he amid the flood
Of mortal ills prevailing:
For still our ancient foe
Doth seek to work us woe;
His craft and power are great
And, armed with cruel hate,
On earth is not his equal.
—Martin Luther

Since those within British Ulster know the others and their intentions—a united Ireland—they have found not only their own case ignored and their own people judged unsympathetic but their nature ignored as well. They feel they face a flood of mortal ills on their own and so in their British Ulster form a fortress. There they take their stand as Protestants.

Why there can never be a united Ireland arises from the nature of Protestants; and, like all else arising from the Irish issue, no-one wants to learn too much about the matter, certainly not about Protestant reality. So this scholar or that puts them into pigeon-holes of class or interest or faction, or stresses their diversity or their innate Irish character, and pays no heed to the real as perceived by the real. These commonplaces, replete with footnotes and rigorous methodologies, or the momentary wisdom of the politicians and journalists, collectively form the received reality, not the reality of Ulster Protestants at all. This reality is thus not only unfashionable, as the Protestants recognise, perhaps overemphasise, but also unpalatable for those who, for whatever reason or ultimate goal, seek an accommodation. It is even uncongenial to those who simply report a scene that varies from experience, a people driven by perceptions not easily imagined in New York or Paris, much less London. Their perceptions are thus not readily accommodated, and for good reason. The Protestants of British Ulster are, whatever else, not accommodating.

There are the Protestants who are more or less as they really are to be found in Northern Ireland, and then there are the Protestants who are as imagined, by others or by themselves, especially imagined by the Irish nationalists. For nationalists the real Protestants are those behind the marches, behind the Orange oratory and the references in the Dáil or at Westminster, as well as those imagined by the republicans who are more Irish than Protestant. None are much like the everyday Protestant of British Ulster, or at least much of the time, for there were Protestants on the road to Dunloy and they are all Ulster Protestants in Ireland and so in this sense Irish. They are not, however, much like alien stereotypes, for the real Protestants are little known. They are certainly little known among Ulster Catholics, who have increasingly been separated from them by the necessities of the Troubles and have always been at a distance in a divided society. And Catholics in the Republic have had even less opportunity to meet Protestants in what remains an equally divided if more subtle society; and almost none have met the Protestants of British Ulster, only television images and caricatures. As for those in Britain, if they contemplate unionists—Protestants of course—at all it is as an irritant, as Irish, as a small factor in the greater game of Westminster politics, now with important votes, sometimes with grievances, but rarely with affection. Further off in Europe or America the stereotype rules OK. Unlike the Protestants of the Republic, the Protestants of British Ulster are not invisible but rather imagined variously, and usually to the advantage of the observer.

Mostly in the Republic local Protestants are assumed to be sound, similar, merely those other Irish attending a different church, even if in reality there is a far greater division than many Catholics accept or recognise. And from Dublin the Protestants of Northern Ireland are seen as different from the locals, Orange unionists, stereotypes, often represented by the bigots and the intransigent, almost never known as everyday people. They are rather shaped in public and often in political discourse to fit political argument or preconceived notions. They are often depicted as amusing, ranting bigots or—worse—mindless sectarian murderers, as if the UVF murdered solely for the pleasure of the deed rather than political purpose, however sinister that purpose. In fact Northern Ireland from the Republic often seems to be filled with hard men, bigots, not all Protestants, dark and dour figures with harsh accents talking on television, marching to and fro, and so not everyday at all.

Polls indicate that in fact many Catholics recognise that each unionist is not a bigot nor every loyalist a paramilitary, that Northern Catholics are not without complexity or even bias. Ulster Protestants may not be congenial but are assumed to be decent if misled about nationalist Ireland, misled by their politicians. Still, there is no evading the fact that Ulster Protestants are different from local Irish Protestants, who are benign and Irish. The Protestants in the North are both alien and Irish, awful and impressive, ordinary and awful. What is agreed is that there is another tradition in Ireland, especially in Northern Ireland: that of the Protestants. There is little recognition, however, of how many kinds of Protestants there are, how complex the tradition, or how different that society is, and a reluctance to accept that the Irish component is not dominant but represents a different Ireland from the one glorified in patriot history or immortalised by regular political usage in the Republic.

The Protestant society of Northern Ireland—British Ulster—enormously diverse in all matters, is at one in opposition to a united Ireland. The British establishment accepts this as natural—they are biased against the Republic as well—and the Dublin establishment as unnatural—they are aware that the unionists are really Irish. Neither Dublin nor London, however, focuses on the Protestant nature of that opposition: Enoch Powell came to Ireland to defend British sovereignty against a nationalist challenge, and Sinn Féin, aspiring to a non-sectarian society, has long been alienated from the Catholic hierarchy. Neither wants to become involved in a sectarian conflict, although the British use religious division as a reason for staying and the IRA the British presence as the reason for such sectarian division. No-one much cares what the Protestants think about religious matters, which should be but are not different from advocacy of the union or opposition to Sinn Féin.

Alas for the advocates of a tolerant and pluralistic world, polities with space for all and governance based on fraternity as well as liberty, in Northern Ireland for

Protestants politics arise from the faith, immutable, indistinguishable, special. And almost all those who most avidly defend British Ulster as a Protestant society, as British, not Irish, are those most fundamental in their Protestant faith. Protestants are unionists, all from firm conviction; but some are more Protestant than others and so more fearful of Rome, more determined in defence of their Ulster, and so less compromising in all matters. And in these matters the absolute convictions of the few colour the whole Protestant ocean, just as the political convictions of the republicans colour the nationalist ocean. In a sense the very capacity to attract more into the fundamentalist structure of resistance weakens the core of that resistance: the more powerful a Paisley the more likely there is to be competition at the core, with those left behind, those marginal and isolated, reliant only on revelation. The more fundamental the Protestant the more separate from the many and the more apt to oppose amalgamation and, of course, assimilation with anyone, much less the Roman Catholics in a united Ireland.

The enduring intransigence of the fundamentalist Protestant to a united Ireland that has moulded all Ulster politics this century is epitomised in the refusal to give an inch: no minor concession, no cosmetic accommodation, nothing. One is saved or not. The basic fear is that to concede is to ensure absolute concession. Outside the gates the sinners have been co-opted by Rome. The fundamentalists suspect as failed Christians not simply the Romans but also many of the more conventional within the gates who have adapted to the times instead of imposing their faith on reality. British Ulster is a mighty fortress, with high walls, brave people and a militant history but somehow vulnerable to betrayal, to a single concession, to one traitor who would open the gate. Salvation can be won only through eternal vigilance—a cold eye cast on those outside the walls, of course, but also doubts about one's own. The revealed truth may be twisted, may lead to compromise: look at O'Neill and Faulkner and even William Craig.

Concession imposed is quite different from sins of commission: one cannot be more British than the British, although one can certainly be more faithful, more redeemed. So Irish Protestants have had concession forced upon their community, but this is the burden of history, not the result of free choice. To give in to accommodation voluntarily is what would destroy the bastion. And the bastion of British Ulster is a vessel of the faith, not a means of governance, not a place but a perception, unwelcome in secular times but no less real, more than real for those caught up in the power of the Lord.

The born-again Christian fears for his faith just as great pride is taken in its power. If there is to be a united Ireland, then some means of attracting those repelled by the concept of a united Ireland, not simply of unity but of cohabitation, must be found. This can hardly be easy—the more so as the nature of the Protestant fundamentalists remains hidden. For them, the absolute, the zealous, the way to salvation has been found—and all about are those misguided, those malevolent, the legions of Rome and the pieties of the conventional Christians. These lost souls hardly know they are lost. They think their life pious. They have been taken in by conventions, the lure of easy money and power, the comfort of the established; and Ireland is filled with these. Northern Ireland is also filled with many Protestant variants. Those zealots roaming the streets of British Ulster in the grip of the Lord, born again, are a very small minority. Many Protestants simply accept that there are many roads to salvation, some similar to theirs and some inappropriate or alien—but that of Rome a dead end. Many Protestant congregations are simple, quiet, doubtful of secular institutions, limited in ceremony. Others are old, elaborate, complex, ancient institutions with rituals, elders, prelates and orders.

There have always been within Christianity those most fanatical in their dedication, most pure, most suspicious of authority, most certain of their own voices. There have always been a disproportionate number of these to be found in Ulster—not that money and land, caste and class can be discarded, only that the faith truly mattered to many who came to plant Ulster with purity as well as to reap temporal rewards, theirs as a result of piety and prudence, battle and the Bible, history and hard work. To deny their new life led in their own way engendered further protest. The Reformation certainly gave ample opportunity for many to protest in their own special way. In Ireland they remained so, protesters against convention, often at times against the Crown but always against the Catholics, the Irish—whatever the term might have meant at one time or another. Some Protestants continue to do so, protesting against the world as found, revelation as offered by the settled and orthodox, seeking instead the fundamentals of the faith and the personal revelation of the Holy Spirit. And once found, most are born again, transformed, enhanced, and zealous in conviction.

The truth pure is not an easy neighbour. Pilgrims and puritans, each has found Christ, discovered the revealed truth, and cannot easily abide those content with sin and sloth and the easy life. So uncompromising at times has been their vision that many have been driven away, despatched to the wilderness or far parts, imprisoned or censored. The existing system appeared often inimical to the faith revealed. The pure in heart have often found conventional society intolerable, and so too conventional society has found them: a constant disruption, a clamour and clatter on matters often long decided and seldom on society's agenda. Often those born again have little formal training, no training in theology and no skills except in disputation although often a total grasp of scripture, for it is the Bible alone that contains all that need be known. Once the sinner is born again in Christ, nothing is ever the same and nothing is ever as important. And this makes nothing easy for those who seek accommodation or even reconciliation.

In this century the fundamentalists, isolated amid the alien fields of Manchester or London or New York, persist, ignoring the damned and the ignorant. Their lives revolve around their special vision. Some are isolated in the backlands or on a frontier, and most are always isolated by conviction and ideological necessity. No matter where found, they create their own world, not monks but missionaries, not hidden in beehive huts but handing out tracts on the street corner: Are you saved? The Christian fundamentalists have always done so, fled the secular and compromised centres of great empires for the fringes. They came to Ireland and to New England, travelled to South Africa, and can yet be found with the word of the Lord at doors in Rio de Janeiro or Melbourne, in chapels in Alabama, and on the road to Dunloy. They do not suffer other denominations gladly, or often at all. Some prosper, like the Mormons in Utah, and some disappear, as have most of the American utopias of the last century. All have caused trouble for the conventional, for they are not for the easy life. They have found the truth, the one truth, the way and the light.

Until time and the constraints of society have an effect, those born again are not readily born into any sort of general community and cannot accept amalgamation or co-operation or tolerate the very presence of the unredeemed unless compelled. And yet often, as in Northern Ireland, objective conditions impose toleration: there is no place to flee to, no power to expel the many, no means of constructing a truly satisfactory earthly garden for the faith. This is as true in British Ulster at the end of the century as it was at the beginning. The other Protestants may live righteous, godly and sober lives, attend chapel every day and say prayers at dawn and grace at meals, but for the fundamentalists such Christians, decent enough individually, are misguided.

All the redeemed feel transported—saved. Those born again into Christ feel different, are different, and expect to be treated differently. To be and to remain fundamentally Christian, their faith must be secured or all else is ashes. Their vision is so compelling that all life is changed, and so all may be at risk. The truth, buttressed by the Bible but imposed by revelation, must be defended in a hostile world. And all are apt to feel beleaguered in a world not yet saved, perhaps beyond saving but capable of corrupting the faith revealed. What is so compellingly powerful is also vulnerable to sin and the arrogance of earthly power.

The newly saved are in every way transformed, and this transformation must at all times be protected, husbanded, and kept apart from the everyday and the temptations of the earthly. Very little is due to Caesar and all to a risen Christ. Such Protestants in Belfast or Portadown are not easy to shift or to corrupt. They are possessed of a most profound vision that requires absolute independence. And few of those not so touched—those engaged in conventional politics or political analysis or the life of the times, especially those within the Roman communion, who sometimes live next door but in a different world—seem to understand just how intransigent and independent are these Irish Protestants. To defend their faith they have co-opted Caesar, imagined a British Ulster as a fortress even if erected amid an ocean of Catholics. By necessity British Ulster will have to do as a promised land. And the land is promised, and cannot be amalgamated into some entity labelled "united Ireland" when union with the ungodly is impossible. One is saved and free, or not. To say "no," as the Protestants have done so often and so regularly, is not a negative posture but a reaffirmation of their faith. Their British Ulster can exist or it cannot: justice and freedom cannot be diluted, are pure and whole and defended zealously by a refusal to accept compromise, a refusal to surrender.

Many Ulster Protestants are not as zealous in their convictions, not born again but simple, plain, and pious. Yet it is the zealots that charge the atmosphere of British Ulster. Even and particularly the republicans—who too have been transformed by truth revealed—fail to grasp the integrity of fundamentalist assumptions, the power offered and requisites demanded by the faith found rather than inherited. Some Protestants feel compelled to take the word to others, but not as many in Northern Ireland, where the prime responsibility is to persist rather than expand.

For Protestants in Northern Ireland their faith must exist within an alien community, an island nation of others, mainly populated with those beyond redemption, who are often led by those who glory in sin. Even in British Ulster they must exist amid a huge minority of Catholics. In fact many in the past, unable to assimilate and unwilling to accept the risk of contamination, moved on from Ulster, from Ireland, seeking space and isolation from threat. In Ireland there is no space and can be no isolation, and few have great faith in good will or toleration or the motives of the others. Even the conventional denominations—Presbyterian or Anglican—no longer have the vitality or often the desire to live in Christ. The flock in Ireland harvested by Rome are a clear and present danger to doctrine, to revelation, and to the most fundamental concepts found in Christ. They have shaped in Irish nationalism a means of expropriating the whole country. The only defence, one not trusted but crucial, has been to rely on the Protestant British state, defender of the faith. The British establishment may not be properly pious but it is Protestant. And, as Protestant, the system is assurance against the power of Rome and British defence against Irish nationalism. In union—the sword and the Bible—there is strength if not always theological agreement.

Yet in Northern Ireland, if not British Ulster, there are Catholics, most Irish nationalists, all an affront, all intolerable but undeniably present. They are simply there and often have been encouraged by British policy or negligence, by London's priorities, the Crown's Catholics. Many of the Protestants have had to find a means of making the intolerable tolerable and accept the reality of Catholic neighbours. Even the most fundamentalist Protestants have had to adjust to their presence. They have done so living absolutely separately in all ways that matter. Personally the faithful may be congenial, but each one is separate from the next one. They are for Protestants separate but not equal: for the Roman faith is flawed and so the Irish Catholic community. This may not be popular, certainly is not politically correct, but it is taken, as is the Gospel, as undeniable. Thus the institutions of British Ulster must defend not simply British civility, the ethos of Britain, but the Protestant community. The minority in British Ulster must be shaped as inferior and subversive, no matter the ethics of the day. The Catholics have long simply been taken as inferior and therefore treated to keep them so. If this is not possible through law it may be managed by custom and attitude. Certainly this was done to effect until the rise of the Troubles in 1969 and the emergence of the IRA.

A great many of those Protestants in British Ulster who seek moderation and understanding, who support fellowship and ecumenical gestures, still find the Roman church distasteful and authoritarian and much that is Irish-Irish unattractive and often inferior. They tolerate the other but accept that their own is the better way—and so says the record and observation. The fundamentalists are apt to believe that their truth and their society are simply the only way, not just the better way and in fact one endangered by any other sect or denomination, almost all other options but those closely allied to the truth as discovered, revealed, impounded and expounded.

The problem is that there is no viable solution to the presence of millions of Catholics, a large number within the gates of British Ulster. If British Ulster were a fortress matters would be easier, but as a concept, not a place, the sanctuary is shaped amid the seditious and heretical, not a walled city on the hill. The fundamentalist muddle of strategies, avowed or not, has been adjusted over time but remains the same: to protect the basic Protestant traditions against all comers—a tradition that cannot tolerate options and does not want to risk co-option by state or church. The fundamentalists may be in a tiny minority, are found crude and abrasive by most Protestants, and may in time, as have most who discover Christ through revelation, become moderate, but for generations their Ulster has produced replacements. There have always been new prophets and fresh preachers with the good word and the hard word. There have been still more of those driven by revelation, often without learning but never without conviction.

Much has changed in Northern Ireland, but the persistence of the most fundamental form of Protestant Christian ideology, incorporated in shifting institutional form, has not. Calvin and Cromwell are alive and well. The attitudes and assumptions of the past, essentially of the generations after the beginning of the Protestant Reformation, permeate Northern Ireland. These are the convictions that drive not simply church service but also majority life. Those most driven, most fundamental, most Protestant configure all life in the province. The central provincial Protestant engine need not be one denomination, this church or that evangelical movement, need not be epitomised by a single divine or a particular congregation, but there is and has always been a centre of gravity for the Protestant majority. Those at the eye of the storm have shifted in name and number, and so too their arrangements and sects, but the storm is, as always, drawing in the new, those born again in Christ, and spinning off the contented and comfortable. In the eye reside the evangelical, committed, convinced, born-again Christians, earnest, puritanical, and absolute. A few are hypocrites, a few seek only power and glory, but most are driven by their vision. In time they or their children may grow easy, adjust to reality, run for office and seek the votes of the dubious, ease into the comfortable, but they have always been replaced by the pilgrims, those captured by the word of God, the reality of Hell, the necessity for redemption and a life born in Christ. And so there has always been a hard core at the Protestant centre and there often have been charismatic spokesmen. This has ensured that there has never been an easy time for the province. The faith just found does not adjust to the everyday.

To the conventional it seems that each generation produced a famous bigot, an orator for the street corner, a sect that readily embarrasses the sophisticated and elegant, the educated and established. Few appreciate the zealot at the front door or primitives speaking in tongues. The Protestants with oak pews, paid choirs and university degrees, those with a sense of the decent and the proper, have been repeatedly shamed by bigots, by the Bible thumped, by sermons filled with Hell fire, by the arrogance of innocent conviction. Yet what can be said against the simple faith, the word revealed, the lives truly led in Christ? However raw the edges of the evangelical, such rough Christians are real.

This old-time religion has shifted, but only in the details of the enemies list, the degrees of threat, or the agenda of danger. Every generation a new levy come to Christ, are born again, and persist with the same dedication shown elsewhere in Ireland only by the republicans—those too of little property, limited learning and an absolute faith that transforms daily life. The most Protestant of the Protestants determine the ethos of British Ulster. They make Ulster indigestible for republicans, unappealing for nationalists, and uncongenial to all in a world where toleration and amalgamation seem the obvious alternative to schism, violence, and chaos. Taken at their own estimate, they cannot be united with anyone or any others. To dislike the fundamentalists, to damn their theology, their assumptions, their pretensions and their arrogance is to reassure them. By their enemies shall you know them: Rome and Canterbury, brick churches and university prelates, are enemies worthy of the faith. The wisdom of the elegant and educated is doctrinal fault. Toleration is to abide sin and so endanger the truth. Co-operation is the handmaiden to co-option and damnation. Few may so believe, but sufficient are the faithful for British Ulster purpose. And this attitude underlies the concepts of uncompromising adamancy; sin is not a matter of degree: one is saved or not, just as one is pregnant or not, and so not an inch can be given.

Unlike many other societies, in Northern Ireland it is not the ruling elite, those with the means of production or divine right, but those most fundamentally Protestant who determine the values and agenda of the community. Everywhere, no matter the diversity of culture or the internal divisions of the community, no matter how many kinds of Protestants there are or varying historical and contemporary preferences, the Ulster fundamentalists impose their veto on all. Unable to initiate change, unwilling to compromise, incapable of rule and inept in power, the fundamentalists can hold to their narrow dream and so never surrender, never give an inch, remain generation after generation beyond assimilation, renewed by conversion.

Such fundamentalists are hardly novel in Western history. The puritan ethic had a long political run in the United States and can still be found in the oratory of political candidates. And America is diverse, no longer a Protestant nation nor one with an Anglo-Saxon majority. The American Christian right, a coalition of Protestants, is a component of politics though not representative, more than a mere faction but hardly dominant. In South Africa the British intruders allowed the Boers freedom to shape their faith. The native Africans could be dominated and the

British fled so that the Afrikaners, generation after generation, kept themselves pure. They were a chosen people in a land redeemed by blood, defended too by the Bible and the sword. Even now with accommodation and compromise accepted, the confusion of toleration is apparent. The faithful are trapped in the heart of black Africa, domination lost. Ireland is small and the physical and psychic space limited. Everyone is trapped here in a sense, although anyone can leave. There is no place to cherish revelation in isolation, as there is in America, or to rely on domination over the natives, as there was in Africa. Still the Irish Protestants have coped in a small space. Those who cannot have emigrated. Those who stay have no need yet for a sudden compromise.

Yet time moves, history moves, and change is inevitable, not stayed by crying "Not an inch." Whatever the advantages and disadvantages for Northern Ireland, for one tradition or the other—or both—there has been change. And the Ulster Protestants for this century and much of the last have suspected that change would not be to their advantage. Their position as a majority in Ulster, long associated not only with social and economic power but also political power, has always meant a special position, special when all Ireland was part of the United Kingdom and special when power was devolved on a provincial government. Ireland has always been special, and so too Ulster—not at all like Finchley or even Scotland. And the Ulster Protestant is surrounded by dangers, unlike the Scot or Londoner. The symbol of all that is dangerous is the concept of a united Ireland—not the one proposed by republicans or by Irish politicians or the theorists and scholars but the one imagined by those on the road to Dunloy. If there is an enormous Protestant religious spectrum, considerable theological and intellectual differences among those divided as well by different class loyalties, experience, and education, only a few are found on the road to Dunloy. There for the Apprentice Boys all is simple: there is us and our rights and there is them and their presumptions, ambitions, and provocations. Elsewhere, everywhere in Northern Ireland almost all are as one on the impossibility of uniting their traditions within a single Irish political entity. And almost all have despaired of making this clear to others.

Catholics are simply too different. While class, location, education and experience divide Irish Catholics too, all are within the same church; their theological differences are slight, even as the congregations argue over organisation, scandal, and rituals. And dissent, the crucial facet of much of Protestant debate, is very limited: doctrine is determined elsewhere; criticism may be found in Chicago or Mexico, even in Rome, but rarely in Kerry or Cork. Not so the Protestants. There are all sorts and kinds of Protestant theologies and churches, with fundamental differences. The Ulster strains split and quarrel, amalgamate and divide, disputatious and intolerant, a constant turmoil of interpretation, Biblical quotation, shifting institutions; the most orthodox congregations persist much as in the past, but on the fringes the quarrels continue. At times it seems that British Ulster is united in nothing except the existence of British Ulster. This is what freedom is taken to mean by Ulster Protestants, and the greatest freedom is simply to possess British Ulster, the freedom from assimilation.

Religion in Ulster matters, as much as or more than in any other Protestant community anywhere, and so the distinctions and disputations do matter. Elegance, wealth, sophistication and education have hardly eroded conviction and conformity of principle. Protestants historically protested against the system, opposed on principle. And in Northern Ireland that protest is fundamental. There are real reasons why Protestant churches split, why congregations divide, why those who are born again in Christ find those in established churches uncongenial, perhaps beyond salvation. Salvation matters, and the Bible teaches the road to that end. And the text read variously as in Northern Ireland means that many roads can be found, if none that lead through Rome. In fact access to all the roads must be open so that all can be redeemed: freedom of choice and the exercise of free will are essential—and not found in Catholic societies. And all in British Ulster, whichever hall or chapel, believe the one right road is important. And the defence of the freedom to choose the one right road and to protest against those who would impose a single, predetermined, orthodox road is patent in Northern Ireland, a province more Protestant than easily imagined elsewhere. Each congregation, even the Church of Ireland, seems more fundamental, more alive to the issues of the Reformation, more suspicious of ceremony, ritual and rite and of imposed authority than congregations in more genial societies. Matters most Protestants in Britain or Australia take either for granted or with a grain of salt engender controversy and conviction in Northern Ireland. And in most cases in British Ulster the simple, the plain, the unadorned, the most fundamental survives and flourishes.

Ulster Protestants are very Protestant, low church if there is an option, evangelical and fundamental even within the more established churches. One has to go to Dublin for a hint of Anglican ceremony, and even there the service is simple. In Belfast the prevailing climate, no matter the name of the church, remains bare, nearly bleak, forthright and popular—even out on Malone Road; so much so that the Protestant quietism, those who eschew clamour and ceremony, those who are apt to witness rather than declaim, tend to be drowned out by the oratory of the saved and the warnings of damnation. Those who protest the most are most noticeable and most fundamental to the provincial scene, but they too engender disputation. This constant theological motion can only take place in an open society; and only by long practice has Ulster shaped a Protestant society that tolerates contradictory revelations. And in shaping this society the majority quietly and without notice has found a means of tolerating the minority, the Roman Catholics among them. Ulster is not only a divided society but also one muddled by mixing of residence, occupation, and habit. There may be less of a mix after twenty-five years of the Troubles, but still the province has overlapping and intermingled people, is mixed in many ways if as few as can be managed with decency and under the law. The Catholic minority is still there, still a threat, still potent, growing greater, and no longer as easy to intimidate. Yet the Protestant ethos has been seen to have survived this generation as the previous ones—but not with ease and not without turmoil and never with assurance for the morrow.

What today is possible is that Ulster Protestants can live a Protestant life. The faith shapes the everyday as well as the agenda at the prayer meeting. For the Protestant, life is an endless, seamless exercise in the faith. And such a life is earnest and pious, and productive. And it is different from the life of a Catholic, feels different in the kitchen or in the club. The Protestant knows himself and knows that few others do so, or there would be no clamour for a united Ireland, no harsh words in London, no apologies for their British Ulster. They know that they are different because they feel so and are so treated. They know their own—but often not without asking. They are not always easily identified on first encounter. There is a scurry to check a name or a background. There is always this necessary effort to find who is who, ours or theirs. Yet each Protestant assumes that among one's own there is an ease and freedom.

Certainly one born again in Christ, newly come to salvation with all exhilaration, feels quite different from those not saved and surely from those loyal to Rome. Yet a life in Christ so lived may appear no different from that of the more conventional Protestant of Down or Derry or even the Catholic across the road. Life may look the same, but it does not feel so, is not perceived so. The routines of the day may be similar, the job done, a service attended, lessons done or the tea taken, but the life of the mind, the agenda of the household, the perception of reality is different. Those recently saved see all more clearly, see God in each action, a God found not simply in the Bible but also in daily observance. A man in love may look no different but he feels utterly changed. So too those who come to Christ. So too assume many Protestants, most Protestants. There is often a very real and very tangible presence: grace said to a God just beyond touch above the table, not to a deity cloaked in ritual and formality, reached through intervention or special institutions and on special days. It is an awesome and fearsome God: a God with thunder; a God whose commandments are not easily ignored; a God of vengeance as well as love; a God that dominates the day and the night. For many the revelation that arrives with the acceptance of Christ transforms everything, brings the great issues of Hell and Heaven, salvation and damnation within touch. Life is not easily lived in the shadow of eternity, not a matter of comfort and ease and trivial concerns.

Those who do not so live must expect less, now and at judgement day. One must suspect those outside the communion, at best misguided and misled and at times dangerous in their ignorance, lost in their heretical, all but pagan ways. A great many Protestants have always felt the necessity of spreading the faith, proselytising, and bringing Christ to those not yet saved—and Ireland, if short on pagans, is filled with those who have not been saved. The pagans apparently are more easily converted to the truth than those trapped in Catholicism. By and large, Catholics have long been considered beyond redemption, beyond salvation, too dazed by the power and glory of Rome to be worth the effort to salvage. Few zealots knock on doors in Catholic estates. Most fundamentalist Protestant churches seek converts among their own, among those who have not been born again but are not beyond hope. Some have sought those neglected by other faiths. In Ireland there has been remarkably little tension arising from the competition over souls—the publicity of the exceptions tending to prove the rule—because of the general self-denying ordinances of the divided society. We are here and they are there—and they in many senses do not exist. God in time will take care of his own in his own way. Nothing is more telling about the rigidity of the division for Ulster Protestants than that the gospel is not preached to the Romans.

The Protestant ethos in place is as difficult to define. This elusiveness is a problem within the divided Ulster society, just as it is for analysts. When Protestant paramilitaries are out seeking any Catholic as target—a symbol, not a person—they rely on geography, not visible characteristics, and so on occasion kill the wrong sort, a Protestant, simply for being in Catholic territory. But beyond the evidence of signifiers—

names and schools and badges—what makes a Protestant pub or a Catholic kitchen different?

Certainly everyone assumes that in private, without the need to adjust to the other tradition, the Protestant or Catholic reverts to a base-line normality. What is discernible that makes the two so lethally different? Those involved feel different, purport to have different values, are both decent but different. How is such a difference detected when all look alike? If one is born again in the blood of the Lamb, responsible, saved, transformed, should this not be visible about the kitchen table, visible at once, visible on the street? If one is a daily communicant, member of the Legion of Mary, and never ventures out without a rosary, should these not show too?

The Protestant assumes that the faith, more vital than all else, does transform the saved. The fear of the Lord is the beginning of wisdom. Yet the great difference is internal, not visible, not a matter of digging with this foot or having a Celtic name. The faith transforms perceived reality and so life. Thus the visitor to Ballymena or the Shankill sees only people—Irish people—not the soul of the saved. Even the saved cannot readily see the presence of the living God, but the presence makes the difference, and the difference is immutable and crucial and vulnerable to assimilation. The great chasm is one of perception rather than great difference in conduct or agenda. What matters to others matters less in Ulster: income, education, skills, or temper. What matters first is the faith, and this in Ulster has determined residence, school, and choice of games. Assuming vast differences ensures that there are such differences, and similarities are considered irrelevant and haphazard. What matters most must be felt, not identified.

All this is often very confusing, even for those living in

the Republic. From a distance there are highly visible similarities: to the citizens of Sligo or Meath the people of Northern Ireland look alike, speak alike, are divided by class and culture as well as by faith. Protestant farmers in the uplands share much with Catholics that they do not share with the landed gentry of the Church of Ireland, who in turn are different from the Church of Ireland workers at Mackie's. Belfast shapes all in Belfast to the city's pattern. Faith in both is vital: both traditions are God-driven, church-going, socially conservative. Yet the Protestants are apt to praise liberty and fraternity and equality. The Protestant must rely on free will to select the proper congregation, the most efficacious form for the faith, often whether there should be an organ for hymns or a flower guild. The small differences matter for the Protestants as well as visible right conduct. Yet the streets of Derry and Strabane are filled with everyday, decent people who do not seem different except to themselves. Each knows just how different.

To the innocent, to the Dáil deputy or the man in the Cork street, all these Ulster people, despite their faith, often because of the intensity of their faithfulness, share much that those across the street or further away do not: a hard accent, a sharp, cold mind, an egotism—and for too long, because of the Troubles, a central role in Irish politics that has warped conventional development and congenial dialogues. Those from the North are dour, dark, assumed cunning, not really pleasant, no matter their denomination. So in the Republic there seem to be even more similarities in Northern Ireland than differences, although the Catholics are more alike than the Protestants, though hardly more alike than the Protestants of the Republic.

In Britain or Europe, in Washington or elsewhere, these

differences are discounted as residue. Even if considered, the nature of the religious basis of British Ulster attitudes is discounted as unpleasant, unpopular, and most especially uncongenial to the necessity of compromise. So the nature of the Protestants of British Ulster is glossed over by all, not simply by republicans who know they are all Irish.

As a result, few in Ireland or elsewhere grasp the real and symbolic nature of a united Ireland for British Ulster: religious oppression disguised as political opportunity. To imagine any accommodation one must begin with the actual nature of the Irish Protestants of Northern Ireland, not what would be convenient. And in large part even in approaching the arena the observers have tended to take everyone as engaged in a zero-sum game, the gain of one the other's loss, when in fact the Protestants and nationalists, the Catholics and unionists, are playing different games. The Protestant plays to persist in isolation, saved and separate from the others in Ireland, and the nationalist plays for an end to history in the triumph of the Irish, all the Irish. For there to be no game at all, both must win or at least see winning as a viable option: the end-game as an end to the game.

8

TWO TRADITIONS, ONE IRELAND

There is nothing civilised about a mob, be it
Protestant or Catholic.—Sam Thompson

Ireland is divided and always has been, by class and
province, into a north and south, into Catholics and
Protestants, into urban and rural. A basic accepted by all is
that Northern Ireland is a divided society, a classic case:
what matters most is whether one is Catholic or Protestant.
This dominates urban and country, rich and poor, clever
and dim. This is not so in the Republic, where various
divisions are of various import. Northern Ireland is truly
divided in its own special way: two traditions continually
evolving, two societies in many ways, permanent,
impenetrable, immutable, quite different but both largely
secularised and culturally homogenised and appearing to
others quite alike.

There are many who see Europe as a melting-pot, boiling
away the indigestible into a thick and nourishing broth,
often with many shared "Western" components: Japanese
cars, American films, Israeli cut diamonds, and many old
imperial habits of exploiting the resources of the far places.
The little national differences in western Europe will

certainly dissolve and are dissolving in the transnational medium: CNN on the hotel television, U2 on the Sony Walkman, English used by all air traffic control, and a common currency only a matter of time. The future is a Spaniard working for a Dutch company at a factory in Germany who appears at an Italian-designed office in tweeds from Scotland run up by a Turkish tailor in Denmark. The French Academy may fret about English words or the Tory backbench about amalgamation, but the trend appears inevitable and ultimately desirable. Europe cannot afford rampant nationalism: it no longer pays. Even violent resurgent nationalism, as in eastern Europe, or nationalism revived as politics, as in France or Austria, or, worse, as cult in Germany, will be tamed, tutored, and incorporated where possible.

The West is not so much awake as one. The future is of similarities, not differences. Special traditions will not be lost in a multicultural if homogeneous Western society but will not engender murder, ethnic cleansing, or pogroms. In Britain the Welsh, Scots, English and new immigrants manage; so too the Flemish and Walloons in Belgium. And all the enormous varieties, traditions and cultures are not lost in the United States but transmuted into Americans, in Australia into Aussies. So too will the Irish; so too should the Irish. As it is, BBC Ulster is really little different from BBC London and often filled with American productions. On the streets of Strabane or Bangor the clothes of the crowds are the same, the Irish accents, if variant, are similar, more different in class than caste. In Brussels over a laptop no-one cares what caste the graduate from Queen's. The sensible assume that in time each and all can share their traditions as they perforce share six counties. After all, all the English share the War of the Roses and the Americans their civil war.

King William or Cromwell, like King Arthur or Robert E. Lee, may in time be neutral, not weapons but truly dead if not gone or even forgiven. And this could be an end to history as weapon, an end to traditions that deny the other, for there is always change. For the sensible and reasoned, sensible and reasoned Irish history may not yet have begun, may yet wait a role that serves all, may be a product of scholars and not patriot oratory, but this could change and should change.

Variant traditions penned into place engender considerable mutual effort, direct and indirect, simply to maintain the stability of their differences. Much must be invested in stability that might in other places be spent elsewhere. Separate but relatively stable traditions are neither easy nor cheap. To maintain the two traditions, Northern Ireland must keep in motion even to remain static: tomorrow cannot be like yesterday unless everyone, Protestant and Catholic, takes great care today. To maintain the integrity of the quarrel between the two traditions the quarrel must be kept up to date, fine-tuned. Most of those involved want their exclusive tradition, to keep their rebel heart or their liberties safe, but not at the cost of murder. So care must be taken to keep friction to a minimum—a simple whirr, a scatter of sparks, but no lethal grinding.

And after generations care so taken remains essential, not entirely natural but essential to ensure civility. And despite the Troubles, most of Northern Ireland appears normal to the innocent eye. Most visitors never even see the shower of sparks, much less the bagged bodies by the roadside. Mostly the two cultures, the two worlds, the two perceptions have coped; so that whatever the merits of the two traditions, thought by most of the involved to be resolute and immutable and advantageous, the constant effort to prevent lethal grating at the edges is usually effective. The long IRA armed campaign is evidence that the institutions of stability need not be truly effective to at least moderate the conflict: the death toll is appalling but equal only to a day's killing in Rwanda or Buchenwald. Yet even in the best of times—the long Stormont years—violence occurred. In Northern Ireland violence is persistent and endemic, a low-grade fever that has never been cured, a condition of existence that even offers secondary benefits to society.

This stable, divided society is never at rest. All the involved must constantly adjust so as not to give offence and so in passage through life to present signifiers—identity signs for one's own as well as the others. Even in the most violent encounters a rule of Brownian motion applies: the bounding, bumping molecules are violent close up but the whole system is stable. Offence may be given but according to regulation. Violence may be done but within limits. As for the everyday, the best adjustment is to evade friction. Everyone in public is in social motion. There are small adjustments, slight, often involuntary tics that produce a constant motion, exchanges, contacts, but the result is the necessary stability of the whole. In isolated, segregated zones there need be less adjustment; in mixed zones with long-established residents or at the common centre, more activity is needed. More care must be taken. There is no doubt, however, that the system is composed of contradictory traditions: two categories, them and us. Everyone may seem similar, but not to those involved, and they are the ones who matter, the traditionalists, always adjusting, always changing and for generations the same in their perceived differences.

To exist, those in Northern Ireland, those who live in British Ulster and without the walls, must meet at the gate in such a way as to avoid constant confrontation, find a way to pass with civility and at times mutual respect, and at times in a shower of sparks. In a prison the republicans or loyalists within their segregated cages need not worry greatly about who is their own and who is from the other lot; but in a mixed prison, like Maghaberry, the signs must be present, even though many are serving life together in a community without political content. Each prisoner knows the tradition of the other. In any mixed area more care must always be taken so that the two traditions can be effectively contained, adjusted to stability. In Maghaberry the former republicans and former loyalists share the reality that they are "former"—have left the segregated for the mixed. Those left behind are still advocates of triumph, still pursue domination or justice, the wiles of the rebel heart or the responsibilities of the defender. Those in mixed society, on the other hand, regardless of their tradition, pursue the everyday goals of everyone else, family and salary, pleasure and profit, getting and spending. In Maghaberry there is less normal to pursue, but even then the two traditions merely co-exist, do not blend. A great many subjects for discussion, just as in the outside world, are avoided—easily avoided, since the other is known to be other and the subjects are easy to recognise as divisive. There need be less constant motion in Maghaberry, because the players have been identified, need no longer be individuals.

In Northern Ireland the confrontation of groups is monitored by the rules of engagement: riots have patterns, marches have routes, and the provocations are shaped by tradition. This means that some may be victims and some may not. In more conventional circumstances it also means that with the introduction of the individual, no matter what the circumstances, a rush into the casualty department of the Royal Victoria Hospital or into the bar of a popular hotel, on first meeting at Queen's University or on accepting a lift on the Ballymena road, with each new prisoner, every new colleague, identity is often the first requirement. What and how things are done depends on who they are done to. Much of the time the whole point is to see that nothing provocative or painful is done at all.

Mostly there is no problem. Many arenas or events are closed to the other tradition by custom or choice. It is only when the ground is open to all—all criminals, all physicians, all second-year students—that adjustment must be made. Over generations, especially the last, these open grounds have been narrowly circumscribed by residence, by custom, by habit and history. There are resorts for each, bars for each, hotels for each, football teams for each, even sports for each, as well as segregated schools, estates, and work-places.

Many reformers simply seek to open more areas for mixing, hardly aware that the great difference is in the tradition, not apparent proximity. What engenders the Troubles is that the militant nationalist tradition has fostered physical force as a means of achieving a satisfactory arena, one opposed to British interests and to the defenders of British Ulster. These defend their own with resort to force, legal or vigilante, effective or no, but always an early choice. The divisions at the harsh edges of the traditions ensure that violence and the traditions never really amalgamate, only share uneasily the same space. Mixing is really not mixing at all but the adjustment of intractable differences. Traditions ensure both endemic violence and persistent stability, but each is apt to assume that such a tradition—their own—is vulnerable to change. No-one feels triumph assured or history's verdict guaranteed; no-one in Northern Ireland is quite certain about tomorrow and so one relies on yesterday for assurance and on one's own for reassurance and suspects forbearance, assimilation and tolerance, even mercy, as eroding necessary defences.

Yet no matter how long the tradition of segregation, the edges of the two traditions still merge, blend in places, some intrusions important and some not. Some arenas are communal: the university common room, the train to Dublin, the centre of a few towns, the planes from London, the chess club. No-one can at first sight tell who is who, and so identity must be established: the badge noted, the newspaper read, the odd word, the hint given, a name, a school, a sign so that offence will not be given, the arena ruined without benefit. Some activities for varying reasons attract those from both sections of the community: intellectual activities, an arts club, or pigeon racing. Some venues hardly need adjustment: one goes into the Roxy to see a film, not to mingle. Others are dominated by a mutual concern without threatening implications: stamp collecting, landscape painting, the lifeboat society. Then intimacy swiftly erodes the need for repeatedly proclaimed identity: it would be a rare member of a chess club who did not know the persuasion of all the members; and after a match who would care that a Catholic won or lost to a Protestant but a true bigot. And there are, of course, many of these in Northern Ireland, but not so many at a chess club. If, however, the arena of chess move. then there may be a problem in another venue. Would the match be in their hall or ours? Would the hall be safe and secure, entail risk, upset the balance, cause trouble?

Cross-tradition contacts cause problems and so are worth the effort only in special cases. And Northern Ireland is filled with special cases, groups and organisations and associations that mix both traditions, friends across the divide, neighbours in each other's kitchen, and even girls dated, men married. This is more the case than admitted and less than the optimistic would like, and at times and places all but unknown, especially in the heartlands of the present conflict. Still, traditional loyalties can become at times secondary, but not often. And the very universality of the violence has encouraged efforts at moderation and amelioration, from mixed schools to special friendships.

No cross-traditional contact is easy or without risks, whatever the rewards. A mixed marriage may be taken as an affront to a segregated area. Mixing is always risky, and permanent risk more so. Such permanent denial of traditional loyalties is for many an erosion of necessary distinction. Some will not have the other, even if a brother or an aunt, in their home. Some parents will not even see their children. But some parents and kin and friends adjust—love over loyalty. Still, for a mixed couple this church or that may be barred, and the pub at the corner, even comfort on the street. Some, once blended, simply move, slip into an area where toleration may exist; some simply leave the province. Yet if escape to a more congenial or more mixed area is denied, everyone has to make do. The couple never really fits anywhere but with each other, always moving their private mixed venue with them, inevitably imposing a more complex level of toleration. The mixed couple imposes strains that generate agitation within the stability provided by the constant minute adjustments. More adjustments are necessary, and some do not care to adjust. It is easier to stay with one's own; at times it is impossible not to do otherwise.

The number of neutral venues after a generation of Troubles is small, and such sites are never as neutral as the involved imagine. One must belong. The Jews, mostly along the Antrim Road with their own synagogue and institute, are lumped as Protestant Jews, for their class, location and political inclinations are more congenial. Everyone must belong to one of the traditions: American politicians or British Labour Party people, suspected by unionists even when Methodist or Unitarian. Always one may hold the same life values, be splendid examples of sound, decent people dedicated to their professions, modest and prudent, but all know the faith of the other and all make adjustments.

Even when harm is seemingly done, prejudice and bias allowed free play, arrogance and provocation the order of the day, much of the display is shaped so as to do no harm by ritualising the insult. Most of those who would do harm wittingly tend to do so in traditional patterns that allow arrogance and fear a role in life without recourse to violence. The faithful march and sing, demonstrate, shout at the crowd, throw pennies from the walls of Derry, or preach treason at Easter over the patriot dead. Riots can be choreographed so that the demonstrator, even throwing stones at the appropriate target at the right moment, can do no real harm. Anger is vented. These are the public institution of control: better the Orangemen on the road to Dunloy than engaged in arson or murder, better graffiti than the Armalite. By such displays, which reinforce the acceptance and often the delight in prejudice, the assumptions of the tribe can be exposed and endorsed, can in fact be displayed with relish. It is far more telling to march back and forth across Ulster, sit at the crossroads in defiance of the RUC or even throw the odd bottle than to resort to the slanders of the pub or to the political speeches that hammer the others and extol the faithful. Everyone who chooses can, on the day, be a public patriot and a secret bigot, a Protestant defender or a republican rebel.

In sum, the constant personal adjustment of individuals, the general opposition to mixed intrusions, the rituals of domination, defence, and intimidation, from the Orange marches to the IRA Easter statement, are both divisive and integrative. In the first place they keep the opposites apart, and in the second they allow a general society to be erected on top of the two traditions. This divided Northern Ireland society is more tangible to the involved than to the visitor. The passing stranger, even an overseas relative, cannot see many of the differences, the divisions that are hidden by good nature, social institutions, and care. What the visitor sees is a people with similar accents, according to class, not national or racial background, people with similar social attitudes, with similar economic problems, dressed alike, living in similar estates or farms, people who must be Irish, are as one. The people and their homes are not quite indistinguishable. There are often the tell-tale tags: painted kerbstones, a badge in a buttonhole, political posters, a Claddagh ring, graffiti. Most are in solid neighbourhoods, some with the painted kerbstones but most only different to the locals. As with other divided societies, where the variation seems so slight, so too in Northern Ireland are the variations small to all but the involved. At present no-one in the melting-pot of New York much cares where one goes to church or temple. No-one in Alabama feels any longer impelled to defend the past by lynching blacks. No-one in elegant Paris wants poor Algerian Berbers imposed on their own street but they find no problem with the elegant rich Arabs next door. In America and Europe bigotry and prejudice are alive and well but unevenly distributed and not the single compelling rubric of society— not even in the American south, although there racial stereotypes, historic attitudes and advantage divide much of society still, but the avowed dream is the same.

In much of the West the differences are there: class differences, national differences, religious differences. Colour and creed matter. Those who came first suspect anyone later. Those with money exist uneasily alongside those without. Differences are at most times insidious but only rarely lead to displays of physical force. This is obviously not everywhere so, for the world is filled with tension, national division, and tribal strife. Often the risk of trouble is there with urban mix, whether with the Copts in Cairo or the Chinese in Malaya, but is worth the slight danger. Not always: the Chinese in Indonesia were slaughtered as communists and the Copts in Cairo are at risk to Islamic zealots. Such a danger may under varying pressure become intense; and then there is Bosnia.

But in the West even the big differences have largely been dissolved in pluralistic societies where even the greatest differences are overshadowed by the advantages of the whole and by the opportunities available. It is still undeniable that much of the Balkans has collapsed into chaos and the edges of the Soviet empire have revealed ancient national hatreds, but these are clashes in borderlands, lands without democratic traditions or appropriate leadership; but Ireland still seems to the innocent so innocent. It is a green and pleasant island, filled with charming people, even if somewhat dour in the North, not a post-colonial Rwanda or the front line of the ancient clash of Greeks and Turks. Ireland should be a plural society where the two traditions can co-exist, and to a remarkable extent it is. In fact all the differences of race, religion and nationality that cause trouble are muted in plural societies, in London or New York or Paris—not a mixed pot but a delicious stew with the parts still tasty. Differences are assumed to add spice, to make society more exciting, the frisson of differences that makes New York or London vital. Social violence may come and go, and in some provincial arenas differences may be institutionalised, but this is because the involved are really different, can be seen at a glance as Chinese or black. Citizens of the Republic often find all from Northern Ireland, regardless of their religion, alike and unappealing. Yet in the province everyone involved assumes that the two traditions are vastly different and at the same time must make every effort not to give offence. Everyone knows that there are differences, differences that are vital.

Such perceptions are hardly altered by the contacts available in Northern Ireland. Friends may work in the same shop for twenty years and have no idea what the other does at Sunday service or believes about salvation. The Troubles have often ensured that even this contact is lost as the peace walls have gone up, the isolated moved out of mixed estates; the fearful Protestant on the border has departed for Antrim and the Catholics too close to the Protestant urban heartland have long since left. Long before the Troubles the two communities remained innocent of the other, no matter how close the orbits of the involved or how often paths crossed. Any contacts were shaped to avoid intimacy and insight, to avoid trouble, or were made by rituals that reduced the individual to symbol. A local lad in the UDR felt that a uniform made him someone else—a defender—and when he was shot without his uniform his own were aggrieved that another Protestant had been murdered. Not even in the killing could there be agreement on who was dead: Protestant or British soldier, local lad or symbol of the Crown—all the same to his family, all one in real life but not in Northern Ireland, where tradition defines reality.

In any case the two traditions knew and know almost

nothing of the form and practice of others but what can be imagined from gossip, corrupt evidence, the bits found in the mass media, and hearsay. Yet both assume, not without reason, that the different traditions shape lives differently. Certainly both Catholic and Protestant have been shaped by a shared but disputed history: battles and laws and institutions arise from or impose differences, so that 1916 means the Somme to one and the Easter Rising to another. This, like other differences, the optimists and reformers would erode. The sensible assume that proper history could be learned or unlearned, tolerance and understanding as a class project. The optimist sees the times changing: Catholics no longer need sit outside a Protestant church for a friend's funeral service. Private mixed schools can be found about Belfast. Bigotry is unfashionable. The historians hope to teach a balanced past, the sociologists to expose the roots of custom, the lawyers to find justice half way between opposing poles. Surely the Protestants could be shown their Irish roots, recognise their contribution to republicanism, to Irish-Ireland? Surely the Catholics could be taught that their history has not simply been a long and violent struggle against English oppression? Surely the differences being learned could be unlearned?

These secular intrusions, the scholars, the law and physical geography or demographic data, do not mellow the integrity of the difference: they are not basic, not a matter of faith but of reason. The involved perceive that at core is the faith, and this faith not only sets one free but also distinguishes one from the other. One may not be able to see faith any more than one can see the differences in each individual, but in the end in Ulster the faith that imposes distinction is what matters, often all that matters.

Each is apt thus to construct an alternative reality: the

imagined other, not the lad at the works or the next-door neighbour but the generalised, the Catholic as stereotype, never met but not without substance. The faith is thus extended into real life, and again one mostly sees what one expects to see. Thus the Protestant stereotype of Catholics is slothful, feckless, impulsive, manipulated, intermittently prone to violence, lacking in discipline and self-restraint, dependent on ritual and form. They live with the promise of weekly forgiveness. They are assured of the promise of salvation—available to all who accept doctrine. And so with doctrine in hand, the Catholics lead less disciplined, less productive and less Christian lives. And they resent the more provident and productive, the Protestants, those persistent and free of clerical bounds and slothful habits.

On a grander plane the Protestant accepts that Catholic doctrine, the agenda of Rome, is innately expansive and so seeks to counter free will and direct access to God with rituals, display, and false promise. They know this well, for they too read patriot history and religious history if from a different book, and know of the saints and the miracles and the superstitions of the others. They know it all down to the decorations and glowing red lights and the smell of wax—an aura absent from the meeting hall and Anglican cathedral.

It is true that a Catholic church is apt to have gilded saints and priests with vestments; but it is also true that the Catholic congregation is no less puritan in assumption and perception. With a few distinguished exceptions, Ireland's Catholic churches are tawdry in decoration, the people not visual, not encouraged by either the prelates or society to savour the pleasures of the eye, much less the body. The Catholic mind, if not the church, is often as stark and bare and simple as the Quaker meeting-house. Many Catholics may look at paintings or Georgian houses, but few see more than signs of wealth or Ascendancy domination. The Irish Catholic has been taught to suspect the sensual, the body, the pleasures that so often delighted the Italian Catholic (who too may have modern churches in lamentable taste) in food and colour and song. The Irish church is often bleak: the odd candle or gaudy mosaic make little impact. More important, the Catholic God, however shaped by ritual or decoration, is often as forbidding as the Protestant God. For Protestants, never through the door, Catholic churches are a mass of plaster saints, false intermediaries, hideous crucifixes, fairy lights and candles and potted incense and confession booths, all shaped to impose the Pope's authority on a subject and submissive people. The forms follow the function, maintain the souls for the benefit of Rome.

To find such a church and such Catholics, the Protestants of Northern Ireland need not scavenge history or theology, need not resort to books or statistics but merely look about and see what they see. They perceive a people that have not been as productive as Protestants—as the British—who have failed to shape a viable state in twenty-six counties, who in the six counties would rather indulge their appetites than build. In effect, having expelled the Catholics from the walled city, from Providence and hope of salvation, the Protestants blame them for being outside, unredeemed, left with fallow land and alien habits and resentments. The victim is at fault; and since even the most dedicated bigot suspects that this interpretation is not without some self-interest, those still within the city are not reassured by simple possession of the truth and so keep the walls in repair. They may be reassured that their faith is sound, but it is not yet secured, even if visibly successful—unlike that of the others.

Everywhere that Rome has sought open competition with

the Protestants, Rome has failed to compete: the Catholic ethos engenders closed cultures, communicants who lack discipline and responsibility and are less productive. Italy and Spain are economic and cultural black-spots, only emerging into the new Europe with the decay of Catholic control. In Ireland the Protestants find evidence for all their assumptions and most of their prejudices: these may be expressed crudely along the Shankill or with discretion on Malone Road but are as one and reinforced by a selection from contemporary events. The Protestant knows Ulster's Catholics, not from observation but from assumption: the other tradition is constructed from legends, a little experience, stereotypes, and feared vices.

The result is that for the Protestants there is a great, largely invisible but very real Catholic world. It is different in kind from their own: long-established, intractable, largely immune to penetration or reform, a maze of regulation and diktat transversed most effectively without thinking, relying on the map supplied by Rome. The Irish Catholics live in this world, where most answers are supplied, devotion shaped by ritual, by the authority of the establishment and by the rules of Rome. They live within the dictates not of right reason but rather of centralised authority. The Catholic religion is a matter of doing as one is told and repeating formulas: the fingering of rosary beads, the walkabouts on Pattern Sunday, the sign of the cross, the bob to the crucifix, and for a long time the parroting of Latin in services that need not be understood to be accepted. Every Protestant knows that the Catholics inhabit this special world, because from birth the individual has been moulded by authority, by repetition and doctrine. Worship is not a matter of revelation or exultation—even the Catholic charismatic movement upsets the Roman hierarchy—but of deeds done and formulas repeated. Heaven is reached through attendance records, not through revelation. The Catholics need only responses to lessons learned and accepted, accepted without challenge and made visible in ceremonies, accepted not as symbol but as reality.

Life within this Irish reality, cunningly delineated by Rome, is quite different from that led by Protestants in Ireland and elsewhere. The others, those ensnared by Rome, cannot resist imposed authority. They may be deeply pious, occasionally produce a soul susceptible to mystical experience, do good, be neighbourly, lead sober and righteous lives, but by and large all assume that if they follow the form most sin may be forgiven and all can thus enter the kingdom of Heaven. Entry for Catholics is essentially by means of a visa granted for good works, obedience, and adherence to the form. Most Protestants see Catholic hypocrisy in the confession, authoritarianism in the clergy, a power structure authorised by the hierarchy, and an easy and comfortable adaptation to a theology that permits if not encourages daily sloth, the sins of omission, and the easy life. All this is in direct opposition to Protestant practice, and experience; the two traditions have little in common, are natural competitors on an often uneven field.

That all this is in opposition to much existing evidence, common sense and reality is another matter: evidence, common sense and even reality have not fared well in much of Ulster. One need but look around to see what was looked for.

Looking not only within the province but out beyond in the Republic, the Protestant sees at best a decent people deluded and at worst the "rogues, vagrants and sturdy beggars" whom Cromwell banished to Montserrat after the victory at Drogheda in 1649. Those who would be critical and seek only failings find them in abundance in their neighbours. Their business practices are either duplicitous or ineffectual. Their family size, their vote and their feckless attitudes towards responsibility and the public good stem directly from their acceptance of the Roman vision. Their daily lives, if often devoid of major sins, are still without the light of the Lord. They are denied the comfort and the revelation of the Bible, are asked to accept, not to question, to make appointed rounds, not to seek Christ. The more fundamental the Protestant the more profound the differences in the life as led are perceived. Those who often know the least at first hand are apt to know the worst about Catholicism.

The fundamentalists certainly know where they stand. Most have no hierarchy, some no rituals, often no hymns. Many have no time for anything but the prospect of judgement and the necessity of leading a principled and exemplary life, godly in all matters and so productive in worldly ones. Even the everyday, the conventional, the members of established congregations feel a fundamental difference with those others across the road, over the peace wall, down in the Republic. The others do not fear God: their God is not a God with thunder but one that can be placated by formulas. They are not saved but deluded by orders and dominations and powers. Those within the Protestant community find what they seek in such a tradition. Such a tradition deals best with general matters. So the most rigorous application may not be true for the family on the next farm or on the estate but is true for all nationalists to some degree, to an observable degree. The Irish hierarchy has permeated the nationalist people. The parish priest determines the values and morals of his own, who they marry, how they transact their business, their family size, and their reading lists. Each Catholic must come to the confessional, not only to be cleared for further sin but also to report any defiance of the Church's regulations. Those regulations internalised—found in even those who profess independence of mind and the virtue of free thinking—have produced a Catholic society where government is merely the secular arm of the bishops, where critical thinking is abolished in favour of acceptance, and where there is no discipline in productivity or capacity but only in acceptance of authority. Irish nationalism is simply the outward form of Catholic control. And differences between the IRA and the Catholic hierarchy are a matter of timing and techniques—means, not ends. The Republic is the form of Catholic Ireland. And if effective in the control and possession of the souls of the Irish, the system is a failure in secular terms, a state unable to keep its citizens at home, provide even frugal comforts, unwilling to let ideas circulate or encourage initiative and enterprise. Most of all, Catholic Ireland has been unable to produce a civic culture that would allow the free play of diversity and the rise of creativity and productivity. What else could be expected from Rome, from the indolent Gaels?

For Protestants the failure of the Republic is so obvious, an axiom, that detailed criticism is often neglected. The failures of Irish Protestant society in the province that parallel those in the Republic are glossed over by the anecdotal evidence of tidy towns, clipped verges, affection for the work ethic, and the visible virtues of a plain people. The rate of unemployment, the misery of the poor, the endless flow of fiscal intervention from London and from Europe does not loom large in Protestant minds. The cost of maintaining British Ulster is seen in the bravery of the RUC, the rigour of the defence, not in the £2,200 a year the British government spends for each person in Northern Ireland—1,580,000, and only 855,000 of those Protestant and eligible to be within the walls. Not mentioned either are the other defensive costs: the shame of the sectarian murders, the corruption of justice, the decay of the civility so prominent in discussion—all casualties of the defence, necessary losses for most.

Protestants do not care to defend their own society. Few even bother to explain the rationale of the Stormont system or the puritanism enforced from the pulpit, the children's swings chained on Sunday or liberal dissent batoned on the streets. Why explain? It is war in any case, and wars are like that. Few want to examine their own. Most Protestants feel in their heart of hearts that they live in a grand wee country, more moral than most, most faults imposed by response to subversion. So it is a land saved by their own exertion from a tide of flawed nationalism—and Catholicism. If the latter assumption is not politically correct, so be it. What is considered truly important is the life as imagined by the decent: grace at meals, moderation in all matters, a stable family, tidy houses and tidy minds, prayers said and the Bible read. There is nothing like this in Kerry or mid-Tyrone, where the fields are rimmed in weeds, the children numerous and without prospects, the parish priest at the door and the tithe to be paid or Hell assured. This vision is especially untroubled because none have been to Kerry or care to go. Protestants, like Catholics, know what they know and if misinformed in detail are not apt to change their perception of the other tradition, a lesser as well as different ethos.

There is no doubt that there is in Northern Ireland a Protestant ethic that differs from the Catholic, that stresses the individual over the community, productivity as criterion of a life well led, that praises plain thinking and a critical mind, an intellect often honed on the Bible. What is also clear, if less so, is that life as led as a Protestant is different from that of the Catholic neighbour; but the difference is not tangible, not in clues or in special private behaviour but in the perceptions of reality. What matters is the assumption about society rather than tolling up the neat fields, polished shoes, or family size. A Protestant, even one with less commitment to the church, lives a life enhanced by the tangible presence of the Saviour. Each day is a religious experience, everyone is judged not by the parish priest or the rules as written but by the living God. The stress on individual responsibility that finds resonance in all British Ulster institutions is assumed to be absent in Catholic Ireland: the other tradition is quite different, relies on the acceptance of authority that has a resonance in all Irish institutions—for the shift from Catholic to Irish is easy for Protestants to make.

How one feels about reality shapes a world that appears quite different to outside observers. Very few Irish Catholic observers—and few Irish Catholics need observe, since they are already informed—can see or sense the perceptions of the Protestants. Their flaws and policies are easy to read but not the content of their character—and that is different from imagined and from that of the Irish Catholic. To the innocent all on a Belfast street look alike and so should be much alike. Yet who can tell the man transfixed by a mystical vision if he keeps still in awe? Who can tell the woman in love if she keeps the secret? Who can tell a Catholic from a Protestant pedestrian or who is who in a pub? Who could tell the family friends visiting Dunloy from the Orangemen who arrived to march until the latter were costumed in provocation and the others stood by the side of the road? Even in confrontation the two traditions do not seem opposites but variants; but the smaller the vital differences the more intensely they can be felt.

It is what those within their own environment feel that makes the difference, and these differences, difficult to see, are not so much contradictory as complementary. The perception of Catholicism and so of Catholics has remained remarkably stable in Northern Ireland. Irish Protestant perceptions neither violate the reality imagined nor fail to pay dividends. Those with no other assets but perception can feel, if not assured of Heaven at least better than the others. Both traditions supply advantage, allow a divided society to operate, impose rules and encourage mistrust and distaste. Invidious distinction has value—and hate too returns considerable interest for little investment. Since individuals are not the focus but religion, individuals can be ignored, befriended but not understood, hated even if never introduced. It is the perception of Catholicism reinforced by selected evidence—all real and much telling—that allows each Protestant to suspect and oppose the pretensions of the other. The more reality introduced into the equation, the more exposure to the individual, the more adjustment may be necessary; for generation after generation such adjustment has been made with ease, without the need for any agonising reappraisal. Great theories are never discarded simply because of flawed evidence until the accumulation of contradictions allows a new general theory; and for some, conversion never comes. A generation of the Troubles has merely reassured Protestants, reaffirmed their assumptions, refined their perceptions and so reinforced their prejudices. The Protestant constable, the B Special or the UDR man at the checkpoint does not need to ask questions: he knows all he needs to know and stands by the side of the road to intimidate, not to investigate. Any nationalist is suspect, and some soon to be punished—for subversion, for being nationalist and ultimately for being Catholic and so seditious, rebellious by nature.

Certainly all these Catholics, rich or poor, nationalist or not, besides their religion share a conviction that they are Irish. This is not necessarily and increasingly not at all so with the Protestants, for Ulster is British. Since Ulster is clearly not part of Britain, where Ulster Protestants are regarded by all as Irish, this requires some translation and engenders some uncertainty. The Ulster Protestant knows what he is not: Catholic. And the more closely the meld of Irish and Catholic, nationalism and religion, the more distance the Protestant seeks. A few deny they are Irish at all, in any way. For the more sensible this is not so easy. Standing at the seaside watching the lights go on in Scotland makes Scotland no closer. What has been done instead is to construct a British Ulster, Protestant in ethos and agenda, British in civility and resource if Irish in location, accent, and custom.

What matters is the faith; but this alone is insufficient in the modern world as identity. In Cyprus, where there has been an inconclusive peace process for a generation, to be Cypriot tells nothing: one must be Greek or Turk. A Greek Cypriot is also Greek Orthodox, as a Turkish Cypriot is Muslim, but both share only hostility and proximity on an island, are Greeks and Turks in Cyprus. British Ulster is the opposite of the Cypriot nation. Cyprus is a legal entity, has real boundaries, laws, a tangible presence that in no way has engendered citizens—these are Greeks or Turks living on the same contested island. British Ulster is imagined, a safe retreat for an Irish Protestant people with standards, values, assumptions, and agenda—all the intangibles beyond institutions and laws.

In Ireland the Protestants are Irish, have been so for centuries, have at times been in rebellion against the greater kingdom, just as at times they have been its most loyal supporters. Protestant Ulster existed before British Ulster existed, when all Ireland was united under the Crown—has from time to time found vital Protestant Ulster interests at variance with the Crown but not often and not for long. Mostly they have no problem with loyalty, but that loyalty is not to a nation or even to a special religion as much to advantage gained historically. It has been an advantage integral to religion and long protected by the Crown, but still a confusing heritage. The Catholics are assumed to have none of these problems. They are Irish. Since the legends and heritage of Gaelic Ireland as displayed by Dublin are not those of most Protestants, the Protestant places less value on what is Irish and on what arises from Ulster and instead perceives the difference that arises from sectarian loyalties as the predominance of the British. Thus various attempts to shape an Ulster identity, to find Celtic ancestors or consider unilateral independence have been ineffectual. What the Protestants perceived is that their religious virtues are congenial with British political civility and capacity. Geography, even cultural geography, does matter but not a great deal. Ethnic purity is not really an issue—who knows who is most Celtic; even the cherished Scottish ancestors are often more Nordic than Celt.

In British Ulster what matters is the identity of those who would not be Catholic but British and are yet in Ireland. In Britain the Ulster Protestant is treated little differently from the Ulster Catholic or for that matter any Irish Catholic. All are assumed to be Irish, all Paddies. So the Ulster Protestant is Irish by accent, by location, and often by choice: an Irish Protestant from British Ulster. It is a complicated and slightly disorienting tradition; it is so much easier for the Catholics who are simply Irish. In fact the Protestant fears that the ease with which a Catholic feels innately Irish indicates all too well the equivalence of Irish Catholicism and Irish nationalism. For, with few contemporary exceptions, the Protestant may be born in Ireland, have an Irish accent, tick "Irish" as an identifying characteristic, but is never an Irish nationalist. For Protestants, Irish nationalism as practised in Ulster is readily visible as Catholic in shape, membership, and attitude.

In fact the others have shaped a mirror image of Protestant institutions, but for sinister purpose. The Catholics have their own masonic orders, their own secret societies, new ones and old ones, to the same end: rebellion. For centuries they had their own rural nightriders, sectarian factions that burned and maimed, just as do the Provos in Tyrone and Armagh. The Provisional IRA is simply the epitome of Irish nationalism for this generation. It is parochial, pious, provincial, narrow in aspiration, sectarian in targets, traditional in organisation. The Provisionals in the country are an aggressive sectarian movement focused on driving out the Protestants. This has always been so with Catholic defenders. In the cities, especially Belfast, it is a radical conspiracy of gunmen seeking vengeance, now with Semtex and Armalites, once with Webleys and before that as Fenian bombers. If the IRA are not Catholic defenders they certainly act as if they are: Catholic aims and aspirations, Catholic symbols and rituals, and in the Republic Catholic friends and advocates.

After a generation of violence, British Ulster cannot see the need to distinguish between Irish Catholicism and Irish nationalism. Some Protestants, especially the gentry and the successful, are fond of their Irish roots, proud of their Irish history. Irish titles might have been given at a discount, but they are still Irish. Others without ancestor charts or family lands are not immune to local patriotism—the fate of the Northern Ireland football team or even at a pinch and to some degree the triumphs of any Irish side. Some are not, delight in the support of the sporting enemies of those teams identified as Irish Catholic—at the Olympics or at a Celtic match against Rangers. Few Protestants are ashamed of being Irish but instead, in Leeds or Bradford, are irritated that all Irish are assumed to be one.

What most Protestants are not is firstly loyal to Ireland. In fact much of the confusion and uncertainty arises in shaping an identity beyond the claim that Ulster is British but not in Britain. Even the perception of a British Ulster, a real place if without unifying institutions, is also a concept conceived by a Protestant population in need of reassurance and not easy to explain. The Protestants are a people who are often united only on the need for a union that ensures their present Protestant freedom within the United Kingdom. British Ulster is not a nation but home and refuge. The other Irish do not have this problem: they have a nation, composed of a Republic, and another pure and whole in each heart. They assume that their national perception is valid for all in Ireland, should be accepted as compulsory through appeal and logic. The proselytising of Irish nationalists has often been visible on many fronts: cultural offers, leadership of the national cause, parity of esteem, a splendid destiny open to the willing. There have always been a few so attracted, but the enormous bulk of Ulster Protestants has seen no advantage in an Irish nation and great risks: fiscal risks from a small, feckless Dublin establishment, national risks as a small, unimportant country, cultural risks from acceptance of a marginal language and literature, and most of all the single great risk of the amalgamation of the faith through erosion, subvention, and the imposition of alien values. The Protestants did not want any movement towards union, do not want any movement at all, want what they have at less cost, not more at great risk, and are not tempted by a dominant role in any future Ireland. None could or can see advantage in all the suggested pacifying arrangements, federalism, or condominium, since all these edifices of lawyers and theorists would mean accommodation with nationalism. What the Protestants want is their own, their British Ulster, defended, secure, imagined but viable. And what they have in British Ulster is inherently better than any other options and one that can be and often is displayed, paraded, deployed in rituals and displays and ever defended. They do not want to be only Irish, Protestants in Ireland. They want what is theirs, won and defended. They do not want but must accept the others among them, or their unpopularity, and so they must make the best of being Irish and the most of Ulster and so continue as before in the Lord's work.

The Ulster Protestant has settled for what has been left, for what can be defended. Partition, whatever the original conditions and rationales, whatever the first hardships and incongruities, is now reality—not because of laws or treaties or the impact of time, not because of a line on a map, not in spite of the Irish Constitution or the claims of nationalists but because the country is and has long been divided by conviction. Here is British Ulster and there are the others. The others that were Protestants are lost and gone for ever; the others that are in the grip of Rome are beyond reason or reach. The threat remains, as always, Rome, and the most urgent the seditious within the six counties. That some

Catholics are content within Northern Ireland is ignored: one is as all, except when met at the golf club and then an exception.

These realities—the loyal Catholics, the Protestants discarded—do not make British Ulster any less real. The Catholics live in Northern Ireland, not British Ulster, and the other Protestants are in the Republic, not Northern Ireland. In fact for a generation it has been British Ulster, not the British, that has seemingly been the target of the IRA. It is British Ulster that contains the hopes, aspirations, attitudes and agenda of a Protestant people of Northern Ireland. And British Ulster is not subject to negotiation. How could it be? It is not even a tangible entity with institutions of governance but is real nonetheless. It is a child not of partition, the Tan War or the agreement of states and governments, not ruled directly or at all, but rather the creation of necessity: a home for the Protestants of the six counties beyond reach of declared enemies and faint-hearted friends.

When the sticker on a unionist's car reads *Six into twenty-six won't go,* this is a simple truth. Six and twenty-six will not make a 32-county Ireland, because the six, the historic core counties, the Protestant province of Northern Ireland, are only the outward and visible sign of British Ulster. Everything about this perception is antipathetic to an Irish republic, to an Ireland filled with Catholics, to the concepts, ideals and triumphs of Irish nationalism. There can be no diversity in unity, no strength, no advantage, nothing but the loss of all that Protestants publicly profess, all that makes them different—and British.

Essentially, even with British persuasion, foreign investment and vast nationalist concessions the citizens of British Ulster cannot imagine an end of partition that would offer advantage. The very fact that the threat of the gunman would go—and the British army—would be an indicator that force as a factor was no longer needed: diplomacy and compromise had effected the change so long desired by the nationalists and so to the advantage of the Catholic Church. In any event, in real life a united Ireland would offer little real economic advantage, certainly not to equal those of Northern Ireland within the United Kingdom, little leverage in the international arena, little personal scope that was available to any British citizen, and, no matter what the law books might say, none of the freedoms so crucial to a modern state. Unity has only costs, not advantage; how unnatural to give up advantage for the theoretical, the arguments of doctored history, the appeal to geography and not reason. In this sense the entire tradition espoused by the nationalists as either shared or exclusively Irish is denied: the farmer in east Tyrone knows full well that the conflict is between them and us, only incidentally us as representatives of the British but in most matters us winners, the planted who have flourished, and them, the displaced and unredeemed. The avowed enemy of the gunmen, the Crown, is delusion: the enemy is Protestant Ireland, now reduced to British Ulster. And if the Crown goes, so too Protestant Ulster, a fortress without hope of relief as Derry once received, an island amid a greater Catholic island. The other tradition is to absorb or expel and so triumph, not to oppose the alien British, who are said by every republican to be cause of every Irish woe, but to eliminate the Protestants of Ulster as different, a constant affront, history's reminder, history's winner, if the triumph is always at risk.

So not an inch must be given, not to the gunmen, not to the appeals of nationalism, not to the disclaimers of Rome or Dublin, not to the initiatives of the alien and self-interested and distant in Washington or Europe or the United Nations; and there must be no mistaking that only in union can a refusal to betray British Ulster be ensured. Only thus can there be no surrender. There is either a British Ulster or there is not. Either the Protestant tradition is valid or it is not: there is no parity, no equivalence, only perceived reality and the facts of a divided society.

The crucial problem is that the two traditions feel mutually exclusive, share no perceived common loyalty. In Ireland those within Protestant Ulster see James II as one with the Pope, no matter what historians say, see their history as theirs alone, not the history of the other Irish. Tone may have been Protestant but he was not a friend or ancestor to British Ulster any more than the Presbyterian rebels of the United Irishmen. The Irishmen who died at the Somme are not esteemed in the Republic, nor are those who fought against the Axis remembered. The traditions share the same events, the same battles, but each is a winner or a loser, each shapes the past as future and excludes the other, no matter what the record says. No matter how attenuated the actuality of the tradition, a matter of lapel badges and rival football teams, or how compelling a commitment to kill or starve to death, the involved believe them mutually exclusive, feel that little is shared and much contested. This contest has been inherited, ritualised, a constant resort even in tranquil times—is tradition itself: the Irish united on division, discord and physical force as a shared value.

And such a tradition requires ultimately, if not today, winners—and there has not been a winner, only Europe's longest war, two centuries of low-intensity conflict between the irreconcilable national aspirations, a clash of destinies, muted, lethal, and seemingly permanent, beyond peace, beyond process, a special tradition. And the future thus belongs to the strong, the determined, the pure in heart, the faithful, those who defend most effectively, sacrifice the most, control the past, belong to the one tradition. For three centuries this has been an aspiration of both: the union or the republic; at times almost a reality, but never a final solution. More than most, despite all their assets and virtues, those within British Ulster fear most of all just such a solution, and the more so because those who advocate with fair hearts and great decency a united Ireland cannot understand that this would be a final solution, an end to British Ulster, not the creation of a new Ireland. The nationalists see Britain outside the engagement and so see but one valid Irish tradition. And the unionists find nothing congenial in the nationalist tradition for British Ulster and much that is alien. Both traditions find a dialectic of defence, one from the British occupation and the other from Irish ambition. Once more both traditions play different games, if with similar rules. Both assume in their heart of hearts that to win is to ensure that the other loses. In the meantime civility demands adjustments and some minimal accommodation.

9

BRITISH ULSTER: THE DETERMINANTS

History of Ireland—lawlessness and turbulency,
robbery and oppression, hatred and revenge, blind
selfishness everywhere—no principle, no heroism.
What can be done with it?—William Allingham

Those who would reason together find Northern Ireland
distressing, just as they found the lethal rivalries of the
South Slavs in Yugoslavia distressing. The British may be
different from the Irish, Dublin and London may have
different perspectives, but the most troubling factor for
many is that the two major traditions in Northern Ireland
seem focused on matters open to reason and so to
adjustment. What really determines the integrity of the
quarrel? Why with so much in common cannot those
involved—sensible, decent, righteous people—adjust their
two traditions?

The optimists are confounded. Even the pessimists find
Ireland's long war excessive vindication. The differences
seem so slight, and elsewhere many of the compelling issues
have long been ameliorated or forgotten in the turmoil of
more cataclysmic events. Yet just as in the past, the steeples
of Tyrone and Fermanagh cast cold, hard-edged shadows.

Why? What determines the intensity and persistence of the quarrel? Why is the gain of one imagined to be the loss of the other every time there is change or suggestion of change? Even change for the good is shaped as contentious at best, more apt to inspire discord than receive welcome. Even peace is perceived as dangerous, if welcome.

In fact the peace process was a triumph of exhaustion as much as an agreed way forward. The gunmen ceased fire because the cost surpassed the expected returns. No-one can speak beyond the general wish for advantage, for expected entitlements, and now, most of all, for an end to fear. Even without murder at the bottom of a lane much still seems the same: certainly the hot summer of 1995 was an indication that the old ways were still to be deployed, even in a new context. Recognition that the context had changed was at least an indication that the determinants of the quarrel were not immutable.

After a generation of the Troubles there has not been much visible change for the better. There are ruins and graves, additional grievances and ruined lives, but what else? The reasoned and optimistic want more. Why cannot the two traditions find if not common ground at least a common language of discourse? Still amid the frantic negotiation of the peace process no-one listens to the other, merely waits until his or her views can be propounded. No-one can imagine the other's position or priorities. No-one really listens, since nearly everyone involved in the political crisis assumes that everyone starts from the same basics. The involved hold not perceptions of reality, not even a negotiable position but rather the revealed truth. They know what they know, start each time from the same line to reach the same conclusions. Adjustment may be in tone or argument but never in assumption or conclusion. The long years of repetition without correction have convinced all that what is repeated is true; and they listen only to what they choose to hear and hear that repeated repeatedly.

Almost all adjustments have been cosmetic, the shaping of formulas rather than addressing the intractable, an excuse to find words to define a grey area between black and white. This is the joy of the bureaucrat, the theorist and the practising politician and is a vital skill in ameliorating conflict, producing agreements, enacting legislation, and keeping a responsible and responsive government viable. Talking about the point, nibbling at the margins of dispute, finding a formula for discord—these are the means necessary for putting acceptance of the inevitable on paper: this means this to the Egyptians and this to the Israelis, and so all can move along towards accommodation and hence advantage; the advantage when perceived will give reality to the formula. This is what diplomats do, the outcome of shuttle diplomacy, the nature of negotiation.

In the Irish case the search for words regardless of the underlying reality is, of course, reasonable if accommodation is desirable but must wait on advantage. Advantage must be sold and has not been, not yet. If Ireland is not to continue as a zero-sum game there must be a grey area of mutual acceptance that will allow time for advantage, real advantage, to emerge. If there is no advantage then the wonders of the formula will not last; the Downing Street Declaration or the Anglo-Irish Agreement were not sufficient unto the formula. Yet even negotiation without resolution has returns: a peace process that gives peace is not without advantage. But talking is done without listening in Ireland and without addressing the perceptions, concepts long evaded by the involved. Empathy is missing and, more to the point, an understanding of the power of perceptions: few listen, fewer hear, and almost no-one can then make use of the message to advantage, especially to mutual advantage. Everyone professes to seek accommodation, justice, and peace, but not compromise or concession. The involved cannot imagine congruence, even when sought.

Almost everyone involved accepts the need for accommodation, for the democratic fashions of the times do not favour the absolute. The most random of killers within the UVF proposes a political agenda as much as does the Catholic hierarchy or the Communist Party of Ireland. Yet the absolutes of Ireland, the unbridgeable gap between opposing perceptions not only of what is desirable but also what is real, have hardly eroded. There has been change, but not all to the good or what might be expected. The Protestants have changed in that considerably fewer first identify themselves with Ulster and more with Britain: the union is more vital than ever. The republicans have changed in that they recognise that rebellious Protestants can deny a national unity and so a united Ireland; but there has been no change in the basic assumptions that once British sovereignty goes so too will Protestant doubts. The Protestants do not want to contemplate their absolute reliance for union on the good will and responsibility of the government of the day in London. Union is an ideological position, a moral posture, integral to identity, and yet could be voted away overnight. British Ulster cannot be so destroyed but cannot be properly defended. The republicans do not want to contemplate the fact that it is not the British who keep the Protestants from adapting to Ireland but themselves, the Irish who are analysed as both alien and unpalatable, inhabitants of a failed entity. The British still assume they are responsible, umpire of the end-game, a part of the solution, responsible and disinterested, not really a player and not really with interests at stake.

Everyone believes that a formula of accommodation exists. All that is needed is that one must accept the present—the revealed truth. British Ulster must be beyond challenge or the Republic a reality. Even the militant will take less than the ideal, but not much less. The others, most of the others at least, want to start the process of uniting the country or continuing the defence of British Ulster or Britain's responsibilities in Ireland and see the future as the present but without the gun. Others seek a more inclusive formula, want to introduce federalism or draft a treaty or change nothing but the rebel heart and so defend Protestant interests. Most accept that talk is cheap but necessary and not easy to refuse; few accept that talk to be effective must lead to costly and necessary adjustment. Talking for effect has been limited to talking to the committed, not to communicating with the others and in some cases not communicating at all. So all are used to talking and many willing to adhere to Western fashions of dignified and decent exchange. Better in all cases to urge toleration and good manners, speak softly and maintain one's perceptions intact.

Often there appears to have been no change in perceived reality, but this is not so: the determinants have changed, even when this cannot be admitted. The Troubles have imposed change, displayed the cost of conviction and shifted some perceptions but hardly touched values and assumptions and seemingly led to an uncompromising impasse. The divisions of Northern society's two traditions seem more pronounced, with less mixing and repeated failures to find a means to peace. Non-sectarian parties, the Peace People, institutionalised mixing and ecumenical conferences have come and gone, or have come and stayed, but have had no real or lasting effect except for individuals and small groups. It is rather that after a generation there are new martyrs, new grievances, and new losses to be made good. Hearts have grown cold. So often nothing seems changed, the province and the people divided and bigotry, segregation and distrust rampant. Even without the gun few hope for more than tomorrow to be like today. Even then the peace process proved vulnerable to impatience, just as the Anglo-Irish Treaty did to the opposition of the supposed beneficiaries.

No-one ever gives up hope. There have been commissions and plans and presidential visits, plans for elections and promises of development, but no emerging common ground or agreed definition on Britain's role or the Republic's function. The search for reconciliation seemingly continues as much from exhaustion as from hope. And at least for seventeen months there was the reality of the peace process and even after the IRA bombs the hope that the gun might not return, not tomorrow anyway. A generation had costed out the price of absolutes for the province: few might want to pay but only a few need play to begin the game again. No-one in the months after the ceasefires could imagine a return to the gun, and so tomorrow and tomorrow stretched out, months and years of process, because recess is far better than recourse to a real armed struggle or the deployment of forces to impose an unpalatable resolution.

In the meantime the Orangemen can march on Dunloy, must march on Dunloy, even if provocation produces visible resistance. Instead of peace in 1995 there was a summer of mutual provocation, arson, and the rituals of venom. And the next year brought accommodation no nearer, only the dreary round of politicians addressing their own. Everyone displayed apparent charity and professed moderation as well as moral righteousness. In the end it was more of the same and so further division of a people so seemingly alike. Great names and important people came and urged peace. The nationalists, especially Sinn Féin, urged movement and the unionists sought immobility. The British found reason for delay that the nationalists found unreasonable.

In the meantime Northern Ireland soldiered on as always, each to his or her own, all imagining their Ireland, a British Ulster that was real but fantasy and a united Ireland bitterly divided. And in February 1996 the IRA lost patience—a quality rare at the centre of the republican world—and there were bombs in London and perhaps an end to the ceasefire but perhaps not to peace as process. Everyone feared that even hope would slip away and the zero-sum game would begin again. Everyone involved feared the other and their own, the mistake, the omission, the blunder that would lead to murder, to the most fearful outcomes. It was all that many in Northern Ireland seemed to have in common with each other or in common with the involved in Dublin and London and Washington. They seemed not so much separate traditions as a single tradition where internal clashes were adjusted by agreed ritual: everyone knew what to do on the road to Dunloy, provocation and response, the same as before, a mutual formality of a singular society.

From afar these Protestants and Catholics still seemed much the same, shared a desire for peace, shared a suspicion of the British political establishment and the priorities of Dublin, shared not just their accent but apparently many of their assumptions; even their views of each other are parallel, not as harsh as each imagines. The people are socially conservative, church-going, taciturn, and if much the same also different from those in the south. And none think more so than those to the south who find even their own Catholic nationalists in the north, much less republicans, uncongenial: too much rectitude, rigid, harsh, self-righteous, arrogant in their long war, not at all popular. The Belfast IRA man with his Bobby Sands lark or Easter Lily, his urban ways, never bog on his boots or ease with a cow, was a stock republican figure. So too were the Ulster political divines, each a type, orators filled with Biblical quotations, limited in vision but not in venom, bigots who encouraged the mindless sectarian defenders. The Southerners may not find either the IRA zealot or the Protestant orator or UVF gunman charming, but they exist. And both have their own self-image and are imagined as stereotypes in Dublin as in London, defined away as intractable and ignored, as in fact are most members of both northern traditions and the Irish in general by the British. The Irish do not ignore the British but exaggerate their involvement and concern, transform them like all the others into stereotypes, perfidious or shrewd but rarely observed and then in passing.

In Ireland distance is measured not in miles but in attitudes and assumptions: a hill farm may be forty miles from Belfast but a century back in time, another world altogether. And Northern Ireland is a special place, beyond the colour of the pillar boxes or the special text of history. Sometimes nothing seems to have changed: King William climbing on his white horse just out of sight down in Sandy Row or the rebel heart still cold. So everyone was worried, anguished and lectured when the Orange marches began in the summer of 1995, the churches and chapels and Orange halls burned, when the old language and ritual of confrontation and provocation emerged almost as soon as the gunmen were off the streets. What had changed? Not Paisley;

not, said Paisley, the IRA. And in the following year, with the IRA bombs in London, Paisley was proved right—again.

What had changed? Much had intensified—fear and loathing and suspicion—but what had really changed? Both sides have been forced to accept the depth of commitment of the other, even as they seek frailty and lack of will. The endless funerals—IRA gunmen, RUC constables, the innocent and transient, the burial ceremonies back in England—have imposed responsibilities and restraint that were less needed when the opposing forces were less effective. Stormont was in a sense a police state that ran out of police as soon as the minority refused to be intimidated. Until 1969 Stormont had seemed immutable, and after 1970–71 no system could be imposed unless acceptable to both nationalist and unionists—and for all practical purpose this meant militant republicans and zealous loyalists. They agreed on nothing but the necessity of the gun and the perfidy of Britain, enemy to one and ally to the other. Pride has not paid well except briefly and only for a very few who savoured the power of the gun. The republicans had at last stopped waiting and had moved into another stage of Irish history, become a major player. The IRA, proud of tradition, persistence, and purity, had its long-sought armed struggle but at enormous cost, a tragedy without a final act.

On the other side the blunders and horrors of the Protestant paramilitary defenders, tolerated in their way by many unionists, made abundantly clear amid the atrocities and random murders that pride in the Protestant tradition did not any longer appear a Christian virtue. And the British were exposed to the cost of official intimidation in a truculent society. Engaged in a dirty war, the British army and RUC not only gobbled resources of money and morale but became contaminated as well.

Whatever the costs, however, the two traditions have spent twenty years at odds. They shared their gradual and mutual loss of innocence, shared the cost of violence, shared the price of pride. London and Dublin, larger, more distant, learned less, hardly learned that their agendas were all but identical: both wanted an end to Irish history and to be left alone. London hardly recognised the addiction of the psychological secondary benefits stemming from their responsibilities to make the Irish accept British example. And Dublin hardly recognised that unity some day meant unity never and so no real change, a posture feared by republicans and denied by unionists.

The two cusps of the Troubles, the IRA and the loyalists, favouring the gun as a necessity, left between them most others who felt that reason might later if not immediately have general takers. Unionists did not want violence, only to be left alone within British Ulster. Nationalists did not want unity any time soon or even at Ulster Protestants' expense, only the prospects and tranquillity in the six counties. The British felt they had no interests but disinterested responsibilities, especially to the Northern Ireland majority. Everyone in Northern Ireland seemed easy and open to negotiation—everyone but the gunmen. Yet most of the negotiation on both sides of the cultural divide was with their own. The moderate nationalists urged concessions on Sinn Féin and a ceasefire on the IRA. The republicans demanded that the other nationalists not run against a hunger-strike candidate. The Unionists sought to re-create a unionist majority to back or oppose a London initiative. The loyalists sought a hearing by the unionists—and were apt to find it offered by the nationalists. The middle ground was rarely crossed—probed and noted but not occupied. Even the IRA and the loyalists maintained erratic and not unprofitable contacts, for in the end, if there were to be an end, they would hold a final veto. But during a generation of turmoil, except for the brief tenure of power-sharing, no lasting bridge was built between the two traditions or beyond the province except the old and often frayed alliances at Westminster and Leinster House.

Intervention by those of good will has either been seen as an intrusion favouring the other or has engendered great enthusiasm that could not be translated into institutional change, or for that matter in changing the habits of perception. The great contemporary crusades of the Peace People indicated real support for "peace": everyone wanted peace, but not at any price, not without justice or in some cases vindication or even at the cost of real change. Those who have actually changed, who perceive reality differently, are still rare. And even change does not produce what the disinterested hope. Most have changed in traditional ways, become more like they were, become more traditional. Some have had to adjust the new reality to old precepts and aspirations, and this they have done. Some have discovered new roles, new responsibilities if seldom responsibility. And whenever and wherever possible the past has been preserved as comfort in troubled times. The visible result in the summer of 1995 was arson, provocation, adamancy, and concern that order might decay. Too little had changed apparently. Certainly in 1995 decency had spokesmen and advocates—but this was always so and hardly deterred the bigots and zealots, barely moderated the seedy prejudices of the comfortable. Northern Ireland has not changed out of all recognition. The old reality has done the adjusting, and not as response to decency, arguments or reason but inevitably in reaction to events. These events have encouraged division and divisiveness even as they have indicated the cost of two traditions.

The efforts to ease mutual hostilities have since 1993 largely been focused on accelerating a peace process rather than contemplating a means of shifting the involved on basic perceptions. There has been ample Irish enthusiasm for peace as negative—an end to the culture of fear and terror—rather than for positive and fundamental adjustments. Those who sell the advantages of permanent peace have noted the reward. The infusion of money and investment, the end of unemployment and the productivity of cross-border institutions are seemingly transitional rewards for a journey without certain destination. The reality of Europe is cited. The American card is there to be played again. Some suggest that changing provincial demographics, changing notions of sovereignty or changing supranational institutions can be reflected in Northern Ireland arrangements. Such arrangements always assume that everyone will win and none lose, instead of the popular and persistent assumption that every gain is a loss, that what is good for the nationalists is bad for the unionists. Spokesmen say they believe in mutual advantage but cannot easily define any real gain other than an end to the killing. The Protestants do not see their role: they kill only in defence, represent the majority, are legitimate.

So no-one has found a third way, a political accommodation that appeals to all or often to any. All the conventions, assemblies and agreements, all the theories suggested and models proposed have been rejected. The only novel prospect with real Protestant vitality was the improbable independent Ulster advocated by spokesmen for the defenders. They, then and later, spoke only for their kith and kin. In politics few Protestants supported an independent Ulster. Fewer claimed an Ulster heritage adequate for a nation. A free Ulster was not a practical option in any case, even for the majority, much less for the nationalists in the six counties. British Ulster must be British—whatever that might mean. Almost no Protestant has any doubts that what this does mean is that the symbols and sinews of the Crown must be present. This is why it is the union that must be defended: to keep Ulster British. Few have changed their minds about their own image and that of the Catholics or about the reliability of London or the ambitions of Dublin. The great slippage has been in the incapacities of the local nationalists: the IRA indicates the power of Irish Catholic nationalism at the gates.

When the Apprentice Boys marched at Dunloy they marched not only to old tunes but to new perceived dangers, to be met by the same means. The Orange hall was empty. The land was filled with Fenians, IRA gunmen and IRA threats, and so a march as in the past was crucial, more for themselves than to intimidate the others. Reality has changed and the change has been recognised, but the Protestants do not want to change, nor the Apprentice Boys, nor the unionists—not that sort of change. Worse, the average Protestant feels neglected, uncertain, disoriented because they, the Fenians, have a secret army and we, the chosen people, have not. This is truly dreadful change and inexplicable. Somehow the Catholics are incompetent in state development but effective in revolution, destruction rather than construction being in their nature. The change, however, has simply made most unionists more determined in their support of the union. Thus the urge for peace, the cost of war, the actual shifts in assumptions, the rise of new fears and new opportunities have resulted in a province remarkably familiar: two traditions, mutually exclusive, provocative and uncompromising, both part of greater tides, producing those engaged in a zero-sum game that has as game-master the Crown.

The sensible have long assumed that congeniality and fraternity can be evoked from familiarity, can encourage mutual purpose and a communality of interests. Pressure to mix, to know the neighbour or to listen has received a sympathetic hearing from the conventional and comfortable, North and South; yet no-one mixes, knows the other or cares to do so. One may march for peace but return to the comfort of old prejudices in the old district, isolated again. Few Protestants, just like the Catholics, see great advantage in mixing.

So whether in one party or two, with or without Stormont, regardless of the fashions of the time or the impact of the Troubles, the Protestants appear much the same. They are not quite, not in perhaps crucial ways. Their response has seemed consistent: concede nothing, oppose any initiative to nationalist advantage. Even during the seventeen months of the ceasefire, when almost everyone in Ireland recognised the general advantage of peace, whatever the direction or pace of the process, the unionists preferred to wait, to do nothing, to act as if nothing had really changed when fearful that still further change was in prospect. This has been the chosen strategy for the defence of British Ulster from the first: change no boundaries, no institutions, no police, programmes, or attitudes—unless compelled. Do nothing and offer not even, as Terence O'Neill did, a kind word. Why offer anything to nationalists who want to take everything? Why appear flexible when Westminster can then take instead of give advantage? And advantage has been taken: old ways have been discredited, old positions abandoned, and old habits maintained only by

great effort. The unionists and so the Protestants have had
to adjust the basics by evasion, by reinterpretation, and by
the use of repetition, rituals and rites as if nothing had
changed when everything has. There has "always" been a
march on Dunloy, but rarely into solid Catholic territory
with the slogans of the IRA on the walls of the Orange hall.
The march and the scuffles are recourse to bluster to hide
weakness. In fact this has largely always been so,
intimidation and visible arrogance arising from fear of the
future as much as from delight in present power. Present
power has always been insufficient. British Ulster and before
that Protestant Ireland has always been special, under threat,
loyal but forgotten.

Ulster society is not going to "change" for the
convenience of accommodation or according to ideological
prescription. The bricks must come from those in place,
together with a few odd struts and buttresses imported. Any
accommodation must first accommodate to Northern
Ireland reality, what the Protestants and Catholics there
imagine, and then to the policies and predilection of the
others in London and Dublin. A whole new plan will not
work unless there is a whole new people, a new Northern
Ireland, a new Ireland or a new Britain arising without
warning. This, like the conversion of the Protestant working
class to republican ideals, does not seem a viable strategic
prospect. Instead, any accommodation must be adjusted to
the present perceptions of the real, not reality that is desired
or should exist. The old must be used to construct anything
new, not simply ignored. Using what exists, however
unpalatable or unappealing such material, is hardly
impossible. A great many churches in Rome are built within
or integrated into surviving imperial structures. Perceptions
of Rome or out of Rome can be used as building stones,

fitted into a structure of advantage—something old, something new, something borrowed and something ignored. In Northern Ireland no-one has either the resources or the ambition to begin again with a scatter of bricks and a brand-new builder's diagram. Most such proposals are found in academic journals and theoretical projections: ideals rising from optimism, wishful thinking, cherished methods, or simply hope. What is actually needed is to use what is there—not bricks but perceptions, complex, manifold, inherited and reworked, some splendid, some secret, but all vital to creating existing reality. It will help if each can be made in some part to see as others do—not accepting such a perception as real but as valid for the other. The republican may accept that for the man on the north Antrim road or in the marching band from Ballykeel a British Ulster is real, not imagined. After all, the Republic has for generations been imagined and no less real for that.

If there is a British Ulster imagined by Protestants, what then? If Rome is more prevalent in Irish society than Irish society accepts, what then? If Ireland is more like Britain in accomplishment and even civility than imagined, what then? Can the involved be brought, reluctant horses all, and shown the water? One need not drink from the mirage to accept that for others the water is real.

And perception must be considered in any arrangement. The traditions of the Protestants are real if often not very traditional, very accurate, very complex or very convincing to others. The rituals and rites that arise from the understanding of those traditions, however, have been highly visible, and given that they seek to offer both reassurance and provocation, to shape arrogance and confidence in such a way as to control potential violence, they have been remarkably effective. The problem after 1994

was that the traditions had not really kept up with events—
or rather the events transformed the needed agenda of the
old marches and displays. In the years before 1968 British
Ulster no longer felt threatened, as it had during the Home
Rule agitation and the Tan War. The Free State and the
Republic limited subversion to oratory. During the world
war IRA republicans proved no threat. The postwar Dublin
anti-partition campaign had been a failure, as had the IRA
campaign called off in 1962.

In 1968 nowhere in Ireland did there appear
countervailing power, and at no time had the Unionists
been as little interested in the rest of the country. The
O'Neill-Lemass meeting was as much a sign of the Republic's
irrelevance to British Ulster as a move towards closer ties. It
was difficult for the bigots and malcontents to find a threat:
who really believed that the IRA or Dublin could endanger
British Ulster after forty years of effective defence? Irish
nationalism had seemingly run its course; and so Orange
displays, the Stormont system and British Ulster could move
on, with a few sectarian flourishes, to other matters. The
emergence of Paisley, the revival of the UVF and the
banning of nationalist ceremonies by William Craig were all
considered minor. This was Northern Ireland politics as
usual. Stormont did not need such defenders.

The arrival of the Troubles after 1969 changed all this.
The IRA's armed struggle, the external demands for reform,
the end of Stormont and the B Specials and the sense of
surety added up to anxiety and a real challenge. A
generation later the "pan-nationalist front" of Dublin, the
SDLP and Sinn Féin was a powerful and determined force;
the IRA had a truly impressive secret army that made
conventional governance even with massive security forces
impossible; and the nationalists had friends in Washington,

in British Labour, and in Europe. The unchallenged constitutional position of Northern Ireland had evaporated and the sympathy of the London establishment and the Tory Party had eroded. The majority position as majority was even at the mercy of statistics: Northern Ireland had 645,000 Catholics (41 per cent and growing), leaving the defence to 855,000 Protestants (54 per cent and fading). Times had changed much faster than the Protestants could easily accept. They, the majority and the victims, felt hard done by, deprived, and endangered. Worse, by 1996 the Protestants felt ineffectual. They had not given an inch but the whole front had receded. The opposition was everywhere and everywhere projecting arguments and conclusions that were at odds with perceived history and actual reality. No-one cared what the majority really thought: consultation in London was rare, and the triumphant nationalists in Dublin pretended a concern that in no way moderated their ultimate aim: reunification.

At Dunloy and Rasharkin in August 1995 the majority felt compelled to march as a sign that their adamancy was untouched: British Ulster would be defended. The fact that at Dunloy the battle had already been lost only made the march more poignant, especially so since the core of the demonstration, the defiance at Derry, would appear at a city now administered by Catholics, with the loyal population withdrawn from the core. Yet British Ulster was still there; the Protestants were still a majority and could not simply be discarded or discounted; the differences and distinction were as always; assumptions might have been challenged by events but not entirely discarded. What was not discarded was the enormous difficulty of adjusting to the other tradition after a generation of violence and years of anguish that few anywhere seemed to understand. The increased divisions within Northern Ireland had simply made common purpose more difficult, except for the general desire for peace. Neither tradition had really learned much about the other except their mutual indomitable persistence. What the majority wanted was to persist, even in ritual, to keep British Ulster as imagined, even after all the changes, a British Ulster that squared the circle by existing for only some of the province, an entity without institutions, civil power or tangible presence but one that needed loyalty and defence. That such a creation might not weather contemporary priorities, the pressures of the "pan-nationalist front" or the commitment of the citizens or warrant the support of London was unwelcome. These were factors few unionists wanted to contemplate, for each indicated that there might be change: a Catholic majority on the way or a failure of nerve in London.

And change was not to the advantage of British Ulster. At Dunloy those loyal to that Ulster marched against the future, not simply in support of the past. What was wanted at Dunloy and what was wanted for British Ulster was as much as possible. And the "possible" interjected complexities into the unionist psyche that were unwelcome. Doing nothing, as in the 1974 strike, had enormous appeal—wait out the peace process while others made the running and the ruining—and doing something entailed risk. Why take risks? In fact the leaders of British Ulster had seldom found effective ways of acting at all. They had turned a refusal to change into a means of adjusting to imposed changes: time did not stand still. It was a Protestant Ulster solution to an Ulster Irish problem, not unlike the republicans' strategy that had transformed repeated failure into a heritage of persistence.

Thus the congenial and not irrational strategy for all

unionists, for the leaders and for the Orangeman and his fife, was to do nothing: not an inch. Others could give away the patrimony—not much but too much: the B Specials, Derry as Protestant, and somehow the special arrogance that the minority could not resist at all, much less in arms. So the overall strategy was immobility. To remain immobile, however, there had to be constant adjustment, not simply to the great players and to major events but to the reality of the province. The constant adjustments that allowed a British Ulster to exist despite the intolerable mixing imposed by the existence of the Catholic population had to be continued, IRA campaign or no, peace process or no.

In Dunloy the lads could come and parade and go home and all would be the same, except that the Catholics would not be intimidated: they had changed too and perceived the demonstration as an intrusion, and so too the Orangemen. Dunloy was in alien hands, the land gone, the old defences abandoned. Part of Ulster had always been lost—now that part could not, as in the past, be simply denied as miserable and Papist but must be accepted as dangerous ground. When that ground was mutually occupied—in dispute or in peace—then the institutions of toleration still worked. In Rasharkin there would be a tomorrow. The trouble could be blamed on outsiders—misguided lads from Ballymena and Ballykeel if judged by Protestants, mindlessly provocative Orangemen if judged by Catholics. Yet the riotous display by the Kick-the-Pope bands was unwelcome by the local Protestants. Provocation would disrupt the steady state needed to make life run on—and life would run on after the bands had gone home to their own.

There had to be no such adjustment in Dunloy or Ballymena. Yet the potential violence was mere scuffle—a new variant of the old rituals, a means of adjudicating the clash of destinies. When such displays are ritualised, with the Apprentice Boys marching about on assigned routes, those who act on the edges, the undesirable elements of both persuasions, seek to expand the envelope of ritual domination. This is both more so and less so after a generation of Troubles: none wants to be too provocative nor too quiescent. The balancing act is more complex but even more important, for within the spirit of both traditions as well as in the lie of the land, admitted or not, accepted or not, the assets are being deployed for potential change. In the meantime Northern Ireland remains stable, despite the incidents and anguish.

Protestants, especially with the shifting demographic tide, seem compelled to assert their claims to a no longer viable territorial domination. There is no point in surrendering an inch even when that inch has long been lost. In 1995 such marches with the outlying violence indicated by the end of the summer the stability, not the fragility, of Northern society, divided, but one on the peace process. The two-traditions system perfected over two centuries has adjusted first to the IRA armed struggle, then to the reality of direct British control, and finally in 1995 to the ceasefire. It was not at all that the more things changed the more they stayed the same but rather that the majority wished this to be so, even acted as if it were so. The more crudely that case was made the more comforting to British Ulster.

To counter, for whatever purpose, the tirades and the slogans of British Ulster, or the increasingly subtle if no less uncompromising proposals of the republicans, with complex and subtle responses has little effect. What is at issue is not open to much reason or to real history but only to advantage clearly perceived in the light of long-held assumptions. Any accommodation must address the perceptions displayed as oratory, bias, habit, and detailed experience. Reality is not what is proposed by scholars, much less by specialists, but what those on the road to Dunloy or those waiting for them imagine it. Reason, subtlety, the drafting of agreements and the balance of the text can come in later if there is to be formal agreement, an adjustment of perceptions to mutual advantage. And if not, the text and reasons may be deployed to hide that fact or to buy time to allow further change. Peace merely as process with only the most limited perceptual changes had a longer life than some Continental governments, if nothing like that of the Cypriot experience—a generation of process.

In the general search for a way forward, a means of adjusting the priorities and assumptions of the involved— that partition represents reality or is artificial, that two traditions can mix without harm to governance or not, that Irish nationalism is largely identical to Irish Catholicism or not—the observers had tended to shape two sides: the nationalists and the unionists, and so in Northern Ireland the Protestants and Catholics. All that complex history, the past rigorously re-created by scholars—not the imagined past displayed on gable ends by the faithful—is reduced just like the political slogans and strategies to the fewest, most acceptable components. Nationalists prefer to ignore the evidence of polls over the years, of voting statistics, public statements and private actions, the fact that many Catholics are content within Northern Ireland even if they are not really part of British Ulster. And, equally to the point, this has always been so. Most Irish Catholics, most of the time, have not wanted to sacrifice for the nation, have been content with their lot or with reform and advantage. Even the militant republican movement has a long history of schism as one faction after another, one generation after another—including the present Sinn Féin—has given up physical force for a political option, often to considerable immediate advantage for nationalism if never to achieve the grail of the republic.

In sum, there are all sorts of players in Ireland and all sorts of Protestants whose various perceptions are the determinants of action. There are rich Protestants and poor, urban Presbyterians and rural Presbyterians, evangelical Christians and those who appear once a year at the Church of Ireland Easter service. There are middle-class Methodists and born-again Baptists, those who go to the same mission as their grandparents and those free-thinkers at Queen's who will not tick "Protestant" in the questionnaire. Some identify for advantage with an Ulster identity and others stress the British connection above all else or admit to being Irish if different. Some live in an area dominated by the Presbyterian Church and others in uplands planted with a different crop. Every Protestant is different, if the same: differences with historical explanation or differences of class and simply cast of mind. There are different agendas, different historical imperatives, and different social and economic and religious heritages. One Protestant is not much like the next—especially to Protestants. Even in Belfast the members of Paisley's Martyrs' Memorial Free Presbyterian Church in Ravenhill Road, that most famous cynosure of Protestant perception, are diverse in many ways: some are richer, some poorer, some with university education and some without, some without politics and others local activists, some taciturn and others congenial. Most are alike of their time and place, their speech and their experience. Their religious convictions are alike, their habits and their lives similarly circumscribed. They are largely members of a class and caste; saved and sober, they come to hear what they expect to hear.

Such a congregation is proper and pious more than anything else, not bigots but certainly prejudiced in favour of their revelation and their creed. They mean no-one harm and find in their own services a comfort and reassurance. They would be uncomfortable at an established church, for even if Presbyterian it would not be Free Presbyterian—too orthodox, too formal, too fancy, too cold and artificial; mostly they have never been in a Church of Ireland church any more than in one of Rome. They are what they are: fundamental in faith, simple in display, good citizens of British Ulster. They are apt to vote their pastor's party. They keep themselves to themselves, lead ordinary lives, cherish piety and productivity. All fear Rome and suspect Dublin, dislike not Catholics—people seldom met—but Catholicism, an ever-present reality. For them the Bible is not simply a book but the basis of analysis: salvation is a matter of life lived. The home must be Christian, prayer needs no intermediaries, each man and woman is free. And each assumes that this responsibility taken ensures a godly life and this in turn produces habits and discipline and dedication that ensure prosperity and a civil society. They are a force not for revolution, despite Paisley's adventures and provocations, but for stability. They have tended to make brave soldiers for their faith and for the Crown. They most of all are and feel Christian, each day and every day.

There is sin and sloth and failure—and redemption. The answer is Christ found, and the return is salvation. All sorts of Protestants in British Ulster are in such matters much the same: Anglican pastors, the elders of the Brethren, the disputatious Presbyterian theologians, and the parson in the wooden hall at Wednesday night prayer meeting citing the

Good Book. All are Protestants, think much alike on the importance of their faith in church and out, are decent people and righteous.

It is not so much that society generates religious fanatics as that the Ulster Protestants take their religion very seriously, all day, at home, at work, in church, or on the march. Political speeches are sermons, and sermons are both recreation and revelation. That many feel their faith threatened means that for many the faith remains the most important facet of life. These convictions are everywhere to be found, varying in degree and in intensity but found throughout the Protestant community. And almost none of this is apparent in casual contact, in conversations with Catholic neighbours or in responses to a reporter. The living presence of God is only apparent to the saved: all others sense nothing but a seriousness of purpose. Time has for two centuries remained still, reinforcing rather than eroding conviction. The benefits and costs of this conviction have changed over the last generation—and the necessity of adjusting to Irish reality has always imposed changes—but the basics have been remarkably stable. Not all the wonders of technology, the homogenisation of Western society, the appeals of the secular, the ebbing of conviction in Britain or the rise of general toleration and ecumenical aspirations have shifted the Ulster Protestants, a chosen people with a special vocation, defenders of a land redeemed in blood and maintained by constant vigilance.

The Protestants are all too aware that their world view has become rare, obsolete, and unfashionable. They know that they are politically incorrect: their fears do not seem valid to others nor their aspirations desirable. They live isolated in a Western world that has other fears and another agenda. They recognise that their reality has been discarded as fanciful, either self-serving or paranoid. And they are anguished that no-one listens or if by chance does so hears little and understands less. What such people seek is reassurance and security in an environment that has grown increasingly hostile. They know that even in Ireland they are really a minority and in Northern Ireland a declining majority. British Ulster has few friends and each year more enemies. And certainly British Ulster would be dismantled by Irish nationalists, could be abandoned by the United Kingdom, and yet is still held by Protestants to be not the best defence but the only effective defence of their faith and way of life. Many feel that if British Ulster goes so do they. Each may seek to defend British Ulster individually, but when written big this is Trimble or Paisley: the great salvos, the uncompromising defence—for the truth is indivisible, not readily defended in parts. Such unionists speak directly to their constituency, to what is expected, to perceptions long held: if they did not they would, like moderates and mumblers, have long ago been relegated to the wings of politics. The great and untarnished truths sell in Ulster, and, as everywhere in mass politics, complexity of thought, humour and concession sell poorly. Conviction arising from convictions is what is wanted and what is acceptable.

So what is acceptable to the Protestants and what is not is shaped in rude terms. And such crudities can be and have been effected, deployed, and defended. In Northern Ireland the great ideas, the defence of individual freedom and the revealed truth were formed into institutions and systems that not only protected what most others considered obsolete and undesirable but did so by imposing injustice as a necessary component of the fortification. Inherent superiority and absolute assurance had to be displayed as well as claimed. And the visible rewards of past triumph

333

made such display effective: persuaded the others, the Catholics, of their inferiority. Time might moderate such display or such injustice, but the truth is still an unmatched asset. Others do not possess it or have denied it. The others may no longer be inherently inferior, and know this, but they do not yet know the power of the Lord and so are excluded from the fellowship of Christ and participation in British Ulster.

In Northern Ireland, Protestant truth as perceived and as revealed was protected and displayed, not imposed but rather used as a rationale for exclusion. The living Protestant tradition arises from the continuing need to defend truth from perceived enemies: it may be truth that brings advantages, that reveals inherent superiority or that will not be admired elsewhere but it is truth that works in Northern Ireland and the truth that shapes British Ulster. As tradition it is exclusive, open only to those whose convictions are Protestant, and therefore difficult, since asymmetrical to an Irish nationalism that in theory is open to all who would be Irish.

The Peace People shaped great universal generalisations, but these rewarded neither the best nor the worst in society, did not establish institutions of the committed, did not reward vengeance, address the returns of hate and bigotry, did not require exchanges of prisoners and symbols, and could not be effected in the crucial middle ground between the banners of a great army and the financing of a minibus for prisoners' families. Nationalism in the province was always divided, as has always been the case between those who could adapt and moderate and those who could not. The republicans have always been a minority but often capable of shaping institutions of resistance within the hidden galaxy of the faithful that makes possible an armed struggle, a secret army, a new generation of recruits. If the Peace People wanted a universal but could find no means of intermingling the perceptions and aspirations of the two traditions, except in the most limited social and economic projects of good will, the republicans, like the advocates of British Ulster, relied on a single tradition, sought not a blend but purity.

The British have refused to accept the rejection by the Irish of the received practices of Britain as best, their refusal to take tutelage in civility and culture. They cannot yet withdraw with magnanimity and in triumph: just to go would indicate an 800-year failure accepted in London that British is not best. Most in Britain find the Irish in general distasteful and alien and mostly uninteresting, unless of course they assimilate and so become different but for name—and a Callaghan can be Prime Minister—for being Catholic is no longer relevant; but the establishment finds them a constant rebuke to the values cherished. To go would be to give up and leave the Ulster Protestants in alien hands. And so the British remain, without declared interests, merely responsibilities, and so defend almost inadvertently those who also oppose the Irish and do accept British authority and superiority much of the time.

In all instances the case for involving the two traditions has proved most congenial on the lowest level and when the British are not involved. Chess clubs work but peace marches do not last, nor cross-cultural political structures of any size. The more general the concept or the initiative the more divisive. The more power the institution has the more toleration is excluded. Mixing is best often done in dribs and drabs: many have a recipe for a great Irish stew but none can find the proper pot.

What must be sought is not the lowest common

denominator of accommodation—for those involved imagine none such exists—nor a grand and unifying concept: peace—for none are long involved in a crusade that marches in a circle—but a nexus of the two traditions that will be perceived as being to the immediate and potential advantage of each. In 1974 peace in the Middle East was possible because the Egyptians thought they had won the war and the Israelis knew they had not.

For once a means must be found in Ireland so that the gains of one tradition will not be seen as losses by the other. What is crucial is what is perceived, not what others imagine. Since the basic convictions of the two traditions are asymmetrical, inclusive and exclusive, if both arising from a revealed truth, there may be room for adjustment: one can more easily tolerate the irrelevant. In any case an accommodation must reward and punish both, empower both traditions, ensure minimal change and maximum returns. Always any such proposition must rest on the perceptions of those involved. The perceptions of all, however marginally related to actuality, are the crucial determinants, and these are not, as often assumed if examined at all, mutually exclusive. They are, if not very pliant, open to manoeuvre on each level: what people imagine they want, what they really want, and what they will accept. What is acceptable may not be what is sought and at times even the involved are uncertain, their perceptions contradictory, certainly illogical, and their aspirations alien to their avowed agenda. Perceptions are determinants but also various, can be mixed and matched to varied ends—if the involved can recognise advantage, offer advantage, accept what is imagined as vital.

Quite obviously for many who want not peace at any price but an end to the killing, the perceptions are not a determinant, simply ignored: those who build models or seek ideals are more apt to ignore prejudice, fantasy and the baser emotions in their project accommodations. Yet for the most part northern perceptions do seem contradictory, engender a reality at odds with compromise, evolve from two traditions, various national assumptions and aspirations not easily adjusted. How can British Ulster be part of an Irish nation? How long can Protestant Northern Ireland bar the march of the Irish nation? How long can nationalists assume they speak for their own people on the national issue—an issue for many no longer? How long will Britain continue to imagine satisfactory benefits from an expensive and unsatisfactory sacrifice because involvement is perceived as responsibility?

As for those involved most directly, can they all agree on the grand issues, the priorities of time, the direction history should take? Such concepts, priorities and directions need not be the same but need not cancel the other. As long as perceptions, the determinant of the issues and the future are not deployed but ignored or denied or opposed as prejudice and so excluded, the necessary adjustment of reality, the shaping of another future will as always wait on events.

10

THE IRISH ARENA

I have been accustomed to understand by Ireland not
merely a country possessing certain geographical
features but a country inhabited by a certain people ...
—Isaac Butt

The Irish traditions, the perceptions of the involved and the
determinants that shape the dynamics of the quarrel all exist
within a perceptual arena: a real Irish garden filled with
lethal toads conjured up by the involved. Few conflicts have
generated so great a literature or so continuing an analytical
and scholarly interest, which has arrayed every discipline,
every methodology and most concerns in thousands of
works. The Irish arena has been fought over, defined and
redefined, weighed and balanced by scholars and specialists
for a generation. Seemingly everything that matters, from
badges and emblems to refinements in trauma surgery, has
been examined; and seemingly often the results have been,
if available to all, pursued only by the specialists. The
everyday people of Ireland, long exhausted by the turmoil
and the dreadful, have often had more than enough of
analysis, as have most everyday people on their own
perceptions of matters: the common wisdom, the received

338

truth, observation and assumption. This is indeed the arena—not the country itself but the galaxy of perceptions, a great whirl of assumptions unevenly distributed, generating light and energy but often indistinct to the distant or uninterested.

Certainly the arena is not limited to Ireland or to Britain, to places or to people or to the present. The past for various purposes has been rewritten front to back, research centres opened, options detailed, conferences held, solutions and accommodations proposed, and journals begun, and so every faction has a historian. And the arena is not the same as it once was: history changes, the future changes, and perceptions change, words have different meanings, slogans appeal to different aspirations and fears. And the aspirations and fears move too. Nationalism in Kerry is not what it once was, nor Orange assurance on the road to Dunloy. All of this has been noted if not always absorbed. The concern has meant that even the uncongenial Protestants have inspired a not unreasonable collection of data. In this, like those in Britain or further away, they are treated as part of the problem, a constant in the arena and so in a sense a determinant factor. They are of the arena and yet partly shape it and so have been the subject of investigation as well as the cause of action.

The written assault on Ireland continues. The peace process has generated dozens of proposals, foundations have given grants, professors have flown in, Sinn Féin is besieged with requests, biographies and surveys are under way: no end is in sight. Social scientists move along the Crumlin Road with check-lists and multiple choices on demand. If the peace process ends or dribbles away with the end of the ceasefire, the only certainty is that other investigators will appear with an appropriate agenda, other check-lists and questionnaires, if the same methodologies. And now the Protestants are a required stop on most academic tours, as once each journalist stopped by one or two shop-fronts to gauge loyalist opinion before returning to base at the Europa Hotel.

What is often neglected by the investigators, who seek only the truth and the best for all, is that much of the Irish arena is not very amenable to many academic disciplines, just as the nuances, such as they were, of loyalist opinion are not apt to be found in an upstairs office during a public chat, any more than a similar visit to the Sinn Féin office in the Falls Road was going to give insight into the republican mind. Much of the arena—the real terrain, not the scholarly maps or the analysis of journalists—lies beyond easy reach in the perceptions of the involved. These perceptions impel action, but even the involved are often unsure what their action will be, or why. When a moment of decision comes, then a decision is made, unpredictable by all: no-one in the class knows who will join the IRA until a desk is vacant, or whether the vote will be given to Paisley's lot until the ballot is marked. Then the uncertain perceptions are concentrated and action taken. Often most distressing to those of good will is the fact that existing evidence indicates that many of these perceptions are strongly, often violently, held and demonstrably false. Still, the lad from Tyrone joins the IRA to seek a united Ireland even if he ends up shooting Protestants at their doorstep and calling it a military operation, and someone votes for Paisley—more for Paisley often than for anyone else. And the vote and the gun are not unreasonably used; it is the perceptions that make them appropriate means, not unreasonable or even false. Even if not false they make reconciliation impossible and accommodation mirage. How indeed can one reconcile what was never one, where agreement never existed? How can there be a united Ireland if Ulster is British?

In fact for the fair and decent some perceptions appear simply wicked: rationales for murder. The prevalence of spite and malice, hate and ancient grievances hidden in popular political or psychological language, traditional duplicity and greed along with new and unsavoury appetites are real enough. Those who marched down the road to Dunloy had real as well as imagined grievances and desires, an agenda that included disdain and pride, anger and resentment, as did those who waited for their arrival. Even if the disinterested find many of the assumptions of the Irish contradictory, vindictive, self-righteous and best avoided if analysis is to provide understanding, those perceptions remain real enough to shape the arena, are the crucial determinants of events. So reason is apt to shy away from the perceptions, for the more reasonable choose not to recognise the advantages of hate or the persistence of malice that makes conciliation difficult. Unfortunately what is decent or politically correct or desirable is often not readily available. The determinants seem to determine the continuation of conflict, just as the country's traditions seemingly encourage the worst, not the best. Yet the strange mix of present perceptions is at the core of the arena, shapes the arena, makes the quarrel and is made by the quarrel. It may not be a reasoned, even a coherent Ireland, may so far be inherently quarrelsome, but it is a real Ireland, perhaps the real Ireland. The rebel heart or the Protestant ethic are hardly imagined, and from them some extract murder and others intractable commitment to a cause. Truth is perceived and reason thus without takers.

Many reasonable suggestions have faltered over the years because they are reasonable. Justice and vengeance are not easy to shape to documentary form nor hate effectively factored into accommodation. A search for justice or even vindication is not without merit; vengeance or hate need not impose murder as a means—perceptions, even the most unpleasant, can not only be edited and changed but may offer entry to accommodation. Not all the perceptions are vile or imaginary, and none are eternal. Even the Irish perceptions change, and some simply vanish. Often, however, what matters is what is assumed. In this book the focus has been on present perceptions that shape action, not on those matters that are tangible, easily quantifiable, the basis of most analytical endeavour.

The major perceptions are often crude and are rarely as ancient as imagined. And some of the oldest and most cherished—the Protestant affection for liberty and the Catholic admiration for sacrifice—can lead to bodies dumped by the side of the road. Such raw perceptions are not only hidden from probing for decency's sake but also hidden at times from the holder, who may be unable to foresee the inevitable actions that arise from such comfortable ideas. These ideas are always adjusted for the times, even if in Ireland time seems to run more slowly. Those who march along the Dunloy road are contemporary, have chosen from experience, have been taught daily, are not simple creatures of history bearing ancient ideas and ideals. They may be their fathers' children but they have been to the school of life and learned as a rite of passage. They can yet learn. Old or new, the ideals arising from imagined reality are apt to be rough. At Dunloy such perceptions displayed as event led only to a scuffle, a confrontation shaped by the old rituals into symbol rather than massacre. They can lead to the most squalid acts or to great bravery and can always be rationalised and elaborated.

At base they are not necessarily base but necessary to action.

Many perceptions in any arena may be complex, but in the shaping of events the crude often play a disproportionate role. *Black is beautiful. Peace, land, and bread.* These ideas fit a perceived reality, are the slogans of revolutionary aspiration or high policy and so are foundation for elaborate concepts. The raw perceptions largely determine the dynamics of the arena. The Irish arena is shaped by the perceptions of those involved, those in Northern Ireland, in the Republic, in Britain and elsewhere. What they see they see; and while much seen is real, some is not, except to the viewer. One person may see a risen people and another a mob caught up in killing. An IRA volunteer sees a dead soldier and the victim's wife her Protestant husband murdered at the door for keeping the peace. In the Irish arena what matters is what the involved assume matters and why. Whether it should or not is another matter.

No-one has ever been very successful at predicting change, not in Ireland, not elsewhere. The Danish physicist Niels Bohr noted that "prediction is very difficult, especially about the future." The safe wager is that tomorrow will be like yesterday, which is often so but not often enough to provide continuity. The favourite does not always win. We are not still in the Garden of Eden.

Yet Ireland from 1922 until 1969, divided and largely at political peace, a torpid, marginal island on the edge of great events, evinced the most limited change. Few countries were as little troubled by the world's catastrophic events, the turmoil of the times and the enormous change in technological capacity and ideological assumption. For Ireland not only were there no great wars and alarms, no occupation, no physical destruction or invasions but also not much day-to-day change. There were a few more cars, the radio came to the village along with electricity; Stormont was built and much later a central bus station in Dublin. There were elections, a few new faces, the arrival of Hollywood films, the drain of the real war, but no unpleasant surprises; not even television greatly upset the traditional, no more than the Hollywood films or English newspapers. There were the same families and classes, the same seasons and fairs, the same political parties and mostly the same politicians. The new was slight, the recession started early and never finished, enterprise eroded. Belfast was bombed and the Americans came. Dublin had shortages, President Kennedy came to Dublin, and de Valera stayed on.

Northern Ireland did not blossom but moved on, stolid, unproductive, stable. The other Ireland was also isolated, also agricultural, provincial and parochial, but the new men deployed enthusiasm, the available talent and almost no resources to establish a democratic state if with limited economic development. That Ireland was also stolid, unproductive, and stable. While there was great accomplishment, new industries and at last an end to TB, as in the North there was limited prosperity, more limited even than that managed by Stormont and Britain. And after forty years Northern Ireland has some of Europe's worst housing, most decayed manufacturing, and most unsavoury political practices.

Ireland had hardly been home to innovation or enterprise, but there had been neither real war nor dreadful want, no holocaust, no great air raids, no ethnic cleansing. There was the unremitting persistence of poverty, awful housing, limited social welfare, class advantage, rural misery, and the ethics of the parish. This began to change with the impact of government money spent on misery, limited private enterprise rewarded, and ideas despatched across borders—radio first, then television, to complement Hollywood and the *News of the World*. Yet there was no revolution, no turmoil, no feel of adventure, only the hint of better times as the sixties came to an end. The Irish interregnum had lasted half a century, one of the most turbulent of centuries, and Irish politics and perceptions had barely changed. Expectations were channelled by the past, even in 1968, as the future unexpectedly arrived in the train of a scruffy band of students. These students, idealists, teeming with radical ideas and old resentments, struggled along the road to Derry carrying slogans, drooping banners and the weight of history to rally against stability. It was not just another march in Ulster.

History began again in 1968. In 1969 events turned violent, to the disappointment of some and to the surprise of almost no-one. Provoking the system, no matter how justified the provocation, guaranteed trouble. And trouble there was: disorder, riot, pogroms, anguish, and arson—not anarchy or chaos but not like the old days. No-one could be sure of tomorrow, and a few began to regret yesterday. The times were particularly curious, because after fifty years perceptions had hardened into certainty. There had been no need to adjust to events and experience, only fit the new bits into the old model. The old truths were still true. Many of these certainties existed as more real than real. Irish nationalism and Ulster unionism emerged at the end of the sixties having learned nothing and forgotten nothing. It was only the tangible presence of violence and the all but tangible sense of movement that concentrated minds. Then each acted as if programmed: the advocates of British Ulster turned on the subversive minority, who turned to an IRA that did not really exist but sprang renewed to use their mission as defenders as a means of fulfilling their role as revolutionaries, while the moderates everywhere hedged and quibbled and sought to moderate the rising turbulence. The British government felt compelled to intervene to discipline the unruly Irish. All the involved defended their perceived historical interests in congenial ways and shaped events to expectations.

No-one can stand too much reality. The most convenient response is to deny the present or to shape it to expectation. Some do nothing, some do what they have always wanted to do and others what they did yesterday. All rationalise without self-analysis or empathy but from doctrine. Everyone, as usual, knew what they knew, and therefore many knew what they should do in changing circumstances. Certainly the rising violence of 1969 activated all those who believed that the gun had a vital role to play—for the defenders of the system, those who would oppose disorder or those who would cause it. For the rest their politics grew to be irrelevant, whether the old pieties of the nationalist or Ulster Unionists or the new ideas of the university. This was not an obstacle to those with firm opinions: they repeated them no matter the action or the name of the game. So in Ireland history began again, and most took their perceptions back with them into the future.

Over the next generation the old perceptions had to be repeatedly fine-tuned to experience until almost the entire country existed with a mix of the old, of reality read as affront, of reasoned analysis and good will and venom. Contradictions seemingly bothered no-one. Some saw history unfold as expected: the republicans manoeuvred into their long-sought armed struggle but could go no further, neither back nor forward. The loyalist defenders finally had a tangible threat but could not reach it with their limited capacity. The British had a turbulent Ireland regarded as tribal struggle. Dublin had responsibilities without capacities, ambition without enthusiasm. None really wanted their heart's desire at any cost once time passed and the cost became clear—no-one, that is, except the few zealots who found a vocation in violence. Only a few will do in Ireland if there is toleration; and so the IRA armed struggle continued, the loyalists killed Catholics at random, the British forces deployed for insurgency, and the psychotics found rationale for murder. No-one wanted to accept that the old agenda had crumbled in the winds of war, an irregular war none had imagined. Politics in Ireland became in large part evading or ignoring violence as much as determining who got what and how much. Most in Ireland and those concerned in Britain wanted what they had always wanted, what they had and more without cost. Increasingly, however, most would take what they could get; but even this always seemed at someone else's expense and so not readily available. What they learned from events seemed to reinforce what they assumed they knew as well as to open novel options—not always welcome.

In Northern Ireland there had always seemed to be a zero-sum game; but because of the emerging crisis there was a spectrum of mutual advantages found in Dublin and London, despite rather than because of existing perceptions. The old ideas and ideals no longer represented either reality or desire, although old habits and old customs were retained. The British found it difficult to imagine the Irish in Dublin as allies, and Dublin found the British difficult, arrogant as always. London, often involved elsewhere, attracted only by the most recent spectacular, was apt to find Irish advantages small, the problem of security paramount, and the future not especially pressing, while in Dublin northern events were often mistakenly assumed to be crucial and British co-operation necessary if embarrassing. Most Anglo-Irish dialogue was halting, because of lack of practice and the retention of old habits, even as new perceptions took over. These new perceptions, involving the need to redefine nationalism and the British connection, gradually offered a prospect of change if not stability. London, like Dublin, essentially wanted peace and quiet on its own terms and so an appropriate and reassuring end to history—not so easy to do on its own, as was discovered after the Anglo-Irish Agreement of 1985 foundered on even involving the moderates of Northern Ireland, as the failure of power-sharing in 1974 indicated.

On the other hand the uncompromising desires of those closest to the vortex remained shaped by perceptions that had not only emerged intact after 1916 but were reinforced by events after 1968. The IRA had applied cherished republican strategy and created what the militants had always wanted: an armed struggle that could not be crushed given the existing arena. For once old perceptions fitted new reality. The Unionists, battered and splintered, emerged as unionists under the direct rule of the Crown, backed by increased military and police forces and years of promises but more fearful of betrayal than ever, many in need of the reassurance supplied by loyalist paramilitaries and all suspicious of any moderate initiative within the unionist establishment. They kept their aspirations and assumptions largely intact and remained proud defenders of a proud province even when joined by the loyalist paramilitaries.

What ever so gradually everyone involved recognised, if haltingly, was that not only had there been change but also that their own perceptions had changed: how could they not? Yet often the old assumptions and agenda, which were contradicted by the new, were retained as still valid. And whatever the agenda, the old habits of mind, the unresolved grievances and inherited prejudices were largely intact. The British found the Irish uncongenial and the Irish found themselves still divided on their nature; everyone advocated change but resented the airs and graces of others, as they had always done.

The resulting muddle was not easily explained, nor were the inevitable conclusions of the new reality taken as inevitable by those who persisted in repeating what was demonstrably inapplicable if not false. London really had no tangible interests but was psychologically deeply involved: history lived not just in Downing Street but in the City and the clubs, in many a colonel's heart. Dublin wanted a united Ireland but not really. They fixed the boundaries of the march of the nation at what their people would pay: very little. The Irish had always been more apt to let the few and faithful sacrifice, if there were no subsidiary cost or no other course, than rally to a crusade. And the faithful in the IRA could not win, could not lose, had a campaign but nowhere to go. They too shifted perspective, and while they could not accept a unionist veto they now could not imagine an Ireland without the consent of the unionists. This, however, proved no problem, because doctrine indicated that the unionists were so inclined only because of the British presence. So the British must go, even if the majority of the province considered themselves British. And this majority had to count on London but could not surrender, but realised that accommodation was inevitable. They lacked not the will but the resources to deny Irish nationalism on their own but could do so to their own. So in many ways no-one gave an inch, surrendered nothing vital yet assumed that the future would be different from the past.

When the peace process moved forward in 1995, that future was tomorrow and tomorrow and tomorrow. The next day, the future, would be like yesterday, nothing resolved and no-one greatly harmed and any great reckoning still distant. What existed was peace as process, no surprises if often disappointment and very considerable sound and motion but no fury: no violence until the core of the republican galaxy lost patience, not so much with the process as with the displays in London, read as arrogance, not just delay, perfidy not political necessity, and set the London bombs of February 1996.

Few imagined that such a peace process could last indefinitely, only hoped for the tomorrow: seventeen months of tomorrow. Much the same thing had happened once before, after 1922, when few could imagine partition as permanent. In 1996 few could continue to imagine tomorrow as absolutely like yesterday. Some had taken great risks to get to the ceasefire, and some saw great challenges emerging from the end to violence; but in 1994 few had foreseen the glacial pace of events. Still, some sort of accommodation appeared inevitable: reason so demanded, and self-interest and the specialists and general expectations. General expectations, however, continued to be expressed in the traditional immoderate and absolute language of general politics, which often hid individual subtlety and toleration. The arson and vandalism, the forced marches and ritual insults of the summer of 1995 were orchestrated for both old and new reasons but indicated that even in the midst of the peace process the intractable perceptions of the involved still found no common ground. In the perceptions of many, all the subtleties, all the complexities imposed by history and the times, all those factors so familiar to scholars and pundits and analysts are minced and made into crude vessels, rude, serviceable, the stuff of politics and bias. National stereotypes are not politically correct, seldom subtle, often misleading, but more often are based on the perception of real observers. All such generalisation may be untrue but all, to persist in the political discourse, must be founded on truth. The truth is more complicated when examined—if examined. It is with the raw perceptions displayed that politicians must cope and must shape to eventual institutions and to effective discourse: one may run against taxes but on election meet the bills; one may threaten harsh and terrible war but on reflection make a deal.

As the peace process moves along, day by day, with or without bombs, what must be addressed are the basic perceptions involved, some now misty, others not admitted and many proposed as viable factors: demands, realities, agendas, and demonstrable truths. The IRA Army Council, narrow, isolated, deeply dedicated, not beyond reason if often beyond reasons, must cope with a very small constituency and answer to history. Their perceptions matter and are neither subtle nor mysterious, liable to adjustment imposed but not liable to permit accommodation that does not fit perceived notions. So too the loyalist paramilitaries, who will resort to murder as long as the majority fears for British Ulster. They have no ideology at all, only fear, anguish and resentment rationalised as a defender's creed, but this is ample for their purposes, for murder. Northern Ireland has long been an arena of clashing destinies, contradictory perceptions, and lethal ideas inherited and adjusted for present purpose. Such purposes have made the province a battleground where the bodies come one by one, lifted from the street corner, carried out of bombed shops, shot down at the end of the lane or on the doorstep. Even if lethal and violent, the arena of the mind, the ideas of the involved, the reality shaped by expectation permits and encourages not simply the IRA, engaged in Europe's longest war, but also the UVF or the Red Hand Commandos, who have recourse to indefensible operations for defending their own.

In this arena of perceptions the Protestants must speak as unionists of various flavours, as British when they are Irish, if of a sort, as a people fearful that tomorrow is not apt to be as easy as yesterday, sometimes as militant, almost always as defenders, if rarely in favour of paramilitary murder. The result, as has been the case for generations, is that the shrill and the uncompromising are apt to ruin any case almost before such a case can be formulated. Even if there were no UVF or if the UDA was no more than benign, a Gresham's Ulster Law would encourage the bad to drive out the good from the Protestant arena and gain a hearing at the cost of reason or moderation. Yet here too there is change. The general acceptance that cautious quiet might be the best response to the peace process has had takers and has generated for over seventeen months a Protestant consensus. If nothing is happening, nothing need be said. Doing nothing is congenial. Even the loyalist paramilitaries do not kill when no threat is imagined. In politics in all of Ireland doing nothing has nearly the appeal of doing the same thing one always did. In Northern Ireland doing nothing assures the Protestants that no wrong step can be taken, nothing given up by mistake. *No surrender* not only has enormous charm but is also what most Protestants truly want. And after 1994 and then after the ceasefires, doing nothing, surrendering nothing, not even the right to speak later, had great effect as a political strategy.

The optimum strategy is to hold British Ulster against a national majority with limited support. The problem has been that the Protestants, the unionists, the defenders of British Ulster have not had title deeds to all of British Ulster, the tangible parts; so that much has been lost over the past generation but not the intangibles. Others could surrender an inch at a time what was beyond the province of British Ulster. Obviously the ultimate political power rests in London, obviously the tangibles of control, finance, soldiers and support are not in the province's hands. All the reassurance from London, all the leverage the Unionist members have at Westminster, the long and special relationship with the British establishment, are not control. And without those British assets British Ulster might be exposed, not as a viable entity but an imaginary one.

Those who build scenarios about future prospects can imagine an Ireland where the unionists are left on their own to defend their own, numbering the guns and the constables and deployment of the Royal Irish Regiment in a new Irish war. Then the rules would change, chaos would come, and the entire country would be ruined—not so fanciful after the collapse of Yugoslavia or the border wars of the old Soviet Union. Such scenarios require that the perceptions of the involved are as proclaimed: not an inch means no surrender on anything—all or nothing, with nothing all but certain. The Arabs demand justice even if the skies fall, which has often been a recipe for continued injustice, humiliation, and misery. The last ditch has charm, and those who would take British Ulster into it are not likely to be those who worry unduly about the viability of a rebellious province or the day after tomorrow. Ulster will be right and Ulster will fight and tomorrow is another day.

Yet in Ulster there have been for a generation those

willing to surrender this to keep that, give an inch and remain largely in control, moderates, some cunning and some idealists—and they have all been discredited and discarded, because the general population has accepted that accommodation is not required, however effectively tooled. They believe that at the end of the day Britain will not coerce the loyalists of Ulster. To scuttle, to discard their proclaimed responsibility would violate not so much their ethics as their self-image as disinterested defenders amid the savage Irish. The British for generations have assumed that they are part of the solution, not the problem; and such an image is not without reality. Who protected the vulnerable Catholics in 1969? Who arrests both loyalists and republicans? Who is responsible to all? Who is in charge not just by right but because the cost of order must be paid by the solvent? And so the British assumption about their role and mission is one of the grand perceptions at play on the Irish issue.

In Ireland it is the perceptions that matter. The Unionists saw the student marchers in 1968 as terminal threat and so overreacted, ruined not just their case but all the opportunities to co-opt, misdirect, adjust, or manipulate. The unionists of 1969 could not help but respond thus to provocation, because they believed what they believed: the IRA was real, nationalism was on the march, radical slogans were cover, not agenda, the provocation to entrenched power as ritual could not be ignored or tolerated. The perception of assurance had to be defended, not the Stormont system. And it was defended in August 1969, not by police but by pogroms. There the cruder perceptions of rebellious Fenians and who would dare to challenge the inherent superiority of the system drove the mobs into the streets. And simply being a mob without any agenda has charm but with just cause can be involvement in high purpose that has tangible returns. Some mobs return home with loot and others with satisfaction. In Belfast the main intention was to clear out the subversives close to the walls. Catholics were burned out or attacked because they were perceived as provocative, vulnerable, dangerous and disruptive but most of all because they were "them".

Thus, while there are no "Protestants", only various individuals of all sorts, all these sorts tend to share certain crude concepts about the nature of society, each shaped by experience and private constructs. These perceptions need not lead to the same conclusions: not very many Protestants were needed to run riot, but in some degree all Protestants shared the perceptions that drove the violent. Unionist politicians understood why the RUC overreacted, and the decent middle class deplored the violence but shared with the violent the belief that Catholicism was a danger to British Ulster. There was a general cause to burn down Bombay Street, just as in time there would be to shoot a Taig taxi-driver. The Protestants recognise the loyalist slogans, even if few accept them as sufficient rationale for murder. Still, everyone understands. British Ulster is under attack. Battle flags have always been slogans: it is peace that requires fine print.

Mostly people are satisfied with prejudice, the ruder stereotypes, the subversive Fenians glimpsed along the road to Dunloy. Slogans that can be written on banners or shouted from a dais have undeniable mass charm, especially for those already convinced that they are listening to revelation. These slogans are the perceptions that are catered to instead of denied by politicians. A whole nation can be reduced to ranks of brown shirts shouting "Sieg heil!" and a century of thought reduced to the inalienable rights to life, liberty, and property, or Paris taken with a Mass or defended with audacity. Slogans and the perceptions they represent are often the crude material out of which complex and elegant accommodations either arise or, if misrepresented, collapse. Perceptions make the arena, shape the drama, often giving it both content and language, and they are not wont to change easily. In Ireland today such slogans have not only deep roots but also present utility, fit experience and expectations, explain much and promise more.

The Irish Catholic for many Protestants may not be as roughly imagined by those who listen only to Orange oratory and accept the slogans of the tribe. In many ways the Catholic next door may be both known and esteemed, personally decent, judged on merit, not as example. Yet on a provincial scale, for Ulster and for Ireland, most Protestants imagine the greater reality roughly, see through a glass darkly. They often claim not to hate or fear Catholics, because they do not know any, but do hate and fear Catholicism, which they know as threat. Did not 30,492 vote for Bobby Sands, convicted gunman? In fact most assume they know Catholics all too well: individuals are simply exceptions. They fear every Catholic but their neighbour. In this they differ little from the Catholic Irish, despite the differing lenses and consequent images. Each assumes that any other role played will be ignored: the farmer in the next field can become an RUC constable and the clerk put up a Sinn Féin poster and still be decent. Decent is only possible in isolation, an exception; any other role transforms one into many, reduces exception to stereotype. All the rationalisation cannot persuade the other that esteem is real or even that toleration is more than passing, for the assumption remains and is often reinforced that each will revert to type if need be, if there is advantage.

Exceptions are not even exceptions but special cases to the general rule.

For much of the century the two traditions in Ireland have known little of the other except what is necessary to know; and what they know they know. Many Catholics, especially in the Republic, know no Protestants, and the few symbolic individuals met are not very much like the Protestants of British Ulster. The Catholic perception of Irish Protestants has almost nothing to do with Ulster Protestant reality. Even the clever, educated and competent in Dublin choose to read whatever lesson is useful. There is no realisation that the border represented a reality of the spirit, not some imagined injustice. The Irish in Dublin lived in a dream world. None knew the Ulster Protestant. The Irish-Irish simply imagined what they wanted: their perception was self-serving, if genteel and well-meaning, but still crude and cruel and at times dangerous.

In Northern Ireland Dublin's assumptions were scandalous, ludicrous. Protestants were assumed to be Irish, creatures kept from their destiny by British special interests. Every Protestant who spoke his or her mind was supposedly a bigot pretending to favour freedom of thought, pretending to be different, pretending not to be Irish. Protestants were assumed to be moulded by the needs of the moment, open to the lure of easy money—the old assumption that the half-crown counted over the Crown—and so not faithful to their own, not Protestants at all but Irish. They were thus creatures, not a proud people. They were all potential subjects of a united Irish society, under the dead hand of Catholic authority. A generation of sacrifice and defence and defiance and Dublin still thought them both intractable and corruptible, rigid about unimportant matters and flexible on principles.

It was not a stereotype that sold well in British Ulster. In the real world there are all sorts of Protestants, all sharing this and that but almost without exception believing that British Ulster is best served by a maintenance of the union. Unlike nationalists—the few militant republicans aside—who aspire, some day, somehow, to a unity that would require no sacrifice, the Protestants are determined to maintain their separate and threatened tradition at all costs. Some can even imagine doing so if abandoned by London, but most assume it will never quite come to that. Almost all share a conviction that their special tradition, their civic culture and their freedoms are endangered by Catholic nationalism. The responsible in Britain may not accept the threat but sometimes do realise the reality of British Ulster loyalty and commitment to the Crown. Their sacrifices may be discounted and their people unloved but their loyalty is not easy to escape. And what they are loyal to is another tradition from that offered by Dublin or the IRA. It is this tradition that flourishes as British Ulster, that holds pride of place. If Whitehall or Westminster or the Crown would betray that Ulster then in the past Ulster has indicated that such loyalty may be reconsidered. This eventuality has been contemplated but has never seriously eroded the commitment to union with England. Many feel that British Ulster can only be defended by such a union; and some of these, including Enoch Powell, have urged every integrative initiative possible to make the province no different from any entity in Britain: not just direct rule but integration. To protect British Ulster, British sovereignty must be inviolate: there must not be two Irelands but rather one kingdom and the Republic. Others see advantage in a devolved parliament: Stormont revisited. Flexibility, however, is limited to the means of union, not its reality. However defined, union is a slogan and a solution.

Ulster independence is an idea after its time. Even Ulster devolution has lost advocates in the trend towards a more perfect union. So far only through such a union can British Ulster be maintained and realised. And British Ulster has always had real and perceived enemies: it is an aspiration and an ideal under siege. Most Protestants perceive two historic dangers: Catholic nationalism and loss of British support. The most visible is the undenied ambition of nationalism as construed at present: a united Ireland sooner or later, a united Ireland as inevitable, just, legal, rising from the support of a majority of the people of Ireland. Nationalists are divided only in timing and means. While the Ulster Protestant recognises that in considerable part the engine of nationalism is fuelled by Catholic energy, a case against the politics of annexation must be made, since few beyond Ireland accept the religious dangers and designs of Rome. Even more important, if less visible, the certainty of any union that relies for security simply on the judgement of the London establishment will be inherently insecure. One cannot be united to a United Kingdom that opts out, and a majority at Westminster could so do any day, any time those in power felt that their special interests so required. Then tomorrow could not be like yesterday, then British Ulster would have to become Ulster and the Protestants a minority—an eventuality that all can imagine but do not care to articulate as a prospect: the reverse of the British Ulster dream of security as the nightmare of abandonment.

The Protestant then marshals forces to defeat Irish nationalism. And nationalism is in Catholic hands—and Protestants know as little of Catholics as Catholics know of them. Thus Irish society is divided without great prospect of understanding or insight, and it is certainly easier to hate at a distance, innocent of the real people. The Orangemen come to Rasharkin from Ballymena or Ballykeel to find Catholics, to intimidate them as a category, as symbols, stereotypes, the others. So the decencies of the long-established churches, the necessary toleration imposed by evolving society and the taste of the ecumenical are lost along the main street of Rasharkin, in the tunes of the Kick-the-Pope bands and by the side of the Dunloy road.

If this is the case, then if there is to be a united Irish people the fundamentalist ethos must be transformed, come to terms with diversity and opportunity. And at present the fundamentalists, as has been the case for generations, give no indication that such a course is likely. What in a united Ireland would be to Protestant advantage as defined by the evangelical? Diversity and toleration are dangers, not desirable. There is no opportunity in an Ireland filled with the unredeemed, who are not worthy of esteem. To be Irish seemingly requires that Protestant history be rewritten, new heroes imagined, old sacrifices forgotten, evasions taken as gospel, another language learned at great expense and no gain, new rules, new games and holidays accepted, and most of all new attitudes: hard work need not be rewarded; caution, precision, enterprise and punctuality would no longer be virtue's reward but duties evaded—and evaded because preferment comes not to the diligent and pious but in Irish-Ireland to the connected. There prosperity is at the mercy of favourites and family favours. There the people are manipulated by the Roman church. There freedom is unknown.

This is worst of all. For fundamentalists, for many Protestants, Irish-Irish society is submissive to domination, suspicious of liberty, apt to forgo responsibility in compliance with established authorities: institutions rule, not reason, ritual replaces revelation, and so the lives of saints replace the truth of the Bible. Some take their analysis straight from a reading of the Bible, some from the observed habits of Irish governance, but all, all unionists and so nearly all Protestants, find Irish national society and all its creatures alien, often abhorrent, certainly uncongenial. There are too many to convert, too many to control—the reason British Ulster has six counties, not nine. What must be done is to hold back the alien tradition at the border, monitor the subversive minority, and stand fast.

It does not matter if this analysis of Ireland is true: for the Protestant there is ample evidence to that effect if evidence were needed.

They, the Ulster Protestants, feel very different, another tradition, people who share nothing but the island. In fact the Irish Protestants are and remain very different, in the best of circumstances poor candidates for a pluralist society until time and opportunity have eroded isolation, co-opted the ambitious. And in Ireland there has never been a time when unity offered opportunity or advantage.

So, seemingly, the nationalists have very little to offer Ulster Protestants that has any appeal. The Protestant does not believe in Tone's analysis or aspirations. The United Irishmen were a momentary convergence of the diverse, united only in opposition to a pressing threat of oppression. And that threat was soon better met by Protestant institutions, by the Orange Order, and then transformed by the new threat from Catholic nationalism. This new danger to the Protestants was best met by co-opting British support rather than opposing British policy. In the end, after a century, if the defence could not prevent Rome rule in twenty-six counties the same has not been true for the heartland, so long planted amid the Irish. In Ulster, always

361

different, always considered a bastion if all else was bargained away in London, the faith could be walled and guarded and the long tradition protected. Just as the nationalists read history as centuries of Anglo-Irish conflict, so did the Protestants read it: the reverse side of patriot history, where conciliation and compromise, peace and prosperity were seldom given more than walk-on parts. History for all Ireland comes raw from desire rather than refined by scholars. The Protestants do not see the whole country as opportunity but as a certain danger. They would like to be content with British Ulster, authorised by the Government of Ireland Act, 1920, then a disaster for unionism in Ireland, now the foundation of the province, would be content if it were not for the reality of the minority and so the ambitions of Catholic nationalism. The Protestants cannot defend themselves without alliance with a government that can never have the same priorities as Antrim and Down. So there is always need for reassurance. The Protestants cannot be fully alone with their special province as long as the others exist as well. And about this nothing can be done. So there is more need for reassurance. As for the rest of the country, no-one wants more: the Republic is a poisoned pawn. The saved and the damned cannot be united. There is only a choice between two traditions opposed in principle. It is either one or the other, as Paisley said during the long, hot summer of 1995: "Ulster or the Irish Republic, freedom or slavery, light or darkness."

The Protestants do not want a united Ireland because there is no united Ireland, only light or darkness. What the Protestants would like is an imagined yesterday when their tradition was in the ascendant, certain, dominant, admired and encouraged, not limited by the London establishment. They want the return of an imagined golden age of assurance that cannot be found in history texts. This is what they really want but cannot quite come to articulate. Instead they say they want to be recognised as British. And they truly do want to be recognised as British—especially by the British. It is in fact this Protestant anxiety that has always created a persistent doubt about any enduring link. It was much of the British establishment that sought Home Rule. At the brink of political defeat, many in Ulster, recognising that all Ireland could not be saved, threatened not simply armed resistance and mutiny but a potential loyalty to the German Kaiser—any comfort in a moment of crisis, like the American colonists in the eighteenth century who wanted to be loyal as long as loyalty was in their special interests. The enduring perception has been that British Ulster must but cannot count on London—and, like many perceptions loose in Ireland, this assumption does not seem without merit. So in a sense the problem was never resolved, despite the Government of Ireland Act and the long, easy tenure of Stormont. There were always those in Britain who were not as loyal to Ulster as Ulster was to Britain.

The Ireland Act, 1949, in reaction to the Republic's withdrawal from the Commonwealth confirmed Ulster as part of the United Kingdom until its parliament decided otherwise—and this from a Labour government. What more could be wanted? In fact it was almost because such legislation was thought necessary and indicated that Northern Ireland was not just like the rest of the kingdom that Unionist opinion was always a mix of arrogance and anguish. Scotland could not vote itself out of the United Kingdom, or Cornwall. Wales did not have a devolved parliament. The police in London did not carry automatic weapons. The province was different, and even the Unionists recognised this, but such a difference did not mean that Ulster was Irish. In reality the repeated assurances after 1969 that the province would not be abandoned as long as the majority so desired fed this perception of potential betrayal. And this anxiety was again supported by considerable tangible evidence, including the public opinion survey regularly taken after 1969 that showed little support in Britain for British Ulster. The Labour Party had little interest in Unionists and abhorred loyalists—spongers; and many members often advocated an all-Ireland solution. Labour was not sound. Even the Conservatives were not solid. Thatcher, a natural unionist, firm advocate of keeping the Irish in their place and the British in Ireland, a friend of the security forces, had signed the Anglo-Irish Agreement.

No-one was safe or sure but their own. So what the Protestants wanted they could not have—the past replayed to their tune over and over—and what they feared they dare not easily speak—betrayal. Why else was the head of the European section of MI6, with the Prime Minister's authorisation, secretly talking to Martin McGuinness, at the core of the republican movement, from November 1990? Why did everyone in power in London and in Belfast lie if such talks were in the general interests? Why would they not lie again? How could British Ulster ever take the word of anyone but their own?

After September 1994 what they could easily take was tomorrow like yesterday if the peace process continued. They were not even sure that they wanted "more". Many now felt that devolution might weaken the union even further. So better to take tomorrow if it were like yesterday, cast a cold eye on the pan-nationalist front, revel in the disarray and confusion arising from the February 1996 bombs in London and try not to alienate the British government. And, of course, what they would get would be in the end what the British establishment decided they should have; and surely this would not be expulsion from the United Kingdom. So even in the most difficult of circumstances there was seemingly nothing the Irish establishment could offer to match direct rule and a future like yesterday. The Irish establishment did not even know what to offer, since they hardly knew what Protestants wanted; when told, they discounted any reality that did not match their own agenda. What they would offer would be what should be wanted, a bigger and a better Ireland. The Protestants repeated again and again that there could be no prospect of prosperity, no release of creativity, no gain in language or literature or creativity from diversity incorporated into some imagined united Ireland. An Irish entity with a Catholic majority ensured that any diversity would be passing. Where were the Protestants in the Republic?

There were other, less appealing disadvantages in any all-Ireland arrangement. For there could be no declared dominance, no special privilege, no pride in inherent superiority assumed, witnessed, even proclaimed. Any all-Ireland solution would be unrewarding in that a parity of esteem, even equal shares, was not what the Protestants wanted. They do not want what the Catholics had, land or saints or heritage or language, whether it was or was not theirs as well. They did not care for esteem from a manipulated people, a failed society. They wanted to be left alone. They really wanted both assurance that they would be left alone and acknowledgement of their special virtues and wondrous history. Obviously the other Irish could not offer them the last, since it contradicted their own historical tradition, their own perceptions, and their own pride, however misguided. And obviously if all that Dublin had to offer as reward British Ulster did not want there could be no deal, no advantage. Being left alone, partitioned off and ruled directly from London was not within the gift of Dublin.

At the end of the century, being left alone seemed as if it should have been a reasonable aspiration, and yet no Protestant was certain that even this could be achieved. They could hardly be left alone when there was a huge and growing minority of those who were inside the province but outside British Ulster. They could not even be left alone to govern the province without interference, given their historical record. They wanted what they could not have and had what they were not sure they could keep. How can one write a treaty to incorporate vengeance? The Protestants in the real world could not have what they really wanted—a golden past—nor the absolute assurance of an eternal British Ulster. They already had what they said they wanted: assurances of the union and direct rule from London. This was enough if true, but in truth in their heart of hearts most assumed that a constant defence of British Ulster was needed, was in fact a clearly defined responsibility. What they would take, of course, was any asset, any assurance, any aid in that defence and oppose any diminution of the union. Dublin clearly had nothing to offer but ashes, shame, defeat, bribes, a hopeless future. Out, out, out.

What no-one could imagine, whatever the militants might say, was whether British Ulster would accept ejection, however disguised, from the United Kingdom, the fearful predicted civil war, and the republicans a swift unionist conversion to nationalism. The republicans therefore might take any arrangement that would facilitate such a conversion, even if the republic were postponed indefinitely. They still wanted what they wanted but would take a path into the future. The others were not so concerned about the future. So while Dublin would take very little—assurances about nationalists in the province—and London might even take a graceful exit but would expect to soldier on, the Protestants were not really sure of their final position, what they would take.

They waited with an eye on the Republic, the immediate threat, the source of the pan-nationalist front. And it is important to remember that for most Protestants the Republic is unknown, distant, not merely a matter of green pillar-boxes and different newspapers but very different, filled with alien political arrangements, a distasteful religion, strange games and habits, filled with Gaelic foreigners who have long advocated annexation as principle. Few visit there except for the Horse Show in August or on the way to the boat-train for matches in Britain. The Republic is a land not only not known but also not wanted, a factor only because of the imperatives of geography.

What amid the constitutional proposals, the good will offered, the formulas and suggested adjustments is the enormous charm of the unpleasant and unmentionable? Scorn for one's neighbour has attractions, whether Tamils or Turks. To cherish invidious distinctions, to enjoy harm done, to hate simply and purely may be secondary benefits, but for many in Ireland at least from time to time these find favour, do pay returns. In fact for long all that has been available for many involved in Ireland is secondary benefits, so that the wonders of the primary have almost been forgotten. There might be war and violence along the Falls and Shankill but there was local pride and mutual antipathy and the pleasures of anger and hate amid the terror. And when the peace process came and the end of terror, many were amazed: streets without soldiers and still secure, visits without trepidation, easy shopping, no fear of the knock on the door. Peace brought enormous and actual benefits. But hate need not be discarded, only become secondary.

Even those who should know better can assume that the peace process is peace rather than mere improvement. Such a process does not erode the charms of prejudice but rather makes them more secure, institutionalises the returns of bigotry, separates development and ignorance. No-one in Ireland, not simply in the province, can remember the primary benefits of a stable, civic culture in a 32-county society. Ireland has never been free but often at peace. Both majorities can remember, often with nostalgia if not accuracy, their tradition paramount, beyond serious challenge. This is of course what many would like: the past replayed with all the edited changes of memory incorporated as real, the assurance of Stormont and a nation once again, almost. And then all the pleasures of prejudice and bias kept.

The problem for Ulster fundamentalists has been not simply their numbers or the perceived and actual power of the Catholic majority in Ireland or even the failure of London to realise fully the dangers inherent in nationalism but rather the lack of either secure isolation or sure defence. Those imagined as natives are still there, organised and waiting. The Catholics are indeed many and even in Ulster all about. There is no place to go but to seek a withdrawal of the spirit, limited physical segregation, and toleration of what must be accepted: the reality of Catholic neighbours. Isolated and monitored, the Catholic can be contained, as the individual kept in place and as faction kept powerless. A generation of the Troubles did not shift basic premises: the old ways had to be continued, the old walls repaired, the route marches made, and the flag displayed. Even if the natives were not intimidated, the loyal would be reassured. Even if the routes now ran through alien fields, past empty churches and abandoned Orange halls, the glorious past could be conjured up. Essentially in 1995 nothing seemingly had changed: British Ulster remained under siege from within and from without, defended by the faith and few friends.

The ideal for many Protestant fundamentalists would be a politically correct Cromwellian solution, respectable ethnic cleansing. There had always been the hope that economic conditions would encourage Catholic emigration. A decline in the size of the minority would have meant an end to two populations separate and unequal. Would that somehow the minority could be sent off to Connacht without need of massacre! Ideally all the Fenians would then be in the Republic and all the Protestants within British Ulster—a real place that would have bounds and borders and be homogeneous. Then there would be no need to tolerate a Catholic neighbour: "Toleration made the world anti-Christian." This is the reverse side of "Brits out"; but for the Protestants a pure British Ulster is not realistic, while for the republicans a united Ireland is not without prospects. The Protestants are left standing guard, left always on the defence and often the defensive.

The primary defence has fallen on the British army and the RUC. The old defence system had been badly frayed, Stormont gone, the Unionist Party split, fair practices in economic and social matters imposed, changes made everywhere without effective unionist response. Yet much has not changed: British Ulster still exists, the faithful know what they fear if not exactly who they are or what they want. And so too have all the others involved in Ireland changed and stayed the same.

The arena is swept by assumptions, perceptions, unarticulated emotions, contradictory conclusions, unstated premises, and various received truths long assumed valid. Some of these are amenable to swift change and some to the slow drip of reason and experience. Everything changes, even Protestant fundamentalism. The change in perception, in what is allowed and what is not, what is real and what is not is rarely subject to law, although laws may accelerate or retard the evolution of perceptions. And perceptions are never immutable. There may be erasures, corrections, additions, and adjustments, some swiftly done, some imperceptible over time.

In Alabama fifty years ago the arbitrary killing of a black man by mobs or secret factions was a constant, unacceptable to the proper, to the written law and to those elsewhere in the nation. In Alabama the ethos of those times allowed vigilante murder. Federal intervention, the new laws, the militancy of the potential victims and the impact of decency and right reason all played a part in changing the ethos; but the practice disappeared because those who might have been involved no longer felt properly justified in such acts. Those who killed—or those like them—hard, rough men, used to guns and big engines and cheap whiskey, often church-going men with simple minds and families to support, still drink at the same roadhouse. They hate the same people, sit on the margins of America, as did their fathers and their grandfathers; and yet they do not drive out on a hot summer night to kill. Times have changed, and so have they—slowly, not a great deal, but enough, helped on their way by the law, by the customs, but mostly by the times. Perceptions have changed, murder can no longer be easily rationalised and so is not done. There is no advantage, not economic or political but most important not psychological, to be gained.

So perceptions are not for ever, not even in Ireland, where history often seems not past but not yet begun. To begin for those who want resolution, accommodation and an end to the gun in Irish politics there must be a recognition that such perceptions are not only present but useful and effective and must so be addressed. Domination and arrogance are real, offer real returns—may not be politically correct but cannot be discounted, much less changed by wish or lecture. Much that has happened in the last generation has not been politically correct and has hardly been understood even by those involved. British Ulster has always offered advantage to those within the walls, to the defenders and the frightened as well as to the powerful and content. The Protestants, even the poorest of these—and these were often the most fundamental in faith—were each special, important, a figure and a participant in a world largely dominated by outside powers and dominations. To be Protestant, to be British, to be of the majority in Northern Ireland was to be engaged in a daily struggle. Life was not only earnest but also gratifying, an adventure, a challenge for even the least gifted and most limited. At the most base each could hate with conviction and approval and at the best sacrifice for the common good: vote the straight ticket, paint the kerbstone, lobby at Westminster. The Ulster arena gave all Protestants all sorts of returns, psychological and practical, real and imagined. This had been so for generations and was so in 1995. The march on Dunloy was not just a walk in the country or a tradition fit for tourists but a defence of all held dear: a march with glory and risk, even if not too much of either. The need for a constant defence of their special tradition enhanced the everyday, and served their interests as well.

A generation of terror beginning in 1970 did not sap the

vitality of British Ulster, even if assets had been lost, precedents breached, and changes imposed. This society, organised as a dream, an ideal, existed to protect the saved, the decent citizens, those British and Protestant, and so need not be extended to involve the others, not British, not Protestant, and not loyal. They were both different and subordinate and should be subservient. The faithful of British Ulster felt that the English had grown soft over time; Labour corrupted the workers, and the Conservatives were seldom unionists. There were in fact none like the Ulster people, none so loyal to the truth, to their tradition, none so misunderstood or endangered. British Ulster was a special society in that it was real but imaginary, existed in many tangibles but mostly in perception. Northern Ireland was by necessity divided into the subordinate and subversive and the majority. The majority lived in British Ulster and the others outside salvation if inside provincial walls.

One of the great cohesive factors was the existence of an ideological threat: a common enemy that gave scope for institutionalised enmity. There were enemies outside in the rest of the country and as disturbing within the six counties. To be defended the loyal had to be identified as friend and the others as seditious; in a crowd everyone seemed much the same. It was easier to disdain in general terms both personally and as strategy. Still, once labelled, all else fell into place: the degree of intimacy, the structure of toleration, the intensity of defence. The besieged cannot be choosy about their weapons: vengeance has served the Irish well, and hate has a low start-up cost; generosity is for those long comfortable in triumph institutionalised, and magnanimity for the old rich. In British Ulster triumph is proclaimed, marched to and spoken of but not realised, and none are so poor as those at risk on the morrow. Reassurance is most easily found in aggression, real or imagined, a marching ritual or the toss of a stone, a church burned or an Orange hall destroyed. Whatever else, hate pays dividends, the cost is low, the grievances real, congenial with assumed tradition and personal experience, and the other options often slow, less exhilarating.

In many ways hate and fear have been institutionalised in Northern Ireland. This is not without rewards, for much violence can thus be moderated, channelled, turned into ritual: riots where few are harmed, marches that do no physical harm, opinions that vent venom over a bar not over a gun barrel. It is seemingly cost-free hate at worst and the structure of Northern Ireland stability at best. But hate is never really without cost. Even the most tolerant and comfortable society can be tainted by such general emotions that give reassurance to the few and fanatic. Less stable societies, instead of harbouring the odd assassin or the small faction, have grand traditions fashioned from splendid ideals as well as noble aspirations and so great hate; so too Northern Ireland. Thus individual venom becomes general, bleeds out even into decent society. The noble and the ideal can be used as rationalisation for the zealot's hate. Such opinions allow or encourage some, both the pure in heart and the warped, to resort to real violence; such violence is then tolerated by an atmosphere shaped by general and traditional perceptions. The crime may be awful but all the faithful at once understand the motive, the provocation, the roots of murder. Hate and glory, vengeance and patriotism, spite, malice and dedication are all involved in simple acts, violent acts, murder from a ditch or in a cell. The boy next door bombs away the centre of town, a nephew murders a stranger—everyone knows why if not who. There are always reasons, and many arise from a cold heart and cunning and in Northern Ireland from long habit and proven returns.

There are always reasons, excuses; no-one of ours is responsible. Each as always sees what they see. A divided society that can only imagine the other can easily imagine a monster, readily see provocation; but first comes fear and hate. Then the others can be made victim without names known or neighbours chosen, a Fenian, a British agent. Fear can be eroded and often without great cost: the peace process ended a culture of terror and has yet to send in a bill. Hate if not freedom is still readily available and not without reward and not so swiftly eroded, not at all as long as the benefits are addictive and accessible. The very decent, those without politics, those who would harm no-one, lend a hand to all. The decent can hate too.

And if there is to be not reconciliation but accommodation, the advantage proposed must show adequate returns, find a means of shifting perception, not merely to end fear by imposed security but to offer better returns than hate at little cost. To resolve conflict the conflict must be seen to be more costly than harmony. Harmony requires investment, time, fine-tuning, patience, and the virtues of conciliation, while hate needs only to harden one's heart—no need to seek a stone: merely to understand atrocity is enough to ensure atrocity, and the politics of atrocity founded on hate returns dividends in kind. In accommodation, advantage is all, not right reason or formulas of agreement, not parity, not promises or cunningly wrought programmes or alignments but the perception of gain over loss. Ideally this would be great and immediate gain over fear and anguish and old losses, pride rewarded, glory achieved, virtues admired, money in the bank, and the cost hardly felt; the dead weight of the past dumped, the future of the nation open, the chosen people returned and redeemed. And perhaps even this is not necessary for stability and tranquillity. Habits change: bears are no longer baited or the deranged kept in chains; no-one is hanged for the theft of bread.

The Irish arena must be accepted, the perceptions of the people recognised as real, and a path to general advantage sought, not the nature of the conflict redefined or the ideal proposed as possible. The real terrain of the Irish conflict is the perception of the involved, not a map constructed from hope, reason, or cunning. Such maps will direct one about the terrain, not change it. The reason the problem has no solution has always been the definition of "problem" and "solution". As long as the involved assume they are in a zero-sum game, our win their loss, their win our loss, then there is nothing to be gained or lost. Yet it is clear that the involved, no matter how fundamental in perception, are not even engaged in the same game. They speak to cross-purposes and hear only their own voices. The arena has been not only a wilderness of mirrors but an echo chamber and can yet be a still point in the turning world of impossible dreams and lethal schemes. There is an opportunity to play to prejudice, to accept that perceptions are not mutually exclusive, even if not complementary. The advantages offered by spite, hate, malice, domination and power are not countered with kind words. The power of the gun is real, as is the weight of history rationalised. Those who kill are complex, many brave, idealistic, lethal, often vile, never without reason and not immune to change. They and theirs must be subject to persuasion, not approbation. Those who refuse to talk to treason fear to talk to no advantage. Those who will not talk at all are not necessarily simply recalcitrant but cunning. Those who seek to marshal the forces of light against those of darkness, those who seek the grail at any cost, those most fundamental in their perceptions must be offered advantage.

In Ireland those within the arena must note that such gain if not at the others' expense is most assuredly in their own interests. Such a game may be different for each player, the goals scored according to special rules, but both traditions can be satisfied, if not fully. Even the most fundamental can be attracted by advantages that weigh more than the traditional returns of arrogance, commitment rewarded, and conviction ensured. Sometimes only a small visible shift is necessary. Sometimes all the idealistic laws and proper attitudes accumulate a real mass; sometimes democratic politics can pay better than pragmatism or appeal to the base. Sometimes exhaustion can rule or the fear of risk. Change is a constant.

The same sort of men with red necks, raw prejudices, drink taken and hate intact sit in the same kind of Alabama roadhouses on a Saturday night, no nicer, no better dressed, no more elegant or educated, but no more there to murder. In the Mississippi Delta or the red hills of Georgia they are as raw and unpleasant, their habits and assumptions as unsavoury; they look the same, lean, formidable, marginal inhabitants of a small, hard world, prey to hate and redemption, brave in war, bitter in hate, good friends and dreadful enemies. They are not an easy constituency. And now they keep their guns on the rack of their pick-ups, drink their beer, and go home to the hills, no killing done as pleasure or duty. Their authorisation has disappeared because the perceived toleration for such conduct was lost. They can no longer have murder explained and so no longer need murder; there is no longer advantage in lynching, in killing as reassurance. What has changed fundamentally in

Alabama is the perception of those most fundamental; those at the raw edge of caste are not the same as they once were.

The Irish arena is filled with lethal perceptions, but even these may be interpreted to immediate advantage. There may not be any final act in Irish history but the country need not be arena for a tragedy in endless acts. Scenarios change; the arena may be made hospitable to other plots and new themes without relying on the hand of God or a change of heart. An arena shaped by perception is in flux. Not everything is possible, but some things are. There may not be an Irish solution to the Irish problem but there is a mix of prospects that might move accommodation forward, shift the priorities of the committed, and make the future less the past repeated. Most assume that the dreams contradict each other—and they do—but Ireland is more complex, more spacious than imagined; even Northern Ireland has room for more than one dream, can be arena to accommodation as well as the fearsome. The Irish arena shaped by dreams and fancies, a matter of the heart, not simply another field, holds the components of general if not mutual satisfaction—or as much as necessary to take the gun out of politics.

II

CONCLUSION

There will be no tomorrow—tomorrow is over.—
Malcolm Lowry

Nothing can be for ever. In Ireland time moves along,
perceptions adjust, and the accepted reality is not really
today like yesterday. As the century comes to an end, the
Irish arena, if enormously different from the past, seems
largely intact: old dreams, old ideals and the old faith have
survived, and done so not greatly mutated by experience.
The old Protestant ascendancy that dominated Northern
Ireland until 1971 may be in disarray, but the same attitudes
are easy to find. The British still assume that Ireland is a
quaint and often dangerous responsibility, if one with less
appeal than a generation ago. Nationalism may not be either
militant or triumphant, plays to mixed reviews and seems
parochial to Dublin 4, but it is still there, still based on
patriot history. Irish history as desired, as written for present
purpose, is new and still addressed to the old issues. Yet
much has changed.

Each generation learns the past anew to contemporary
purpose, edits, adjusts, and discards. History is of course not
lived but written and in Ireland often not read but assumed.

History is malleable, and perceptions are not for ever—even those held yesterday may not do for tomorrow. Still, past may be prologue. In Ireland this has often meant tragedy, not farce. Yet there is always something new. And so history more often serves as rationale than as determinant. Irish history rules OK, as long as to our rules now. Objective conditions, the tangible, the accepted legacy, advantage, ambition and the personal all mix as the past perceived, as Irish history on demand.

In Ireland the historical ingredients have been relatively stable for much of the century, the pool of people and ideas static. Old attitudes as much as specific grievance have been passed along in a stable society that, despite the gloss of the new, has retained much. And much that endangers the tranquillity of Northern Ireland has seemingly been a constant, even if much has changed. There, in six counties, the mix incorporates disputation, disdain, two traditions, old habits shared by all, and the relevance of unresolved quarrels and assumptions. For those in more stable societies, for those in Kerry or Kent, this has often been unwelcome. It has seemed as if the new wars of Ireland are just like old wars fought over old issues, as if violence has been institutionalised, not moderated. It has certainly appeared as if the Irish are incorrigible—even to the Irish, Protestant or Catholic, north or south, who are often in despair at the latest Irish debacle. What is past is present. This is in part because the system has used the old banners, the old quarrels within a new context. The words are the same but the music is different and so many are out of step on the same road.

Nationalists want a system evolving out of the irreconcilable dreams of the past to encompass both traditions. No-one has found such a formula. Many in

Ireland and in Britain prefer their own recipe and prefer to wait for vindication. A grand accommodation seems chimerical. Everyone soldiers on—even peace has come as process and that liable to interruption. Still, given all, given spectacular failures elsewhere, the Irish traditions have adjusted to advantage, conflicting perceptions have been institutionalised, a divided country and divided tradition have been divisive but, as such matters go, not especially deadly. Once there was partition there was stability and stagnation for British Ulster and for republicans hopes until 1969. The system adjusted and coped. The centre—London, Dublin, and Belfast—held. So the "system" worked.

Endemic violence is not novel, in Ireland or elsewhere. Bandits along the road need not unduly upset travel and commerce, only raise the cost. The existing Irish system as it evolved offers neither triumph nor stability but instead both monitors and moderates the very violence that it encourages. There is cost and lack of comfort, but life goes on. Thus most of those involved seem to be caught in a tragedy with endless acts. The long cycles often seem the only valid ones: the siege mentality, the politics of paranoia, persistent social division, lethal dreams unresolved, grievances unresolved and the British still involved, and so all still engaged in a zero-sum game. Nothing is decided and yet everything goes on as if it were soon to be—rather like the peace process unfolded. Most assume that any grand agreement must come shaped by these persistent historical imperatives that impose impossible conditions. The particular and novel are assumed alien. The contingent and unforeseen appear to have only a passing role and initiative difficult in a circle closed by the past.

Such a circle has closed in violence and closed out chaos. Mostly this century the centre has held, and when there has been violence there have been limits, even over the last generation. Three thousand dead may seem appalling, but for a generation the roads have taken more than the gun. There are rules and limits to Irish violence. These permit much while denying all, so that most of the time most of Ireland is stable. Still, each generation in Ireland and outside it has found that there is an "Irish problem"—at times tangential to major interests, almost always so to British interest. And almost all, the involved, the responsible and the disinterested, always assumed that a major factor was the clash of conflicting traditions, history at play. Yet for much of the last two centuries the arena is empty of contention, the grievances latent, no-one killed and London hardly aware of Ireland. Even with the present Troubles this is often so: the countryside is peaceful, the violence random, limited, occasionally spectacular but of low intensity, and Westminster empty when Ireland is on the agenda until a bomb goes off. There is always a feeling that the low-grade Irish fever might peak, to the disadvantage of all, but this has seldom happened and then not for long: the centre has managed to grip history.

The prospect of trouble in Northern Ireland may be a constant, confined by rituals and rites but still a chronic malady, because none can imagine an accommodation that offers all advantage. There seems to be no cure that will appeal to all, much less all equally. If the centre has so far held it is because there has always been available force: detention, the British army, coercion and imposed control to counter bombs or pogroms or murder from a ditch. The bombs and the disputations and repression seemingly arise from irremediable Irish divisions and Anglo-Irish divisions. Those in Northern Ireland in any case often perceived themselves very different, holding aspirations that would deny the others' dreams. Each wants both justice and the control of history, not just their cause vindicated or humiliation given—all these have been won or lost and to no avail. What is wanted is history written to dictation, a real and legitimate British Ulster, an Irish republic, one and free, the British tutelage praised and continued, and the past adjusted to fund the future.

What should be wanted is an arrangement that assures all that their dreams will be manifested, that British Ulster exists and so too a united Ireland, Britain there and gone, everyone content. There is in fact no need to kill the dreams but only to adjust matters to perceived mutual gain— everyone gains: let time work to advantage, eroding difference, so that the players are reassured. They can assume that their past will be prologue to a satisfactory future, a future that may always recede but is not worth seeking by force.

Obviously this has not been done. The dreams will not wait and are contradictory: no Irish republic can incorporate a British Ulster, no united Ireland can be imagined by a London dubious of Irish capacities. Somehow no Irish nation is easy to imagine that is not defined by opposition to the British. The nationalists assume an end to history: free at last—but to what purpose? What is Ireland then? The Protestants assume an end to them, assimilation as Irish, and so remain wedded to the defence of their tradition on all fronts and at great cost. They do not want to end in the boneyard of Irish history. The British find it difficult to imagine an end to their historic mission, for the Irish are not yet refined from the base ore but still need oversight. What everyone wants is a grand epilogue or at least the game to go on until the prospect of mate is real. Such an end-game has been elusive. The big issues seem too big. The great questions of state and nation, legitimacy and sovereignty, prohibit any efforts to reconcile the traditions. What is the point of peace as process, peace in pieces, if in the end the integrity of the quarrel is untouched? And nothing this century has changed the assumptions of the involved: not violence, not partial triumph or defeat, not the odds. Seemingly if history as a recurring confrontation is to end, somehow the circle must be squared. Either Ireland is one or not. And if not, how is it to be shaped as one?

None can imagine an arena where all are content. After a generation it is difficult to imagine a Northern Ireland where all are secure, much less satisfied. What all have been apt to assume is that the quarrel is symmetrical, but this is not the case. Not only do the nationalists and unionists want different things but they cannot even have what they profess to want. Any "triumph" can only be achieved at the expense of the others. If there are no others about then there is no triumph: who would march to Dunloy if there were none by the side of the road, and how can there be parity of esteem in a new Ireland that the unionists define as demeaning? Defeated, the other would then not be the same, would no longer fit the definition of the defeated. To win there must be a constant enemy, someone on the side of the road to humiliate, someone to blame for history's flaws. In 1922–23 the IRA burned down the big houses of the ascendancy as convenient vengeance against history: the real enemy was the Irish people who denied the dream.

Enemies are vital within Irish history. The Anti-Christ wrapped in republican banners is real, as is perfidious Albion dressed as an RUC reservist, barman by day, British proxy by night. Everyone has written in a role for the other, Fenian or bigot, Paddy or Brit. Time has allowed the clashing dreams to incorporate the enemy as essential. Each depends on the other to play the appropriate role—and the play never ends, simply must be re-read again. The drama never seems to change. The British cannot leave Ireland without accepting that British is not best, and so they demonstrate that this is so by staying. Ireland brings out the worst in the British. And Dublin cannot rest easy as long as nationalists are dominated, cannot truly admit the end of the dream of a single nation even when the eventuality is undesired and the nationalists of Northern Ireland as unwanted as the Protestants. And the republicans and unionists soldier on in perpetual battle, even when no shots are fired, one eager for all to be Irish and the other not to be assimilated by those Irish. All require the others to reinforce their basic assumptions. And a basic assumption of all is that even if Dublin and London have complementary interests, the two traditions in Northern Ireland have not. Dublin can be satisfied with compromise, having given up the payments on the great dream, and the British have no avowed interests but the good of the Northern Ireland majority—whatever that might be. In theory they could be one, unlike the republicans and unionists. These two are engaged in achieving asymmetrical aspirations, united in distrust, a desire for vindication, suspicion of others, and the conviction that to gain imposes loss on the other.

In fact both see the other as different. The Protestants face Irish Catholics, and the republicans need to convert unionists loyal to Britain. Neither tradition can easily imagine that reconciliation does not mean eradication of their own vitality. The future if the same is intolerable to republicans and if different unacceptable to unionists. Northern Ireland must accept that the past assumptions are imposed on future prospects—and history has proved to those who seek such proof that the two traditions must exist in constant opposition rather than in tandem. The divided society should fall but does not, part light, part darkness, part Protestant, part Catholic, part Irish and part not, and these parts not symmetrical. Each wants to win but not at all costs. Each wants triumph but has settled for persistence. None want to be instructed that the game is not worth winning, is beyond winning. None can easily imagine that the shifting, evolving arrangements encompass more than one game. Both traditions in Northern Ireland and both Dublin and London accept the symmetry of a quarrel that is not symmetrical at all. Protestants and Catholics, as do Dublin and London, want different things—as well as justice and control of history.

On a small island at the edge of Europe, on the far margin of turmoil and revolution, Ireland has somehow always offered a special, even romantic if narrow stage for great ideas, great confrontations. There in bitter intimacy the dreams and horrors of the West have often been displayed on a small scale. At times the great issues have found only slight echo: some ideas did not sell, some horrors were avoided. No monster ruled, no great class struggle split the country, no modern authoritarian ideology found fertile soil. Ireland has not been a universal Petri dish. Yet for the analytical if not for the Irish, the country within small compass has been the arena for great issues: freedom and faith, the nation and the church, peasant aspirations and the rights of man. Here various means have been deployed or devised: revolution, guerrilla war, popular democracy, class mobilisation, subversion and ethnic cleansing, plebiscites, conspiracy or devolved government. There is often, if not always, a special Irish example—and often the Irish example is archetype. The national liberation struggle invented by Irish republicans from 1916 to 1923 mixed old habits, old ideals and attitudes and new technologies, applied theories and the opportunities and vulnerabilities of the moment to produce a means into the future that proved an export item. The boycott began with Boycott, and the transnational Fenians have many descendants today. In Ireland the contradictions of revealed truth and institutionalised faith, the loss of the imagined past, the language and the nation, the morality of the murder and the poetics of oppression are to be found, often still found alive as rubric or issue. Irish history has been variously reconstructed for varied uses, been filled for the foreign with archetypes, the gunman and the wit, the poet and the rebel. The Irish experience, whatever the tradition in Ireland, is valid wherever the great issues matter. Beauty need not always be terrible, but much of the terror of Ireland's history has enriched far fields. What happens in Ireland has often mattered, seeps through to those uncertain where Ireland lies, of who played what part or the names of battles but know of the Irish. Many know of the Great Famine still, and Bobby Sands, and others the successful within the diaspora, the priest in Africa and the president in the Oval Office. Everyone knows the Irish—or something of the Irish.

None know the same Irish as do the Irish. Late and soon and all too often shaped as a lost cause, they have been a people whose prologue is the past and whose future has been determined rather than explored or shaped to contemporary usage. The Irish know themselves, not by looking into their own hearts as much as by looking back to the imperatives of their past. They are not so much damned as undaunted and ineffectual at transforming their legacy into contemporary currency of value, but indomitable: they wait on history, they persist, survive.

Any analysis of any aspect of the Irish problem suffers from two problems. First, any general theory often seems to fit the reality as well as any other. So no theory need contradict the others. All theories work, none predominate, and so each can write history from appropriate selections to a desired end. And second, all investigations are hampered by the refusal of reality to remain in place; the very words have various meanings, the scope of the arena shifts, the point of focus determines the result, so that an uncertainty principle is at work: any probe distorts the data. Only the professionals try to divorce their agenda from the text; the rest, including the committed scholar, adjust the past to the text and so control the future. History is created from the singularity of the study, each time anew and not even at times limited by the record. Any history will do, and all history is shaped to make do, to make reality work. And so there is no consensus and yet no contradiction.

The various factions in dispute perceived the past and so the future as theirs. Their analysis is valid, proves out. The IRA purports to be engaged in an armed struggle against the British, and so sovereignty is the issue. The faithful know this, and even others—enemies, friends, and the disinterested—accept it. A republican victory, however, must be won largely against the interests and personnel of Protestant Ireland defending a different tradition. Many find this obvious and the Protestants ominous. The IRA fight as nationalists but their victims die as Protestants. So from London the Irish struggle is sectarian, requiring the British as monitors and protectors, but in Dublin it is a national concern, though somehow Irish responsibilities often parallel those of Britain. And no-one is wrong or anyone quite right. The nationalists want progress and the unionists security and London to dictate the degree of both instead of

Dublin. The Catholics say they want nothing and the Protestants assume they want everything. It is an Irish problem beyond solution, an Anglo-Irish problem largely confined in six small divided counties and beyond efficient reach of Dublin or London. It is a war of liberation, the last phase of colonialism, a sectarian war, a tribal war, a class struggle disguised by religion and nationalism, or a religious confrontation hidden by national banners that reveal the actual purpose of the national struggle. It is certainly a struggle—all agree on this—but with the basic nature revealed according to the proffered text, a text that varies according to aspiration. All agree, none more than the involved, that it is a long struggle, determined by very old rules; not all recognise the same rules but all accept that history rules.

Yet the Irish arena is renewed for contemporary use each year. The imperatives of history may fit but they do not determine the action: that is shaped by the perceptions of the moment. And always those at the core cite precedent, read their history, not that of others, know what they know, and what they know matters because it matters.

And around it goes. Yet what goes around does not come around in quite the same form. These Irish are not those. The Earls in flight left behind not the Irish but peasants— not worth the trip, a different Irish back then. Then those most Irish were aristocrats and overlords, not the many with no property, no visibility, no importance. That was then; that Ireland was filled with those quite different from the winners and losers at the Boyne—or Vinegar Hill: there the British troops, speaking Irish and German as well as English, killed the rebels of Wexford. Times change and so too definitions. The Protestants of Ulster live in a different Ulster than their ancestors: even the bounds and counties are different: the province with nine counties cherished by nationalists was limned by Elizabeth, not Irish patriots. The republic established in every Irish heart a century ago is not found in Dublin—or in many Irish hearts. The men of no property hire televisions and are on the dole, are not the same as those led by Tone. Perceptions change if not the violence.

And the violence of the last generation has imposed change, not all recognised, not all articulated. Violence has paid, but strange wages unevenly distributed. So a united Ireland—a chimera or a certainty, a golden dream or a cover for Rome—has shifted meanings and defenders and advocates and always to the advantage of those concerned. And Protestants in Northern Ireland are what one makes of them, what they make of themselves, and this is not always clear, and what others make of them, and this is not always to advantage. The struggle is often more compelling than the goal. Some want to sacrifice and serve, not succeed. Others want vengeance defined as justice. And some want unity, but with conditions that ensure that partition will be permanent. The perceptions of the involved are complex, contradictory, and often covert—just like the Irish, just like the British in Ireland.

So, for there to be accommodation at least some of the hidden dynamics must be manipulated to the advantage of all, certainly so that persistence alone no longer pays as well. Persistence will always pay. What must be offered is what Oliver Twist wanted, what most want: "more." At least "more" of what the involved say they want, "more" perhaps of what they really want, but most of all at least what they will take to adjust to resolution without recourse, today or tomorrow, to lethal means. Then the dreams can wait on events and Irish reality can be shaped to imagination, not by a gunman at the end of the lane ready to kill for the cause, for history's sake. Then, without the gun, all involved in Ireland, near and far, would be able to imagine a future, if not perfect then possibly without murder as means.

And suddenly, unexpectedly, there was a ceasefire. Ireland was again—for the time being—at peace. The peace process that improbably seemed to offer a way out of the Troubles, out of the past, has fascinated many, most especially because it was not only unexpected but inexplicable. There was no agreement, not even really talks, no prospect of accommodation. There remained clashing destinies without the prospect of resolution. There were still in Ireland dreams that kill and do not die, immortal and lethal. There were still institutions and establishments that persisted in proven error, individuals who in mass could be transformed from decent into deadly. And all the aspirations that have riven Ireland for two centuries remained for seventeen months inexplicably in equilibrium, Ireland at peace, Britain with an Irish problem unresolved but with peace. It was the kind of peace that passeth understanding. It lasted from day to day, solved nothing and solved everything, allowed the militant to march and those who wanted merely to be left alone to get along.

Even the IRA bombs of February 1996 did not doom the process, only the prospects of a sure tomorrow, the prospects of any formal resolution. As a warning that the process must appear to proceed, the bombs concentrated minds. At the very least something must appear to be happening: peace must process towards some end beyond tomorrow. The February bombs indicated that any process must at least promise advantage. Still, for seventeen months the whole country ticked along. The Irish, the British, everyone was praised for restraint, admired for cunning, cited for sense and sensibility seldom shown elsewhere—and all at no cost. The Orangemen could still march. The IRA was still there as in the past, waiting for an appropriate moment to act if need be. Taoisigh could come and go and the process continue. Anyone in Belfast could go to the films without fear or in Tyrone to town without taking a detour. The British troops could stay in the barracks and the prisoners foresee release. And nothing at all happened. It was an Irish solution to an Irish problem: peace by process somehow constructed out of bits and pieces no-one imagined existed and few dared to adjust. And, like many Irish institutions, there was not only a lack of precision but also a lack of pragmatism: the process did not work very well or without some violence. Still, the cost was low, few lives were lost, there was hope, and things could be worse. Even if there were to be bombs and talks this would be part of a process, and that was better than simply bombs and endless funerals.

Such a peace by process evolving out of the turmoil of the Troubles was special, different, but not unique. There is peace by process in Cyprus and prosperity for all, and the Greeks and Turks no nearer to amity this year than last century, a millennium of confrontation, oppression, and discord on hold. This will not of course do for Ireland or for Irish republicans, for in Cyprus the Greeks denied by Athens have no place to go and the Turks with a grand army no intention or need to concede advantage. Elsewhere dreams tend to fade with victory in the field or the arrival of novel advantage or final solutions. Even in Cyprus most Greeks would be content with "more" in Cyprus rather than the lost dream of *énosis*—union with Greece—which in July 1974 evoked a Turkish invasion and the Athenian denial.

Often lost causes are truly lost. The aspirations that have elsewhere driven rebellion and great wars have elsewhere faded, been transmuted into parochial rivalries and history texts. None rally for the Old Pretender. The Norse are gone, and monarchy has little appeal. The guerrillas of the sixties lie in shallow graves or lie about their past. Arafat rides into his office in a limousine. Dreams do die out; some causes are lost for ever. Some causes can be revived: Perón returned from exile, a Greater Serbia. There have always been long waves that produce religious fundamentalism or ambitions among the parochial and denied, cycles of challenge and response, revolution and reaction. Often history is ransacked for rationalisation to explain a Zulu nation or an Islamic republic. The old ways are often lethal, tribal wars and pogroms. And there can be new variants: drug empires to rival the great companies of the Indies, and transnational terrorists to replace pirates. There is change, growth, continuity and novelty, low-intensity violence or technological change, weapons of mass destruction and millions of pounds gone in the City of London with the detonation of a lorry at the Baltic Exchange in 1992 or in Singapore through electronic fraud. It is history as action, history as the clash of interests, history as a surprise. No-one knows the rules in advance, except that many assume that history rules—our history, not theirs.

So too in Ireland, much changes and much stays the same. History is what one makes of it. Cromwell came to Ireland for 284 days and is there still. The Vikings came for centuries and left only a few shards, some genes, faint traces. Nothing is for ever, certainly not the past as perceived. The perceptions, the dreams, reality as translated shift and slide at times with imprecision and at times mutate into new, viable forms. Ireland is not simply trapped in history. History seems caught in stopped replay: nothing happening, churning action visible but no movement, the image frozen.

This is illusion. In 1994 the Troubles were no longer yesterday repeated but evolving into a peace process. The analysis of the involved had shifted the definition of advantage and the prospects of the possible. It was possible to talk not about talks but about the shape of tomorrow. There was no great cost to the process, and the profits still came each day. Almost everywhere the everyday people lived like that, day by day. In Ireland the days beyond the gun with dreams on hold stretched out, months, more months, seventeen months of process—and at no cost, and no resolution. And always the feel of a high-wire act: a wrong move and the past will return, the body count will begin again and none claim responsibility. No-one ever claims responsibility for initiating harm, only for responding to provocation: repression, revolution, the British army in the kitchen, the bomb on the bus are always responses, not determinants. And for seventeen months no-one felt provoked sufficiently to alter yesterday's expectations. And so there was peace until the London bombs of February 1996, and then process again, perhaps peace again.

How can peace be a perpetual motion machine that offers more than is demanded? Even for an island of saints and miracles and sacred wells, few ever imagined such a spectre and yet all benefited—so far all still benefit to a degree. True, the process went only so far and then the IRA lost patience. Yet the restraint of the militant has indicated that such a process can again be shaped to advantage if at greater cost and at greater risk: too much delight was taken at the low cost for the involved. The IRA in the interim have lost much of the constituency for physical force—so too the loyalists, who felt no need to murder as defenders when there was no longer an attack. For republicans the constituency of the IRA is very small, untouched by great marches and popular protest. They answer to patriot history, not to the populace, to the Pope or to the Peace People. They can be denied, however, and have been denied in the past, and so must consider the need for nationalist toleration, consider the risks of denial by the core of their own, even consider the prospect of process as opposed to military matters. Matters for all have grown more complex. The peace process offered few precedents. It was not yet like the old truces, not like the old republican splits, not like anything else. Everything changed.

What had not changed were certain basics: the aspirations of the republican movement, a responsibility to history that could no longer easily be postponed day by day, the suspicion by all in Ireland of perfidious Albion, the inability of London to focus on Ireland, and the advantages of doing nothing for the defenders of British Ulster. There had to be a feeling of movement but no actual motion—at least until those who could move agreed on the advantages to be sought by the continuation of the process. Only London really has the power to make the great move, and London was distracted.

What frightens most of the everyday people now is the fear of the past, to be part of history once again. Most would be content with tomorrow like yesterday. Most people at most times have been so content—a few, the Americans, expected more on the morrow, and some expect disaster. The Irish have always felt they are threatened by disaster, have risen from horror, may again have the land ruined, their hearts broken—but not today. And this has mostly been the case. For the Irish, history is always there, waiting. In Ireland there are those who each year near the solstice put pebbles in a Kerry field and those in Tyrone or

Woodvale who will kill to impose a dream, to make history move more rapidly.

What happens next, what happens at all in Ireland—history once again, nothing much, a real transformation, or the death of dreams—matters very little on a grand scale. Yet to all the Irish—for they will pay any costs—and to those involved in the clash of destinies Ireland matters a great deal. Ireland in fact has always mattered more than numbers, size, scope or intensity—a few thousand dead in a generation, no more than die of malaria each day in small African countries or are buried and forgotten in the irregular wars of central Asia. It is not numbers that matter but proximity, visibility, empathy, and relevance. Ireland has always offered insight if not example.

For centuries those in Ireland who would turn experience into prose or into poetry have written out the drama of Ireland and have sometimes been driven out of Ireland as too real, too provocative. Those without Irish connections or with an alien eye have for a generation sought explanation and understanding, sought to find out what mattered most in Ireland in a time of terror—often hardly troubled that the country ran on the everyday rhythms: school attended, milk collected, taxes paid, the crops in and the computers bought. And now everyone still wants to know the state of play. What is to happen tomorrow, are the dreams still valid, are the old tunes still there, has the last ditch been passed? And most of all can the circle of Northern Ireland be squared, can the long zero-sum game be solved, can everyone be a winner or at least none a loser? Can the peace process evolve by intention or by luck, through management or arrangement, into an end of history? Can there be an Ireland without lethal schism, perhaps still with hate but no longer with horror? Can there be an end to the gun in politics if not to the dreams? Can the present process be made permanent? Could accommodation truly come?

Some have predicted that chaos will come if change is imposed, if this is not done or that not accepted. The Protestants will not tolerate real change but would prefer to bring Northern Ireland down around their heads rather than compromise on the union. A few assume another Armageddon possible, and promise one. Some assume that British Ulster is beyond persuasion, would implode or explode, rush into exile or to civil war. And most assume that with the union the IRA will go on as before, the square circle. All are apt to predict what fits their own agenda, seek no change or much change as the only practical option. In fact no-one can predict what would or what might happen in a future when perception of advantage and opportunity were in flux. Prediction is very difficult in any case, especially when the comfortable past offers no precedent.

So the concerned, as always, seek in history congenial examples and in analysis general answers to special Irish prospects. Mostly, clever or dim, profound or parrots, as always they find what they seek, Irish nationalism as various, the British establishment as imperial, the Protestants as Irish or the Irish as Catholics. Until February 1996 there were those who hoped that all that need be done was to wait, wait until the peace process became addictive, wait until the republicans' ardour died and so too in time their dream. Others wanted to wait only until the next general election, or until British Ulster was really under threat. Those who wanted to wait often did so, because no-one had to pay for waiting. And then in February 1996 the first payment on the bill became due: waiting is not for ever, one must wait on something. And even then payment is wanted. Process must offer advantage to all, not simply to those who see waiting as sufficient strategy.

A great many optimists and many pragmatists continue to believe that the peace process can be extended, be effective and lead to accommodation. Those who seek solutions to the great and persistent quarrels, the intractable and uncompromising, if they rely on common sense, decency, right reason and the erosion of reality are often disappointed. Even compelling force, historically far more popular, has limitations in resolving deadly quarrels. France and Germany fought for centuries, as did France and England, and now there is one Europe filled with military cemeteries, old battlefields, neglected monuments, and fields of poppies. Nothing has lasted for ever. No means is sure. Nothing ever worked very well for Ireland. Thus the integrity of the Irish troubles, the persistence of Europe's longest if least intense war, is special; the problem so far is that there is no solution. The persistence of the Irish problem arises from the power of contradictory dreams, limited coercion, and the cunning rules of engagement. No-one wins everything and everyone loses something, and tomorrow is another day not unlike yesterday. History rules.

What most want for Ireland, those in Ireland and out of Ireland, is peace, of course, but peace with justice. For this there must be some vindication of perceived grievance, if without great cost but with general benefit. There must be advantage, resolution, an end to history as now played. In the end what all want is the assurance that tomorrow will be like yesterday, not by some happy accident but by agreement and intention, not subject to sudden change but because all are agreed. This would be solution enough, whatever the problem. The aspirations and ambitions of all need not be satisfied: all do not have to win everything, but all must feel no need to resort to physical force, to tolerate a return of the gun. What is wanted is not so much a solution as a final resolution: here history as tragedy stops.

While nothing in the real world may be final, in the midst of the peace process, day by day, what most began to imagine was an agreed accommodation, not an endless squabble as in Cyprus nor perhaps a neat and final end. What is wanted is the past past—not, as in the Balkans, merely on hold, not as in Ireland today with no-one willing to deny their dream of the morrow. For this the dreams have to be adjusted so that they can be accommodated— perceived as possible, cherished and potent and protected from time, projected into time.

There are, more or less, three options, to some degree each appealing to such concerns, each viable and none ideal— certainly not ideal as far as the Protestants are concerned; for centuries nothing has for them been final but rather only effective. What is needed is something that is effective for everyone at a cost within paying.

First, the most obvious prospect is that tomorrow will be like yesterday, that some sort of peace process can be continued until the passions and aspirations of the involved erode, are corrupted by time and tangible returns. In 1995, within months the intangibles had apparently changed: the rationalisation for recourse to the gun had seemingly disappeared. The very process, with a lack of momentum that the Protestants took as advantage and the British as of no consequence, was seen by republicans as loss. There was no longer advantage in process. Doing nothing meant for the IRA having been done to. Even Dublin recognised that at least something must be seen to be done but could generate no sense of urgency elsewhere. Yet doing nothing has great appeal. The benefits of doing nothing are always enormous, cost-free, politically congenial, and allow wisdom to be awarded and cunning displayed and none the poorer. So in Northern Ireland peace without even need of a piece of paper emerged, after a time peace without any need for there to be a process. So doing nearly nothing finally resulted in nothing: an easy option failed. Given all, there would still be those who would prefer nothing done—even at the risk of a return to the violent past. Some believe anything done a risky choice. And doing nothing could impose change—erode, for example, the capacity of the IRA to act.

For two centuries the militant republican movement has felt morally justified in recourse to physical force to achieve a free Ireland, variously defined but always one separated from England, independent, a nation once again. This presumption has from time to time generated a generic and extensive toleration of a campaign of violence and at others of singular rebellious acts against those in authority—alien, arrogant, not Irish at all. Thus the Fenians spoke for all Ireland and those who maimed the landlord's cattle spoke the resentment of the poor. In fact the very term "physical force" has entered usage to make conventional, acceptable and decent such recourse to violence—physical force, not violence. In a sense such violence in Ireland is authorised or rationalised, recognised, treated as special. Everyone understood the reasoning and rules of the Troubles, even if disapproving. The authorities, denying the legitimacy of the armed struggle, still make special rules and revoke them at risk. Generation after generation, as Ireland's grievances were ameliorated and opportunity offered, the history of conciliation, toleration, arrangements and co-operation, ignored by patriots, rebels, and defenders, the republicans persisted. Their power was eroded by Irish advantage gained, first within the United Kingdom and then without. The dream was achieved incrementally, with each concession denied and then granted. The republicans never gave up hope of achieving all, and increasingly the most endangered, the Protestants of Ulster, sought survival through increased militancy and the link with Britain. Increasingly each incremental nationalist gain was smaller and engendered less national commitment to all: the Irish-Irish were all but content and the Irish Protestants all but besieged. And there matters rested.

In fact a not unreasonable assumption is that by the end of this century the accumulated advantage of compromise and conciliation, the changing circumstances of Ireland and Britain, the balance of assets and the correlation of forces will have been so great that in the future those who seek toleration for their use of physical force will no longer find it. The long dream will die for lack of takers. None caught in the incandescent vision of the republic will kill without prospect of return—though most can find, have found in the flutter of an aspen leaf the winds of change. So what is needed is a process that will erode toleration. Time serves authority. History will close on a perpetual check—no mate, no triumph, just tomorrow as yesterday until there is no more game, the players expire and so too history.

This was a reasonable expectation, but in the past such expectation has repeatedly been confounded by the persistence and power of the republican dream. So doing nothing is more difficult than first imagined; but still a reasonable strategy is doing very little. Certainly it is the chosen course for British Ulster. Hold firm, trust in the union, persist, and the republicans will never be able to win on their own. Of course British Ulster cannot win on its own, even exist alone, but that is another matter. Doing nothing over a generation but persisting has so far kept British Ulster safe, if battered and beleaguered. British Ulster need not hold out for ever but only until nationalism is at last reconciled to reality. And what need be done to effect this most desirable and elusive eventuality is nothing: wait on the morrow, wait for the core of the republican faithful to die away. If this is the case—and many sensible and astute observers feel that it is—then nothing at all is needed, although most would prefer some outward and visible indicator. Even if there is nothing much to show for the peace process, nearly everyone wants something as closure: a bit of signed paper as a symbol that all is past and not prologue. Treaties have not brought peace to Ireland, but this has not reduced their attraction, for each has given nationalism something and so reduced its capacity to seek all. This could mean that at last the militant republicans would be left behind to die off, historical artefacts too few to resort to the gun. Thus even British Ulster can see the advantage of doing something to ensure that nothing is done to them.

If nothing is not sufficient, if doing nothing merely ensures that sooner rather than later the quarrel emerges again, that the dream of a united Ireland still has takers and legitimacy, then something more serious must be done. Doing something more than expected, something dramatic and detailed and constitutional, is crucial and is or should be today's agenda. Nearly everyone accepts that sooner or later there must be a product. What is needed is something symbolic and real, actual concessions by all as the middle option between nothing and everything. This in some form is what was imagined by most of those who negotiated the peace process in the first place. The militant nationalists, not all by any means Sinn Féin, foresaw a political and constitutional way open to a united Ireland. The unionists, not all in Northern Ireland, intended to make sure that this aspiration was imaginary by shaping any agreement to defend the perceived rights of British Ulster within the United Kingdom. Those rights could be adjusted or skewed, the outer ramparts could be ceded, but any middle-ground accommodation would still see a British guarantee in place, visible or invisible, tangibly in place because the establishment in London was still loath to give up what was seen as a clearly defined responsibility, if self-declared. Most nationalists would be content with much rather than aspire to a unity few really wanted any longer. In the end the republicans would see, and properly so, such an agreement as a betrayal of the dream, no matter how congenial in terms, broad in national support, resented by the unionists and feared by the Protestants of British Ulster. It would not be what was wanted even if only grudgingly accepted in London and no matter how generously praised as triumph in Dublin and Washington and Europe. Sinn Féin was determined that this would not happen, that the product would not be closure but gate. The shrewd felt that time would close the gate. The legitimacy of physical force would have gone and so too the IRA. The republicans might oppose the Ireland that such an agreement created, but, unlike the other treaties, too much would have been won to permit armed resistance. Everyone has a different product in mind, but all agree that the present process must lead to something. The problem is that unless the republican dream dies off, the something imagined is not enough.

The only reason the unionists might be brought aboard would be their perception that such an agreement, however wondrous and popular, would close rather than open constitutional and political means towards a united Ireland. The British would cling to sovereignty and the Protestants to unionism and so would have forged with Dublin and the others still another barrier to the march of the nation. This would not do for Sinn Féin but might for those less faithful. Who can really imagine a practical united Ireland? Any future republican position, narrow, unpopular, short on reason and assets, would attract few and alienate many, so that the vast majority could hope that this time the scope and elegance of the accommodation—a formal matter, a national solution—would for ever end toleration for physical force. This time the arrangement would signal that the dream was terminal, too much won and what was still left not worth the cost. Anyway, who could imagine a united Ireland imposed by coercion? Who could even imagine the Protestants of Ulster persuaded into such an entity? Surely the republicans, the gunmen, would this time accept the final arrangement as final?

And no-one could be really sure. No-one has ever been really sure that such a dream can be condemned to extinction by a majority, by logic, or by the direction of events. So far it has not been. An accommodation that leaves the British in Ireland and so reassures the Protestants of Ulster—although this logically should not be the case—may not be any more effective than doing nothing much at all. British Ulster feels that the present arrangement is sufficient. Why make concessions in the hope of converting republicans, who alone cannot challenge the present unless the present is changed, concessions made?

What is left is shaping a grand accommodation that offers those militant republicans a way into the future, a process without the gun that would allow the Protestants of Northern Ireland some day to choose Ireland over British

Ulster. And so the unionists would have to be persuaded that it is to their advantage to break the connection with the British, abandon the union, so as to better protect British Ulster. The British, who have been less than forthcoming on the nature of their returns on an Irish present, would have to see advantage as well, would, like all the others, have to take what they have said they want instead of what they really want. And Dublin will take whatever the republicans want, who must assume that the Protestants do not want what they say they want. Such an Ireland, not united, not for ever partitioned, not British but incorporating British Ulster, is in detail difficult to imagine but in concept possible. Everyone must receive their heart's avowed desire, but not at the expense of the others nor with reservations so as to postpone what they really want until another day.

What this means is that the republicans must continue to believe that the Irish Protestants are really Irish—and this is not beyond reason. It also means that the Irish Protestants must be given a means of defending British Ulster greater than the union. This is a most improbable aspiration, since seemingly the great magnet that holds the disparate Protestant majority of the province as one, overrides economic and social interests, overrides doctrinal and ideological differences, proves stronger than class and caste, is the loyalty to the union. That union makes possible freedom, self-esteem, arrogance, and security, rewards the faith, protects the Protestants, makes possible the ideal.

And yet that loyalty has always been conditional. The union is a means, not an end but a strategy for defending British Ulster, an entity seldom described but very real. British Ulster is not a failed entity at all but one that has survived, survived the loss of the whole of Ireland, the loss of Stormont, the erosions of reform, the rise of the IRA—

survived and persisted. It encompasses all Protestants who seek to be free of Rome rule, safe from a united Ireland with a Catholic majority, secure from the ambitions of nationalism espoused by the Catholic majority in Ireland. The union is thus a means, not an end—which is why from time to time loyalists have attacked the British army, for their loyalty is to British Ulster, not the British. The two are often identical, both British, both within the United Kingdom, both sharing the same civility and social diligence, both with shared history and ideals. In America in the years leading to the revolution most colonists wanted to be left alone to their own advantage; if being British was not to advantage then their loyalty was withdrawn—and so their secret army, a militia of defence, at Lexington fired the shot heard around the world to ensure life, liberty, and most especially the pursuit of happiness. In Northern Ireland the Protestants have none of the advantages of distance and numbers but also want most of all to be left alone but within the United Kingdom. The Americans wanted to create a nation, but the Irish Protestants want only to be left alone and yet fear that this is what the British may do.

The defence of British Ulster in the end rests with the British, not with Ulster. And in London, Northern Ireland is seen as special, uncongenial, often ungrateful, and perhaps not worth the cost of care. The British establishment has said so from time to time. The British people make this clear, not just in polls but in pubs and in person: "No Ulster banknotes here, Paddy." The innocent might assume that such general distaste, coupled with the high cost of the province, would persuade all, the people and the politicians, to end the Irish connection, the source of too many ills. This has not been the case. The British support their army, dislike the Irish, but feel that the last generation has been the best of a bad lot. What else is to be done? No-one wants to scuttle. It would be difficult to dump those who, however uncongenial, have accepted British example and tutelage, who, unlike the other Irish, want to be British. No-one much wants to have to police the province with an army. And no-one in Britain, except a few, really care very much.

The Americans in 1776 could aspire to independence, but not British Ulster. How could they then be British, and how could they afford a proper defence? And a defence is necessary—a symbolic defence along the road to Dunloy and a real defence with British assets on call. The province is home to a huge and growing minority, a clear and present danger, intolerable but tolerated. The Protestants cannot, because of the times and their vision, maintain the natives in bondage, expel or absorb the alien, imagine a final solution. The Americans could deal with the natives found there, and so too the Afrikaners; numbers did not matter much. Cromwell dealt with the Irish natives. British Ulster is shaped not to deal with the Catholic Irish but to control them. As it is, there are too many to control easily, even with aid from Britain. In Northern Ireland numbers matter: 645,000 Catholics and only 855,000 Protestants. So the promised province has always been at risk. British Ulster may be special, a grand place, not a country, not a nation, a special place, and so specially threatened. The Catholics cannot be treated like the Zulus, the Republic cannot be ignored, and the basic rules of the game do not allow British Ulster a victory but only to persist.

The two great principles within British Ulster have been, first, the need for reassurance from Britain, because the province is different and difficult, and then a defence best served by the union against the threats from the Irish majority. If an accommodation could be fashioned that would offer the majority in the province the reality of a defence more secure than the union, then the involved might under appropriate psychological and symbolic conditions be so inclined. There could be advantage to the end of British sovereignty, for British Ulster is special, a perception, not a place.

If such a defence against Rome was not necessarily a permanent and impenetrable barrier to the Republic—if the Irish Protestants might yet decide to be Irish, as republican ideology insists—then what purpose would the gun have in Irish politics? If the Protestant Irish could decide at some future time that Rome was no threat, that unity in steps had advantage, that reality had changed—if in fact, as the republicans always believed, they were more Irish than imagined, more Irish than Protestant, more Irish than British—then movement, if glacial, towards unity might well take place. And if not, not. Then the republicans had misread the future and the future would unfold to Ulster Protestant expectations. British Ulster would be safe and British and in Ireland, with all the entitlements intact: passports and voting and pensions, the colour of the pillar-boxes a matter of negotiation, and any stamp will do.

While the other British provinces scattered within the Commonwealth are not threatened by Rome, they have adjusted to other challenges: varied religions, strange immigrations, uneasy natives, and exotic locales. No-one in British Ulster really cares about the fate of British Honduras or British Columbia. What they want is what they want; and all are as one on what they do not want: incorporation and so assimilation into a united Ireland. They want to stay as they are—and they are Protestants.

What so few in nationalist Ireland seem to grasp is that the Protestants of Northern Ireland, committed to the most fundamental ideals of their religion as well as to the congeniality of the British tradition, are very different. Excluding historical loyalties, the long service and involvement within the United Kingdom and the imperial past as recalled, few fundamentalist Protestants have ever readily assimilated into pluralist societies. Time, adaptation, temptation and co-option may erode their special isolation, but in Ulster this has not yet been the case. There each Protestant generation finds commitment even more necessary, more fundamental. They feel besieged and so are besieged, perhaps betrayed, never understood, their special difference not apparent. Their lives from a distance appear the same as those of their Catholic neighbours: same football clubs, similar houses and cars, one street much like the next but for the kerbstones; but their perception of reality, their values and agenda and expectations are quite different. They are different in fact from most other Protestants, those in Britain, those in more established churches, those not at risk, even many of those in Northern Ireland. They are more fundamental, more Protestant, more fearful, and more dedicated to their vocation. And so their perceptions have largely become those of Protestant Northern Ireland, not always as crudely put but as real. As long as the Protestants assume they are in danger of submersion in a nationalist majority then they are going to be less Irish than Protestant. This means they are going to continue to look to Britain as protector of British Ulster.

For the Protestants of Northern Ireland to see advantage in one Ireland, in being Irish, in being united with the other Irish, however tenuously—much less in any sort of united Ireland—then much must change. This is not change in promises or programmes, not constitutional adjustments, not the promise of esteem—not Dublin's to give—not jobs for the boys, nothing tangible available to the nationalists, but a change in Protestant perceptions. Reality must change. And there has been no such change this century. Rome is still perceived as a threat and the Irish state as feckless, nationalism a cover for Catholicism, and their own future at risk. To protect that future one must understand them and their past as perceived, as lived, accept the enormous differences, the reality of the fears—not all unfounded—and the relevance of their analysis. This means that before anyone can do more than imagine a united Ireland—as imaginary in any case as British Ulster and as real—everyone must recognise the obstacles to a united Ireland. Ulster Protestants cannot match the Irish Catholics in numbers, and so will not mix. Ireland then must be separate and equal, one and divided. Coercion could actually—power does come from the gun—accelerate a London withdrawal under various banners but could not unite Ireland. Coercion would make any united Ireland a cover for the triumph of the majority, would fail to unite all with the common name of Irish. Achieving a united Ireland is sufficient challenge, the more so since only one player has this as aim and none are yet truly engaged in the fundamentals. Few in fact realise that what they say they want and what they truly want vary: what they can get is a matter for process and must come only in relation to the adjustment and deployment of existing perceptions. These shape the dynamics of the Irish problem—a problem with many explanations and contradictory aspirations, not all exclusive but most hidden.

In a sense what each really wants is a perpetual triumph over the perceived competitor for control of the past and the future. This requires that the historic mission be continued, despite the existence of a perpetual if ineffectual opponent. The Irish in general want to be accepted as different from

the British, a nation once again, and in particular
triumphant over the system's Northern Ireland garrison—
loyalists, all Protestants. Thus historical grievances will be
assuaged and vengeance over reality and domination
ensured and so the avowed republican principles denied. To
succeed, republican history, a tale of confrontation and
persistence, must continue the struggle until the Protestants
are Irish, not simply conquered or absorbed but Irish and
Protestant. The British want their role in Irish history, their
assigned and necessary mission to transform the Irish to
enterprise and civility, to be accepted as just and continuing:
eight hundred years and at last proved right in using might
for right's sake. Those responsible for policy in London will
thus at last receive general recognition for the necessity and
accomplishment of the long crusade, waged without special
interests, special favour, or special returns, a millennium of
decency imposed by appropriate means.

For such an outcome to be effective, however, the
necessity for that crusade must exist. Just as to be a nation
once again Ireland still feels the need of the British
challenge to shape any future mission in opposition, so the
British need the Irish commitment in order to be an imperial
arbiter still: without the Irish the British will not be as
British, as righteous, as right. As for the Protestants of
Northern Ireland, they seek the rights, privileges and
legitimacy of the properly dominant, those successful by
wont and by history's judgement, over an awesome and
dangerous if scruffy opponent. They want to be triumphant
in their role and mission, justice accepted as due over a
sullen if potentially dangerous enemy, always in place to
ensure the unity of God's chosen people. They need the
Catholics as nationalist enemy as much as the republicans
need no Protestants as loyal to the Crown. It is as if one

could not be Irish without Britain, British without the Irish to tutor, Protestant in Northern Ireland without Catholics to fear and disdain. Thus each cannot achieve their heart's desire without the presence of the other, and so each has fashioned a more congenial public and often private aspiration: peace with justice.

This means that the British cannot imagine peace unless justice is theirs to impose, the Irish justice without all grievance repented and repaid, and British Ulster—the least in power, the most at risk—justice to shape the province to majority agenda. Translated for public consumption, this has meant that Britain offers to do what a consensus in Northern Ireland suggests—and there is no prospect of such a consensus, so the mission continues. The Irish are willing to accept victory over history in incremental steps, and so any beginning will now be good enough—even for republicans, who have long had to persist without general national support and may yet have to do so again. And the Protestants of Northern Ireland will accept that as a predominant majority protected by Britain the most effective role is to surrender nothing, to persist. Everyone must persist to ensure that justice can be assured—this is what is wanted—and so the prospect of accommodation is not great. How can the dynamic that generates the dialectic of opposites without prospect of a final synthesis of history emerging be ended if it is not recognised? Stability has come as perpetual confrontation and conflict—a steady state institutionalised, always different, always the same but never offering culmination: a complex, multiple Irish dialectic. In Irish history synthesis has been elusive.

What each claims to want is neither a continuation of that dialectic nor justice on their own terms over history but rather minimal basic concessions that would deny the

411

irreducible aspirations of the others. What is necessary is that each receive concession in such a way that the aspirations of the other are not present but possible. The British still have a role and mission in Ireland, if not legally that of the past; the Irish, especially the republicans, can anticipate a means towards a future united Ireland by the beginning of incremental moves for a more united Ireland; and the majority in Northern Ireland can accept that such a union can be more effectively denied by new rights, powers, and privilege—concessions—than the union with Britain as at present constructed. There can be promise of a united Ireland, prospect of British concern, but for the Protestants assurance that if not dominant their British Ulster will be safe in their own hands—safe because all recognise that this is to the advantage of all. The British will underwrite Ulster as duty to the Protestants, as always, and the nationalists because they recognise that without a united Ireland by consent there cannot be a united Ireland. All must perceive their own advantage to be greater than loss. Each must accept an arrangement that in time will erode the necessity for losers, for rewriting history, for vengeance and vindication, because gradually the rewards even of the day, the assurance that tomorrow will be much as yesterday, will outweigh the risks of great gain, grand dreams, the old causes. Each must also perceive their own advantage the greatest, their reading of history most accurate, their prospects most assured, and so take this as victory. All must win and all must not seem to lose except to the others, but none need accept history as written by others. Thus the Egyptians still feel they won the October War in 1974 and so the peace, and so too do the Israelis. And so both are right. In Ireland too, in time, perhaps all will win and none lose.

And if the accommodation is appropriately designed,

such benefits will begin on the morrow, accumulate, outweigh intangible grievance, make possible the adjustment of the lethal dreams to the everyday world. The dream of a united Ireland need not be abandoned because unlikely or beyond easy reach and must not be sought merely out of reflex. What matters most is an adjustment of the dream to both reality and means other than those so long cherished by the core of republicans. There must be an acceptance that unity could as well as should come by other means, that the dream lives, even if realisation is not in prospect. If there is to be an Irish people of two traditions, such an eventuality will come slowly, voluntarily, often grudgingly, at great cost to all and perhaps, with luck, to considerable benefit to each.

To imagine there is a formula for this is as foolish as the search for a redress of old grievance under republican banners or recourse to comfortable slogans instead of sacrifice. If a united Ireland is truly an Irish aspiration then costs will have to be paid. So far payment in lives and in money, in ease and decency by adherence to old ways and roles, has been costly: not for most but for those most concerned. Any accommodation must ensure that at least no-one need any longer assume advantage in recourse to force—and perhaps accept that force is not only not cost-efficient but actually counter-productive. As for the other costs, these would be real, would require a change of priorities, a change in roles as missions change, change in agenda, and always money, time, and enormous effort. There is no convincing evidence that very many in the Republic want to pay those costs or have ever wanted t pay those costs, rather only to achieve vicarious satisfacti n in the belief that the end is desirable if the means too 'ear. And with vast resources, Britain has been willing to pa the

Irish costs for the returns of secondary benefits, reassurance of the vitality of their long imperial role and their imperial mission to Ireland. And in so doing for a century the Anglo-Irish quarrel has ensured that all will pay but for secondary benefits—and always it seems that those who must pay the most are the Irish Protestants, who have watched for much of the century the inroads of Catholic ambition, which offers armed struggle or assimilation. It is no wonder the Protestants of Northern Ireland find the charms of nationalism so scant, devious, and preposterous. It is no wonder they fear that the British may lose interest in secondary benefits. It may not excuse the deployment of any means in the defence of British Ulster, epitomised by the Stormont system, which was as much about the display and distribution of assets as administration and governance; but it goes far to explain the paranoid style found in Northern Ireland. And the Ulster Protestant has real enemies as well as imagined ones, has evidence of the fate of Protestants in an Irish Catholic state, now a republic, a partner in the pan-nationalist front, always dominated by the ethos of Rome, a state created by British concession in 1921, a state that anticipates Britain as persuader, ally in the end of British Ulster. The nature of Protestants' anger is real. Their fears are real and cannot be contradicted by simple reason or eliminated by coercion. They will not be persuaded or driven against their personal interests and will not concede or compromise the integrity of their tradition. None can easily imagine any defence of that integrity but the union, and all can easily imagine what any all-Ireland solution truly means: an end to British Ulster. Any nationalist gain, so too a Catholic gain, would be at Protestant expense.

For a generation there have been those who sought a way out of the zero-sum game, to solve the Protestant dilemma.

The advocates of a grand accommodation often felt that if there were to be a resolution that was not to be perceived as imposed to the disadvantage of one player then other precedents must be offered. Elsewhere, however, examples were and are mixed. Dividing small islands has not always proved a happy solution, any more than uniting other ones. In fact a great many of the parallels sought only reveal special cases: Hispaniola so clearly divided; Sri Lanka so bitterly wracked by rebellion; Cyprus a state without a nation caught in the midst of talks about talks, always on the eve of war; Corsica divided on whether to be French or special. Divided nations, like South Africa and Palestine, have simply moved from one confrontation to another without permanent resolution, today awful but better than expected yesterday—no small accomplishment. Combined nations like the Soviet Union and Yugoslavia have indicated the power of exclusive dreams, inchoate nations, the old as new and the failure of the new man imagined by Marx. Germany has united, but the Basques of ETA persist in an armed struggle. All are special, as is any divided society, any planter regimes or colonial imposition or arenas where two traditions clash.

In the end, the history and example of others do not really matter in Northern Ireland. Ulster may not be *sui generis* but everyone in the province assumes so and so acts: parochial is as parochial does. The key and the core of the Irish problem has been reduced to adjusting British Ulster to a future world acceptable to the others—the nationalists and the British establishment. What must work must work for British Ulster, must be adjusted not simply to Ireland but there to the most virulent and intransigent. The gunmen and paramilitaries, the zealous and zealots must be, if grudgingly or unwittingly, incorporated. Killing must go out of fashion. Those raw and angry people, bigots all, narrow, brutal, sitting in the upstairs room of a Portadown pub must have a world where they need not defend their assumptions by sectarian murder. They may well continue to hate Fenians but feel no necessity to prowl the streets with a gun, only to go on drinking while the chat moves on to football or the weather. Ideally, those who benefit from hate must be given advantage and yet not allowed to institutionalise their assumptions, not only no sectarian murder but no sectarian advantage. Those who seek vengeance must be dissuaded from doing so with a gun. Those who would die for a united Ireland or to oppose it must see the advantage of living, sacrificing for a more complex interim cause.

Once murder cannot be legitimised and so rationalised, then all else may be possible: comfort, ease, development, enterprise, creativity and even progress measured both statistically and in loyalty to the future as imagined. If the great perceptions can become engaged in an accommodation, then the details can be evolved, the nature of flags and emblems, multiple citizenship, guarantees and laws and money and this police force and that postage stamp. All the pragmatists and theorists can devise formulas that will allow British Ulster to be in but not of Ireland, Britain no longer sovereign but responsibly involved, nationalism content with the morrow and the conversion of the Protestants. All can have multiple advantages and entitlements, various passports, duly elected representatives despatched to various bodies, diverse loyalties, assurance of protection and fair shares for all.

Not all of this can come all at once or without enormous adjustment and novel institutions, but Anglo-Irish relations have always been a muddle of practice and habit, the written and the accepted. The Irishman who works and votes in Liverpool, belongs to British organisations, goes home for Christmas to Kerry, where he contributes to Sinn Féin, speaks Irish and feels neither special nor divided is in the end himself, and so content. So too could British Ulster exist, protected, cherished, safe and separate and special and not on any map but in Protestant hearts.

Then the clauses of lawyers or the welfare programmes, housing allocations or import regulations can be adjusted to advantage. Such adjustments, arising from any real accommodation or any grand scheme, would be enormous. None can really imagine the simple practical obstacles to peace. Most of British Ulster is employed for war: 45 per cent of the Northern Ireland work force are employed by the security establishment; tens of thousands are armed; others are in offices, under contract defending the system, buying and selling and paying off the mortgage. In Britain 44 per cent of the budget of MI5 is spent on the Irish; and then there are the police, the military, MI6 and various bureaucrats who deal with Irish matters and would have to continue to deal with Irish matters for the foreseeable future. The province cannot be clipped away from Britain, cannot be changed by colouring in the map. Partition in 1921 divided one Ireland but not others, and so too Northern Ireland cannot be easily transformed, Ireland made one or muddled into two parts that are separate but one, nor the United Kingdom stay and go. And even then who will make good the returns of violence that have all but been institutionalised?

There are benefits to chaos, whole industries evolved to cope with violence; glaziers do well and black taxis, hospital staffs are adjusted to trauma wards, and construction companies to bomb damage. Peace would be costly, and not only at first. Who would pay, and how much? How could the province be policed to general satisfaction? Who would make the rules, and who obey them? What colour would the pillar-boxes be? Would there be a Northern Ireland passport? And who would pay the piper?

Certainly a grand accommodation acceptable to republicans and Protestants would create a cottage industry of planners and bureaucrats and duplicated authorities that might even replace the armed forces as major employers. Certainly armies of bureaucrats, accountants, lawyers, housing experts and specialists on human rights, family relations, citizenship and pensions would have to draft an arrangement whereby British Ulster would be British and Irish, stay the same and be seen to change. The politicians and theorists, the lawyers and diplomats can always offer binational institutions and triple citizenships, provincial majority advantage, assurances to the minority. There will be suggestions, options, plans, demands about the control of the armed forces and police. There will be the enormous real costs, with the British on call for more than money.

All of these, however daunting, can be worked out and can be in time part of the solution, not the problem. Some countries use the dollar as currency without problems, and sterling was once everyday currency in Kerry as well as Antrim and Sussex. The arrangements arising from the basic accommodation may be complex: the settlement cannot settle everything, only open prospects, only assuage fears and encourage hopes and in so doing begin the institutionalisation of transition, a transition that can be imagined permanent or fleeting. Nothing can be done until there is a complementarity of perception: the grand accommodation that will allow the evolution of the practical.

What is needed is for the republicans to assume that such

an arrangement could lead to a united Ireland, a more united Ireland, and for the Protestants the conviction that British Ulster is now safer than before, just as congenial to civility and enterprise and freedom—and separate—and never, never at risk, never in danger of amalgamation with the Catholic majority. Each can then anticipate a history not unlike their aspirations but one that is not exclusive, allows the other a role. In time all may hope that the future is as imagined, that change is possible or not, that time moves to advantage.

Time has certainly entered the republican calculation: all but a few would wait on tomorrow if the prospects were not unpromising. Complexity too has entered republican considerations: one cannot unite the whole people of Ireland if three-quarters of a million Protestants refuse. What the Protestants want is institutionalised refusal. They might, then, accept a British Ulster—not a Northern Ireland—that they control and can keep in all ways decent and British, keep all the advantages now offered. They cannot now imagine life except with the freedom that Britain guarantees: they are a redeemed people reliant on the Bible but without sufficient power to resist the national majority. At the minimum what the fundamentalists want is to be left alone, protected against assimilation. This British Ulster guarantees. And the display of this reality in the greater Northern Ireland is a secondary but undeniable benefit, as is the discomfort of the Fenians. Many would like to continue to display their power and pride. Who would not? Many would like to dominate the others—hardly a special flaw, but few can admit more than the superiority of their tradition's qualities. And these qualities are often admirable, not merely the sectarian pleasure in humiliation.

The Protestant virtues and sacrifices, if poorly repaid in

provincial prosperity, are real, have been symbolised by the
service to the Crown, the war memorials, the uniforms of
the police, the assumptions of the sermons and patriot
oratory. Few imagine their loyalty as provisional or their
virtues with a reverse side of arrogance. So these symbols are
often more difficult to cede than reality. For those within
British Ulster to accept a London decision to give up the
symbolic sovereignty necessary to neutralise republican
legitimacy there must be enormous advantage. Such a denial
by the British can only be given as a willing, magnanimous
act that reassures the Protestants and themselves. And the
British have the power to make a first move—though few in
Ireland, seized on national issues, ever understand how little
time and concern the British invest in Northern Ireland.
And so there is great momentum for doing nothing, holding
on to the last bastion, keeping faith with the loyalists—not
because of perceived advantage but out of habit.

In any accommodation, advantage must outweigh habit,
offer more than sovereignty, legitimacy, and responsibility:
Britain too must gain, and more than an end to the Irish
problem. British Ulster must gain, real gains and perceived
gains, and may be allowed to feel such gain at republican
advantage. The republicans say they are Irish and so
malleable; and so if they control their own identity there
should be no need for anxiety. Few Irish Protestants can
imagine becoming Irish, as expected—but then, say the
faithful republicans, they would not, or not until the
sovereignty goes. And if in return for the disappearance of
British sovereignty British Ulster gains rather than loses, and
gains what the nationalists see as acceptable, not
domination but security of tenure, not absolute control, a
return to the past and absolute reassurance for the future of
British Ulster, then the Protestants may feel that they have

not surrendered but triumphed, taken more than the inch offered, are still superior in tradition and values than the others—can even march on Dunloy, but in a different context.

What has to be on offer to Protestant Ulster is a resolution in two parts. There must be the perception of gain, the reaffirmation of symbolic certainties, and in addition the real control of their own destiny, not simply written guarantees. There must be money in the bank, promises on paper, but recognition of their Ulster, their own police and laws and most of all a perpetual if calibrated veto on any movement towards matters Irish. There must be no means for the nationalists to narrow this control without agreement. If British Ulster wants greater national co-operation, this is a matter for British Ulster. If a single Olympic team offers advantage, then this would be possible; if not, not. If a joint tourist board would return half-crowns, then this might be possible, if wanted. If a seat at the United Nations were on offer for all-Ireland, perhaps one for Ulster too, then these might be considered. And most within British Ulster assume that what they want is to be left alone, even if the key is that all advantages would be weighted by the Northern Ireland majority, a majority that in a sense would have all the privileges and rights of being British and none of the costs. Whatever the tangible costs the British state might have to pay, they would be less than a new butcher's bill, less than the inevitable reappearance of the Irish problem in British political affairs, would in any case hardly be greater than that incurred if the province were within the United Kingdom. If the tangible costs are not unreasonable, then all that Britain need be persuaded of is that the long mission to the Irish has not been flawed, that at last stewardship is over—the Irish no longer violent, wicked, and vile, most importantly no longer on any London agenda: free at last. The Irish would be no more than island neighbours of various sorts, some perhaps British citizens too, some special and loyal, some not, but none ever again seeking through physical force to establish a special kind of Ireland. Whatever emerges in Ireland would no longer be a British responsibility, though not without interest and not without cost.

Would the Protestants of Ulster accept such an arrangement, a grand Irish solution instead of a small one or nothing at all, an end to British sovereignty but not at the cost of the defence of British Ulster? After all, reasonable Ulster unionists, the moderate and the elegant, have often suggested something similar. And after all, the Ulster paramilitary defenders have suggested a free Ulster, free of British control, free to defend against Irish threats. In the real world such initiatives, from the elegant or those of no property, are an aberration. British Ulster now is committed as in the past to union, even if the commitment is provisional. The only appeal to any change would be a more effective defence of British Ulster than the union; and so far neither the threat of persuasion, the erosion of the majority's numbers or the lack of steel in London has changed Protestant views. Ulster must rely on the union.

The fact that a grand arrangement, however complex and novel, however curious, involving layers of governance and accommodation, from rules for county councils to provincial security institutions and the national concerns of Dublin and London, could appear viable, is as nothing. Why change what has worked? Why build elaborate theoretical castles around an end to British sovereignty when the United Kingdom is and will be united? Those who are apt to say "no," those who oppose any change, those who hate or abhor pretensions of equality, must see advantage. What do they get? Those who will never give an inch or change their view of the evils of Rome or the priorities of the Apprentice Boys, those who are without wit or reason, and most of all those with both who are simply transported by the revealed truth, must see advantage. And that advantage would have to be highly visible, tangible and a comfort to confound all others and ensure the future.

To repeat "no" for nearly a century to advantage lends a certain weight to suspicion of any novelty. To imagine an end to the union, the great political foundation of British Ulster, is for many unthinkable. Could the British Ulster of the Free Presbyterian Church, of the UVF, of those who loathe all Catholics imagine an end to British sovereignty, no matter how great the advantage? Would not the existence of the symbols of the Crown, so long maintained in each British Ulster heart, be worth even more than the risks of any betrayal by that Crown? Would not the very word "Ireland" written over any solution have the same impact that a mysterious and powerless Council of Ireland had on Protestant temper in 1974? Would the faithful still want to march to Dunloy on their own; would it be as effective to intimidate without the authorisation of the Crown; would the abandoned church and the empty Orange hall be then omen, not goad? And so what prospect for an accommodation that would adjust Ireland so that the future is open to unity but the means of preventing it in the hands of the Protestants?

The sure and safe wager is very little prospect. Not all want to reason together. Few like to contemplate a future that does not appeal even if it is inevitable: tomorrow may not come, the Catholic birth rate may change, the IRA may go away, Protestants may move back into Dunloy parish.

Doing nothing and holding firm have paid, and to manoeuvre is to risk what is now assumed safe. Dunloy may be lost, but not Antrim. Almost all Protestants feel that union is still the best option, regardless of the rather limited risks or more often because the risks are limited and known: perfidious Albion never quite as perfidious as possible, always in the heel of the hunt rampant against Rome. Even if the majority of the Protestants did so desire, British Ulster has long been subject to Gresham's Law: the extreme drives out the moderate. In the past the raucous, the raw hatred and bigotry have all played well, better than all else. Because many live intensely, believe with great intensity and see fundamental issues where others want an easy life, refusing to surrender old positions even for better new ones is not an easy or likely course. The faithful and fundamental want what they want, not necessarily what others offer as advantage: they want differences intense, loyalty rewarded, domination ensured. Most of all they want as little to do with Catholic Ireland and as strong ties with Protestant Britain as can be managed; the removal of British sovereignty would be assumed disaster.

Would Ian Paisley tolerate a British Ulster without a Union Jack, no matter how effective and advantageous the arrangement? He who speaks for a real constituency, speaks to the fears and anguish of his own, does not imagine Rome of the Anti-Christ but perceives it as real, knows in his heart of hearts and can find citation in the Bible just how great are the risks to his own, to the saved, those redeemed. Not likely. Most, including Paisley, are apt to see the province still engaged in a zero-sum game.

Change is not likely to be to Protestant advantage, and radical change more dangerous still. What more radical than the disappearance of the Union Jack, the withdrawal of a sovereignty that in the end has reassured those loyal to the Crown for centuries? Yet nothing is quite impossible, because almost without noticing, the unlikely can happen; the intangibles beyond polls and perception can transform reality. Easter 1916 changed Ireland, and so too the Government of Ireland Act of 1920. And the peace process changed Ireland. No IRA directive, no loyalist ceasefire, no talks in Dublin or London, no prospects good, bad or indifferent have transformed Ireland over the last two years as much as the shift in Irish and British perceptions of the possible—even the necessary. No-one planned for a peace process. No-one imagined peace as process. No-one can yet grasp that the Troubles as shaped for a generation are over, even if no-one is yet sure if Ireland has entered an end-game or a prologue to more trouble. Yet the Irish arena has changed, because no-one, not the gunmen nor their mothers, not their friends, not the bigots nor the ideologues can any longer easily accept killing for a dream, for an ideal, however valid. As long as there is a sense of the possible, the republicans have narrow options, and as long as they do not feel the need to resort to physical force there is no need to defend British Ulster with a gun. And so there is room to manoeuvre, do something, do the same thing, do a little, do a lot.

It is possible to burn a church, smear graffiti on an Orange hall, revert to old habits and hatreds; but the medium of action has changed. The same people are there, there at Dunloy, along the side of the road or marching to the hateful tunes from the past. The same hatreds and assumptions abound; but if there is a process towards peace then authorisation to kill can be revoked. There will always be a market for hate and fear, for malevolence and enmity, for the hard word. Peace does not mean propriety or an end to prejudice: the same harsh minds and cruel words can exist, will exist, but not necessarily the gun. A great accommodation ensures only that the killing does not begin again—no second thoughts, no bombs as wake-up calls. A great accommodation ensures that the existing dreams are only slightly adjusted, that the worse does not automatically negate adjustment, because a role is allowed for hate and spite and rancour. In Ireland to hope for differences compromised, mutual justice, malice for none and amity as a universal would be foolish: not even an angel would volunteer to run on such a programme. There are limits to polite society and great staying power in bigotry. To adjust to rancour and malice and spite, to allow a role for the awful, to urge advantage as well as decency, is simply shrewd. At the same time to neglect the decent and tolerant, the reasoned and restrained, would be foolish: the good need not be abandoned as an asset. These deployed graces of reconciliation, proclaimed and often to hand during any movement towards conciliation, have always been insufficient. Any long-range aspirations in Northern Ireland should take into account the depth of distaste, suspicion and scorn always present in the province and at the end of the century especially so. Hate is close-woven in both traditions. Decent people hate with a passion seldom seen even among their own.

So the arena of perception, the stage for negotiation or adjustment, as always appears fallow, less than promising, Somehow, sometimes there has been peace but not promise, not for Protestants and so not for Ireland. All that most ever hoped was that tomorrow was not worse than yesterday. Yesterday has always had a certain charm in Ireland, for it is amenable to editing. In 1996 the Protestants' world has closed and narrowed, events seem to pass them by, and only their enemies act on history. No-one consults. No-one listens. The British Prime Minister must discuss matters or risk an election, but most assume such discussion to be a last resort, not a happy choice. So no-one really listens. Those who chatter and comment in Ireland or in Britain always claim that the Protestants are understood, when obviously they are not. And there is little seemingly to be done. To shout louder makes no friends, even if the faithful are reassured. And British Ulster needs to be reassured.

Beyond the churches, civil society has all but ceased: there is no politics, no vital civil life. The rising generation seemingly lacks ambition, discipline, or a commitment to education. There is all but institutionalised frustration, a nostalgia not only for the great arrogance of the past but even for the challenges that generated an active defence. Now all that is gone and the future uncertain and unpleasant. There is still room for hate and anguish and anger if not for duty discovered, responsibility deployed, and certainly not conciliation. And no matter how awful and awesome this perceptual Protestant landscape, the peace process must not be simply endured but also adjusted to offer advantage to British Ulster. The gains as perceived by the Protestants must outweigh the costs as imagined. The peace process has changed perceptions as the Peace People did not—not changed them fundamentally, not changed history as imagined, not changed the returns of hate nor the hope of vengeance, but changed the costing of the quarrel. Such a change means that for mutual advantage all the involved can see a reason for such a process, even if each imagines a completely different culmination: the British continuing at no greater cost, the Irish national dream forwarded, and British Ulster safe and separate—and all find pleasure in an end to the culture of terror and in the inevitable ensuing general, global admiration for movement towards conciliation.

These are the rewards of process, but for process to be

427

made permanent it must be made sufficiently promising. So a grand accommodation may have a chance. The option of doing nothing has already revealed the risks, with the London bombs, but also the advantages for British Ulster—nothing ventured and so far nothing lost. The option of doing something but not too much always has appeal for politicians, but unless the something is enough then everyone must wait to see if the republican dream can survive into a new century as it has through the last two. So a grand accommodation involving British sovereignty and British Ulster's security and republican aspirations—squaring the circle by persuading all that the process is four-square and sound—is not without merit. Any direction has risks, including a refusal to move at all.

What is real in Ireland is what is assumed real. What matters in Ireland is what matters to the Irish, and to the British. The good and decent believe in reason, the politicians in arrangements, the pastors in God's word, the scholarly in facts deployed, the lawyers in law, and the dreamers in the gun. All believe that their past is prologue and none that in Ireland more often than not history is invention and always a burden, not a legacy, not reason but rationalisation. Many would like tomorrow cancelled, none more than the Protestants. Yet tomorrow can offer a nexus where the shifting perceptions of all can be adjusted to a grand accommodation: tomorrow might well be better and more certain than today. Then again not. Some always want to repeat yesterday. Some push their own solution, their own perception as universal, their adjustments or constitutions or concessions. Few incorporate malignancy or address the contradictory perceptions abroad in Ireland. And few even factor in the reality of British Ulster, further alienating the Protestants, who in response become even more intractable. Many of the responsible feel that great solutions might best wait on others, on better days, the rise of moderation or the powers that be. How can one move into a future so contorted by past assumptions and present priorities? How to get away from the legacy and burden of the past, the unease and confrontations of the present? How does one get back to the future?

The wise may want to leave well enough alone. Those with power have other agendas, always have other agendas and other priorities; the British, who must make the great first move, have inevitably waited too late, because Ireland is seldom of interest until too late.

The optimists want to do something; even those who opt for inaction tend to accept that probably now something will be done. The Protestants, of course, fear it will be done to them, and the others suspect that not enough will be done for them. Everyone wants no trouble and at no cost, wants their own agenda passed—and why not? At least all agree that something is to be done, but will doing something prove adequate? Would not this be the time to do a great deal, change history, not agendas, change the name of the game? So who would stand for great change, expect great change? Who fancies a different tomorrow, even if one shaped by yesterday, which so far has been evil ancestor? Who could imagine the end of history, physical force discarded, the defence of British Ulster unnecessary, imagine a great alliance or at least an agreed synthesis variously perceived? Who is available to craft great change? The sensible would suggest wagering on the short term, letting tomorrow wait on tomorrow, posterity wait on habit.

What the Irish and the British need to do is go back to the future, not hope for the best: deploy the perceptions of all to ensure that yesterday can become an effective tomorrow, that today is not dangerous, that a united Ireland waits on Ireland united, and that on time.

SOURCES

There are two major varieties of sources for any study of living perceptions: those observed and those written—the analysis of the disinterested, the work of the involved, the books of scholars, and the tracts of the times. In the first case each investigator is special, with a special perspective, arrives at the arena for varying purposes, and creates a text out of a mix of motives that largely determine the contents as well as the context. So I am me—an alien eye, an observer who first arrived long ago without Irish connections and a mind as near a blank slate as possible on Irish matters. Since then I have spent a very long time in Ireland, have friends and enemies, have been seconded and adopted, married into Kerry, associated with subversives, have a gallery deal, a publisher, have those who like my work and those who do not.

Whatever else, however, I am not Irish and wait in fact to write a book on who the Irish truly are for my last published exercise, when I shall be too feeble to be savaged for long.

As for the sources, even the last generation has generated such a library that there are bibliographies of bibliographies. For this the truly interested can see my "Sources" section in *The Irish Troubles: a Generation of Political Violence, 1967–1993,* a survey that each year would require additions

430

and corrections and a survey I shall not append in adjusted form here: enough is enough. There are as well all the sources for comparative references: the attitudes of those involved in the October War in the Middle East or the evolution of the Cyprus crisis. Each generates another substantial bibliography. If one wants to drop in the relative development of Norway and Ireland in this century, both starting more or less from scratch, marginal rural societies without enormous natural resources (this was long before North Sea oil) incorporated into greater states, then there is anecdotal material, novels and memoirs, travel books—and the scholars. For example, the recent *The State in the Modernisation Process: the Case of Norway, 1850–1970* (Ad Notam Cyldendal AS, Oslo, 1994) might lead on to Thorvald Gran, through all the relevant works on the state of politics and economics in Scandinavia: Gudmund Hernes, Peter Katzenstein, Johan Olsen and Jonas Pontusson, Bo Rothstein, Tim Knudsen et al. It is difficult to imagine any but the most dedicated comparative scholars searching very far afield, given the library of works on Ireland and contemporary Irish practice and problems.

If one ventures further back into conventional Irish history (back to my one ancestor connection with Ireland, the arrival of St Leger as Lord Deputy to modernise the country by introducing Tudor interests over Celtic habit) then there are truly whole libraries. So one can venture neither beyond Ireland nor back in time without encountering sources if not beyond number then surely beyond need. One cannot carry the works on theology or the clash of ambitions, on Cromwell or the rise of modern nationalism, much less contemplate listing them. I once reviewed a splendid work on the Presbyterian Church in Ireland, an exercise that revealed an enormous accumulation of analysis and history focused on matters that at best I was vaguely aware of and more often came to innocent of data: very complicated, schismatic and independent these Ulster Presbyterians I had first met far removed in the valley of Virginia. All the Protestant congregations have their own history and often their historians; each presents the innocent with the complexities of reality that lie behind the easy generalisations.

As for the Roman Catholic Church in Ireland, it is much the same but more so: more complications, more data, more work done, more good and more bad, whole careers invested in bishops or schism, vast numbers of pages, most different. There is too much to read—even for the specialist, certainly for me. Much the same is going to be the case for anyone who ventures into the past, into the nature of existing societies, into fields where perceptions are not readily apparent or rather the seemingly obvious is delusion presented as reality.

Mostly, then, my sources are my experience in Ireland over a generation, academically and analytically, mainly spent on matters of politics, especially violent politics in general and the republican movement in particular. Mostly my reading has been so focused or for pleasure, even enlightenment, on contemporary Irish work, poetry, fiction, the dark side of matters instead of the delights of the IRA or INLA. And for the rest there is time spent painting and wandering, in conversations on this and that, on Irish matters in London or Washington or even the Middle East, in a lifetime on the margin of events. These are my sources, not the ones I might have chosen had this book been a project from the first instead of one no-one else seemed interested in pursuing. What certainly has made the text easier to pursue is that a secondary benefit of the Troubles

has been that enormous flood of works on modern Ireland—
and finally and at last works on the Protestants, often
neglected, regularly misunderstood, and rarely subject of
affection. As a Protestant of sorts (all American Episcopalians
—Anglicans—would in British Ulster be considered less than
sound, if still Protestant) I at least found all the Irish strange,
not just one set. And so all the scholarly aid and comfort in
understanding the nature of the Northern Ireland Protestant
was welcome, from the first real essay into the field by Sarah
Nelson—I was her external examiner at Strathclyde, which
indicates how narrow the array of specialists was then and to
an extent now. Since then both journalists and scholars
have investigated the Protestants, not always to their liking,
at times it seems never to their liking. Most of their own
work is not very convincing, except to the committed and
convinced, but often very interesting. I had a review of Ian
Paisley's daughter go unprinted because I suspected that I
found it useful reading for one and all as an unintentional
insight into the Northern Protestant mind rather than as an
apologia for her father. In any case it was and is an
interesting book—all sorts of Irish can write, even from
venues least expected—and none should deny that her
father is an enormously effective orator, a man with a
command of his constituency and his text, not for most
external examiners but a talent nevertheless.

If one reads sources, however, to find more to read,
chooses to avoid the narrowly academic, the evidence of the
involved, the numbers and charts of the social scientists and
the ephemeral and fugitive of the moment—seeks one or
two really good books, then try Sarah Nelson's *Ulster's
Uncertain Defenders: Loyalists and the Northern Ireland Conflict*
(Appletree, Belfast, 1984) or any of the grand works of
Steven Bruce, for example *The Edge of the Union: the Ulster*

Loyalist Political Vision (Oxford University Press, Oxford, 1994) and for the spectacular the series by Martin Dillon on several of the "spectaculars" of the Troubles, for example *The Shankill Butchers: a Case Study of Mass Murder* (Hutchinson, London, 1989).

There is not really a very satisfactory work simply on Northern Protestants as they are—rather than as they act politically—although there are good works on the nature of a divided society close up and narrow: see the classic *Prejudice and Tolerance in Ulster: a Study of Neighbours and "Strangers" in a Border Community* by Rosemary Harris (Manchester University Press, Manchester, 1972). And for one Protestant's return to his roots there is Geoffrey Beattie's recent *We Are the People: Journeys through the Heart of Protestant Ulster* (Heinemann, London, 1992); or for a selection of those on both sides of the divide see Tony Parker's *May the Lord in His Mercy be Kind to Belfast* (Henry Holt, New York, 1993).

The Catholics of Ireland do better with the late John Whyte's classic *Church and State in Modern Ireland, 1923–1979* (Gill and Macmillan, Dublin, 1980). For a more general study there is the splendid *Ireland, 1912–1985: Politics and Society* by J. J. Lee (Cambridge University Press, Cambridge, 1989). And so even with this swift and abbreviated list there is the prospect of a project, not "additional reading" for the airport or train.

As for the nature of the Irish, along with the annual book on "Irish Houses and Horses" there is usually one on "The Irish"—some academic, some vitriolic, fewer now than once but still a genre that has generated no consensus and one that seldom does more than add a wee chapter on the others in Northern Ireland, Catholics or Protestants.